p. 308   a key means to transcend our
daily cares is to wholeheartedly
savor our physical pleasures.
our sensual needs must not be
denigrated, but prized and
hallowed

Walking the Path of ChristoSophia

Exploring the Hidden Tradition in Christian Spirituality

Cynthia Avens & Richard Zelley

authorHOUSE™

1663 LIBERTY DRIVE, SUITE 200
BLOOMINGTON, INDIANA 47403
(800) 839-8640
WWW.AUTHORHOUSE.COM

First published by AuthorHouse 12/09/05

ISBN: 1-4208-3492-4 (sc)

Library of Congress Control Number: 2005903760

Printed in the United States of America
Bloomington, Indiana

This book is printed on acid-free paper.

This book is dedicated to The ChristoSophia Community

Whose faith inspires us
Whose hope encourages us
Whose love sustains us

PREFACE

Writing this book is part of our journey along the Path of ChristoSophia. In the past we have walked this path separately; now we walk it together. Along the way we have met others who are also walking this path. Like pilgrims of long ago who journeyed to holy sites and told their stories to each other as they traveled, our pilgrimage today along the Path of ChristoSophia requires that we share the stories of our spiritual quests. As we share the wisdom that we have gained through our individual soul journeys we are engaged in the process by which the story of Christ continues to unfold in a way that is meaningful for us today.

CYNTHIA'S STORY:

For as far back as I can remember I have had a deep inner spiritual life. As a child my spiritual experiences were given meaning through the stories and symbols of Christianity which I learned from my family and the Methodist church that was central to our lives. As I grew older, I continued to actively participate in the church with the hopes of deepening my spirituality. However, I began to feel increasingly disappointed and bored with my experiences in church. Many times I even left a church service feeling quite depressed because the sense of spiritual presence that I had so eagerly sought was missing. I began to search for the spiritual experience in many Protestant churches of various denominations, but never felt that this need was fulfilled. During this time I also attended some Roman Catholic and Eastern Orthodox services and was often drawn to the beauty and the mystery of the liturgy. In one service at St. Patrick's Cathedral which I attended during a trip to New York City, I felt a deep spiritual presence which I had not experienced in a church since my childhood. However, I realized that this way was ultimately closed to me also because, as a non-Catholic, I could not participate in the sacrament of Communion, the central mystery of the Mass. Although I deeply love both the Roman Catholic and the Eastern Orthodox liturgies, I could not convert to either faith because I strongly disagree with the churches' positions on many basic issues. In particular, I could not join an institution which has such a rigidly patriarchal attitude and hierarchical structure. After many years it became apparent to me that my long search for a meaningful spirituality within the institutional Christian Church appeared to be a failure. However, I never considered leaving the path of Christianity altogether. I always believed that in the essence of Christianity was hidden the deep spiritual truth that I was searching for. This conviction became especially clear to me when I read Carlos Castaneda's books about his apprenticeship with the Indian sorcerer Don Juan who advised him to travel on a path that has "heart."[1]

At this time I had the profound insight that for me the "path with a heart" was Christianity for surely its essence is found in Christ's message of love. As I struggled to reconcile what I perceived as the essential "heart" of Christianity with my experiences in Christian churches, I heard these words as though Christ were speaking them to me, "Ask, and it will be given to you; seek, and you will find; knock, and it will be opened to you." (Matt. 7:7) This vivid inner experience gave me the encouragement and strength which I very much needed to continue my quest at a time when I often felt confused and discouraged.

This spiritual search was also the primary motivating force behind my decision to study psychology in college. I wanted to better understand the "psyche," the soul. I was particularly intrigued with the theories of the psychoanalyst Carl Jung. His work on archetypal symbolism helped provide a broader context for my understanding of religion, and the application of his techniques of dream interpretation and active imagination provided a much greater depth of spiritual experience than any I had encountered in church. I have found Jungian psychology to be a very useful tool for enriching my spiritual insights and practices; however, psychology by itself could not satisfy my needs for a living faith. Thus I continued the quest for an authentic spirituality rooted in Christian tradition which ultimately led me to the Path of ChristoSophia.

RICHARD'S STORY:

My spiritual quest has led me through a wide spectrum of Christian denominations. I was raised in the Society of Friends (Quakers), my father's heritage, and in the Episcopal church of my mother. From a very young age I was especially influenced by the peace and tranquility that I experienced in Quaker Meeting. This has been the basis of a deep personal faith in Christ that has sustained me to the present day.

While in high school, I belonged to an organization which encouraged its members to visit the worship services of many different Christian denominations. Thus, I experienced a wide variety of Christian practices and had an opportunity to question and discuss the varying doctrines with the respective clergy. I began to question much of what I had been taught and felt the need to search for a deeper understanding of the teachings and divinity of Christ. This quest took many twists and turns during college and graduate school and finally led to Eastern Orthodoxy. During those church visitations during high school, I had attended a Greek Orthodox church but didn't understand much of what was going on since the service was in Greek. Even so, I was fascinated by all the icons, chant, and symbolism of the liturgy. The Eastern Orthodox church that I eventually joined was an American, English-language church where I was able to explore deeply the mystical symbolism for which I had quested so long. The teachings and divinity of Christ came alive for me and I entered into studies for the priesthood. I received ordination and eventually became dean of an Eastern Orthodox seminary. However, after a number of years I became disillusioned with the rigid ethnicity and patriarchal hierarchy of the institutional Orthodox Church.

The mystical traditions and doctrines of Eastern Orthodoxy still resonate deeply within me. Having studied Carl Jung's analytical psychology for many years, I have attempted to connect Orthodox mystical symbolism with Jung's theory of the archetypes of the collective unconscious. This has resulted in the realization that there is a Path of ChristoSophia not totally contained within institutional Christianity.

Thus we both came to the realization in our own ways, after many years of struggle, that although we deeply desired to develop our Christian spirituality we personally could not do so in the Church as it exists today. This began our quest, through prayer, meditation, and study, to discover a way of revisioning our Christian tradition so that it would continue to be spiritually meaningful for us. The purpose of this book is to share what we have learned from our quest along the Path of ChristoSophia with those who are also struggling to achieve a personally authentic Christianity. It is not our intention to disparage the Christian Church; many people continue to find within this institution a viable means for developing and expressing their spirituality. But there are increasing numbers of people today who find themselves in the same dilemma that we did; those whose souls are rooted in the Christian tradition, but who find themselves alienated from the contemporary Christian Church. The Path of ChristoSophia offers an alternative for resolving this conflict.

TABLE OF CONTENTS

good + bad things to keep + things to reject from Gnostic Christianity

Chapter X has given me another way to view communion, so that it will be meaningful to me. I now have 2 ways: the Borg/Crossan Passover meal (protection against death + food for the journey); and as the Grail - the symbol of bringing the feminine back into Christianity, into God, into Christ.

Introduction

"Make me to know your ways, O Lord;
teach me your paths."

Psalm 25:4

1

CHAPTER I: THE BYPATHS OF CHRISTIAN TRADITION

> Along the great highroads of the world everything seems
> desolate and outworn. Instinctively the modern man
> leaves the trodden ways to explore the by-paths . . .[1]

Although we have been devout spiritual seekers within Christian tradition for many years, we have not felt spiritually fulfilled within the institutional Christian Church. The following metaphor illuminates this seemingly paradoxical situation, which many like us experience today. For most people the Christian Church is like a busy interstate highway, with its gentle curves and gradients, well marked traffic signs, easy entrances and exits, and comfortable rest stops along the way. Just as an interstate highway facilitates the efficient movement of large numbers of people to a distant city, so the institution of the Christian Church facilitates the efficient movement of large numbers of people to the City of God. However, just as some people are called by a sense of adventure to leave the monotony of the interstate highway for less traveled, more picturesque byroads, many people such as ourselves have left the institutional Christian Church today to travel along the spiritual bypaths.

When we leave the interstate highway, we immediately gain a heightened awareness of the landscape as we travel along the byroad. Whereas the builders of the interstate have cut through mountains and filled in swamps to maintain the gentle gradient, the byroad follows the natural contours of the land and we feel closer to nature as we journey on our way. We feel even closer to nature when we forsake our car and set off by foot through the countryside, where we can smell the earth, feel the breeze, hear the birds and insects, and see the great variety of life all around us. The physical effort required in walking the bypaths also helps build our stamina and endurance. In a similar way, walking along "spiritual bypaths" can strengthen the spirit. Walking along bypaths is a much simpler way of traveling, but it requires more exertion and commitment. Thus, there have been only a few hardy pilgrims who have traveled the spiritual bypaths of Christian tradition throughout the ages. Their explorations reveal a hidden tradition within Christianity which is vital for us to rediscover today. Unfortunately, many of these significant bypaths within the Christian tradition have been poorly maintained, barricaded, and even destroyed in the process of building the Church. We believe that the major problem of Christianity today is the suppression of those elements within its tradition which recognize the feminine dimension of the Divine, the presence of the sacred within the natural world, and the value of mystical experience. Today, many seekers are striving to recover these elements of Christian spirituality through their journeys along the feminine, nature, and mystical bypaths. There they eventually find that the bypaths merge into an essential unity, forming one Path. We refer to this path as the Path of ChristoSophia because we believe that the discovery of the sacred Feminine is at the center of the hidden tradition in Christian spirituality.

PROBLEMS WITHIN CHRISTIANITY
The Repression of the Feminine

As young children, our first image of God was of an old man with a long white beard sitting on a throne. This image of the Divine which was conveyed to us by the churches of our childhood was that of the ultimate patriarch. As we grew up and developed greater spiritual maturity, of course we recognized that this portrayal of God was much too narrow and simplistic. However, at a deep level our earliest image of God leaves its imprint on our psyches and influences our spirituality in unconscious ways. The Church

4

through its use of religious language, art, and dogma continually reinforces this patriarchal image of God as the absolute King and Judge.

This perception of God poses special problems for women. As Cynthia explains, "It was difficult for me as a woman to discover the deepest core of my spirituality in an institution which presented solely masculine images for deity - as God the Father and Christ the Son. I also found it difficult to trust my own spiritual experience when the Church required adherence to a ready-made system of beliefs. I eventually realized that these difficulties were due to the suppression of the feminine within the institutional Church."

The masculine elements of law and judgment have been emphasized on the interstate highway of the Church while the feminine elements of feeling and intuition have generally been ignored. This suppression of the feminine aspects of spiritual experience corresponds to a hierarchical structure within the Church which has traditionally devalued the position of women. This patriarchal, hierarchical organization of the Christian Church has served to reinforce the "dominator" model of human relationships based on power and control rather than a "partnership" model based on equality and cooperation.[2]

The Domination of Nature

Throughout our lives, many of our deepest spiritual experiences have occurred in a natural setting. For example, on one memorable May evening we stood in the center of a stone circle in Cornwall under a full moon. Like many others who have stood in this stone circle for thousands of years, we felt a sense of great awe and wonder as we experienced the feminine energies of moon and earth and a deep sense of connection with all creation. We have had many similar experiences much closer to home, while sitting on a rock in the middle of a mountain stream or walking along the edge of the ocean and watching the sunrise. At these times, there is an overwhelming sense of the Divine within the natural world. Therefore, the traditional Christian view of the transcendent God who is separate from nature has never corresponded to our experience. In addition, we are deeply distressed by the ecological devastation that has been wrought by this dualistic separation of God from the physical world. Traditional Christian theology has emphasized man's dominion over nature, contributing to his control and exploitation of the natural world.

Historically the Church has also taken a very negative view towards the human body, for it is part of the world of matter. Thus the body and sexuality have often been condemned as evil by the Christian Church, rather than being celebrated as an expression of the Divine.

The Loss of the Mystical

Richard illustrates the loss of the mystical element of Christianity in the following story: "When I was serving as an Orthodox priest, a very distraught woman came to my church late one night. She told me that her sister had just died in a distant city and she had immediately gone to her Roman Catholic priest to have prayers said for her sister's soul. When she asked to light a prayer candle, the priest told her in a very rational manner that there was no purpose for this superstitious practice any longer. However, in the ancient tradition of the Church, the priest's blessing of a candle for prayer serves the mystical purpose of invoking an angelic presence. This woman's experience exemplifies the erosion of belief in the mystical, even within the liturgical churches."

Mysticism is defined as "direct experience of ultimate reality."[3] From this definition we can see how far removed most of us are from the experience of the mystical in our daily lives. It is very difficult for people today to believe in any reality that transcends the world of the senses. We accept only truth which is based on "scientific facts" and discount that truth which is based on feeling and intuition. Yet at the core of all religions is the reality of the mystical realm, the belief in a spiritual dimension that is not immediately apparent to the senses. In Christian tradition, this is seen, for example, in the belief that the sacraments are outer signs of the invisible, sacred grace of God. However, the institutional Church provides little instruction in understanding the deeper, mystical meaning of the sacraments. It also provides little guidance in inner spiritual practices such as prayer, contemplation, and meditation that help us get in contact with the mystical realm. A major problem of the Church today is that is has largely given up its unique function of helping people to experience the reality of the spiritual world.

The Imbalance of Eros and Logos

The concepts of "eros" and "logos" as defined by Carl Jung have helped us to better understand these problems of the Christian Church. Jung borrowed the terms "eros" and "logos" from the ancient Greeks to describe aspects of the human psyche. He said, "Eros is an interweaving; logos is differentiating knowledge, clarifying light; eros is relatedness; logos is discrimination and detachment."[4]   Logos refers to our rational nature, while eros is associated with our emotional nature; logos is associated with the mind and eros with the soul. We function through our logos nature when we are analyzing a problem, defining and classifying things, and developing rules and regulations. We express our eros nature through our intuition, instincts, and creativity. Our logos nature seeks predictability, security and structure, while our eros nature desires spontaneity, freedom, and flexibility. When we strive to be self-sufficient and independent we are expressing our logos nature, and when we desire love and intimacy we are motivated by the needs of eros. Since the time of the ancient Greek culture, logos has been associated with the masculine mode of consciousness and eros with the feminine mode.

The attainment of knowledge, which is highly valued in our Western culture, is a logos activity. Yet, the cultivation of wisdom, which is central to our eros nature, is neglected in the modern world. As members of the Makuna tribe of Columbia say, "Knowledge cuts up the world into little pieces, while wisdom makes it whole."[5] Our modern scientific pursuit of knowledge is based on the extreme development of the logos function, which attempts to understand phenomena by reducing them to their smallest parts. On the other hand, the search for wisdom requires us to develop the ability to perceive things holistically.

An intuitive, holistic vision that is inspired by eros perceives the interconnectedness of all things. All beings are connected within a web of relationships in this view, for the essence of eros is relatedness. It is through our eros nature that we can feel our connection to other people, animals, rocks, trees, stars, and ultimately God. Eros expresses itself in our experience of communion with the cosmos and unity with the Divine. This is the basis for the mystical experience. It is the relatedness of eros that is sorely lacking in our modern Western society. Logos qualities have dominated Western culture since the Renaissance and caused a subsequent devaluing of our eros nature. This is the root of most of the problems that we are experiencing today: the two sides of human nature are out of balance and the resulting one-sidedness has been very destructive. For example, the logos sense of separateness and independence without the counterbalancing eros sense of relatedness has led to the alienation which is so prevalent in our modern world. Likewise, the emphasis on logos characteristics of rationality, logic, and analysis without the eros qualities of intuition, emotion, and holistic perception has led to the horrors of modern mechanized warfare.

The problems of the institutional Church are also due to the imbalance in which the logos qualities have been dominant for centuries. The Christian Church has often looked upon eros qualities of intuition, emotion, and instinct with suspicion and sometimes even contempt. This overemphasis on logos qualities has led the Church to define "Christian" very narrowly, as someone who adheres to the doctrines and follows the rules which have been dictated by the Church hierarchy. One is classified as a "true Christian" only if one accepts the revelation of Christ as it has been interpreted by the authorities of the Church and become fixed in dogma. Those who do not conform to these prescriptions are labeled "heretics." However, the eros approach views revelation as a flowing, organic, evolving process which is not limited to any historical time period or interpretation by religious authority. The spiritual seeker, by remaining open to her eros qualities of feeling and intuition, will more readily discover this revelation on the bypaths.

The Misunderstanding of Archetype and Symbol

Central to this approach to revelation is an understanding of the relationship between symbol and archetype. Carl Jung defines archetype as a "primordial image" or "motif" within the collective unconscious, the universal aspect of the psyche that is shared by all human beings. However, an archetype is more than simply an image; it is emotionally charged or "numinous," and thus possesses the power for transformation.[6] Symbols may be looked upon as the clothing or outer manifestation of archetypes. By accepting Jung's concept of the universality and permanence of archetypes, we can think of symbols as the unique and variable emergence of the essential archetype in any given culture and era. For example, the numinous image of the resurrected god has been symbolized in various guises throughout human history: as Dumuzi in ancient Sumer, Osiris in Egypt, Dionysius in Greece, and Attis in Rome. The representation of this archetype in Christian tradition is, of course, Jesus of Nazareth. For the devout Christian, Jesus Christ as the symbol of the Savior-God carries all of the powerful numinosity of the archetype.

Symbols must be understood through the eros functions of imagination and intuition. A danger that is prevalent in all religions is that the logos nature, in its attempt to define and categorize the symbols of its tradition, misses the meaning of the underlying archetype. It is of utmost importance to understand that symbols are not **the** archetype, but only point **to** the archetype which is ultimately unknown. A symbol by its very nature is not fixed or rigid, but inherently expresses multiple meanings. This is why the imaginative and creative aspects of eros are necessary for the interpretation of symbols. Logos attempts to concretely define religious symbols, which are so commonly found in institutional religions, indicate a profound misunderstanding of the relationship between symbol and underlying archetype. It is this misguided practice of literalizing religious symbols, rather than cultivating an openness to symbolic meanings, which so frequently lies beneath the accusations of "heresy" against pilgrims who walk on the bypaths.

The Concept of Heresy

Modern Biblical scholarship has confirmed that there was a tremendous diversity of pathways in early Christianity. These reflected the varying interpretations of the numerous religious symbols that were emerging during this unique historical period.

As Elaine Pagels points out, "during the first and second centuries, Christians scattered throughout the world, from Rome to Asia, Africa, Egypt, and Gaul, read and revered quite different traditions, and various groups of Christians perceived Jesus and his message very differently."[7] Many of these early Christian bypaths developed an eros approach to revelation and spirituality, and emphasized an intensely personal relationship to the Divine. A respect for the feminine, the natural world, and mystical experience was often found as a corollary to the value placed upon eros on these bypaths. However, out of the turbulence caused by the many conflicting versions of Christianity during its first few centuries, a movement developed with the purpose of forming one universal Church. This was important in the political realm in order to consolidate the power of the Church in its position against the authorities of the secular state. Thus the Council of Nicaea was convened in 325 CE and one orthodox creed was defined to be binding for all Christians. The dogma of the Trinity was established at this time, and all true Christians were expected to profess belief in "the Holy Ghost, the Lord, Giver of Life, who proceedeth from the Father, Who with the Father and the Son together is worshipped and glorified..."[8] No other interpretation of Christian thought was now acceptable to the Church. After many debates, the texts that would form the exclusive canon for the Christian Bible were selected. The resulting New Testament, which contains only a small portion of the Christian sacred writings of the time, is thus "a highly censored and distorted version of ancient religious literature."[9] Through this process, the Christian Church increasingly emphasized the logos characteristics through its definition of dogma and development of ecclesiastical structure. When Christianity became the official religion of the Roman Empire in 380 CE, it became even more entrenched in the patriarchal foundation of the Greco-Roman civilization. All other versions of Christianity that posed a threat to the power of the Roman Church hierarchy were persecuted and often destroyed.[10] This was the fate of many of the spiritual bypaths which were branded "heretical," such as the various gnostic sects. The diversity of early Christianity was virtually eliminated by the dominant Church. Thus, the official version of Christianity that developed into the institutional Church was founded on the Roman legal model of a patriarchal, hierarchical, urban society. The problems of Christianity, which stem from an excessive emphasis on logos and corresponding neglect of eros aspects of human nature, have been inherent from the beginning for the institutional Church. As Martin Palmer says, "The imposition of one cultural model of Christianity - the Western model - has been the cause of immense problems..." Then he raises the question which for us has been the most basic one in our quest for a personally authentic spirituality: "Do we have to accept the baggage of Western theology in order to be Christians?"[11] The answer that we have found is "No."

THE SIGNIFICANCE OF CHRISTIANITY

We can understand the decision that many thoughtful, compassionate people have made to leave Christianity because of the Church's history of intolerance and negativity towards the body, the natural world, and women. However, we believe that there are many reasons why it is important for those of us who live in Western culture and were raised as Christians to stay within our tradition and commit ourselves to discovering the spiritual treasures which are hidden within it. In order to do this, we must make a distinction between Christianity as an institution and the life and teachings of Jesus Christ. As Gregory Bateson says, "we have lost the core of Christianity."[12] We believe that this essential core of Christianity, which has been lost through the building of the interstate highway of the Christian Church, is Christ's message of love. Jesus, through his words and his actions, emphasized the primacy of love in a society where both Roman and Jew were bound to the law. This message of Christ is still relevant, and in fact even more necessary, for our world today. We desperately need to follow Christ's way of love and develop the eros qualities of compassion, wisdom and wholeness in order to bring healing to our world. As Arthur Versluis says, "when one draws on the full scope of Christian tradition...one finds that Christianity itself offers great riches and much guidance in our present situation."[13]

11

We also believe, as Christian tradition teaches, that the incarnation of Jesus Christ was a unique event, with profound significance for humanity and all of creation. Christianity continues to have great value as the container for the Christ-mystery. Jesus Christ is the culminating figure in a long series of dying and resurrected gods, such as Osiris, Tammuz, Adonis, and Dionysius, whose rites were celebrated in the Greco-Roman mystery religions. But the significance of Jesus Christ is that in him the archetypal Savior-God is united with the concrete, physical human being. As Jean Houston says, "The resurrection story of Jesus differs radically from that of the traditional mystery cult figures. By being historical, by living a human existence in space and time, Jesus brought a new experience to the transpersonal and archetypal dimension of God-Identity."[14] The Christian faith is based on the central mystery of the Incarnation, in which the Eternal enters the temporal world and the Divine enters into human life.

The manifestation of the archetypal Christ within the historical figure of Jesus of Nazareth marks a turning point in the evolution of human consciousness. Jesus provides us with a model for the fully realized divine potential within human beings. He calls us to follow him in the task of actualizing our own divine essence, the "Godseed" which is planted within our human body.[15] In this sense the apostle Paul proclaims to the early Christians that they already possess the "first fruits of the Spirit" (Romans 8:23). The divine seeds which have borne this fruit signify the beginning of a spiritual process which will eventually culminate in complete transformation for those who follow the way of Christ. For Jesus Christ, as the human being who is also divine, reveals to us the result of the process of divinization, the possibilities for humanity when the spiritual fruit is fully ripened.

Carl Jung describes the divine essence within the human being, which we see fully actualized in the figure of Jesus Christ, as the archetype of the "Self." The Self archetype is expressed in symbols of totality and drives our growth toward individuation or wholeness. Jung claims, "Christ exemplifies the archetype of the Self. He represents a totality of a divine or heavenly kind...Christ is an embodiment of the God-image..."[16] Thus Jung believes that

12

Jesus Christ has major psychological significance as the supreme representative of the Self archetype in Western culture. Emma Jung also explains the importance of the Christ image for our culture because "all the contemporary symbolic images of the Self, such as the fish, the cross, the Son of Man and others, have crystallized around it from out of the depths of the collective unconscious."[17] Because of the central importance of Jesus Christ to the Western psyche, Carl Jung warns Westerners against looking to Eastern religions to develop their spirituality. He advises those of us who are rooted in Western culture to work with our own cultural symbols which have been shaped by our Judeo-Christian heritage.[18] In the terms of Jung's analytical psychology, to follow Christ means to commit ourselves to the quest for our own spiritual wholeness.

There is great spiritual treasure to be found within Christian tradition to aid us in this quest. One of the reasons that many people leave their own tradition to seek spiritual truth elsewhere is that we tend to see more of the ideal when we look at other religions. For example, we may compare the holiness of Buddhist monks to that of average Christians, or the esoteric mysteries of Eastern scriptures to the commonplace stories of the Bible. In such cases, the foreign and unfamiliar religions may appear to be much more spiritual than our own tradition. However, we can find the same spirituality in our own religious tradition if we delve deeply enough. If we approach our familiar Scriptures with fresh eyes, as though reading them for the first time, we will discover a wealth of spiritual truth. If we examine the lives of Christian saints and study the Christian mystic literature, we will find a holiness and mysticism as profound as that of any other religion.

The Jungian analyst Thomas Moore, in his book *The Care of the Soul*, also claims that "one obvious potential source of spiritual renewal is the religious tradition in which we were brought up."[19] He suggests that we bring a fresh imagination to the insights of our inherited religion and act as a "reformer" within it, just as Luther and Buddha did. This is the task for the contemporary seeker who walks on the spiritual bypaths, whose experiences can serve as the basis for a continuing renewal of our spirituality as well as ensuring that Christianity remains a "living tradition."[20]

An analogy of the spiritual quest that has been especially meaningful for us is the widely known description of all the world's spiritual traditions as paths ascending the same mountain. All true paths will eventually lead to the top of the mountain; the spiritual experience of Enlightenment, Divine Love, or Union with the Beloved is the same regardless of its name. The paths draw closer and closer together the nearer they are to the top. But the great tragedy of humanity is that most of us spend our time and energy at the bottom of the mountain, trying to convince others to go along with us on our path instead of committing ourselves to the rigorous journey of climbing the mountain. If we stay at the base of the mountain, arguing over which path is the "right" one, we will never proceed very far on our spiritual quest.

We came to a point in our own spiritual quests where we realized that we were firmly committed to the Christian path, even though we saw many problems in the institutional Church. In facing our disappointments and frustrations with the Christian Church, we had to make the decision not to go back down the mountain to begin another road. Instead, we made the commitment to stay on the same path but to explore it more fully and deeply, realizing that in doing so we would be drawing closer in communion to the other spiritual paths. It was through this process that we came to discover the bypaths of Christian tradition and realized that we were actually walking on the Path of ChristoSophia.

This is the path of the heart which follows the essence of Christ's message, the inclusive way of love rather than the divisiveness which results from an emphasis on dogma. This path provides an alternative Christianity that stresses the eros qualities of the heart, the feminine, and the mystical. It is an alternative "Church of Love"[21] which has always existed like a hidden, underground spring beneath the visible structure of institutional Christianity. This spring has welled up at various periods throughout Christian history, in the gnostic versions of Christianity which proliferated in the first few centuries, then in the Middle Ages with the troubadours and mystics, and again today as eros qualities re-emerge in our modern world.

THE TRANSFORMATION OF CHRISTIANITY

Our current time is very similar in many ways to the historical period during which Christ lived and the Christian community was born. Both are times of great crisis and confusion, when the traditional culture no longer seems to provide order and meaning to life. Both are times when the old religious forms no longer seem to work for many people and the culture is in a state of transition, waiting for the new forms to emerge. It was in such a time of upheaval, very much like ours, that Jesus arrived to provide the new stories and symbols which were to transform his culture and provide meaning for most of Western civilization for almost 2000 years. In referring to this process, Jesus said, "no one puts new wine into old wineskins...one puts new wine into fresh wineskins." (Mark 2:22) Jesus brought "fresh wineskins" in the form of his teachings and parables which carried the "new wine" of eros - love and relatedness - to a patriarchal, legalistic society which had been dominated by logos for centuries. The early Christian communities continued the process of creating "fresh wineskins" in the form of symbols and stories to hold the new spiritual truths brought by Christ.

Today we find ourselves in a similar situation to these early Christians. The old containers no longer hold authentic spiritual experience for most people in this time of massive cultural upheaval. Many people have become totally alienated from religion and believe only in a scientific, materialist worldview that leaves life devoid of meaning and purpose. Others have turned back in an attempt to revitalize the old forms of religion, such as the patriarchal foundation of fundamentalist Christianity. However, we believe that neither of these approaches provides a truly viable container for the future. While we may bring much of value from the old forms, what we ultimately need are new containers which will express the valuable essence of Christianity in a form that is meaningful for us today. We must go **through** Christianity to further develop the symbols and myths of Christian tradition for the renewal and evolution of consciousness in our Western culture.

As Jean Houston says, "Whenever a society is in a state of breakdown and breakthrough...it often requires the new social

15

alignment that myth can bring. The myth does not have to be new; it can be a very old myth seen in ways that mediate and refocus the issues of the time."[22] We need to re-tell the Christian story in a new way that is compatible with the scientific discoveries and the culture of our own age. In doing so, we recognize that many Christian stories have been told throughout the ages; the theme of God's revelation through Christ has been expressed in many variations in different times and places. As Thomas Berry explains, Christian tradition is a "process" which continually expresses itself in new forms rather than a fixed system of belief or behavior.[23] The forms of Christianity must continue to evolve, as they have throughout history, in order to meet the critical needs of our present age. A renewed Christianity can be the source for a mythos which provides meaning in our time of paradigm shift when values, beliefs, and world views are undergoing tremendous transformation.

There are many positive aspects of our current age that can aid this renewal of the Christian mythos. Modern discoveries and scholarship have brought new perspectives to our understanding of Christian tradition and an awareness of new possibilities for its future. Recent research in history and theology has clarified the context in which early Christian beliefs and practices developed, thus helping us to discern the difference between the essence of Christianity and its outmoded forms. The work of feminist theologians in particular has challenged us to re-examine many of the old forms of Christianity that are embedded in a rigidly patriarchal system. In addition, archaeological discoveries such as the Dead Sea Scrolls and the Gnostic Gospels have brought to light some of the variety of the spiritual bypaths that were destroyed through the building of the interstate Christian Church. Study of these scriptures is providing alternative viewpoints and fresh insights into Christian symbols, stories and teachings.

We can also obtain a broader perspective and deeper understanding of our own tradition by exploring other spiritual paths. We have much more opportunity to do this today because we live in a global society where the tremendous variety of spiritual paths from diverse cultures and different historical periods are now available to us. The danger in this situation is that we may simply stay at the base of the mountain, to use our earlier analogy, as we superficially try out one path after another. However, if we follow the path of our own spiritual tradition far enough, we will become aware of the underlying oneness of spiritual truth. The symbols and stories of all religions are the outward containers that hold an inner, universal meaning. Through this process, we can perceive more clearly the essence of Christianity, that divine wisdom which is shared by all authentic spiritual paths. We can then cast off those old containers that are obstacles to our path in this current age, and allow the new containers for spiritual truth which are relevant to our time to emerge.

It may seem paradoxical that the Christian mythos has such a tremendous potential for renewal in a society as rational and materialistic as ours. But it is the very fact that our scientific, secular society has not been able to provide a sense of coherence and meaning for people's lives that some form of spiritual renewal must occur. As Carl Jung points out, when the polarities of the psyche become too unbalanced, an "enantiodromia" occurs and the side which has been repressed has to regain balance.[24] In a time when logos characteristics have been excessively dominant for many centuries, in both our religious institutions and society as a whole, the eros qualities must reappear to restore a psychic equilibrium. In a time when "scientism" is the religious faith for a majority of people in the West, even those who nominally call themselves "Christians," authentic spirituality must re-emerge to provide a sense of meaning and wholeness to life.

In addition, a secular society such as ours offers much greater freedom to explore various spiritual paths. In the past, in an "Age of Faith," there was great persecution of those who openly strayed from the interstate highway of the institutional Church, which was seen as the only true way to salvation. The Church generally labeled the bypaths as "heretical," so that many individual seekers were discouraged from pursuing alternative visions of Christianity. Today there no longer exists a single Christian Church in the West which wields the monolithic power that it once did. Many of our institutions, both religious and secular, seem to be breaking apart. While we see the negative consequences of this fragmentation, it

17

is nevertheless this very situation which is making it much more possible to gain access to the spiritual bypaths. And in our current critical situation, many more people are recognizing the necessity of searching for a renewal of the Christian mythos along these bypaths. As Carl Jung also points out, we are living in a time of "kairos," the right time for the transformation of our myths and symbols.[25] Renewal of the Christian mythos can bring about a balance in the psyche and in society through the recovery of eros. The new containers of story and symbol, which express the essence of Christianity, will be created through the activity of both rational scholarship and the visionary imagination. In this way fresh insights into Biblical history and theology will combine with the discovery of repressed archetypal elements to forge a new form of Christianity in which eros and logos are dynamically balanced.

One important characteristic of this transformation will be a changed view of the Bible as "myth with meaning" instead of "history with a moral."[26] The Church Fathers, under the influence of Greco-Roman thought, did not understand that the foundation of the Bible was the mythology of the Near East. This led to an emphasis on dogma, ideology and literal interpretations of the Bible by the institutional Church. In this view, the Bible contains only one, fixed Truth to which all Christians must subscribe. A major transformation occurs, however, when one instead reads the Bible as mythology. From this perspective, any interpretation of the Bible is not seen as the Truth but as one of many possible symbolic meanings. As Joseph Campbell explains, myth reveals psychological and spiritual truths rather than historical and scientific facts. Because mythic images represent universal processes of the psyche, the archetypes referred to by Carl Jung, they must be interpreted symbolically rather than as literal descriptions of specific persons or events.[27] Reading the Bible mythologically engages the heart and soul, not just the mind. The intuitive and feeling functions must be used to discover the multiple levels of symbolic meaning contained in Biblical stories. Discovering for oneself the unending possibilities which are found in the mythology of the Bible opens up a much richer and deeper understanding of Scripture. This is the wisdom of the Bible to be gained on the bypaths.

Another significant characteristic of transformed Christianity will be an emphasis on the Cosmic Christ as well as the historical Jesus. As Matthew Fox points out, Christianity has emphasized the role of the historical Jesus since the time of the Enlightenment. The Cosmic Christ is "the 'pattern that connects' all the atoms and galaxies of the universe, a pattern of divine love and justice that all creatures and all humans bear within them...this image of God present in all things."[28] The Cosmic Christ is the eternal "I - am" or Being, and is also the divinity which is within each one of us. In Jesus of Nazareth the eternal Word and Wisdom of God – ChristoSophia – became manifest within humanity. It is this union of the Cosmic Christ and the historical Jesus that is the basis for Christ mysticism.[29] The Divine, through Christ, is connected to all of humanity and the entire cosmos. This is the central way that Christ is experienced on the bypaths.

The renewed emphasis on the Cosmic Christ also forms the basis for the panentheistic view that is crucial for a transformed Christianity. Panentheism refers to the recognition that the Divine is both transcendent **and** immanent within all of creation. To develop this perspective we must go beyond the confining "either/or" of logical thinking to the "both/and" thinking of expanded awareness. It is this type of thought that is necessary in order to understand the divine/human union in Christ Jesus, as well as the transcendent/immanent union within the Cosmic Christ.

These transformative characteristics of Christianity which are encountered on the bypaths are consistent with the emerging paradigm as described by many contemporary thinkers. Just as visionary scientists and social activists have realized that contemporary problems cannot be solved by the ways of thinking that have dominated Western culture, so have spiritual visionaries recognized that the problems of the institutional Christian Church cannot be resolved without a change in perception. Our culture as a whole, including religion, is making a shift from the dualistic, patriarchal paradigm which has existed for at least three millennia to a holistic, ecological, partnership world view.[30] In this new paradigm, nonconceptual ways of knowing such as intuition and feeling are as accepted as analytical, logical reasoning. The spiritual life embraces both rational study and mystical experience. The ecological view of the emerging paradigm is replacing our Western culture's emphasis on domination and control over nature with a perception of humanity's embeddedness in nature and an emphasis on spiritually reconnecting with the natural world. The emerging paradigm that stresses partnership is shown in a spiritual community based on cooperation and equality, rather than the hierarchical power which is emphasized in the institutional Church.

Pilgrims who walk on the spiritual bypaths today are blazing the trail for a transformed Christianity which is consistent with the new paradigm emerging in our culture. The feminine, nature, and mystical bypaths, which for many centuries have been blocked and destroyed by the institutional Christian Church, are being reopened and rebuilt today as a part of this process of cultural transformation. For the holistic view, which perceives the interconnectedness of all things, is the central feature of the feminine bypath. The recognition of the divine within nature re-sacralizes the natural world, which is the essence of the nature bypath. The recognition of the Cosmic Christ as the divine within the human soul gives the potential to achieve union with God, the central aim of the mystical bypath. Because these bypaths are so interrelated, we find that when walking upon any one of them we are in fact traveling upon all three. Therefore, we can set out on the feminine bypath, the nature bypath, or the mystical bypath in order to begin our pilgrimage on the Path of ChristoSophia.

The Feminine Bypath

". . .all her paths are peace"

Proverbs 3:17

CHAPTER II: DISCOVERING THE FEMININE BYPATH

Connectedness is the vision at the heart of feminist spirituality.[1]

Feminist spirituality is the essence of the Path of ChristoSophia. It is this essential feminine vision which has been lost through the centuries by massive construction of the interstate highway of Christianity. Just as the interstate highway system symbolizes the masculine approach to travel in its linear, rational design, so does interstate Christianity emphasize masculine qualities such as authority, law and judgment in its organization as well as its image of deity. However, traveling the Path of ChristoSophia is like walking along a meandering bypath close to nature, where one encounters the feminine qualities of spiritual experience and the Divine.

It is the vision of connectedness as the central aspect of the feminine bypath that also underlies the nature and the mystical bypaths. On the feminine bypath one readily perceives the interconnectedness of all creation, the "web of life," so that one's spiritual experience necessarily becomes grounded in a respect and appreciation for nature. On the feminine bypath one also becomes conscious of the connectedness of the soul with the Divine. It is this experience of union with divinity which is the hallmark of the mystical way.

THE "FEMINIST SPIRITUALITY" OF JESUS

By looking at the teachings of Christ, we see that the central core of his message was the practice of the feminine values of love and compassion. In fact Jesus' teachings were so radical essentially because of their feminine nature which opposed the masculine values that were paramount in his society as well as our own. His sayings such as "love your enemies" (Matt. 5:44), "Do not judge" (Matt. 7:1), and "Whoever becomes humble like this child is the greatest in the kingdom of heaven" (Matt. 18:4) emphasize the virtues of forgiveness, peace, and humility, which are just as difficult to practice in our own day as they were in his. In addition, Jesus conveyed his message of love and unity primarily through metaphors and parables, which require a feminine mode of intuitive receptivity in order to understand their meaning. Logical, analytical thinking cannot penetrate the essence of his message. Perhaps a major reason that so many women were attracted to Jesus' ministry is that his message and means of communicating it express a feminine mode of consciousness.[2]

Jesus also showed his opposition to the patriarchal social conventions of his day through his treatment of women. As Riane Eisler points out, Jesus' teachings embodied a "partnership" model for human relationships based on the equality of men and women, rather than the "dominator" model of male superiority which was the unquestioned norm of the time.[3] In such actions as his conversation with the Samaritan woman (John 8:3-11) and his forgiveness of the sinful woman (Luke 7:37-50), Jesus displayed an esteem for women of all backgrounds, in all situations, which shocked even his closest disciples.

Jesus used his interactions with women as examples to challenge the sexual biases of his culture which discriminated against women. In his reply to Martha's rebuke of her sister Mary for listening to Jesus' teachings while she herself worked, he upheld the right of women to concentrate on spiritual matters rather than conventional domestic activities (Luke 10: 38-42). His reply to the accusers of the woman caught in adultery, "Let anyone among you who is without sin be the first to throw a stone at her" (John 8:7), reveals their hypocrisy in a society where a woman's seduction was punished much more severely than a man's lust. Likewise, his admonition that "everyone who looks at a woman with lust has already committed adultery with her in his heart" (Matt. 5:28) shifts the responsibility for sexuality onto the man's motives rather than projecting blame onto the woman in her traditional role as "temptress."[4]

It is therefore not surprising that women played a central role in the life of Christ: his mother Mary, Martha and Mary of Bethany, and Mary Magdalene are prime examples. Women traveled with him as disciples and provided their resources for his ministry (Luke 8: 2-3). According to Gospel accounts, women were the first to encounter the resurrected Jesus and were instrumental in forming the early group of his followers after this event. As the early Christian communities developed and practiced the feminine virtues preached by Christ, spiritual equality for men and women was the norm. In the letters of Paul, women are addressed as prominent leaders, evangelists, apostles and prophets within the early Christian community. Because the first Christians met in homes, which were the primary domain of women, it was natural that they would play significant roles in the beginning of the Christian movement.[5]

However, this "theology of equality" which was the foundation of early Christianity was drastically altered during subsequent centuries of Christianity. The conflicting perspectives on women's roles in the Church can be seen in these two verses from the New Testament: "there is no longer male or female; for all of you are one in Christ Jesus" (Galatians 3:28) in contrast to "Let a woman learn in silence with full submission" (1 Timothy 2:11).[6] Unfortunately, it was the latter viewpoint which became dominant as the early Christian bypath developed into the interstate highway of the Christian Church.

THE SUPPRESSION OF THE FEMININE IN CHRISTIANITY

It is often surprising for people to realize that the message and practices of Christ, as well as his earliest followers, placed a high value on the feminine because historically Christianity has expressed exactly the opposite point of view. As Margaret Starbird says,

"Institutional Christianity, which has nurtured Western civilization for nearly two thousand years, may have been built over a gigantic flaw in doctrine - a theological 'San Andreas Fault': the denial of the Feminine."[7] However, the suppression of feminine values and the condemnation of women's leadership roles in the Christian Church can be traced primarily to historical and cultural circumstances rather than to intrinsic theological doctrines.[8]

This early, radical religious movement underwent profound changes during its first centuries as it developed into the accepted religion of the Roman State. During this process of transformation, Christianity increasingly abandoned the challenge to authority and conventions which marked its beginnings and instead adopted the prevailing norms and practices of the Greco-Roman culture in which it was now firmly enmeshed. This had a major impact on gender stereotyping within the Christian Church. The gender beliefs of the Greeks and Romans were based on a sharp differentiation between male and female nature, and the public and private sphere. Public places were viewed as the domain of men. Roles and activities in the public sphere were not acceptable for the proper, chaste woman. Instead the domain of women was the household, and upper class women especially could wield much power and influence within this private sphere. This was the case with many women in the early Church, who acted as leaders for congregations meeting in their homes. The suppression of women's leadership roles within the Church was due largely to the movement of Christianity from the private sphere into the public realm.[9]

This transition to the public sphere was marked by the conversion of many members of the Roman ruling class to Christianity in the third century. This resulted in the incorporation of new forms of leadership within the Church based on the Roman model. The Church became a political body with a hierarchical structure of governance. A division developed between clergy and laity, and a stratification of power defined their positions. As this hierarchy of political power developed within the Church, women increasingly lost the personal power they had wielded in the private sphere.

In the fourth century, this change in leadership patterns was shown in the development of the Christian temple which was patterned after the Roman basilica. Because the pre-Christian basilica was the center of civic authority, the interstate Church took over this model to reinforce its patriarchal structure and emphasis on rule by law. The role of the Christian bishop was patterned on that of the Roman magistrate as a dispenser of judgment. As the meeting place for worship was moved from the private sphere of the "house church" to the public realm of the basilica, Christians adhered to the Greco-Roman social conventions by further denying women leadership roles in the now public religion.[10]

It was this process of institutionalization during the third and fourth centuries which transformed the small bypath of the early Christian movement into the interstate highway of the Christian Church. As an "institution" is characterized by a patriarchal, hierarchical structure, Christianity became increasingly dominated by the masculine qualities of power, order, and control. Therefore it is not surprising that the feminine values preached and practiced by Christ were suppressed and women lost their roles as leaders within the Church. And without a powerful "feminine voice," the Christian Church developed in even more masculine dominated ways in the ensuing centuries.

A crucial event in this development occurred when St. Augustine's teachings on sin and sexuality were accepted in the early fifth century as a foundation for building the interstate Church. Augustine's interpretation of the story of Adam and Eve (Genesis 2:8-3:24) as an explanation for the existence of "original sin" eventually prevailed over earlier interpretations of the story which had stressed humanity's freedom to choose good or evil. According to Augustine, all humanity is "fallen" due to Adam's sin. "Original sin" is conferred through the process of conception and is closely linked to sexuality.[11] Thus Augustine instilled a profoundly dualistic viewpoint in Western Christianity in which the spiritual world and the "fallen," material world are antagonistic to each other. As men were identified with the positive side of spirit, culture, and intellect, and women were identified with the negative side of body, nature, and sexuality, the position of women became devalued even further.

Again, it was the historical and cultural conditions which supported the construction of the interstate Church that led to the acceptance of Augustine's dualistic views rather than the life-affirming perspectives of other Christians which were prominent at the time. The Church was gaining much greater temporal power as it became even more closely linked with the Roman State, and Augustine's view of "original sin" validated the power of both Church and State to govern humans who could not be trusted to make their own free choices.[12] As the patriarchal structure of the Christian Church developed, its primary value was obedience to law and authority. But the passions of instinctive sexuality are unpredictable, and they resist efforts to enforce obedience and control.[13] Thus the male rulers of the Church readily accepted Augustine's equation of sin with the sexual passions which seemed to be beyond willful control.

With the incorporation of Augustine's views, the interstate Church built its theology upon the belief that "sexuality was no longer a way to the divine but a positive obstacle."[14] This dualistic view led to the rise of the monastic tradition and its practice of asceticism in order to overcome the temptations of the body. During the sixth century this negative attitude toward sexuality led to the requirement of a vow of celibacy for priests in the Western Church. All of these developments were profoundly damaging to the feminine element and the position of women in the Church. With sex seen as evil, women were often perceived as temptresses or, even worse, as agents of the Devil. A woman could become "spiritual" only by renouncing her natural sexuality. But even a celibate woman could not separate herself from her sexual functions in her monthly reproductive cycle. The belief that all women therefore were "unclean" at times was used to further limit the roles of women within the Church.[15]

But as the status of the feminine steadily eroded through the centuries while the interstate highway of Christianity was built, a paradoxical veneration of the Virgin Mary slowly evolved. By the Middle Ages a Cult of the Virgin had developed in which Mary as the "Mother of God" and "Queen of Heaven" was worshiped in a virtually similar manner to the Great Goddesses of antiquity. In this way the archetypal Mother Goddess, so severely repressed by the Christian Church, found a way to at least partially manifest through the person of Mary. However, in keeping with the Church's negative views towards sexuality, a major focus for the veneration of Mary became her "purity" as a virgin. The instinctive, passionate, lusty elements of the Great Goddess continued to be denied access in the interstate Church.

The Protestant Reformation in the sixteenth century brought both positive and negative changes in the Church's attitudes toward women and sexuality. Martin Luther taught that the body was good since it was made in the image of God, that sexuality was divinely created, and that marriage rather than celibacy was the will of God.[16] However, the Protestant addition to the interstate Church has also had the effect of further removing the feminine aspects of the image of God. Protestantism arose during a new cultural phase of patriarchal development, when great strides in scientific and technological innovation led to increased forms of centralized authority by political powers. This centralization of power was mirrored in the reformed concept of deity. According to the Protestants, sinful humanity was completely dependent upon the grace of God alone for salvation. The Roman Catholic Church, in its devotion to Mary and the female saints, had provided a valuable avenue to the feminine element of the Divine. But according to the Protestants, intermediaries to God such as Mary and the saints were not necessary. Mary was no longer presented in the majestic images of divinity as Queen of Heaven or Mother of the Redeemer, but instead appeared in Protestantism only in the human image of humble, faithful virgin.[17] When the significant roles of Mary and the female saints were suppressed and the "superstitious" practices of intercession were condemned, Christians who followed the Protestant route on the interstate highway of Christianity lost their primary access to the feminine dimension of the Divine.

In tracing the development of the interstate Church, we can see why "the Fisherman of Nazareth has long ceased to bear much relationship to historical Christianity."[18] The feminist spirituality that was the essence of Christ's Good News for men and women was completely submerged as the institution of the Christian Church developed. Within several centuries this feminist spirituality could still be clearly found only on the small bypaths. Since the Church incorporated the patriarchal, hierarchical power structure of its society, it was threatened by the feminine values emphasized by Christ. Thus the history of the Christian Church became a record of the deliberate destruction of the bypaths which honored the feminine as the core of the Christian message.

THE NEED FOR THE FEMININE IN CHRISTIANITY

We live today in very different historical and social conditions than did the builders of the interstate Church. They denied the value of the feminine in order to adapt to the conditions of their society, a process which was necessary for amassing the power and wealth needed to build such a complex structure as the Christian Church. However, the cultural conditions that we live in today require that we reclaim the feminine element which lies submerged within Christianity. To do this we must realize that neither the denial of the feminine aspect of deity nor the devaluation of women is divinely ordained, nor is the patriarchal, hierarchical structure of the Christian Church the only valid possibility for its form. We must see these one-sided aspects of the Christian Church for the culturally conditioned artifacts that they are, rather than the products of divine revelation. Doing this can allow us to explore the bypaths where the feminine voice can still be heard. And it is indeed crucial for pilgrims on the Path of ChristoSophia to reclaim the feminine in order for Christianity to continue to be a viable religion for many in our changing world. Our entire planet is in desperate need of the return of feminine values today. Christianity, which has been such a powerful force in Western civilization, must acknowledge how its denial of the feminine has greatly contributed to the conflicts and catastrophes of our modern world. The followers of Christ have a spiritual responsibility to be true to the vision of their Savior in proclaiming and practicing his message of feminist spirituality.

Central to this task is the restoration of the archetype of the Divine Feminine to Christianity. The archetype of the Great Mother or Goddess is an image which is innate to the human psyche.[19] She appears in different forms throughout human history and diverse cultures. Her names are many; among them are Isis, Athena, Rhiannon, Kali, and Kuan-Yin. She appears in a "light" form with qualities of love, compassion and fertility, as well as a "dark" form with qualities of anger, chaos, and destruction. However, in patriarchal Western civilization, where the Divine is imaged only as a masculine Father God, the great archetype of feminine deity has been repressed within the psyche. The result has been a one-sided development of masculine consciousness in individuals as well as in society. We have developed extraordinary powers of rational, logical, analytical thinking, which have brought incredible advances in science and technology. But we have dismissed those equally important powers of the repressed feminine consciousness such as intuition, feeling, and holistic thinking. The result of this lack of balance is the current world we live in, perched on the brink of ecological catastrophe or nuclear annihilation.

Healing this devastating imbalance within the larger world must begin with the spiritual healing of our own individual selves. As both women **and** men, we must bring to consciousness the feminine archetype within the psyche in order to be healed of this imbalance and thus made "whole." Reclaiming the feminine God-image within our own cultural and religious tradition is a major step in helping us develop and integrate the feminine within ourselves.

The limited symbol system of the interstate Church, which emphasizes only the masculine polarity, cannot adequately help individuals in their spiritual growth toward wholeness. This narrow image of the Divine as male also limits our experience of God. Many qualities which are part of the archetypal Divine Feminine, such as darkness, chaos, and destruction, are relegated to the Devil rather than God. Recognition of the "dark side of the Goddess" would have a profound effect on our experience of the Divine, and help greatly to overcome the dualistic views which have plagued Christianity. Acceptance of a more inclusive image of deity, which includes both the light and dark aspects of the Divine Feminine, will likely increase our awareness of both the majesty and the mystery of God.[20] Acceptance of the feminine mode of consciousness within ourselves will also lead to an increased value upon the "nonrational" aspects of spiritual experience such as intuition, mysticism, and visionary experiences which the Church has generally viewed suspiciously. In this way our means for spiritual growth, as well as our experience of the Divine, can be deepened.

For these reasons it is extremely valuable for both women and men to affirm the archetypal Divine Feminine. However, it is especially important for women to do so. Thousands of years of patriarchal history have left their mark on the collective psyche of women. The interstate highway of Christianity was built upon the attitude that women were inferior to men, and they could not be spiritual unless they "became men." Christians were not taught to "celebrate femaleness as providing a unique avenue of access to God, or see in femaleness a profound experience of the divine."[21] In fact they were taught just the opposite: the female body was the source of evil, and sexuality, which a woman cannot separate from herself due to her monthly cycles, is sinful. This misogynist attitude which permeated our entire Western culture has engendered the feelings of inferiority, helplessness, and depression which are so commonly found in women. When a Christian woman looks to her cultural symbol for deity, she does not find a figure with whom she can identify in her essential femininity. This creates a barrier between her and the Divine because she cannot relate to God from her deepest self.

Thus incorporating feminine symbols of the Divine into theology and ritual can be a tremendously liberating spiritual experience for women. When a woman can look to an image of the Divine Feminine in both her light and dark aspects, she is more able to develop all of these complex qualities within herself. The model of a Divine Woman with strength, creativity and independence helps a woman to find her own powerful center within. She is able to affirm her feminine qualities, her body, and her sexuality, and feels validated in her deepest being. She no longer feels alienated from herself or from God.

Such a woman who finds her own spiritual autonomy will no longer be willing to accept an inferior role to man, either in a personal relationship or in a spiritual community. The ideal of an equal partnership between men and women is also supported by an image of God which includes both feminine and masculine dimensions. For a male God-image supports the patriarchal system.

As Mary Daly says, "So long as God is perceived as male, then the male is God."[22]   However, when both the masculine and feminine element are represented in the Divine, then men and women are valued equally.   Roles are based on personal qualities rather than simply gender. Thus the intrasexual harmony of the Divine becomes a model which humans can attempt to imitate in their own interpersonal relationships.[23]

When we witness the confusion and destruction brought about by the imbalances of our present world, it seems that to follow Christ today involves the struggle to liberate ourselves from the bonds of patriarchy which set men against women, spirit against nature, and morality against sexuality. The archetype of the Divine Feminine must be restored in our current age for the healing of ourselves, our relationships, and our planet. We will then discover the truth in the statement: "If we, like Jesus, can be inspired by the feminine aspect of God, we may be able to bring good news to our still all too patriarchal society."[24]

RESTORING THE FEMININE TO CHRISTIANITY

Once we have recognized the importance of restoring the feminine to Christianity, the following pragmatic questions arise: After almost 2000 years of a patriarchal mind-set, is it still possible to reclaim the feminine element which has been so severely suppressed by the Christian Church? And if so, how do we go about communicating the fundamental feminist nature of Christ's message to a society which is still caught in the throes of patriarchy? Our search for the answers to these questions must begin on the feminine bypath where our discoveries can lead to fresh, new ways of interpreting the basis of Scriptures, the role of women within the Bible and the Christian Church, and the images and language used to denote the Divine.

Feminist Interpretation of Scriptures

Our first question, regarding the possibility of reclaiming the feminine element in Christianity, has been answered in a strongly affirmative manner by a number of feminist theologians who are re-interpreting the meaning of Scripture and re-assessing the history of Christianity. They emphasize that the process of restoring the feminine dimension to Christianity must begin with a continual questioning of the underlying patriarchal values and attitudes found in the Scriptures, the teachings, and the structure of the Christian Church. The basis for questioning these patriarchal biases lies in Christ's teachings and practice of egalitarianism. Acknowledging the "feminist spirituality" of Christ leads to the consequent realization that patriarchalism is not inherent to Christianity. But throughout most of the Church's history theological scholarship was the province solely of men, and was conducted through a "patriarchal template" which shaped the thoughts and perceptions of individuals and entire societies.[25] Thus theology and Biblical scholarship served to maintain the interests of the patriarchal hierarchy of the Church. This situation is beginning to change today since women have recently begun the academic study of theology. The recognition of endemic male bias in theological studies has led these feminist theologians to question both the interpretation of Scriptural texts as well as the process by which certain documents were accepted or rejected for inclusion in the New Testament.

A pioneer in feminist theological scholarship was Elizabeth Cady Stanton, initiator of The Woman's Bible which was published in 1895 and 1898. In this work she attempted to re-interpret all the Biblical passages concerning women in light of patriarchal bias. Cady Stanton took a historical-critical approach to understanding the Bible, recognizing that historical and cultural conditions determine how divine revelation is expressed. She did not believe the Bible to be the literal "word of God" but understood it as an androcentric text, written by men and reflecting male interests and power. Her major insight was that the Bible can be used in the political struggle to limit women's freedom and power because it expresses the viewpoint of a patriarchal culture.[26]

An example of a contemporary theologian who is re-examining the history of Christianity through a feminist perspective is Elisabeth Schussler Fiorenza. She turns a questioning eye to the selection process of the canon of Christianity. There were many texts available to the early Christians but only certain ones were accepted by the Church Fathers in the fourth century as authoritative

Scripture. These were the documents which now comprise the New Testament of the Bible. As Fiorenza points out, the Christian canon was determined during a period in which there was great conflict over women's leadership roles in the Church. Those texts were eventually selected which supported barring women from positions of power within the Church. Thus "the canon is a record of the historical winners."[27]

Recognizing this fact calls for a "hermeneutics of suspicion,"[28] in which Biblical interpretation questions the patriarchal foundation of its texts. We must "learn to read the silences" of the Biblical documents in order to obtain clues to the egalitarian nature of the early Christian community.[29] For example, the canonical texts do not contain one story or statement in which Jesus supports the patriarchal views of his culture or calls for the submission of women. This is especially surprising considering the patriarchal context in which these stories were written. Thus this observation of what the New Testament does not contain strongly supports the view that Christ promoted equality between men and women.[30]

In a similar manner, it can be assumed that the references to women contained in the New Testament mention only a small portion of women's contributions to the early Christian movement. The official writings of the Church neglected and devalued women, so much information about the roles of women has probably been completely lost to history.[31] Yet enough material does exist in the New Testament to allow feminist theologians to begin to re-interpret the role of women and the understanding of deity in the early Christian movement.

However, considering its patriarchal bias, we must also broaden the sources of information we use beyond the accepted texts of the New Testament. There were many small Christian groups which were suppressed by the builders of the interstate highway of Christianity, and there were many texts with varying perspectives which were rejected from the official canon. Some of these alternative interpretations of the feminine element within Christianity can still be found on the feminine bypath. For example, an exploration of the gospels of various gnostic Christian sects reveals an often very different view of the feminine aspects of the Divine and the roles of female disciples of Christ. Seeing the "Christian story" told from such a different perspective can give us fresh insights and critical questions to ask of the traditional texts that we have been conditioned to accept. Thus a feminist study of early Christianity must extend to all Christian groups and texts, including the historical "losers" in the ideological struggles. The crucial test for the acceptance of the validity of various texts today must be the extent to which they express the essential feminist spirituality of Christ.[32]

Re-interpretation of Feminine Figures in the Bible

We have seen that with the aid of contemporary feminist theological scholarship it is indeed possible to reclaim the feminine elements within the Christian tradition. We must now turn to the second question, how do we go about communicating this feminist spirituality to a world which has so long subscribed to patriarchal interpretations of the Christian message? One of the ways, based on the approach of feminist theologians who look for those clues to the feminine presence which can be gleaned from even exceedingly androcentric texts, is to re-examine the women who appear in the Bible and re-interpret their significance. We must look beneath the surface of the text's presentation of the women figures to examine their deeper meaning. This is the approach taken by Ann Belford Ulanov in her book *The Female Ancestors of Christ*. She examines specifically the four female ancestors which are listed in the genealogy of Christ (Matthew 1:1-16): Tamar, Rahab, Ruth and Bathsheba. She raises the provocative question of why only these four women are included among the long list of males in Christ's genealogical history. Her intriguing answer is that the presence of these women in Christ's genealogy represent the feminine elements which must be included in our lives, and therefore in even a highly patriarchal religion. "These women bring with them the vital, deeply needed elements of the left-out feminine. It is as if the impulse to include the feminine begins on God's side, through these female ancestors from whom in time God will be born."[33]

What are these feminine elements which are represented by the female ancestors of Christ? According to Ulanov, Tamar symbolizes the "primordial power of women's sexuality."[34] She plays the role of a "temple prostitute," which demonstrates the connection between sexuality and spirituality (Genesis 38). Rahab is a prostitute who engages in the paradoxical behavior of "betraying as the way to be faithful to God."[35] By being disloyal to her own people as she helps the Hebrew men escape, she plays the role of traitor and trickster (Joshua 2: 1-24). These two women who are singled out as contributors to the bloodline of Jesus contain elements of the dark side of the Goddess: instinctive sexuality, self-assertive power, cunning intelligence, and destructive potential. Thus all aspects of the feminine are included in the genealogy of Christ, and therefore symbolically within him. Ruth, whose story makes up an entire book in the Hebrew Bible, represents the "initiating woman who makes things happen."[36] She is an example of the strong, independent woman who follows her heart by remaining loyal to the mother-in-law that she loves.

The Biblical accounts of Tamar, Rahab and Ruth relate to actual experiences of women who live within their bodies and act from the center of their deepest being. They do not passively submit to social conventions or to their "fates," but strive to fulfill God's will as they intuitively perceive it. The stories of these women present an authentic and positive image of the feminine in her many guises. The story of Bathsheba, however, depicts a different image. She is seduced by King David, who then arranges for her husband to be killed in battle so that he may marry her (Samuel 11). In the case of Bathsheba, "the feminine is not seen in its own right...but only as satellite to a masculine consciousness...the results for the kingdom...are disastrous. The kingdom is split in two."[37] This situation is symbolic of the condition of patriarchal culture in which the masculine and feminine elements are split off from each other, with all the disastrous consequences that ensue.

The inclusion of these four women in Christ's genealogy appears to symbolize the feminine aspects of being which will be united with the masculine in the incarnation of Christ. The honest portrayal of the living experiences of these women in the Biblical texts seems to prefigure Christ's own attitude toward women. For "Jesus redeems women from being seen only in terms of men's images of her. She is fully herself, to be judged, forgiven, blessed."[38]

Another contemporary woman who has accomplished an insightful and liberating reinterpretation of the feminine figures within the Bible is Miriam Therese Winter. She has set as her task to mine the "wealth of womanwisdom which is yet to be found in the word of God."[39] In a series of books, *WomanWitness*, *WomanWisdom*, and *WomanWord*, she uses a feminist perspective to reconstruct the lives of women who are mentioned in the Hebrew Scriptures, the Apocrypha, and the New Testament. She brings back the names of "forgotten" women of the Bible to our collective memory. These include Mary the wife of Cleopas who was a female disciple that probably stood at the foot of the cross,[40] Dorcas who was a disciple that was raised from the dead by the apostle Peter,[41] Euodia and Syntyche who appear to have been leaders in the Christian community at Philippi,[42] and numerous other women whose important roles in Biblical history have been glossed over in the traditional narratives.

In addition to bringing the names of these unknown women into the foreground of Scriptural narrative, Miriam Winter re-tells the stories of the few well-known women of the Bible such as Mary the mother of Jesus and Mary Magdalene from their perspectives as females. She provides an interpretive context for Scripture readings referring to women which causes us to reflect on the patriarchal biases inherent in the Biblical representations of these women's lives and roles. She presents us with fresh images of Biblical women which relate their experiences and trials to the struggles of women today. For example, her feminist interpretation of Mary's story replaces the image of Mary who has been distanced by theological doctrines with a portrayal of Mary as a woman with whom contemporary women can identify. It is especially women who can share Mary's awe when encountering the mystery of creation, celebration of the joy of giving birth, and pain at the suffering of her beloved child. Women share in the "primal priesthood" of Mary who, as female, was chosen first by the Creator to "lead the opening liturgy" in the preparation for Christ's incarnation.[43] The creative, transformative power of the feminine is revealed in Mary who serves as the vessel through which "will come the liberating force to make old structures new."[44] This image of Mary as a spiritually powerful, yet very human, woman can serve today to help liberate us from the oppressive structures of a patriarchal world.

Re-interpretation of the Roles of Women in Christianity

A vital part of the process of re-examining the significance of women who appear in the Bible involves re-interpreting the roles of women who are presented in the New Testament as followers of Christ or members of the early Christian community. A primary goal of feminist theology is to "restore the history of Christian beginnings to women. It claims the Christian past as woman's own past, not just as a male past in which women participated only on the fringes or were not active at all."[45]

There is sufficient evidence to make the claim that women's roles were equal to those of men in the early stages of Christianity. Several women are mentioned specifically as disciples of Jesus: Mary Magdalene, Joanna and Susanna (Luke 8:1-3). They traveled with him and provided for the needs of the group of disciples out of their own resources. The fact that these women are mentioned at all in the patriarchal context of the New Testament is evidence that they probably played very important roles within the group of Christ's followers. This passage also indicates that there were many other women among the disciples of Christ. Unfortunately, they are lost to us due to the virtual erasing of the names of women from the pages of the Christian story by the Church.

One woman whose name has not been forgotten, but instead has been besmirched by the patriarchal reformulations of the Church, is Mary Magdalene. It is apparent even from reading the Biblical accounts that Mary Magdalene played a very significant role in Christ's band of followers. In fact, in the Gospel of John it is Mary Magdalene who provides "the model for discipleship" rather than Peter.[46] It is Mary Magdalene who bravely stays at the cross during the crucifixion, who is the first to witness the risen Christ, and who is told to carry the message of Christ's resurrection to the other disciples. In this sense she is truly the first apostle. But in the sixth century her role was completely refashioned by the Church Fathers in order to serve the purposes of the patriarchal hierarchy.[47] Thus today when most people hear the name of Mary Magdalene they think of a penitent whore, which is a tragic distortion of the character presented in the Gospels as the most faithful disciple who is the first to truly understand the full meaning of Christ's revelation. In recognizing that the evidence points to the importance of Mary Magdalene's role among the disciples, we can begin to look for further clues about the significance of other women in the early Christian community. The historical record of this time supports the view that women played a primary role in developing the Christian movement. For instance, in the first few centuries of its existence Christians had to defend themselves against the charge that their religion was a religion for women.[48] And the fact that bitter controversy raged in the second and third centuries regarding women's leadership roles in the Church indicate that during the process of institutionalization, the Church was striving to overcome earlier forms of Christian theology and practice that accepted women's leadership. An example of this is the diatribe by Tertullian, a Church Father of the late second century, against women who dared to teach, exorcise, heal or baptize. The fact that he so strongly attacked these activities indicates that their practice must have been fairly common among Christian women.[49]

There are also records of the important contributions of women to the early Church contained in the texts of the New Testament. Because the canon of Christianity was selected with an aim to suppress women's power, the fact that these references exist at all provides very strong evidence that women were leaders in developing the early Christian communities. This was particularly true during the first two centuries after Christ's resurrection when congregations met in homes. Women's social role as household manager in Roman society equipped them to provide the leadership for early Christian groups which met in "house-churches." Women of higher social class and greater wealth often served as patrons for these first Christian communities.[50] Some of these women who were leaders of house churches that are mentioned in the Bible include: Mary, the mother of John Mark, who presided over a congregation which met in her home in Jerusalem (Acts 12:12); Lydia in Thyatira (Acts 16:15); Phoebe in Cenchreae (Rom. 16:1); Nympha in Laodicea (Col. 4:15); and Apphia in Colossae (Philemon 2).[51]

The authentic letters of the apostle Paul further support the prominence of women in early Church leadership. Paul refers to women by titles which are the same or comparable to those given to men. He refers to Phoebe, the leader of the house church at Cenchreae, as "diakonos" (or deacon) and as his patron. In the Letter to the Romans he refers to Prisca, who leads a house church with her husband Aquila and has served as a missionary with Paul, as an equal "co-worker." He also uses this term to refer to the women Mary, Trypaena, Tryphosa, and Persis.[52] He salutes Junia as "prominent among the apostles." Other important women members of the Roman congregation greeted by Paul are Julia, Olympas, the mother of Rufus, and the sister of Nereus.

As seen from this sampling of Paul's references to women, these female leaders of the Christian community were recognized by Paul as fellow apostles, prophets, teachers, and missionaries. There is increasing historical evidence that women served as priests, deacons, presbyters, and even bishops in the early Christian Church.[53]

Thus a venerable tradition of egalitarianism exists within Christianity. Christ himself accepted women as equal to men, and this practice of equality was carried on by the first Christians in direct contrast to the patriarchal social norms of their culture. Men and women in the early Church performed various roles depending upon their personal qualities and abilities rather than their gender. An important step toward reclaiming the feminine in Christianity is to recognize the significant contributions of women to Christianity and to honor their achievements in order to balance the male dominance which developed within the Church. The next step is to restore the original equal partnership between men and women in their service to the Lord.

The Incorporation of Feminine God-Language and Images

One of the major tasks that we must undertake in order to communicate the feminist vision of Christ's message is to correct for the masculine imagery of the Godhead emphasized by the Church. We need to identify and express images of the feminine dimension of the Divine which may be found within Christian tradition along the spiritual bypaths. This process is often met with great resistance by those who are traveling on the interstate highway of Christianity. Sometimes they raise a very important question: doesn't the use of feminine images of deity further polarize the masculine-feminine duality? It is true of course that the Divine as pure Spirit is not gender-specific. We must never forget that "the eternal God is neither male nor female, but Mystery, a Presence, Power, Love."[54] But the limitations of our human language make it impossible to describe the Infinite. Therefore we must realize that all language and images used to describe the Divine are metaphors and symbols. For example, God as "Father" is a metaphor; it is not a literal description of the gender of God. But changing the gender term such as in the Lord's Prayer, "Our Mother who art in Heaven," inevitably meets with strong emotions either of hostility or surprise and elation. The reason for this is because the use of exclusively masculine imagery for God has led to the implicit conclusion that God is male.[55] With the use of feminine language this assumption is overthrown, which proves very threatening to those who have felt secure within the patriarchal context of Christianity. For others the recognition of a feminine image of deity opens up new possibilities which can bring a sense of joy, wonder, and vitality. This is a crucial step in the restoration of the feminine to Christianity because "we literally cannot imagine what we have no models and images for."[56] The incorporation of feminine God-language and symbolism can help provide us with those images for the dimension of the Divine that has been suppressed for thousands of years.

Support for this transformed image of the Divine can be found in the very first page of the Bible, in the original version of the Creation story: "So God created humankind in his image, in the image of God he created them; male and female he created them" (Genesis 1:27). All humans, both male and female, are created "in the image of God." This indicates that God is composed equally of both masculine and feminine elements, and our God-image should include both of these polarities. Although the Bible as an androcentric text favors masculine metaphors for the Divine such as father (Psalms 103:13), husband (Hosea 2:16), king ((Psalms 98:6), and warrior (Exodus 15:3), there are also feminine metaphors which can be found if we look closely enough. For example, God is variously symbolized as a woman in labor (Isaiah 42:14), a mother (Isaiah 49:15), a midwife (Psalms 22:9) and a mistress (Psalms 123:2).[57] These feminine metaphors of God need to be recovered and emphasized more in order to restore equality to the image of God as both male and female. Another important issue in this regard involves the examination of Biblical texts in order to eliminate masculine God-language which is due to biases in translation. It is understood today that the process of translation involves an interpretation of the text, and the male-biased translators of the Hebrew and Greek versions of the Bible often substituted masculine language for a term which was originally generic. The task for the translator today is to restore the gender-inclusive meaning to those texts which do not intend to portray the Divine as a masculine deity.[58] For example, the word "Elohim" which frequently appears in the Hebrew scriptures is a plural word which refers to both gods and goddesses.[59] The usual translation of "Elohim" as simply "God" loses the feminine aspect of deity which is contained in this name. Other Hebrew terms for the Divine which have a specifically feminine connotation include "Shaddai" and "Shekinah." The root word of "Shaddai" means "mountain" or "breast",[60] both of which are feminine associations, so when this name for deity is used in the Bible it seemingly refers to the feminine dimension of the Divine. Shekinah, an Aramaic word which refers to the Divine Presence,[61] has also traditionally been perceived as feminine. These original Hebrew terms for deity can be used in translations of Scripture as well as prayers and rituals. In this way the Biblical image of the Divine will be revealed as much more multifaceted than is the current image of the single male God.

We can also draw inspiration from the visionaries of other historical time periods who recognized the need to restore the feminine to Western culture. This attempt reached its height with devotion to "the Lady" as expressed by the troubadours, who were poets and musicians of the 11th-13th centuries. The chivalric ideal of love for an earthly yet unobtainable woman was matched by the spiritual love of the Divine Feminine. Sometimes this Divine Woman took the form of Mary Magdalene but in most cases, particularly after the Inquisition, she was the Blessed Virgin Mary,

Mother of Christ and Queen of Heaven. The cult of the feminine which flourished during the Middle Ages "contained the seeds of a whole new value system that was struggling to take root in Europe... (which) put new emphasis on the Gospel teachings of equality and fraternity along with a new emphasis on the world, the flesh, and the feminine."[62]

This renewed value for the feminine in turn influenced many of the medieval mystics, who were receptive to experiencing the feminine dimension of the Divine. Their visionary experiences sometimes resulted in the use of feminine God-language. For example, Julian of Norwich emphasized the motherhood of God and even referred to "Christ as our true Mother."[63] As we strive today to develop new forms of language and symbols which express the feminine dimension of the Divine, we may look to those who have traveled before us on the feminine bypath and share their paradoxical images of a God who integrates the polarities of masculine and feminine but is ultimately transcendent to both.

Development of the Symbol of Sophia

Of utmost importance to the restoration of the feminine to Christianity is the discovery and development of the symbol of Sophia, a representation of the Divine Feminine who appears in the Hebrew Scriptures, the Apocrypha, and the New Testament. Sophia, whose name is Greek for Wisdom, is the most relevant symbol of the Goddess archetype in Judeo-Christian culture. According to Arthur Versluis, "...the doctrines surrounding Sophia represent another revelation within the Christian tradition - a revelation which can be found in the very earliest Christian writings, which reappeared in the twelfth and thirteenth centuries..."[64] The Sophianic revelation within Christian tradition is to be found primarily on those bypaths which have given expression to the archetypal feminine, such as gnosticism and medieval mysticism.

It appears that while "all roads lead to Rome," all the bypaths lead to Sophia. All the roads which make up the interstate highway system of the Christian Church emanate from the primary position of the Church in Rome within Christian history. But the labyrinthine passages of the bypaths within Christian tradition ultimately converge at the center where Sophia is found. It is the vision of Sophia which we can perceive as the "connectedness...at the heart of feminist spirituality"[65] as we walk along the Path of ChristoSophia. Sophia symbolizes the Divine Feminine, the "web of life" which characterizes the world of nature, and the presence of the divine within the human soul which yearns for mystical union. Thus Sophia is the essence of the Path of ChristoSophia, for it is she who connects the feminine, the nature, and the mystical bypaths. We will examine her role within the hidden tradition of Christian spirituality more fully in the next chapters.

CHAPTER III: SOPHIA

In her coming all good things came to me,
And of her hands riches not to be numbered.
All of these I delighted in, since Sophia brings them,
But as yet I did not know She was their mother.

Wisdom 7:11-12

As the ancient writer of the verse above refers to his ignorance about Sophia, who is the source of life's blessings, he also expresses the condition of most people in our modern Western world. As a whole, we still do not "know" this powerful figure of the Great Mother as she lives within our Western tradition. The Goddess archetype that resides within the psyche of all human beings takes the form of personified Wisdom in Judaism and Christianity. Her name is "Hochma" in Hebrew, "Sophia" in Greek.

The great spiritual task for modern human beings is to once again "know" this Divine Feminine presence within all of creation and within our own souls. However, as we begin the search for Sophia, we also experience the truth of the Biblical writer's words:

> But where shall Sophia be found?...
> Mortals do not know the way...
> It is hid from the eyes of all living...

Job 28: 12, 13, 21

For this symbol of the Divine Feminine is certainly hidden within most of Christian tradition. As Erich Neumann states, "In the patriarchal development of the Judeo-Christian West, with its masculine, monotheistic trend toward abstraction, the goddess, as a feminine figure of wisdom, was disenthroned and repressed. She survived only secretly, for the most part on heretical and revolutionary bypaths."[1] It is therefore on these "bypaths," which comprise the Path of ChristoSophia, that we must search for the hidden Goddess in Christianity. We can travel this path with the assurance that Sophia seeks to make her Wisdom known to humankind:

> Does not Sophia call,
> And does not understanding raise her voice?
> To you, O people, I call,
> And my cry is to all that live.

> Proverbs 8:1;4

As the Goddess in her myriad forms calls with renewed vigor to humankind today, so can Sophia's call be heard clearly by those who are listening for her. We are living today in a world of chaos and confusion. It is precisely in times such as these that Sophia calls most strongly. It appears that Sophia emerges, and re-emerges, from her hidden places at critical periods of cultural transformation, during those times of paradigm shift when new perceptions, values, and world views are needed. Today it is imperative that we listen to her call, heed her words of wisdom, and mediate the healing qualities of the Divine Feminine into the world. Sophia's Wisdom can help us develop the new image of a "cosmos of connectedness"[2] and thereby overcome the divisions which separate us from the Earth, from other human beings, and from our true selves. As the Russian Sophiologist Sergei Bulgakov states, "The future of living Christianity rests with the sophianic interpretation of the world and its destiny."[3] It is even more probable that the future of planet Earth and all her creatures depends upon humanity's development of the sophianic view which recognizes and celebrates the interconnectedness of all creation.

This sophianic perspective is a leitmotiv that occurs repeatedly in the Old Testament, New Testament, and Apocrypha texts of the Bible. However, since it is a theme which is generally disguised within the Biblical literature, the traveler on the feminine bypath must learn how to recognize the presence of Sophia as she appears in her many veiled forms. In order to do this, it is first necessary to know where to look for the hidden leitmotiv of Sophia within Christian tradition.

SOPHIA'S HIDING PLACES WITHIN CHRISTIAN TRADITION

Jewish Theology

Since the roots of the Christian concept of deity are found within Judaism, it is important to recognize how the Divine Feminine was incorporated into the Jewish image of God. While most people view Judaism as a strictly patriarchal religion, there has been an underlying current of Goddess worship throughout its history.[4] The early Hebrews were influenced by neighboring Canaanite tribes and their worship of goddesses such as Asherah, Astarte and Anath. The characteristics of the Canaanite goddess were later absorbed into the figure of the Hebrew Hochma - Wisdom.[5] For example, Asherah was symbolized as a tree, and Proverbs 3:18 describes Wisdom as a "tree of life." The role of Hochma, or Sophia as she became known in the Septuagint translation of the Hebrew Scriptures, is seen most clearly in Jewish Wisdom theology, which appears to be an attempt to incorporate elements of the goddess cults into Judaism.[6] This theology is expressed in the Wisdom literature of the Hebrew Bible and the Apocrypha, including the books of Proverbs, Job, Ecclesiastes, Sirach (Ecclesiasticus) and The Wisdom of Solomon, which were written during the fifth through the first centuries BCE.[7] At first Sophia appeared as a hypostasis or personification of an attribute of God, in this case God's wisdom. However, Sophia grew in importance until she eventually played the role of a virtual goddess within Hellenistic Judaism. As an archetypal expression of the Divine Feminine, she shared many of the qualities of the Great Goddesses of antiquity. Sophia as the pre-existent creatress is similar to the Egyptian Isis; as the Goddess of order and justice she resembles the Egyptian Maat; and in her connections with the Earth and the harvest she corresponds to the Greek Demeter.[8] As a manifestation of these archetypal qualities of the feminine deity, it is apparent as Elisabeth Schüssler Fiorenza says that "Divine Sophia is Israel's God in the language and Gestalt of the goddess."[9]

However, since Judaism is a monotheistic religion which could not openly allow the presence of a goddess within its mainstream theology, the meaning of Sophia is ambiguous within the Hebrew texts. That the writers of the Wisdom literature intended her to be understood in a personified form, Sophia, rather than as an abstract concept, Wisdom, can be clearly seen in this passage:

> Get Sophia; get insight.
> Do not forsake her, and she will keep you;
> Love her, and she will guard you...
> Prize her highly, and she will exalt you;
> She will honor you if you embrace her.
> She will place on your head a fair garland;
> She will bestow on you a beautiful crown.
>
> Proverbs 4:5-6; 8-9

In very concrete terms, the author portrays this image of Sophia as a living woman. The powers that are ascribed to her - her ability to "keep," "guard," "exalt," "honor," "bestow a beautiful crown" - indicate her role as a goddess figure.

Sophia's relationship to the only God of Judaism is described by the Biblical texts in a variety of ways, as may be seen in the following passages:

> The Lord created me at the beginning of his work,
> The first of his acts of long ago.
> Ages ago I was set up,
> At the first, before the beginning of the Earth.
>
> Proverbs 8: 21

In this declaration, Sophia claims to be the "first creation" of God. The Divine Feminine is not equal to God, but was created in the beginning, prior to the rest of creation.

> The Lord by Sophia founded the earth.
>
> Proverbs 3: 19

Here Sophia is viewed as co-creator with God. The Earth was created through the mediation of Sophia with the Lord.

> When he marked out the foundations of the earth,
> Then I was beside him, like a master worker;
> And I was daily his delight,
> Rejoicing before him always...

Proverbs 8:29-30

This passage expands on Sophia's position as co-creator with God. Her role is that of a "master worker" who actually builds the creation which has been designed by the Lord. In her "rejoicing" before God she is seen as the source of joy in creation.

> For she is a breath of the power of God,
> And a pure emanation of the glory of the Almighty...
> For she is a reflection of eternal light,
> A spotless mirror of the working of God,
> And an image of his goodness.

Wisdom 7:25-26

In these lines, the Divine Feminine can be seen as a flowing stream of power and glory radiating from the Source. Divine light, creativity, and goodness are manifested through her.

As these examples show, the presence of Sophia as a personification of the Divine Feminine is a strong theme that appears in many of the texts of the Hebrew Scriptures. Although her role is ambiguous and often disguised, nevertheless Sophia is recognized as the first creation of God, as mediator between God and the world, and as the expression of joy and goodness in creation. This sophianic theme was understood and further developed by those Jews who became Christians in the first centuries following Christ's death and resurrection.

Jesus Christ

The attributes of the Divine Feminine can be readily seen in the figure of Jesus Christ as presented in the texts of the New Testament and the Apocrypha. As Jesus proclaimed the primacy of love over the law, he emphasized the importance of eros qualities such as caring and compassion. This can be clearly seen in his teachings such as the Beatitudes (Matthew 5:3-12) which extol the feminine values of meekness, mercy, purity, and peacemaking. Jesus taught primarily through parables, containing the wisdom of paradox, the truth which to the rational mind appears to be contradictory. It is only through the eros quality of intuition that the parable can be understood, for it expresses the Wisdom of Sophia whose function is to integrate the apparent contradictions. Jesus often used feminine imagery in his teachings, as in his comparisons of the Kingdom of Heaven to the "grain of mustard seed," (Matthew 13:31) "leaven hidden in meal," (Matthew 13:33) and "pearl of great value." (Matthew 13:45) Jesus' actions also clearly reflect his feminine values: his loving inclusiveness of all people, especially the downtrodden and the outcasts of society; his compassion which prompted him to teach and to heal; and his forgiveness of others even when he was betrayed and crucified. Although many Christians today recognize that the teachings and actions of Jesus emphasize these eros qualities, few understand that this is due to the direct influence of Sophia in the manifestation of the Christ. The concept of the Word (Logos) linked with Wisdom (Sophia) was a tradition in the Wisdom theology of Judaism before the birth of Jesus. For example, a passage written in the first century BCE states, "O God...who have made all things by your word, and by your wisdom have formed humankind." (The Wisdom of Solomon 9:1-2) This statement proclaims Word and Wisdom as joint mediators between God and the world. However, by the beginning of the Christian era Sophia's attributes were subsumed under the Logos in Hellenistic Judaism, due in large part to the teachings of the Jewish philosopher Philo. The earliest Christians were profoundly influenced by the concept of the Logos held by their contemporaries, the Hellenistic Jews, as they sought to explain the person and purpose of Jesus Christ. Thus the Christology of the early Christians was based on the belief in Jesus Christ as Logos incarnate ("the Word made flesh"), to whom the attributes of Sophia were transferred.[10] During the first few centuries of Christianity Jesus Christ was actually viewed as the incarnation of Sophia. The early Christian missionary movement preached the gospel of the resurrected Christ as the life-renewing Sophia-Spirit. As Elisabeth Schussler Fiorenza says, "The proclamation of Jesus Christ as the Sophia of God and the cosmic Lord functions in the Christian community as the foundational myth."[11]

This interpretation of Christ as the incarnation of Sophia can be seen in the opening lines of the Gospel of John:

> In the beginning was the Word,
> And the Word was with God,
> And the Word was God.
> He was in the beginning with God.
> All things came into being through him...
>
> John 1:1-3

In this passage, John equates the Word, "Logos," with the figure of Jesus Christ who he substitutes for the Sophia of the Wisdom literature. We have only to recall the passages in Proverbs cited in the previous section to see how Sophia's role as pre-existent deity and co-creator with God has been transferred to Christ.

The Gospels show many connections between Christ and Sophia. Feminine imagery once used to describe Sophia, such as "living water," "bread of life," and "the true vine" are now applied to Christ. Many sayings of Christ parallel those of Sophia. For example, we are told by Jesus to "Take my yoke upon you" (Matthew 11:29) just as we have been previously instructed to "Put your neck under her (Sophia's) yoke." (Sirach 51:26) We also see a similarity between Christ's statement, "those who lose their life for my sake will find it" (Matthew 10:39) and Sophia's statement, "whoever finds me finds life." (Proverbs 8:35)[12]

The Apostle Paul also applies the language and concepts of Sophia found in the Wisdom literature to Christ. His identification of Christ with Sophia is shown in passages such as:

> Christ Jesus, who became for us Sophia from God...
>
> 1 Corinthians 1:30

> Christ the Power of God and the Sophia of God...
>
> 1 Corinthians 1:24

> We speak God's Sophia, secret and hidden, which God decreed before the ages for our glory.
>
> 1 Corinthians 2:7

Sophia, now "secret and hidden," can be identified with Christ in this passage. As in the Gospel of John, Christ takes on the identity of Sophia who was with God in the beginning. Throughout Paul's writings, references to Christ echo earlier descriptions of Sophia: He is present at the beginning of creation, co-creator with God, the Savior, the Law, and Life.[13] However as these roles of Sophia became increasingly submerged in the figure of Christ during subsequent centuries, the Sophianic nature of Christ truly became a "hidden secret" to most Christians.

The Holy Spirit

It is the third person of the Trinity which has most commonly been represented with feminine imagery in the Christian Church. It is understandable that the Divine Feminine would find an easier access to manifestation through the Holy Spirit since the gender of this aspect of the Trinity is not specific, as it is in the Father and the Son. In fact, the original Hebrew meaning for the word "Spirit" was "ruach," a feminine term. Translated into Greek, "Spirit" became "pneuma," a neutral term. The final suppression of the feminine meaning of "Spirit" came with the Roman translation of the word into "spiritus," a masculine term. It is significant that in the Eastern Orthodox Church, where Greek remained the official language, the earliest view of the Holy Spirit as feminine still exists today. The Orthodox Church possesses an unbroken line of tradition that worships the Holy Spirit as Holy (Hagia) Sophia.

Yet even within Western Christendom the ancient feminine associations with the Holy Spirit still linger on and proclaim the presence of Sophia to us today. In her role as the Holy Spirit, Sophia is often referred to as the "breath" or "wind" of God's power. For example, "She is a breath of the power of God." (Wisdom 7:25) In Genesis, Sophia's acts of creation with God in her role of Holy Spirit can be clearly seen: "The earth was a formless void and darkness covered the face of the deep, while a wind from God (in other translations, "the Spirit of God") swept over the face of the waters." (Genesis 1:2)

In the early Christian Church, the Holy Spirit also assumed many of Sophia's attributes. The Spirit is considered to be feminine in many Christian texts, especially in the Apocrypha and Gnostic scriptures. In some of these texts the Holy Spirit is portrayed as the Mother which corresponds to the Father and Son of the Trinity. For example, in the Gospel of the Hebrews Jesus refers to "my mother, the Holy Spirit," and in the Gospel of Philip he refers to the Spirit as "Mother of many."[14]

In the texts contained in the New Testament, the Holy Spirit is often represented by the feminine symbol of the dove. This carries on the long tradition of the dove as sacred to the Goddess in pre-Christian times. A well-known example of the dove symbolizing the Holy Spirit that occurs in all four gospels is the instance of Jesus' baptism. As described in the Gospel of Matthew, "And when Jesus had been baptized, just as he came up from the water, suddenly the heavens were opened to him and he saw the Spirit of God descending like a dove and alighting on him. And a voice from heaven said, 'This is my Son, the Beloved, with whom I am well pleased.'" (Matthew 3:16-17) There is powerful feminine symbolism in this account, both in the dove and in the water which in the ritual of baptism is transformed into the "Water of Life." The sparser account of Jesus' baptism in the Gospel of John reads: "And John testified, "I saw the Spirit descending from heaven like a dove, and it remained on him.'" (John 1:32) The fact that the Holy Spirit **remained** on Jesus seems to be paramount in John's eyes. It is possible that the Spirit of Sophia, symbolized by the dove, descends upon Jesus at this time and unites with him, thus creating the Christ-Sophia synthesis which was recognized in the early Christian Church.

Another powerful incident that depicts Sophia as Holy Spirit occurred at Pentecost. As the event is recorded in The Acts of the Apostles: "suddenly from heaven there came a sound like the rush of a violent wind, and it filled the entire house where they were sitting. Divided tongues, as of fire, appeared among them, and a tongue rested on each of them. All of them were filled with the Holy Spirit and began to speak in other languages, as the Spirit gave them ability." (Acts 2: 2-4) The "mighty wind" and "tongues of fire" are both symbols of the creative power of the Divine Feminine. At Pentecost, the resurrected Christ as Sophia-Spirit entered each person present. This can be interpreted to mean that the living Christ continues to work today through the Sophia-Spirit within us.

The Trinity

In addition to seeking the hidden Sophia in the three persons of the Trinity, she may also be recognized in the nature of the Godhead itself. It is in Sophia that the Father, Son, and Holy Spirit have their Being. This was the view of some Russian mystics such as Vladimir Solovyev and Sergei Bulgakov. Solovyev (1853-1900) was a philosopher-poet whose mystical experiences with Sophia led him to develop his unique view of the Divine Feminine which inspired the philosophical and religious tradition called Sophiology in modern Russia. Solovyev described Sophia as the "substance" of the Trinity, "the divine principle of all-in-oneness, which is the Wisdom of God."[15] Solovyev's ideas had a great influence on many Russian writers, philosophers and theologians in the early twentieth century. One of these was Sergei Bulgakov (1871-1944), a Russian Orthodox priest whose own conversion to Christianity occurred as a result of his mystical encounter with Sophia. Bulgakov devoted his life to formulating a rational, theoretical framework for his mystical illuminations of Sophia, and defending his Sophianic theology against the conservative members of the Orthodox Church who accused him of heresy. Bulgakov describes Sophia as "the nature of God...a living...loving substance, ground, and principle."[16] She is "the ever-present power of God, the divine essence."[17] In Bulgakov's view Sophia is the ousia or substance of the Godhead. Sophia is distinct from the three hypostases, or persons of the Trinity, yet cannot exist independently of them. The Father, Son and Holy Spirit possess Ousia-Sophia, but each possesses her in a different way, according to its own properties.[18] Bulgakov's rational theological explanation of Sophia does not conceive of her as a person but rather as an abstract concept.

The Blessed Virgin Mary

At the opposite pole from the abstraction of Sophia as Godhead stands the manifestation of Sophia within the concrete human form of the Virgin Mary. For many Christians, particularly Roman Catholics, Mary has provided access to the Divine Feminine within an otherwise overwhelmingly masculine dominated religion. Within the Church, the doctrines of the Theotokos, the Immaculate Conception, and the Assumption have served to reinforce the symbolic potency of the Blessed Virgin Mary as a carrier of the archetype of the Divine Feminine. In the fifth century, Mary was given the title "Theotokos," "God-bearer" in Greek, more commonly stated as "Mother of God." This appellation gives her the symbolic meaning of the Great Mother or Goddess archetype. Mary as "Theotokos" can be associated with all the mother goddesses of antiquity who gave birth to divine sons. Mary had to be a pure and holy vessel in order to be capable of giving birth to the Son of God. Thus the doctrine of the Immaculate Conception recognizes Mary as the perfect woman, born without sin. This doctrine infers that Mary is the physical manifestation of the pure and perfect Goddess, the embodiment of the Divine Sophia. The acknowledgement of the Divine Feminine within the person of Mary was completed in the twentieth century when the doctrine of the Assumption of Mary into Heaven was formally recognized by the Roman Catholic church. This doctrine stated that Mary was assumed body and soul into Heaven, thus bringing her from the earthly to the transcendent realm. Mary was now officially accepted as the primary mediator between the human and the divine, a role which has traditionally been ascribed to Sophia. Texts of the Bible and Apocrypha that referred to Sophia were transposed into litanies to the Blessed Virgin Mary. Wisdom titles such as "Mirror of Justice, Seat of Wisdom" and "Gate of Heaven" were ascribed to Mary.[19]

An intriguing phenomenon, which further supports the Sophianic aspect of the Blessed Virgin Mary, is the mysterious Black Madonna images that exist throughout Europe. These icons appear to represent a continuation of the worship of the Goddess of life, death and rebirth.[20] In their dark aspect they are symbolic of the Black Goddess, and therefore seem particularly anomalous in Christianity which emphasizes the positive, beneficent, light qualities of the Virgin. However, it is in the mysterious dark images of the Black Madonnas that we find the greatest hidden secrets of Wisdom - the Wisdom of the Black Goddess which is imperative for us to understand today.

It is very significant that the recent increasing discovery of Black Madonna statues and renewed interest in them parallels the increase in purported visions of the Blessed Virgin Mary. These sightings of Mary are one instance of the return of the Goddess in our time. Contemporary Marian visions often portray the "black" aspects of the Divine Feminine in her apocalyptic messages of warning and challenge to us. For example, in her famous appearances at Medjugorge, Yugoslavia in 1981, the Virgin made repeated calls to penance and prayer.[21] Sophia in her form of the Black Goddess is calling to us today through the Black Madonna icons and through the apocalyptic Marian visions to heed her Wisdom and change our ways.

SOPHIA'S RETURN

In reviewing the places where the Divine Feminine is hidden within Christian tradition, it is apparent that the interstate highway of the institutional Church has generally ignored, and often denied, Sophia. The Divine Feminine could not find a home within the patriarchal world view of Western civilization. Even though, as we have seen, the early Christians apparently did acknowledge the presence of Sophia as a figure of great importance, the building of the interstate highway Church demanded that she be suppressed. The order and structure that was required in the institutionalization of Christianity placed a premium on ideology and dogma. Thus St. Paul, who claimed that "Jesus is our Sophia," had to carefully choose his words so that they would not be perceived as gnostic interpretations, for the gnostics emphasized the place of Sophia in their teachings. The early Christian Church which was vying for dominance with the gnostics in the first centuries after Jesus' death therefore suppressed the role of Sophia in order to clearly distinguish its beliefs from those of the gnostics. In addition, as the Christian Church developed and formalized its doctrines, it was feared that the open acceptance of Sophia would endanger the Trinitarian dogma.[22] Thus Sophia was driven into her hiding places in Christian tradition primarily because her eros qualities posed a threat to the dominant logos characteristics of the increasingly institutionalized Church which demanded dogmatic systems of belief.

Therefore it is on the bypaths of Christian tradition that we may best search for Sophia. As we travel along the bypaths we can look in the underbrush, peer into tree hollows and dark caves, and gaze into still pools of water where we will be most likely to find the hiding places of Sophia. However, once we have discovered her, we realize that through these thousands of years of hiding, Sophia's power has become diminished. She is no longer the mighty symbol of the Divine Feminine as were the Great Goddesses of antiquity. When Sophia was viewed by the Hebrews as the personification of an attribute of a masculine God, his first creation, or the mediator between God and Earth, she lost her autonomous power as a feminine symbol of the Divine. Later, Sophia lost even her unique identity to the figure of Jesus Christ, and the symbol of the Divine Feminine subsequently became so hidden as to be lost to most Christians. When Sophia is associated with the Holy Spirit, her role is ambiguous and she is not clearly seen as the numinous feminine figure of power and wisdom. Identifying Sophia with the Godhead results in the abstractions which are characteristic of logos conceptualization, however it is the ability to relate to her personhood which brings the balance of eros qualities which are vital to her meaning for us. When Sophia's attributes are transferred to the Virgin, the result is a limited image of the archetypal Feminine because Mary is human, not divine. Mary plays the submissive role of a "handmaiden"; she is the passive vessel for the divine incarnation. As such, the appropriation of the Blessed Virgin Mary as the symbol for the Divine Feminine within Christianity robs Sophia of her potent strength and independence. In all of these instances where Wisdom is hidden within Christian tradition, Sophia loses the breadth of her powers, autonomy, and divinity, becoming a truncated symbol of the Divine Feminine. However, she does not have to remain so. As Susan Cole says, "The quest for Sophia was by no means completed in the early Church... she is a substantial if hidden and unfinished presence in the New Testament. This presence of Sophia in the Christian scriptures as well as in the Hebrew tradition despite, or perhaps even because of, its unfinished nature, provides contemporary spirituality with a figure of great possibility."[23] Sophia's revelation, the revealing of herself, within Christian tradition is not finished. At this crucial time in our Earth's history, Sophia must be liberated from her hiding places to return to us with the might and glory of the ancient Goddess. Sophia's return in her full power is most likely to occur first along the winding bypaths rather than in the interstate Church which still emphasizes legalistic doctrines and patriarchal dogmas. As Fiorenza points out, Christian theology uses masculine imagery for God, yet insists that God's Reality cannot be ultimately expressed in human language or experience. This is the meaning of the second commandment: "To fix God to a definite form and man-made image would mean idolatry."[24]

There are many possibilities for new forms and images of deity as Sophia returns from hiding and reveals herself in all her fullness as the symbol of the Divine Feminine. As Sophia emerges we will recognize the feminine aspect of each of the persons of the Trinity. Thus the Father will be seen as the Mother and Father Creator, the Son will be seen as the embodiment of both Wisdom and Word, and the Holy Spirit will be seen as both feminine and masculine. An approach which seems to hold great promise for the anamnesis of Sophia is the Russian mystics' view of Sophia as the nature or essence of God. Each of the persons of the Trinity participate in the divine nature, yet remain independent of each other.

This can be conceptualized by looking at the following medieval symbol of the Mystery of the Trinity:

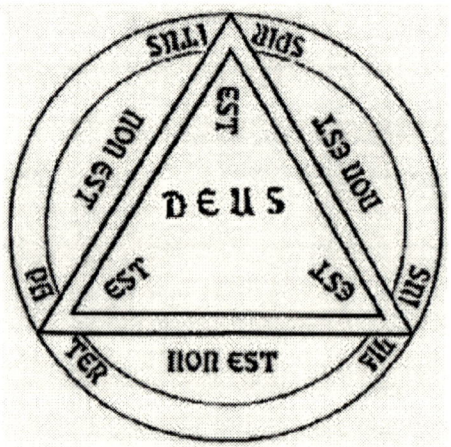

If we understand the "Deus" as Godhead to be Sophia, the image becomes a symbol of Bulgakov's mystical insight:

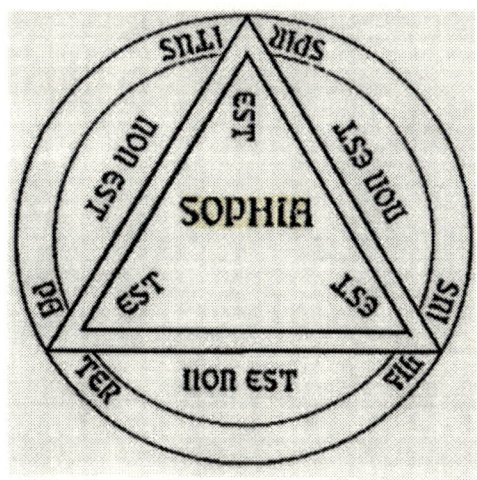

The Father, Son and Holy Spirit each possesses the divine essence, Sophia, but in different ways. This symbol avoids simplistic dualism by portraying the paradox that Sophia is interdependent with each of the persons of the Trinity, yet remains distinct from each of them.

One way that this Mystery may be expressed is through envisioning the second person of the Trinity as "ChristoSophia." Sophia proclaims today, "Christ and I, Sophia, are **one**!" But **oneness** does not mean **sameness**. The unity of Christ and Sophia must be seen as a differentiated wholeness, a dynamic balance between "Word" and "Wisdom." Instead of disguising Sophia in the figure of Christ as the early Christians did, the term "ChristoSophia" assures that the attributes of both are clearly expressed. Referring to the second person of the Trinity as "ChristoSophia" also emphasizes the personhood of Sophia rather than intellectualizing her as an abstract concept. When the incarnation of the Divine is expressed as "ChristoSophia" it becomes possible for us to relate in a personal way to the power and wisdom of the archetypal Feminine.

A visual image that beautifully expresses this Mystery is the "Glorification of the Virgin" motif that frequently appears in medieval Christian art. For example, the golden mosaic in the apse of the church of Santa Maria in Trastavere, Rome, depicts the Virgin Mary and Jesus seated together on the Throne of Heaven. This numinous image of the transcendent Queen of Heaven reveals the Virgin Mary as Sophia, the feminine power that permeates the cosmos, just as it shows the resurrected Lord Jesus as Christ, the masculine power that rules over creation. The artistic depiction of their joint reign in Heaven symbolically expresses the spiritual truth of ChristoSophia – a unity which, in our world of polarities, is differentiated as masculine and feminine aspects of God.

Church of Santa Maria in Trastevere, Rome

THE ATTRIBUTES OF SOPHIA

The Light and the Dark

As a symbol of the Great Goddess archetype, Sophia's attributes are all inclusive, encompassing both the light and the dark sides of existence. In her light aspects, Sophia's qualities include peace, joy, love and life; in her dark aspects, they include chaos, sorrow, purgation, and death. Sophia's action is seen in the eternal round of creation and destruction, life which is born and then dies to be born again.

It is Sophia's light aspect that is most readily seen in the Biblical texts. Wisdom is to be desired above all else, for "Happy are those who find Sophia...all her paths are peace." (Proverbs 3:13,17) It is Sophia that brings peace and joy into the world and into the human heart. "You will find the rest she gives, and she will be changed into joy for you." (Ecclesiasticus 6:28) As we recognize Sophia "rejoicing in his (God's) inhabited world and delighting in the human race" (Proverbs 8:31) she serves as a model for us to follow as we appreciate the joys of created life. Sophia's Wisdom teaches us that life is Original Blessing, as Matthew Fox points out.[25]

One of the symptoms of Sophia's diminishment of power in the Judeo-Christian tradition is that her dark aspects as the Divine Feminine have generally been denied. While we can find hints of the beautiful, beneficent Great Goddess within the Biblical texts, the Black Goddess is hidden even further from view. In Wisdom 7:22-23 these adjectives are used to describe Sophia: "intelligent, holy, unique, manifold, subtle, mobile, clear, unpolluted, distinct, invulnerable, loving the good, keen, irresistible, beneficent, humane, steadfast, sure, free from anxiety, all-powerful, overseeing all, and penetrating through all spirits that are intelligent, pure and altogether subtle." These are all characteristics of the light and illuminating Goddess. However, the dark Goddess aspect of Sophia is vitally important to the understanding of the Christian mythos. The blackness of the Void prior to creation is the realm of Sophia, for she existed in the beginning and it was out of her darkness that the cosmos was created. Sophia as the "darkness upon the face of the deep" was the dark maternal womb which gave birth to the dawning light of creation. It is this same darkness which is the Wisdom of the Earth and the body, the Wisdom of nature which knows the eternal cycles of life and death. It is the same dark aspect of the Goddess that the mystic experiences in the Dark Night of the Soul, the purgative trials of doubt and despair which precede the experience of illumination. The Black Goddess aspect of ChristoSophia was present in the suffering of Jesus during his Passion, and the blackness of the tomb was the dark maternal womb of Sophia that gave birth to Christ in his resurrected form.

Sophia appears to us in our lives in her dark aspect whenever we experience sorrow, grief, or depression. As we become aware of Sophia's cycles of life and death and our own place as mortal beings within this cycle, we experience the sorrows that accompany the loss of life and love. Yet, through our sadness we are learning the dark side of Sophia's Wisdom. As Thomas Moore points out, "Melancholy thoughts carve out an interior space where wisdom can take up residence."[26] Sorrow and grief create the dark inner places where Sophia can be found. The creation of our own souls depends as much on the Wisdom of suffering as it does on the Wisdom of joy.

When Sophia speaks in her role as the Black Goddess she issues warnings to us and challenges us to change our ways. She calls out, "Give heed to my reproof!" (Proverbs 1:23) When Sophia's words of warning are not listened to, the dark Goddess can enact just retribution:

> Because I have called and you refused to listen,
> Have stretched out my hand and no one has heeded,
> And you have ignored all my counsel
> And would have none of my reproof,
> I also will laugh at your calamity;
> I will mock when panic strikes you.

> Proverbs 1:24-26

We can hear these words today if we listen to the voice of the Wisdom of the Earth. If we human beings do not heed the reproofs of Sophia, as conveyed to us in the tremendous ecological devastation of our planet, we can expect the chastisement of the Black Goddess in the cycle of destruction that we have set in motion.

The critical need today is to acknowledge both the light and dark aspects of the Goddess as we experience her in the world and within ourselves. Within Western culture we have historically emphasized the light and repressed the dark side. However, both are necessary if we are to experience life in its wholeness and encounter Sophia in the full power of the Goddess. Since the dark has been so strongly repressed in Western culture, this is the side of Sophia that is currently calling to us most strongly. The growing awareness of the icons of the Black Madonna and the challenging voice of the Blessed Virgin Mary in people's visionary experiences are both examples of the forceful return of the dark Goddess, emphasizing the crucial need for us to heed her call and follow her Wisdom.

A symbol that may prove especially beneficial to us as we attempt to integrate the light and the dark aspects of the Divine Feminine is the caduceus. The physician's symbol of a wand with two entwining serpents is commonly associated with the god Hermes, but actually it has a much more ancient history as the symbol of the healing Mother Goddess. One interpretation of the meaning of this symbol is that the wand or staff represents power and the two snakes represent wisdom.[27] Thus the caduceus may be seen as symbolizing Sophia's Staff of Feminine Power and Wisdom. The two entwining snakes may be visualized as light and dark, then metamorphosing into two circulating bands of light and dark energy. This symbolizes the uniting of the opposites in a dynamic equilibrium; the forces of life and death in the harmony which results in rebirth. Entwining snakes are also a symbol of the fertility of the Goddess. Today this "fertility" may be viewed as the transformative creative power which must emerge out of the synthesis of the dark and light in order to bring healing to our world.

Creator and Creation

Sophia in her light and dark aspects also integrates the usual dichotomy which exists between creator and creation. For "Sophia is twofold...above and before creation and 'in' creation. The world is created in Sophia and Sophia, at the same time, is in the world, throughout it..."[28] That Sophia is the creative power of the universe is shown in the statement: "O Lord, how manifold are thy works! In Sophia you have made them all." (Psalm 104:24) At the same time, Sophia is the emanation of God through all of creation, for "She pervades and penetrates all things." (Book of Wisdom of Solomon, 7:24) Vladimir Solovyev described this understanding of Sophia's dual nature as the transcendent figure of Wisdom and the "World-soul" or the presence of God in creation. Sergei Bulgakov later expressed the same meaning with his terms the Divine Sophia and the "creaturely Sophia" which was the created world.[29] The Way of Wisdom leads to an understanding of the paradoxical unity of these two attributes of Sophia. This is the basis for a panentheistic view that recognizes the Divine as transcendent and at the same time immanent within nature.

Probably the most important implication of this awareness for us today lies in the acknowledgement that every created thing is seeded with the Divine. "To admit this is to affirm the fundamentally divine character of the world, based upon this identity of the principle of divine Wisdom in God and in the creature."[30] Sophia is present in every animal, plant, and mineral, in every planet of the solar system and every star in the cosmos, and within the body and soul of every single human being. To recognize her presence informs us of the sacredness of the natural world.

SOPHIA'S MESSAGE

It is on the bypaths of the Path of ChristoSophia, in the deep stillness of the forest, that we can most clearly hear the call of Sophia today. On the interstate highway it is harder to hear her voice above the noise of the traffic, but on the bypaths we can hear her calling to us through every rock, tree, flower, and animal. Sophia's call is increasingly urgent during this time of transformation in which we live as she cries out to us to hear her message of wholeness and follow her way of wisdom.

The Transformation of Eve

Sophia's message of wholeness requires us to reinterpret the traditional meaning of the story of Adam and Eve. Historically the Christian Church has taught that Eve brought sin into the world by eating the apple of the Tree of Knowledge. In the light of Sophia's message, this sin can be interpreted as the recognition of duality; i.e. the knowledge of good and evil which was gained by eating the apple. The result was a "fall from Grace," a "fall" from the paradisal world of unity into a world of separation. This is the world that we now inhabit, marked by our sense of separation from other human beings, from the Earth, from God, and from our true selves. The story of Adam and Eve mythically reveals the process of dawning consciousness as it occurred within the human species, and as it is recapitulated within each individual. The development of the "ego," a sense of one's separate being, is a necessary step in the psychic development of the individual as well as the human race. However, at this critical juncture in the history of our species, Sophia tells us it is time for her to transform Eve. It is she who brings wholeness by integrating the dualities: the masculine and the feminine, the human and the Divine, the light and the dark, the creator and the creation. Like the two entwining snakes on the caduceus, the polarities of life are transformed into a differentiated and balanced wholeness through the power of Sophia.

Sophia's message integrates the masculine-feminine dichotomy through the acceptance of the feminine dimension of the Trinity. She replaces the exclusively masculine image of God with an image of the divine Mother and Father, co-creators of the universe. She provides a very powerful symbol of the integration of masculine and feminine in ChristoSophia, the acknowledgement of Jesus Christ as the incarnation of Sophia and of the resurrected Christ as Sophia-Spirit which lives within the hearts of all those who walk the Path of ChristoSophia and follow the Way of Wisdom. Sophia's call to heal the masculine-feminine split is of crucial importance today for bringing a much-needed balance to our own souls and to our relationships. As Carl Jung has emphasized, it is necessary for us to accept and develop the contrasexual element within our own psyches in order to grow into our true individuated selves.[31] An image of the Divine which develops and integrates both the masculine and feminine poles would be an enormous help to achieving this task within the individual psyche. Individuals who have integrated their own masculine and feminine sides are then most capable of relating to each other as autonomous individuals engaged in the task of partnership, as described by Riane Eisler.[32] Ever since Adam and Eve developed consciousness of their own maleness and femaleness, and God gave women the task of "childbearing" and men the task of "toiling in the ground," men and women have been polarized and in conflict with each other. Human history records the repression of the feminine pole and the corresponding dominance of men over women. Sophia's message today is that the divisions which separate males and females from each other must be overcome, and a "new Adam" and a "new Eve" must return to the Garden as fully equal partners. We must develop the spirit of ChristoSophia in our relationships as men and women so that our partnerships involve two differentiated individuals who unite to create a dynamic unity from their own positions of wholeness.

It is also imperative in this time for our relationship with the planet Earth to be transformed through Sophia's message of wholeness. Sophia's transformation of Eve involves healing the split between human beings and the rest of the natural world. When Adam and Eve were driven out of the Garden of Eden and God said, "Cursed is the ground because of you," (Gen. 3:17) the material world of nature became separated from the spiritual world of God. This dichotomy between matter and spirit which is at the root of Western culture has resulted in the worship of God as a transcendent being and a corresponding neglect, and often even a hatred, of the natural world. The human race is just now finally beginning to understand the dire consequences of this viewpoint as we witness the increasing destruction of our Earth. However, Sophia calls to us today to change our image of the Divine as we recognize that her role is twofold: She is both the creator and the creation itself. The panentheistic message of Sophia integrates the duality of the transcendent and immanent deity. Our recognition of the sacredness of the natural world changes our relationship with the Earth from the exploitation of dominance to a caring partnership.

The dualities of light and dark are also integrated in the creator and the earthly aspects of Sophia. Wisdom in her transcendent form is the source of light, joy, peace, and love. In her aspect as the World-Soul, the elements of the dark Goddess appear for it is through creation that the continuous cycle of birth, death and rebirth is manifested. The serpent in the Garden of Eden represents the dark aspect of Sophia as the Wisdom of the Earth. The serpent which tempted Eve, and has subsequently become a symbol for evil, is a primordial symbol of the Divine Feminine in her Black Goddess role. As the patriarchal worldview gained dominance, this ancient symbol of the Goddess became hated and feared and its true meaning was lost along with the feminine image of deity. Sophia's message to us today is that the Divine Feminine in all her aspects, dark as well as light, must be reclaimed from the patriarchal world view.

Her message particularly applies to our attitudes toward sexuality and erotic love, realms of the dark Goddess which are also symbolized by the serpent. The traditional interpretation of the Garden of Eden story is that Adam and Eve's "fall" included their recognition of their nakedness and therefore their sexuality. The Christian Church has had a devastating impact on the world by its usual equation of sex with sin. But the dark Goddess celebrates the erotic love and sexuality which is inherent in created life. Sophia's message today summons us to appreciate the joys of the body and honor the sacredness of sexuality. As the Divine and the creation are united in Sophia, so are spirituality and sexuality no longer separate but instead are united in the sacred symbol of the serpent. Thus, Sophia's transformation of Eve involves restoring the serpent as a powerful symbol of the Divine Feminine, and integrating its dark wisdom with that of the transcendent Sophia.

The dichotomy of the Divine and the human are also united in Sophia as the creator and the creation. Traditional Christianity has always had as its core belief that Christ is both God and man. Sophia's message further expands this concept of the God/human union. Sophia is transcendent and is also within all creation, including human beings. This means that **all** people are both human and divine. We have the seeds of divinity within us, and may grow increasingly in our divine nature by developing the ChristoSophia spirit within. Yet, we go even a further step with Sophia in recognizing the divine nature of **all** creation. Sophia's dual aspect means that every created thing - tree, rock, animal, star, and human being - has an essence that is divine. Thus, Christ as God/man shows us the sacredness of human life; Sophia as Goddess/cosmos demonstrates the sacredness of All.

New Perception

As we are instructed to "acquire Sophia, acquire perception," (Proverbs 4:5) it is apparent that Sophia is identified with perception. Sophia's message brings a new perception that integrates the dualities of existence. It is the perception of the interconnectedness of all life and the wisdom that comes from that awareness; it is the perception of creation as a blessing and the joy that comes from that recognition.

This message of Sophia's is symbolized by the wholeness of the apple which grows on the Tree of Life in the Garden of Eden. Sophia's Tree of Wisdom is identical to the Tree of Life, for it is known that "She is a tree of life to those who lay hold of her." (Proverbs 3:18) Whereas Eve's apple from the Tree of Knowledge brought the awareness of duality, Sophia's apple from the Tree of Life brings the wisdom of wholeness. Within her apple are found the five seeds of Wisdom. Sophia instructs us to eat these seeds, thus taking her Wisdom within and assimilating it in our deepest being. This is an organic process by which Wisdom is the fruit which grows from a new perception. Eating the seeds of the apple of Wisdom leads to an "ecosophianic perspective of Nature"[33] as we recognize Sophia's presence in all things.

Reconciliation with God

Sophia is not only the divine presence in creation but is also the means for its salvation. Thus, Sophia gives us the message of assurance in our fragmented modern world that she is continuing the process of reconciliation with God which was begun by Jesus Christ two thousand years ago. The essence of Christian doctrine is that Christ's incarnation, death and resurrection provided a turning point in human history because the sin of Adam was now redeemed by Christ for the sake of all humanity. Sophia is currently returning from her long centuries of hiding to claim her powerful role as Savior with Christ. She proclaims her message that it is through the union of Christ's Love and Sophia's Wisdom, the dynamic equilibrium of the Loving-Wisdom of ChristoSophia, that the reconciliation process continues in our age.

Through this process of reconciliation, "Sophia leads...back to the wholeness of Paradise."[34] But the original state of paradisal unity is now the differentiated Oneness characteristic of the transformed consciousness. Jean Houston describes this process as she traces the psychospiritual evolution of human beings. The "pre-individual" human who was continuous with the natural world prior to ego development is mythically represented by Adam and Eve prior to the "fall." The "post-individual" or "planetary person" which is now in the process of emerging, consistent with the return of the feminine archetype, is "a far more realized being who exists in an ecological continuum with the realities of inner and outer worlds..."[35]

The need today, Sophia tells us, is for the reconciliation of humans with God manifest in all creation. No longer can we afford to view God, or ourselves, as separate from the Earth. In recognizing the divine presence of Sophia within all created things, the sacredness of nature is restored. With the Wisdom of Sophia we can now return to the Garden of Paradise and experience the unity with God and all the other creatures of Earth and still retain our hard-won individual consciousness. It is the Russian Sophiologists in our modern era who have emphasized the redemptive role of Sophia in restoring the unity between Heaven and Earth, between God and creation. Vladimir Solovyev's view was that Sophia, as World-soul, in the past had been in a state of Oneness with the Father, in the present exists in a condition of separation from God, and in the future will experience reunion with God. This is the meaning of the historical process and the purpose of all creation. The redemption of Sophia as World-soul will be accomplished through her reuniting with the unfallen, transcendent Sophia.[36]

The Russian theologian Nicolai Berdaeyev stated that because the fall of human beings brought suffering into the world, it is through the redemption of human beings that all creation will experience salvation from suffering. He believed that "...not only human beings, but grass, birds, trees, animals, fish, and rocks must also experience salvation, and that truly spiritual vows must encompass all of creation, which cries out for salvation."[37] Sophia's message of reconciliation today is for all of creation, not just humanity. Through her transformation of Eve, the entire cosmos is restored to a state of interconnected wholeness.

Sophia's process of reconciliation can by symbolized by the rainbow. The rainbow which appeared to the Hebrews after the flood was certainly a symbol of God's reconciliation with the human race. However, God said the rainbow is to be "the sign of the covenant which I make between me and you and every living creature that is with you." (Genesis 9:12) This statement of divine reconciliation with all the creatures of Earth suggests the loving inclusiveness of Sophia. Similarly, Vladimir Solovyev refers to Sophia in one of his poems as "the rainbow reconciling heaven and earth."[38] The rainbow is a visual image that reminds us that "Heaven stoops toward Earth; the world is not only a world in itself, it is also the world in God, and God abides not only in heaven but also on Earth."[39] In the rainbow, Sophia unites her transcendent and her earthly dimension, creating a divine synthesis which symbolizes the restoration of the unity between God and creation.

SOPHIA'S CO-CREATORS

A prophecy which is well known on Iona, an island off the western coast of Scotland, foretells that the Savior will come again in the form of a woman, rising suddenly in the hopes and dreams of many people.[40] It is possible that the Second Coming of Christ so long anticipated by Christians is actually the re-emergence of the Divine Feminine through the Loving-Wisdom of ChristoSophia within the human heart. The fulfillment of the prophecy of Iona is occurring today on the bypaths where Sophia is making her first emergence from her hiding places within Christian tradition.

With Sophia's rebirth into human consciousness, nature is again seen in its sacred dimensions; the entire cosmos is seen as a manifestation of the Divine; all human beings are seen as souls who bear Sophia within them. With this transformed consciousness we are called by Sophia to be co-creators with her in the world, helping her to usher in the new "Sophianic millennium."[41] Pilgrims on the Path of ChristoSophia are called to be channels for the revelation of Sophia into the world, for she is hidden to us no longer. We are called to be co-creators with Sophia in the process of reconciling humanity with God as manifest in all creation. As Susan Cole says, "By bridging the supposed gap between creator and creation, Sophia provides exactly the image needed to make us aware of our own collective power, not as God's puppets, but as co-creators - or potential destroyers - of this planet."[42]

72

There are a number of trailblazers upon the feminine bypath today who are bringing to us the riches of wisdom that they have discovered, in the form of symbols and stories that express the Sophianic nature of the new mythos. They are marking the trail for others who are seeking the way of Wisdom through their applications of Sophianic language and imagery to meditation, prayer, and ritual. One of these trailblazers is Aurora Terrenus, whose book *Sophia of the Bible* provides a poetic reinterpretation of the Wisdom scriptures of the Bible which can be used as scripture readings in worship services or for private prayer and meditation. Her beautiful and contemporary expression of Biblical texts helps one experience the Spirit of Sophia, the "holy spirit that lives within...the Spirit of Wisdom separate and one with the Spirit of Love."[43]

Other trailblazers on the feminine bypath are Susan Cole, Marian Ronan, and Hal Taussig, whose book *Wisdom's Feast: Sophia in Study and Celebration* provides a wealth of resources for those who are seeking the Divine Feminine; these include experiential exercises based on Biblical Sophia themes, scripture readings from the Wisdom tradition, prayer services which are centered upon the figure of Sophia, hymns which praise Sophia, and a variety of Sophianic liturgies. The association between Jesus and Sophia is clearly revealed in the "Sophia Eucharist" which is based on the passage in Proverbs 9 that describes the table of Sophia. Those who join in this celebration participate in a liturgy that is based upon scripture from the Wisdom tradition and partake of the bread, fruit, milk, wine and honey from Sophia's Table.[44]

Other deeply emotive worship services in which Sophia takes the conventional role of Christ include the Crucifixion of Sophia, which symbolizes the suffering of the Divine Feminine and all women throughout patriarchal history, and the Resurrection of Sophia which marks the emergence of the Divine Feminine in our world today as well as the liberation of women from their bonds of oppression.[45]

In a similar way, Jann Aldredge-Clanton provides worship services which emphasize the resurrected Christ-Sophia in her book *In Search of Christ-Sophia: An Inclusive Christology for Liberating Christians.* Her liturgies are designed to celebrate the seasonal cycle, for she says, "The sacred seasons themselves lie in need of resurrection. Through new and creative interpretations and symbols, they can come to life again. Christ-Sophia invites us to experience the seasons of the Christian year in new ways."[46] In another book, *Praying with Christ-Sophia: Services for Healing and Renewal*, Jann Aldredge-Clanton provides additional prayers, litanies and stories that emphasize the feminine aspect of the Divine. It includes services for traditional holy days of the Church such as Palm Sunday, Easter, and Pentecost, but also nontraditional, pagan celebrations such as the Winter and Summer Solstices and secular celebrations such as Earth Day and Independence Day. The diversity of these occasions for joyful thanksgiving demonstrates the nature of Sophianic inclusiveness. The author also shares her collection of hymns which honor Christ-Sophia. In a similar revisioning of traditional Christian themes in a Sophianic perspective, many of these songs are based on traditional melodies but contain new words which celebrate Christ-Sophia. For example, the hymn "O Come, Christ-Sophia" is sung to the tune of "O Come, All Ye Faithful."[47]

Those who walk on the feminine bypath can use these resources as an inspiration for birthing the new mythos which recognizes both the feminine and masculine dimensions of deity and celebrates the inclusiveness of ChristoSophia. For at the depth of Sophia's call to us to be co-creators with her lies the great Mystery. It is the Mystery of the seed of divinity within each of us, which in turn connects us to the entire cosmos; it is the Mystery of the inner Wisdom that unites those who journey on all true spiritual paths. Sophia restores the balance of the eros qualities of love and wisdom into our world where logos qualities have been dominant for thousands of years. These eros qualities cannot be defined precisely or encapsulated within dogmatic systems. The Wisdom of Sophia is ultimately beyond all words, beyond all concepts, beyond all human understanding. The pilgrim on the bypaths must truly **experience** the great Mystery of ChristoSophia within the heart. It is from the fertile depths of this Mystery within the human heart that Sophia is reborn in our current age, thus fulfilling the prophecy of Iona. The manifestation of Sophia's transformative powers in the world today depends upon our co-creation with her. We become her partners in creative transformation by remaining open to her Mystery, experiencing the Loving-Wisdom of ChristoSophia, and mediating the healing qualities of the Divine Feminine into the world.

CHAPTER IV: GNOSTIC CHRISTIANITY

Jesus said, "When you make the male and female one
and the same...then you will enter the kingdom."[1]

The "kingdom" which Jesus refers to in this quote from *The Gospel of Thomas* is a metaphor for "gnosis." The term "gnosis" is a Greek word which literally means "knowledge," however it is knowledge of a spiritual rather than an intellectual nature. Gnosis might be more appropriately defined as "inner wisdom," for it is a knowledge of the heart rather than of the mind.[2] Thus gnosis derives from the eros functions of intuitive insight instead of the logos qualities of factual analysis. The source for this wisdom is one's own spiritual experience rather than the teachings of authorities or collective systems of belief. The ultimate liberating wisdom for the gnostic comes from the experience of the Divine within his or her own being. Thus knowledge of one's true Self and knowledge of the Divine are integrally connected in gnosis. As the gnostic scholar Elaine Pagels says, "to know oneself, at the deepest level, is simultaneously to know God; this is the secret of gnosis."[3] The gnostic realizes that the Kingdom of God is an inner kingdom; it symbolizes the transformation of consciousness which is the hallmark of gnosis.[4] The quote of Jesus from *The Gospel of Thomas* reveals that the integration of the masculine and the feminine is a chief requirement for gaining entry into this kingdom; in other words, in order to achieve gnosis. It is this inclusion of the feminine element which makes the exploration of gnostic Christianity so very important for pilgrims walking on the feminine bypath.

GNOSTIC CHRISTIANITY AS A BYPATH

Although the beginnings of gnosticism are shrouded in mystery, it is known that it developed independently as a Hellenistic religion which pre-dated Christianity. With the rise of the early Christian community, Christian concepts became incorporated into gnosticism and resulted in a uniquely Christian form of gnosis.[5] During this time period pagan, Jewish, and Christian gnostic groups existed simultaneously. Thus gnosticism was a spiritual movement which exhibited an amazing diversity. A variety of gnostic communities, Christian and non-Christian, held widely divergent systems of belief and practiced quite different religious rituals. However, gnostic Christianity appears to have been firmly imbedded in the early Christian movement and gnostic Christians considered themselves to be authentic Christians.[6] Even those texts which were accepted into the canon of the New Testament express some gnostic ideas. Although the Apostle Paul officially opposed the gnostic teachings, many of his concepts are consistent with gnostic ideas. The writings of the Apostle John, including the Gospel of John and three epistles, also contain many gnostic characteristics.[7] A number of important early Christian theologians, such as Basilides and Valentinus of the second century, were especially known as great gnostic teachers. Some followers of Valentinus even believed that **only** the gnostics were true Christians. According to the leaders of the Western school of Valentinus, however, the true Church consisted of both catholic and gnostic Christians. The majority of Christians, they believed, did not recognize the spiritual element of the Church. This most important aspect of the Church was open only to those who possessed gnosis.[8] Thus, as early as the second century after Christ's death and resurrection, there were Christian theologians whose understanding of Christianity included both the interstate highway of religion for the masses as well as the bypaths for the few seekers of gnosis.

Early Christianity was marked by its diversity of thought and practice, and gnostic forms were accepted by many as entirely valid expressions of this spiritual movement. It was only later that gnostic concepts were labeled "heresy" as the interstate highway of the Christian Church was built. Just as the contours of the land are bulldozed and flattened in order to construct the interstate highway, so early variations in Christian doctrine were destroyed as dogma became regularized in the process of institutionalizing Christianity. The richness and beauty of gnostic symbolism and mythology were thus lost to mainstream Christianity. Gnostic Christianity differed from the institutional form of Christianity in that it possessed no structured Church or theology, no prescribed doctrines or rules, no set canon of scriptures. Gnostic Christians traveled the bypaths of personal spiritual experience rather than the collective highway of organized religion. Travelers on the interstate highway of Christianity found well marked traffic signs posted by the authorities to direct their way in the form of creeds of belief and moral prescriptions which were presented and enforced by the clergy; seekers on the gnostic bypath instead discovered their own "signs" in the wilderness of the soul by paying attention to their feelings, intuitions, dreams and visions. The gnostic perceived revelation to be a continually unfolding process and therefore looked inward to attain a progressively greater understanding of truth. Thus the gnostics could not accept an external authority in the form of church or creed which attempted to confine inner spiritual experience in order to make it consistent with a revelation which had become fossilized at one historical point in time.

The eros aspects of human nature which produced the imaginative, inspired upwelling of religious symbols in gnostic mythology came into direct conflict with the dominant logos characteristics of the institutional Church which was preoccupied with defining its dogmas and organizing its administrative structures. Gnostic Christianity posed a threat to the Church Fathers, the builders of the interstate Church, because the eros nature of gnostic illumination resulted in an immense variety of symbolic imagery which could not be compartmentalized and systematized. As the bishop Irenaeus, one of the chief critics of the gnostics in the second century, complained, "Every day every one of them invents something new, and none of them is considered perfect unless he is productive in this way."[9] Gnostics claimed their own spiritual authority based on personal revelation, which challenged the Church's official position as the sole representative of Christ in the world. The patriarchal hierarchy of the emerging institutional Church could not control the individual discovery and expression of gnosis, and gnostic revelatory experiences which differed from official Church teaching came to be labeled as "heretical."

The formal suppression of gnostic variants of Christianity was completed when Christianity became the official religion of Rome, for then it became especially important to present a religion which was simple and clear enough for the masses to understand. The complexities of gnostic thought and symbolism certainly did not meet these criteria. In the early fourth century the Emperor Constantine issued edicts which prohibited gnostic Christians from meeting together and called for the burning of gnostic gospels. The gnostic tradition was then forced underground, but has surfaced through the centuries in other sects such as the Cathars of the Middle Ages, the visions of Christian mystics, the tales of the quest for the Holy Grail, the studies of alchemy, and the mysteries of Kabbalism.[10] Today we see a re-emergence of this perennial spiritual perspective in the work of Jungian psychologists and the discoveries of pilgrims walking on the feminine bypath.

The restoration of the gnostic pathway, which was barricaded for so long, has been especially helped by the fortuitous discovery of 52 gnostic texts near Nag Hammadi, Egypt, in 1945. These texts were among those which had been labeled heretical by the Church, and were probably placed in a large urn and buried in the mountainous area near Nag Hammadi by some unknown monk to keep them from the eyes of church authorities. There they remained for nearly 1600 years, until finally discovered accidentally in our modern era by Arab peasants. This gnostic literature consisted of Coptic translations, written in approximately 350-400 CE, of original Greek manuscripts. The dates of the original manuscripts are disputed; however, some were probably written before 150 CE and some perhaps written as early as 50-100 CE, which would make them even older than the gospels of the New Testament. Included in the Nag Hammadi texts were alternative early Christian gospels such as *The Gospel of Thomas, The Gospel of Philip, The Gospel of Truth, The Gospel to the Egyptians,* and *The Gospel of Mary,* and works attributed to Jesus' followers such as *The Apocryphon of James, The Apocryphon of John, The Apocalypse of Paul, The Apocalypse of Peter, The Letter of Peter to Philip,* and *The Acts of Peter and the Twelve Apostles.*

It seems very significant that this aspect of the hidden tradition of Christian spirituality was literally hidden in the earth, awaiting the social and spiritual transformations of our modern era until they were uncovered. The discovery at Nag Hammadi has profound implications for our search for the symbols and images which can renew the Christian mythos in our current age. These closed scriptures of early Christianity have now been opened to us, and we are able to discover for ourselves the wisdom which has been hidden for so long within their pages. Previously our understanding of gnostic Christianity was limited for the most part to the polemical writings of church authorities such as Irenaeus and Tertullian who bitterly opposed, and probably misrepresented, gnostic teachings and practices. The scholarly process of interpreting and understanding the gnostic texts is still ongoing, but a primary result of this research has already been to show that the bypaths of early Christianity were much more numerous and diverse than was previously realized. The gnostic literature contains many stories and sayings attributed to Jesus which are similar to the works contained in the New Testament, but there are also intriguing differences which can motivate us to look for new and deeper meanings in the texts. The image of Jesus that emerges in the gnostic gospels is much more complex and paradoxical than in the gospels of the New Testament. A major value of reading on our own the texts of the Nag Hammadi Library, which have been available in an English translation since 1988,[11] is that the juxtaposition of the familiar and the strange can jolt us out of our conditioned ways of thinking about the Bible. The gnostic texts can help us "open our eyes" as we approach the Christian stories and symbols and thereby gain new insights, which lead us further along the bypath in our quest for gnosis.

MAJOR CONCEPTS OF GNOSTICISM

The difference between the religious concepts of gnostic and conventional Christians is explained by the Jungian psychologist June Singer as: "Gnostic mythology...reads everything in a direction opposite from orthodox theology. What is true in a limited world view is false in an unlimited worldview...Gnosis does not negate conventional wisdom; rather it holds up to it a reflective glass that reveals the side that was hidden before."[12] Exploring the gnostic bypath enables us to discover this hidden wisdom of Christianity which provides alternative views regarding the creation of the world, the relationship between humanity and the Divine, the nature of Jesus Christ, and the meaning of salvation. It is especially on this bypath that the Divine Feminine emerges from her hiding places in Christian tradition to guide us on our way.

The basic gnostic myth postulates an original Unity which differentiates upon entering the world of time and space, causing the light of the One to shatter into fragments which creates all forms - good and evil - as they fall through various levels of density. Eventually the fragments of light which fall from the divine realm are hidden as "divine sparks" within the human being.[13]

The pre-existent One is often referred to as the "unknown God" because its absolute transcendence cannot be conceived by human thought or language. This unknown God is androgynous in nature. The differentiation of the archetypal androgyne results in the creation of masculine and feminine images of divine powers in gnostic cosmology, which is reflected in the creation of males and females on earth.

In contrast to the transcendent realm of divine Light, the gnostics perceive this world of birth, death, and fate as a realm of darkness. Various gnostic myths which describe the creation of the world are attempts to explain the reasons for humanity's apparent condition of alienation from God and the resulting darkness of ignorance. Yet there exists the spark of the divine in human beings which connects them to the transcendent deity. It is only through the liberation of this divine spark within the human soul, which is achieved through gnosis, that one can escape from this prison world of darkness and unite with the divine Light. For gnostics, the Great Work involves freeing and reuniting all the fragments of divine light which are scattered throughout creation.

Thus the gnostic view of salvation differs markedly from the view which became dominant in the institutional Church. Gnostic Christians emphasized that human beings need to be saved from ignorance rather than sin. Salvation is not achieved through repentance and faith, but through a process of awakening from the slumber of mortal existence to the awareness of the divine spirit which exists within the Self. The purpose of the "living Jesus" which is revealed in the gnostic texts is to act as a guide to help us in this process of dispelling the illusions of darkness and gaining enlightenment.[14]

Jesus Christ is only one of many redeemer figures which appear in gnostic mythology. Gnostic Christians were more concerned with the cosmic, archetypal dimension of Jesus rather than the historical figure. In this sense they emphasized what we refer to as the "Cosmic Christ." The gnostic "living Jesus" exists eternally as the transcendent power which animates the universe as well as the divine spark within the human soul. For the gnostic Christian, "accepting the Savior" means to acknowledge the presence of the indwelling spirit of Christ and thus to re-enter the Kingdom of Heaven. The inner path which one travels to return to the Kingdom is one which leads from this earthly world of fragmentation to the original condition of unity. According to David Fideler, "In the gnostic view, this path, the nature of Christ, is not a static form of salvation but the very incarnation of saving gnosis itself."[15] This is the Path of ChristoSophia that the gnostic follows in her quest to achieve spiritual wholeness. For the pilgrim who achieves this quest, who attains gnosis, is then as *The Gospel of Philip* tells us, "no longer a Christian, but a Christ."[16]

The traveler on the gnostic bypath must always keep in mind that gnostic scriptures are an expression of mythology rather than historical facts. These spiritual adepts of early Christianity attempted to convey the knowledge gained by gnosis in the language of the soul which we know as myth. Literal interpretation of the gnostic religious imagery prevents us from understanding their deeper spiritual truths and blocks our own progress on the pathway to gnosis. Instead we must emulate the practice of the gnostics themselves in using our eros functions of intuition and imagination to seek the varied and complex layers of symbolic meaning which are expressed in gnostic myths.

In our modern era Jungian psychology has made a major contribution to deepening our understanding of gnostic mythology. Carl Jung was profoundly impressed by the similarities between the symbolic imagery found in gnostic texts and his own dreams and visions. He believed that the myths created by the gnostics were the product of their direct visionary experiences of the archetypal realm.[17] Jung's understanding that myths are expressions of archetypes, the universal processes of the psyche, explains why gnostic symbols consistently reappear among human beings throughout history, even when threatened with persecution for heresy. For even when the gnostic bypath is closed off by the authorities, gnostic images will continue to emerge spontaneously from the depths of the human soul.

Many Jungian psychologists have been very helpful guides on the gnostic bypath for they have provided an interpretation of gnostic imagery in the psychological language of contemporary Western culture. In this way the universal truths which are found in symbols that often appear strange and bizarre can be more clearly seen. A major insight of Jungian psychology is that gnosis is the mythological expression of the experience of the Self,[18] the archetype of wholeness or totality. Aspects of the Self archetype which have generally been repressed by the Church, such as the feminine and the dark side, can be readily found on the gnostic bypath. In the terms of Jungian psychology, the search for gnosis is the quest for individuation or wholeness. The gnostic's goal is not to be morally "perfect," but to be spiritually "whole." A major step in this journey toward wholeness is the integration of the masculine and the feminine aspects of the psyche. Therefore the feminine, in both her light and dark images, is a primary figure in gnostic mythology.

The Jungian emphasis on wholeness as the underlying theme of gnostic mythology appears to contradict the usual view of gnosticism as a religion of dualism. In gnostic thought we find the oppositions

of light and dark, body and spirit, humanity and God. I_
scholars use the criteria of dualism as the defining cha_
determining whether or not to label a text as "gnostic."
is important to keep in mind that there were an incredib.. ..
gnostic groups with diverse perspectives and interpretations which
are reflected in widely differing texts. Much of the gnostic mythology
does express a dualistic attitude, in which the material world is
seen as a realm of darkness and evil. But we must not oversimplify
the dualistic position, for the definition of gnosticism which was
formulated by the Congress of Messina in 1966 recognized the
"monistic background"[19] behind the gnostic dualistic concepts. The
essential idea of gnosticism is the divine spark within the soul which
inextricably connects the human being to the unity of the unknown
God.

Elaine Pagels points out that Valentinus, the most influential
spokesman for Christian gnosticism, did not promote a dualistic
concept of God. The Valentinians taught that there was a difference
between the images of God as father, king, or creator, and the
ultimate source of being which they called "the depth."[20] All of
the beautiful and terrifying divine powers which are so colorfully
depicted in gnostic texts are manifestations of the unknown God,
representations of the underlying Monad. As Pagels points out, the
Valentinian text *Tripartite Tractate* emphasizes the "theme of the
oneness of God."[21]

Other gnostic texts also contain passages which refute the
dualistic worldview which is usually ascribed to gnosticism. For
example, *The Gospel of Philip* states, "Light and darkness, life and
death, right and left are brothers of one another. Because of this
neither are the good good, nor the evil evil, nor is life life, nor death
death."[22] This saying warns us against perceiving the world in the
simplistic terms of dualism. For nothing in this world is precisely
what it seems to be, and those things that appear to be opposites are
actually closely related to each other. In the *Gospel of Thomas*, Jesus
says, "The kingdom is inside of you, and it is outside of you."[23] Here
again the dualistic separation between spirit and matter is shown to
be false, for the Divine can be found both in the inner spiritual world
and the outer material world.

The view that gnosticism is a dualistic religion which rejects the physical world often seems to be based upon a literal interpretation of gnostic myths. Although this was surely the interpretation given by many of the gnostics themselves, particularly since they lived in a dualistic culture, it also points out the dangers of literalizing religious symbols. We must always keep in mind the mythical and mystical context of gnostic scriptures, in which gnosis is communicated through paradox. For it is only through paradoxical wisdom where the opposites are joined that one can begin to approach the unity of the God who is unknown to human reason and sensibility. Thus a dualistic perception of the world actually appears to be due to the **lack** of gnosis. It is probable that the gnostic initiate recognized the apparent dualities of the temporal world as well as the nonduality of eternal Being, the unknown One. Today the recognition and integration of these opposites must be the goal of the modern pilgrim who seeks gnosis. And the task that is of utmost importance in this quest is to integrate the repressed feminine element within the psyche and within the Godhead. It is only in this way that we will enter into the kingdom of the "living Jesus."

IMAGES OF THE FEMININE IN GNOSTIC CHRISTIANITY

Gnostic Christianity is one of the major track ways of the feminine bypath. Gnosis, which relies on the eros activities of nonrational, intuitive, imaginative thought, entails a feminine mode of consciousness. Gnostic seekers who opened themselves to spiritual revelation through dreams and visions were more receptive to the feminine face of the deity. The Divine Feminine which had been forced into hiding during the building of the interstate Church could reveal herself fully to the pilgrims on the bypaths who opened their hearts to her wisdom. Thus the mysteries of the feminine became an essential aspect of the gnostic conception of deity.

The feminine names and images for the Divine provided by gnostic Christianity can help us to balance the exclusive masculine imagery of the Godhead that is found in the interstate Church. The gnostics acknowledged that the Divine is not gender specific in their reference to an androgynous "Unknown God," the "One," the primal source of All. But they also utilized both masculine and feminine images to symbolically express the underlying unity of the Divine. Gnostic mythology expresses the paradoxical image of a God who unites the masculine and feminine elements in a dynamic balance, yet is ultimately transcendent to both. The complex variety of feminine symbols in gnostic myth provides us with many models for her inclusion in our image of deity.

The Divine Dyad

Many gnostic Christians symbolized the unity of the One through the image of an androgynous divine being. Elaine Pagels says that according to this gnostic belief "the divine is to be understood in terms of a harmonious, dynamic relationship of opposites."[24] She describes the view of the gnostic Christian Valentinus that "God is essentially indescribable...But...can be imagined as a dyad; consisting, in one part, of the Ineffable, the Depth, the Primal Father; and, in the other, of Grace, Silence, the Womb and 'Mother of the All.'"[25] This Father-Mother God is the creative source which manifests as an interplay of masculine and feminine energies throughout every level of creation, including that of the human soul.[26]

The image of God as a dyad which unites male and female elements affects one's response to the Divine. Pagels makes reference to a gnostic group whose prayer began, "From Thee, Father, and through Thee, Mother, the two immortal names, Parents of the divine being..."[27] Through their prayer these gnostics were in touch with an image of deity which was fuller and more complete than the one presented in the prayers of the institutional Church.

The androgynous concept of God also led gnostic Christians to different views of the Trinity than those which were taught by the Church. Many of the gnostic texts describe a complex creation of divine powers, in which a male and female deity unites at each level to produce another pair of male and female powers. For example, *The Gospel of Truth*, a gnostic Christian text which was perhaps actually written by Valentinus, describes the creation of the original Ogdoad of Aeons (divine powers.) From the primal masculine power of the Fore-Father, or Abyss, and the feminine power of Thought, Ennoia, came forth the masculine Mind, Nous, and the feminine

Truth, Aletheia. This divine couple then produced the masculine Word and feminine Life, which in turn brought forth the masculine Man and the feminine Church. Further emanations developed from these original dyads, resulting in the Pleroma, the fullness of the divine realm, which consists of a hierarchical arrangement of thirty divine powers.[28]

As Anne Baring and Jules Cashford point out, "The Gnostic myth is the first to express the fourfold image of Mother, Father, Daughter and Son...and to offer an image of the totality of human experience in life in these four divine figures."[29] Thus the gnostic concept of the Pleroma of divine powers, which presents a complex image of deity incorporating an equal balance of masculine and feminine elements, is quite different from the traditional concept of the Trinity. The original tetrad of Mother, Father, Daughter and Son expresses an image of wholeness which is not found in the Christian Trinity. It is a quaternity image which includes the feminine element, and thus symbolizes the archetypal Self.[30]

Other gnostic texts refer to the concept of the Trinity, but in a manner which differs significantly from the dogma of the Church. In conventional Christian theology, the gender of the Holy Spirit is usually depicted as either male or neutral. However, as we have seen, there are suggestions even here of a feminine nature of the Holy Spirit. Gnostic Christianity brings the Divine Feminine in the form of the Holy Spirit clearly into the open. For example, in *The Apocryphon of John*, God appears to John and says, "I am the Father, I am the Mother, I am the Son."[31] In this trinitarian image of God, the usual place of the Holy Spirit is represented by the feminine aspect of deity in the form of "Mother." *The Gospel of the Egyptians* presents a similar image of the Trinity emerging from the transcendent, invisible Spirit: "Three powers came forth from him; they are the Father, the Mother, and the Son."[32] From this original trinity are brought forth a host of divine powers which constitute the Pleroma.

The Gospel of Philip says, "Some said, 'Mary conceived by the holy spirit.' They are in error. They do not know what they are saying. When did a woman ever conceive by a woman?"[33] This passage shows that the gnostic writers of this text clearly believed that the nature of the Holy Spirit was female, for this is the case upon which they built their argument that Mary could not conceive by her.

As these examples have shown, the gnostic religious literature presents many images of feminine divinities as equal counterparts to the masculine deities. But some of its most intriguing, powerful depictions of the feminine face of God are autonomous figures of female deities.

The Archetypal Goddess

Images of the Divine Feminine appear in gnostic literature which have many similarities with the ancient Great Goddess figures of Sumer, Babylonia, and Egypt. One particularly fascinating example is found in the treatise *The Thunder: Perfect Mind* which records the revelation of a divine female. The monologue begins: "I was sent forth from the power, and I have come to those who reflect upon me, and I have been found among those who seek after me."[34] The Divine Feminine was sent forth from the original Source to Earth where she may be found by true spiritual seekers. In this passage her role is similar to the Sophia of the Hebrew Wisdom literature, who is an "emanation of the glory of the Almighty" (Wisdom 7:25) and states that "those who seek me diligently find me." (Proverbs 8:17)

The deity of *The Thunder: Perfect Mind* claims, "I am the first and the last."[35] Here she identifies herself as the primal, eternal divine power. Then follows a series of paradoxical statements, including:

> I am the honored one and the scorned one.
> I am the whore and the holy one.
> I am the wife and the virgin.
> I am the mother and the daughter...
> I am knowledge and ignorance.
> I am shame and boldness.
> I am shameless; I am ashamed.
> I am strength and I am fear.
> I am war and peace...
> I am the one who has been hated everywhere
> and who has been loved everywhere.
> I am the one whom they call Life
> and you have called Death...[36]

In these self-references both the light and dark sides of the Divine Feminine are integrated in an image of wholeness. The deity who speaks in *The Thunder: Perfect Mind* unites the polarities of existence because she encompasses the All. One of the names that is given to this gnostic female deity is Barbelo. *The Apocryphon of John* describes how Barbelo is brought forth from the transcendent Spirit.:

> . . .his thought performed a deed and she came forth, namely she who had appeared before him in the shine of his light. This is the first power which was before all of them and which came forth from his mind...The first power, the glory of Barbelo...she glorified the virginal Spirit and it was she who praised him, because thanks to him she had come forth. This is the first thought, his image; she became the womb of everything for it is she who is prior to them all...[37]

In this passage Barbelo shows similarities to the feminine deity in *The Thunder: Perfect Mind* and the Sophia of the Wisdom literature as she also is the first emanation of the invisible Spirit. As the divine womb, she also appears to be related to the pagan Mother Goddesses of antiquity. She completes this role by giving birth to the Divine Son, as so many Mother Goddesses have done before her. As *The Apocryphon of John* relates, she conceives from the Father of Light and brings forth "a spark of light"[38] which is the Christ. The gnostics who wrote this text envisioned Christ to be the union of the divine opposites of male and female, for he is the "only-begotten child of the Mother-Father."[39]

Another name under which the Divine Feminine often appears in gnostic texts is Protennoia, "First Thought." *The Trimorphic Protennoia* begins,

> I am Protennoia, the Thought that dwells in the Light. I am the movement that dwells in the All, she in whom the All takes its stand, the first-born among those who came to be, she who exists before the All...I am invisible within the Thought of the Invisible One. I am revealed in the immeasurable, ineffable things. I am incomprehensible, dwelling in the incomprehensible. I move in every creature.[40]

Protennoia shares similar characteristics with the gnostic goddess figures already referred to in that she is the first creation, the Thought which emanates from the Light of the Spirit, the creative source of the All. The one who is "incomprehensible" yet also the one to "move in every creature" shows features of the Great Goddess who is simultaneously transcendent and immanent. In another passage in this treatise Protennoia states, "I exist before the All, and I am the All, since I exist in everyone."[41] In this statement we also see the union of the eternal, transcendent Divine Feminine with all of creation. She is the "divine spark" which exists in everyone and connects us to the eternal realm of the Pleroma as well as all of manifest creation. Protennoia's links with Divine Wisdom are also seen in her statement, "It is through me that Gnosis comes forth."[42] She is the source of the inner wisdom sought by the gnostic.

The Gnostic Sophia

All of the images of the Divine Feminine which we have examined - the unnamed deity in *The Thunder: Perfect Mind*, Barbelo, Protennoia - are actually expressions of the primary female figure in gnosticism - Sophia. Kurt Rudolph says of Sophia that "She belongs to the oldest and most important elements of the structure of Gnosis."[43] Gnostic scriptures expand and enrich the image of Sophia which is presented in the Hebrew Wisdom literature. However, gnosticism does not contain just one accepted version of the myth of Sophia but instead presents a multitude of images of the Divine Feminine in which her various facets unite and separate in a kaleidoscopic manner throughout the diverse myths. This multiplicity of symbolic imagery further affirms the gnostic realization that the Divine cannot be known through human reason or limited by human concepts.

The essence of the gnostic Sophianic myth, which appears in so many different forms, describes the descent of the Divine Feminine from the celestial realm to the material world. Many versions of the myth base the impetus for this "fall" on Sophia's error, her pride which causes her to want to create autonomously without her consort or her overwhelming desire for the High God. This folly brings about her alienation from the Pleroma and correspondingly all the negative conditions of the world. In some gnostic systems the error of Sophia brings forth the Demiurge, the creator of this world, who is perceived as a jealous and malicious god. In this way these gnostics are able to explain the existence of evil, for the god of this world of darkness is not the unknown High God.

The suffering of Sophia is a central theme of the myth of her exile. The painful emotions she experiences when she realizes that she is alone and abandoned - sorrow, despair, fear, and ignorance-are transformed into the four elements of earth, water, fire, and air, and as such become the very substance out of which our world is built. Sophia suffers also because of her compassion for the Earth, which she acknowledges was created as the result of her error. Thus she becomes "the spirit of the world," watching over it and caring for it like the mother of a deformed child.[44]

The mythic suffering of Sophia symbolizes the archetypal suffering of the feminine. This is the suffering that we experience today in the repression of the Divine Feminine in our culture, the suppression of the eros aspects of human nature, and the dualistic split between matter and spirit. This myth continues to have significant meaning for us today because it is the feminine which has "fallen" and must be restored in order to bring wholeness to the world and the soul.

The next sequence in the mythological process occurs when the High God recognizes Sophia's repentant suffering and sends salvation to her. This may be in the form of Christ, who serves as a guide to lead her back to the supernal realm of the Pleroma. But through her compassion a part of her remains with the world. Often her nature is represented in two forms - as the transcendent goddess figure and the fallen Sophia who goes by the name "Achamoth" or "Prunikos." She then represents the figure of the Great Goddess who is both Virgin and Whore, spiritual and sensual, because she encompasses the All. The dual nature of Sophia recognized by the gnostics was later reflected in the views of the Russian Sophiologists such as Solovyev and Bulgakov who perceived Sophia as both transcendent and present within the world. The gnostic images of Sophia convey the paradoxical attributes of the Divine Feminine. She unites the Light Goddess in her qualities of compassion, love, and life with the

Black Goddess elements of chaos, sorrow, and death. Recognition of the "fallen" Sophia who remains in our world can help restore the dynamic power of the Black Goddess which has been especially repressed in Western culture.

The mythic theme of Sophia's fall, repentance, and redemption represents the spiritual quest of the human soul. The feminine nature of the soul is revealed in this passage from *The Exegesis On the Soul*: "Wise men of old gave the soul a feminine name. Indeed she is female in her nature as well."[45] Sophia symbolizes the presence of the divine spark within the soul which has fallen from the transcendent, eternal realm into a physical body and yearns for mystical union with God. The "fall" of Sophia in the gnostic vision was a cosmic event which resulted in the creation of the world, rather than the Church's concept of the "fall" of humanity which resulted in sin and death. Sophia's "fall" occurred through the process of differentiation out of an original Unity, and led to the separation of spirit and matter. Redemption, according to the gnostic view, entails a reuniting of the soul with the Divine through the transforming wisdom of gnosis. Just as Sophia remains in the earthly world while returning to the heavenly realms, so the soul which has attained gnosis continues to live in the physical body while at the same time maintaining consciousness of the Divine.

The gnostic bypath openly reveals the relationship between Christ and Sophia which was apparently understood by many in the early Christian communities but later became hidden as the interstate Church was built. Christ takes on a number of roles in relation to Sophia in the gnostic texts: as her savior, her divine consort, and her son. As Sophia appears in a dual nature in gnostic texts, so does Jesus Christ appear in the two forms of celestial Christ and earthly Jesus. Christ, as a being of light who exists in the Pleroma, temporarily unites with the earthly body of Jesus to function as the gnostic revealer. It is the heavenly Christ who rescues Sophia in her fallen state by leading her back to the Divine. As he states in *Pistis Sophia*, "I led forth Pistis Sophia...and Pistis Sophia gazed upon her enemies, from whom I had taken their light-power. And I led Pistis Sophia forth from chaos..."[46] This redemptive role serves as the model for the actions of Jesus as the savior of humanity on

Earth. Christ as the savior or liberator of Sophia is also her consort in the divine realm.[47] The theme of "divine syzygy,"[48] the union of Sophia with her male divine counterpart, is an essential element in gnosticism. The cosmic Fall will be healed and the Pleroma will be restored to its original wholeness in the fullness of time when Sophia and Christ enter the bridal chamber and unite in marriage.[49]

In other gnostic texts Sophia is the consort of the High God and mother of Christ. We have already seen in *The Apocryphon of John* that Sophia in the form of Barbelo conceived Christ. A passage in *The Sophia of Jesus Christ* states, "First Man is called Begetter, Self-perfected Mind. He reflected with Great Sophia, his consort, and revealed his first-begotten, androgynous son...Now first-begotten is called Christ."[50] In this text Sophia is both the mother of Christ and also the feminine half of his androgynous nature, which is also called "Love."[51]

The gnostic Sophia's roles in the earthly realm are similar in many respects to those which the Church attributed to Jesus Christ. In the gnostic view she is the primary mediator between God and the world. As Hans Jonas points out, in the theology of the Valentinian Christians, "the suffering of Sophia, not that of Christ, is the central fact, doctrinally and emotionally."[52] Sophia, through her own suffering and redemption, initiates the liberating quest for gnosis for all of humanity. She is a model of the "saved savior" who has attained the wisdom of wholeness and can thus guide others who seek this way. Jean Houston refers to Sophia's role as the gnostic revealer when she says, "Sophia provides the balance between masculine and feminine spiritual principles that the gnostic Jesus spoke of as necessary for the full development of life in the kingdom."[53]

The many similarities between the functions of Christ and Sophia suggest that perhaps the view of some early Christians that Jesus Christ was the incarnation of Sophia actually reflected these gnostic beliefs. One reason that the figure of Sophia was so vehemently suppressed in the Church was probably because the authorities were trying so hard to distinguish the interstate Church from the gnostic bypath. Sophia was much more comfortable walking along the variety of meandering bypaths rather than confining herself to the linear course of the interstate highway. Therefore the role of this numinous figure in gnostic mythology was transposed by the Church into the Virgin Mary, Mother of God and Queen of Heaven, who serves as mediator between God and humans. But as such the Divine Feminine has lost much of her power as a symbol of wholeness for Mary does not represent the dark elements of the goddess which are essential to the gnostic Sophia.

We can look to the gnostic figure of Sophia today to deepen and broaden the image of the Divine Feminine which was perceived by the early Christian community. Gnostic myths which represent Christ and Sophia as consorts provide a powerful symbol with which to express the mystical concept of ChristoSophia. An image of Christ and Sophia as the divine couple integrates the archetypal feminine, repressed for so long in Western culture, with the masculine deity. ChristoSophia symbolizes the paradoxical condition of differentiated wholeness, which is the goal of the gnostic's quest. It is the union of Christ and Sophia, Love and Wisdom, within the human soul which gives birth to the divine child of the Self. This is the gnostic salvation process which is mirrored in the outer world of creation. It is through the union of Christ and Sophia, the dynamic integration of masculine and feminine energies, that the entire cosmos will be restored to a state of wholeness. Thus the symbol of ChristoSophia represents the union of the Divine and the soul of the human being, as well as the union of God and all creation.

Eve and the Serpent

Many of the gnostic texts portray an alternative view of Eve, the female companion of Adam, in a manner which is consistent with the gnostic creation and redemption myths. The Church traditionally portrays Eve as the original female human being who gullibly listened to the evil counsel of the serpent in the Garden of Eden and coaxed her husband Adam into eating the forbidden fruit of the Tree of Knowledge. This myth was interpreted by St. Augustine as an explanation for the existence of "original sin" in human beings which was transmitted from Adam and Eve to each succeeding generation. The interstate Church which accepted Augustine's interpretation was thus built on a foundation that emphasized human sinfulness and guilt, and perceived woman as the source of temptation and the serpent as a symbol of evil. This interpretation of the meaning of the mythic "fall of Adam and Eve" was a major source of the devaluation of the feminine by the Church. Gnostic views of the meaning of this myth were radically different from that of the Church. According to *The Gospel of Philip*, the story explains that the tragedy of the human condition results from the separation of the masculine and the feminine. According to this gnostic gospel, "When Eve was still in Adam death did not exist. When she was separated from him death came into being. If he enters again and attains his former self, death will be no more."[54] When the original unity of the androgynous human was broken, the awareness of duality brought death. The "fall of Adam and Eve" recapitulates the "fall of the gnostic Sophia"; the mythic tragedy of the original humans reflects the cosmic tragedy of the Divine Feminine. Adam and Eve's expulsion from the paradisal unity of the Garden of Eden is analogous to Sophia's exile from the fullness of the Pleroma. In both myths the underlying theme is the experience of alienation from the Divine, which paradoxically is the condition which is necessary to initiate the development of consciousness. The gnostics' deeper understanding of the symbolic meaning of the myth had its corollary in a positive view of the role of Eve. In a number of gnostic creation narratives Eve appears as another form of Sophia for she represents the personification of gnosis. She is the archetypal feminine power whose task it is to awaken and instruct Adam.

In *The Apocryphon of John* the consort of Adam is called Epinoia, meaning "insight," which signifies her positive relationship to him. The text reads, "he sent...a helper to Adam, luminous Epinoia which comes out of him, who is called Life. And she assists the whole creature, by toiling with him and by restoring him to his fullness... the Epinoia of the light which was in him, she is the one who was to awaken his thinking."[55] The value of the feminine is clearly seen in this story, for Epinoia is a figure of light and life, the helpmate and teacher of Adam, who brings him to consciousness and restores his wholeness. In the traditional interpretation of the Genesis story Adam and Eve are literalized as man and woman, but the mythic account in *The Apocryphon of John* reveals that Adam and Epinoia can also symbolize the physical body and the soul of the human being. For

Epinoia represents the feminine nature of the human soul, whose light provides the inner illumination of divine consciousness.

A similar version of the myth is told in *The Hypostasis of the Archons*, in which the consort of Adam is referred to as a "spirit-endowed woman." She commands Adam to arise from his deep sleep of ignorance, and he says to her, "It is you who have given me life; you will be called 'Mother of the living.' For it is she who is my mother. It is she who is the physician, and the woman, and she who has given birth."[56] Here the feminine companion of Adam is also viewed as his superior spiritually. He honors her roles as birth-giver and physician, which refer to the creative and healing properties of the feminine. In this passage the woman who gives life to Adam, and is therefore the mother of all humanity, resonates with the image of the ancient Mother Goddesses.

One of the most dramatic reversals of gnostic interpretation of traditional symbolic meanings involves the role of the serpent in the Garden of Eden. The Church depicted the snake as a creature of treachery and deceit whose evil counsel brought about the "fall" and therefore all the ills of humankind. The negative associations with the serpent as a symbol of evil and also the instinctive nature became linked in Western culture. However, in gnostic creation myths the snake is often a symbol of wisdom. *The Hypostasis of the Archons* makes clear the connection between the Divine Feminine and the serpent in this passage: "the female spiritual principle came in the snake, the instructor."[57] The archetypal power of the feminine which was embodied in Eve has now been transformed into the serpent, who also is the agent of spiritual illumination. The serpent explains the reason for the creator god's forbidding Adam and Eve to eat the fruit of the Tree of Knowledge of Good and Evil according to a gnostic belief that the creator of this earthly world is an inferior, even evil, deity. For "the snake, the instructor, said, 'With death you shall not die; for it is out of jealousy that he said this to you. Rather your eyes shall open and you shall come to be like gods, recognizing evil and good.'"[58] The illuminating serpent encourages the primal humans to overcome the blind obedience based on fear in order to attain an increase in consciousness. The serpent's instructions to Adam and Eve are actually a message to all human beings to "open one's eyes" from the sleep of unconscious, conditioned living, and in this way became aware of one's true spiritual nature. For the gnostic, eating the fruit of the Tree of Knowledge was not a sinful act of disobedience against the divine will, but instead was a highly desirable act for the purpose of attaining gnosis. The result of Adam and Eve eating the fruit of the Tree of Knowledge was that "they recognized that they were naked of the spiritual element."[59] They were not ashamed of their physical bodies, which is the usual interpretation given to the awareness of their nakedness, but they recognized the true state of their souls which lacked the spiritual element. This recognition of their condition of alienation from the divine Spirit marked the beginning of human consciousness, for the animals do not suffer from this existential awareness.

The liberating function of the snake in the Garden of Eden caused some gnostic groups to identify the serpent with Christ himself. *The Testimony of Truth* portrays the serpent as the wisest of all the animals who reveals the nature of the malicious, jealous creator god to Adam and Eve. The serpent performs the role of the gnostic revealer and symbolizes both divine Wisdom and Christ. A passage in the text refers to the serpent of Moses as a symbol of Christ: "For this is Christ; those who believed in him have received life. Those who did not believe will die."[60]

The gnostic symbolic interpretations of the snake in the Garden of Eden recall the earlier associations of the serpent with the archetypal Great Goddess. In ancient religions which worshipped the Divine Feminine, the serpent was honored as a symbol of life, immortality, healing and wisdom. All of these attributes are seen in the gnostic serpent in the Garden of Eden. Mary Condren points out that the essence of serpent symbolism in goddess religions is its "dual nature and simultaneous capacity for good and evil."[61] The dual nature of the gnostic serpent is seen in its association with the Tree of the Knowledge of Good and Evil, and also as a representation of Sophia in her spiritual as well as her earthly domains. The gnostic serpent in the Garden of Eden integrates the opposites of good and evil, life and death, masculine and feminine. The interstate highway of Christianity recognized only the serpent of the instincts and therefore denigrated the serpent as evil, but seekers on the gnostic bypath also recognized its other form as the serpent of illumination. Restoring this knowledge is a very important step in reclaiming the numinous power of the serpent as a symbol of the Divine Feminine in both her light and dark aspects.

The seeker on the gnostic bypath discovers that the ultimate meaning of the Garden of Eden myth is the recognition and integration of the polarities of existence. The myth symbolically expresses the paradox of human consciousness as a "fall" from the experience of unity into separation. The subsequent recognition of the dualities of existence is necessary in order for the human ego to emerge from its original unconscious wholeness. But this awareness of separate self also entails a loss of contact with the divine ground of being. The gnostics perceived the story of the events which took place in the Garden of Eden as a symbolic explanation for the tragedy of the ordinary human condition rather than an illustration of human sin.

In Christian tradition the purpose of salvation is based on the meaning given to humanity's "fall." According to the doctrines of the Church, Christ offered himself as a sacrifice to redeem the innate sinful nature of humanity which is based in the "original sin" of Adam and Eve. In gnostic interpretations, the liberating function of Christ was to reunite the opposites which are symbolically expressed in the creation of Adam and Eve. As *The Gospel of Philip* states, "Christ came to repair the separation which was from the beginning and again unite the two, and to give life to those who died as a result of the separation and unite them."[62] Christ's purpose is to restore wholeness through a reuniting of the masculine and the feminine. Eve as a representative of Sophia aids in this task by manifesting the eros functions of spiritual insight. It is through the symbolic union of Adam and Eve, the integration of logos and eros, that one attains the wholeness of life which Christ proclaims.

Mary Magdalene

The union of the masculine and the feminine is portrayed by a number of gnostic texts in their depiction of the relationship between Jesus and Mary Magdalene. The importance of Mary Magdalene's role as disciple of Christ is seen even in the texts which were accepted for inclusion in the New Testament, although her later recasting as the penitent whore by the patriarchal Church greatly devalued her status. For those who are only familiar with the common characterizations of Mary Magdalene, the gnostic scriptures present a surprising, but perhaps truer, picture of the power and wisdom of this female disciple as well as the nature of her special relationship with Jesus. The gnostic scriptures portray Mary Magdalene as the beloved of Jesus. *The Gospel of Philip* refers to the Magdalene as "the one who was called his companion."[63] The meaning of the Greek term for "companion" is understood to be consort or sexual partner.[64] This meaning is supported in the statement from the same gospel that Jesus "loved her more than all the disciples and used to kiss her often."[65] Here again it is important to guard against mere literalizing of the intimate relationship between Jesus and Mary Magdalene, and instead to consider the underlying meaning which is symbolized by this partnership. Mary Magdalene appears as a representation of the divine Sophia, and her relationship with Jesus in the earthly realm mirrors the union of Christ and Sophia in the fullness of the Pleroma. Mary Magdalene as the human consort of Jesus is a symbolic image of Holy Sophia as the spiritual consort of the Christ. In the gnostic scriptures Jesus and his beloved partner, Mary Magdalene, can be viewed as the earthly manifestation of the archetypal principle of ChristoSophia, the divine union of the masculine and feminine energies which interact as a differentiated wholeness.

Mary Magdalene also represents the model of the gnostic disciple. *The Dialogue of the Savior* refers to her as "a woman who understood completely,"[66] meaning that she had fully attained the wholeness of gnosis. This is perhaps due to her unique relationship with Jesus Christ which enabled her to receive a special revelation from him that was hidden to others. In *The Gospel of Mary* this hidden revelation is made explicit. Mary Magdalene's secret wisdom was based on her experience of a visionary dialogue with the risen Lord. Mary's primary role among the disciples is first demonstrated when Christ departed from his disciples, for it was Mary who comforted the grieving disciples, strengthened their resolve, and "turned their hearts to the Good."[67] She assumed the role of gnostic revealer after the resurrection of Christ when she said, "What is hidden from you I will proclaim to you."[68] Peter then asked, "Did he really speak with a woman without our knowledge and not openly? Are we to turn about and all listen to her? Did he prefer her to us?"[69] Peter's confrontation with Mary Magdalene, which is also described in several other gnostic texts, indicates the arguments that were developing between the institutional Church and gnostic Christianity.[70] Peter, as the "Rock" upon which the foundation of the interstate Church was built, questioned the spiritual authority of women and the validity of personal revelation. On the other hand, Mary Magdalene carried on the functions of the gnostic revealer after Christ's resurrection as she shared the wisdom gained from her inner experience of the continuing presence of Christ. She responded to Peter as many other gnostic visionaries have probably felt when faced with similar uncomprehending accusations: "Mary wept and said to Peter, 'My brother Peter, what do you think? Do you think that I thought this up myself in my heart, or that I am lying about the Savior?"[71] The disciple Levi then supported Mary's position in his answer to Peter, "if the Savior made her worthy, who are you indeed to reject her? Surely the Savior knows her very well. That is why he loved her more than us."[72] This response was also a challenge to the authorities of the Church, represented by Peter, who determine the truth or falsity of spiritual claims based on prescribed external criteria. Levi pointed out that personal spiritual experience is a gift from God which cannot be validated by any external authority but only by the heart.

The stark contrasts in the attitudes of Peter and Mary have led some commentators to differentiate between the tradition of Peter which formed the Roman Catholic Church and the tradition of Mary Magdalene which underlies gnostic Christianity.[73] Since gnostic illumination is a function of eros, it is not surprising that it was a woman who mediated this gnosis to the disciples after Christ's resurrection. In this way Mary Magdalene performs the earthly role of the gnostic Sophia. Like Sophia, she remains in the world after the departure of Jesus to continue his redemptive function of guiding others toward gnosis. Like Sophia, she also symbolizes the divine spark within the human being which seeks union with the Cosmic Christ. Mary Magdalene's value as a human woman who embodies the archetypal Divine Feminine is that she can readily serve as a model for those who seek mystical union with Christ. It is through her openness to the wisdom of gnosis that she "knows" and unites with Christ.

On the interstate highway of the Christian Church the symbol of "Mary" as representative of the Divine Feminine was split apart into two opposed images: the Virgin Mary and Mary Magdalene. The ancient symbolism of the Great Goddess and her Son-Lover[74] is hidden in this duality for Jesus Christ is the son of the Virgin Mary and, according to gnostic tradition, the lover of Mary Magdalene. Likewise, the Church has sundered the wholeness of the Great Goddess in her light and dark aspects, for the White Goddess is associated with the purity of the Virgin Mary and the Black Goddess with the sinfulness of Mary Magdalene. The gnostic image of Mary Magdalene re-unites the light and dark aspects of the goddess as a potent representative of the divine Sophia.

WOMEN'S ROLES IN GNOSTIC CHRISTIANITY

Mary Magdalene's prominent position among the disciples in gnostic texts is indicative of a greater role for women in gnostic Christianity. Peter's refutation of Mary's authority was based in large part on the fact that she was a woman and therefore could not possess a hidden wisdom unknown to the male disciples. This was the viewpoint that formed the hierarchical structure of the institutional Church which traced authority in a direct descent from the original male apostles of Christ. However, in the gnostic Christian communities, spiritual authority was based on inner vision, so the testimony of a female such as Mary Magdalene was equal to that of any of the other disciples.[75] This is why we see in *The Gospel of Mary* the unique occurrence of a female who acts as spiritual instructor to the male disciples. The acceptance of Mary Magdalene's spiritual authority by the gnostic Christians is further seen in the fact that the gnostic text *The Gospel of Mary* is the only known gospel to be named after a female. It is possible that this gospel was even written by Mary Magdalene herself.[76] Scholars have suggested that other gnostic texts were perhaps also written by women, including *Pistis Sophia*,[77] *The Thought of Norea*,[78] and *The Exegesis on the Soul*.[79] If this were the case, it would provide further support for the gnostic Christians' perception that women's spiritual vision is equal to men's.

Other female figures in addition to Mary Magdalene appear prominently in the gnostic texts as valued followers of Jesus. *The Sophia of Jesus Christ* refers to the twelve disciples and seven women who followed Christ; *Pistis Sophia* refers to four women who gathered with the other disciples after the resurrection - Mary Magdalene, Mary the mother of Jesus, Martha, and Salome; and *The Gospel of Philip* refers to three Marys who were always with the Lord - his mother, his sister, and the Magdalene. The gnostic texts make explicit the importance of these women's roles which can only be inferred from the writings of the New Testament. It is shown that they are also true disciples of Christ.[80]

Perhaps we can gain a clearer view of Jesus' attitudes toward women from the gnostic scriptures than from the texts of the New Testament which were selected according to a patriarchal bias. The egalitarian views of Jesus, apparent even in the New Testament gospels, were incorporated by the early Christian movement and appear to have been retained more fully in gnostic communities than in the institutional Church. In gnostic sects women functioned as priests, prophets, teachers, healers, and perhaps even bishops.[81] They continued to serve in roles equal to men, as had been the practice among the earliest Christian groups, even after the Church barred women from these roles. It appears that women were especially attracted to gnostic sects, in part because they were able to hold positions of leadership which were closed to them in the institutional Church.[82] In addition, the greater openness to women in gnostic Christianity was matched by a greater emphasis on feminine modes of consciousness such as visionary insight and creative imagination. The importance that these eros functions were given in gnostic Christianity, in contrast to the dominance of logos characteristics in the interstate Church, was probably another reason that many women found the gnostic bypath to be especially appealing.

The value which gnostic Christianity accorded to the feminine, as seen in greater equality for women and the primacy of eros in gnostic revelation, challenged the patriarchal hierarchy of the institutional Church. Many of the criticisms by church authorities were directed toward the egalitarian practices of gnostic communities. For example, Tertullian's virulent attack against the gnostic Christians especially condemned the despicable acts of "heretical women" who considered themselves equal to men: "how brazen they are! They dare to teach, to dispute, to exorcize, to promise cures, even perhaps to baptize."[83] The absence of a hierarchy of power, with male superiority as its basic feature, threatened the order and control which were necessary in the process of institutionalizing Christianity. Therefore texts which indicated the importance of women's roles in the early Christian movement were excluded by the authorities from the canon of scriptures which comprised the New Testament. This was especially true for those texts which revealed the prominent position of Mary Magdalene among the disciples. Her status posed such a threat to the male hierarchy that her entire image had to be refashioned by the Church in order to devalue her position. For this reason the beloved companion of Jesus which was depicted in *The Gospel of Mary* became transformed into the penitent whore in the popular mind. The historical misrepresentation of Mary Magdalene is a metaphor for the subordination of women within the institutional Church. Recovering the gnostic image of Mary Magdalene as a woman of spiritual power and wisdom who played a significant role among the disciples can provide us with a model for women's leadership in the Christian community today.[84]

The sharply contrasting attitudes toward women which are found along the interstate highway of the institutional Church and the gnostic bypath are reflections of their differing views of deity. The Church's repression of the feminine dimension of the Divine was matched by the suppression of women's social and spiritual roles. On the other hand, the gnostic Christians recognized the importance of the Divine Feminine in their vision of a dynamic interaction of feminine and masculine energies which produces wholeness. Differences in perception of the feminine are also shown in contrasting interpretations of the role of Eve. The Church's justification of its demands for women's subordination to men was usually based on reference to Eve as the secondary creation, formed from the rib of Adam, and as temptress whose sin caused the "fall" of humankind. However, in the gnostic texts the figure of Eve symbolizes the positive attributes of the feminine spiritual principle. Her role in awakening, instructing, and healing Adam reveals the spiritual power of the feminine. Gnostic Christianity presents the primordial human female Eve, like the prominent female disciple Mary Magdalene, as a model for women's valuable roles in the spiritual community.

It is important to realize that gnostic Christianity, although giving the feminine a much more dominant place than does the institutional Church, also contains elements which denigrate the feminine. There were tremendous differences between various gnostic groups; some such as the Valentinian Christians considered women to be equal to men,[85] but others devalued women in a manner similar to the interstate Church. Gnostic mythology presents many powerful, numinous figures of the Divine Feminine, but in many accounts it is she who is responsible for the creation of this world of darkness and sorrows. Many gnostic texts emphasize the spiritual authority of female figures, but others claim that only males can enter the Kingdom. Therefore it is apparent that gnostic Christianity does not present a view of the feminine which is completely untarnished by patriarchal attitudes. The negative attitudes toward women which were the cultural norm often prevailed even along this bypath. Gnostic Christianity provides only the beginnings of a movement toward spiritual and social equality for women.[86] The vision of an equal partnership between men and women in spiritual service, which we may briefly glimpse along the gnostic bypath, is an ideal which remains to be fully realized.

GNOSTIC RITUALS

The union of the feminine and the masculine, a central tenet of the gnostic conception of the Kingdom of God, is symbolically expressed in a number of gnostic rituals. This motif is clearly seen in the primary gnostic sacrament of the bridal chamber. *The Gospel of Philip* states that the bridal chamber is "the holy of the holies" in which "the redemption takes place."[87] The bridal chamber is the sacred temenos in which the redemptive act is accomplished as the divine spark within the human soul is reunited with the Godhead. The meaning of this sacred rite derives from the gnostic myth of Sophia's "fall" which disrupted the original Unity and the subsequent reunion with her consort Christ. This mythic theme of the separation and reunion of divine partners is mirrored at the human level in the differentiation of the sexes as expressed in the story of Adam and Eve. As *The Gospel of Philip* states,

> If the woman had not separated from the man, she should not die with the man. His separation became the beginning of death. Because of this Christ came to repair the separation which was from the beginning and again unite the two, and to give life to those who died as a result of the separation and unite them. But the woman is united to her husband in the bridal chamber. Indeed those who have united in the bridal chamber will no longer be separated.[88]

The separation of Adam and Eve, which destroyed the primordial state of androgynous unity, brought death into the world through the recognition of duality. Christ's redeeming mission was to heal this separation which defines human experience and restore the condition of wholeness. Christ brings the liberating gnosis through which the initiate who unites with the Divine in the bridal chamber overcomes the illusion of separation which characterizes ordinary human consciousness and thus attains the knowledge of eternal life.

The mystery of the union that takes place in the bridal chamber is prefigured in the "hieros gamos,"[89] or divine marriage, which takes place in the Pleroma and begets all creation. *The Gospel of Philip* explains:

> The father of everything united with the virgin who came down, and a fire shone for him on that day. He appeared in the great bridal chamber. Therefore, his body came into being on that very day. It left the bridal chamber as one who came into being from the bridegroom and the bride.
> So Jesus established everything in it through these. It is fitting for each of the disciples to enter into his rest.[90]

The primal union of the divine Father and Mother in the celestial bridal chamber serves as the model which Christ reveals to his earthly followers by which they too may attain wholeness. The divine marriage symbolizes the integration of the masculine and feminine polarities within the human soul. As Stephen Hoeller says, "In modern terms one might define this mystery as a sacred rite of individuation wherein the person becomes a true **individuum**, or indivisible unity."[91]

Thus we see that the central symbol of the bridal chamber in gnostic Christianity has many complex levels of meaning: it represents the re-uniting of male and female who have suffered the separation of Adam and Eve; the synthesis of the masculine and feminine aspects within the psyche; the union of the feminine soul with the divine bridegroom; the hieros gamos of the archetypal Masculine and Feminine which gives birth to all creation.

It appears that the actual ritual of the bridal chamber was a mystical ceremony which enacted the "spiritual marriage" rather than sexual practices as claimed by some critics of gnosticism. In the consummation of this sacred rite, the spirit of the gnostic initiate was united with the fullness of the Pleroma while still embodied in this world.[92] *The Gospel of Philip* describes the condition of one who has achieved the fulfillment of the bridal chamber: "If anyone becomes a son of the bridal chamber, he will receive the light. If anyone does not receive it while he is here, he will not be able to receive it in the other place...The world has become the eternal realm (aeon), for the eternal realm is fullness for him."[93] This passage describes the mystical illumination which dissolves all appearances of separation. The light of the bridal chamber enables the gnostic to see the unity of the earthly and the transcendent worlds, the temporal and the eternal realms. It is necessary to unite with the Divine while still in this world in order to bring the fullness of the Pleroma into everyday, human life.

The gnostic Christian celebration of the eucharist was also a ritual of transformation which brought illuminating gnosis to the participant. *The Gospel of Philip* describes the meaning of the eucharist for Valentinian gnostic Christians: "The cup of prayer contains wine and water...And it is full of the holy spirit, and it belongs to the wholly perfect man. When we drink this, we shall receive for ourselves the perfect man."[94] The "water of life" contained in the gnostic cup symbolizes illuminating gnosis[95] which has the power to transform the recipient into "the perfect man," the image of unity and completion. The deeper meaning of the gnostic eucharist is parallel to that of the sacred rite of the bridal chamber; it conveys an experience of the original wholeness of the Pleroma.[96]

The union of masculine and feminine, central to the gnostic concept of the Pleroma, is also found in the symbolism of the eucharist. The cup of prayer contains both the "perfect man" and the "holy spirit," which we have seen is regarded as a feminine figure by gnostic Christians. Another passage in *The Gospel of Philip* which presents similar symbolism signifies the importance of the eucharist ritual: "His flesh is the word, and his blood is the holy spirit."[97] Partaking of Christ's flesh and blood unites the masculine word (Logos) and feminine holy spirit within oneself, which is the way that one gains entrance to the inner Kingdom.

The importance of the Divine Feminine presence in the gnostic eucharistic rite is seen clearly in this invocation from *The Acts of Thomas*:

> Come, gift of the Most High. Come, perfect compassion;
> come, intercourse with the male. Come, holy Spirit...
> Come, hidden mother; come, you who are manifest by
> your deeds and supply joy and rest to those bound up
> with you. Come and take part with us in this eucharist
> which we perform in your name, and in the love-feast
> (agape) for which we are assembled at your invitation.[98]

This prayer addresses the figure of the gnostic Sophia as though she is the ancient Great Goddess. The archetypal Feminine is asked to preside at the "love-feast" of the eucharist as she has done at the sacred feasts of the goddess cults throughout history.[99]

The ritual of the round dance, recorded in *The Acts of John* and possibly performed by gnostic Christians, possesses a symbolic meaning that is similar to the eucharist sacrament. Before his arrest Jesus sang a hymn as his disciples held hands and danced in a circle around him. In *The Acts of John* the round dance takes the place of the Last Supper, and Carl Jung has pointed out the similarity of the symbolism between the two final acts that Jesus performed with his disciples. In the rite of the eucharist, which is based upon the records of the Last Supper in the gospels of the New Testament, the Christian takes within himself the body and blood of Christ. In the ritual of the round dance, as described in the gnostic text, the disciples perform a circular movement around Christ in the center. As Jung says, in both activities "Christ is taken into the midst of the disciples."[100] For the gnostic, this symbolism refers to the realization of the inner Christ, the spark of divine light within the soul. As Jesus says in his hymn, "Now if you follow my dance, see yourself in Me who am speaking."[101]

The round dance of Christ beautifully expresses the image of wholeness. The circle with a center point symbolizes the incarnation of deity,[102] therefore the round dance itself depicts the meaning of Christ. The symbolic image unites Christ in the center with his disciples who form the circle around him, thus expressing the incarnation of the Divine on Earth and the presence of the Divine within the human being. The hymn which Christ sings contains the statements:

> I will be saved,
> And I will save. - Amen.
> I will be loosed,
> And I will loose. - Amen.
> I will be wounded,
> And I will wound. - Amen.
> I will be born, And I will bear. - Amen.
> I will eat, And I will be eaten. - Amen.
> I will hear, And I will be heard. - Amen.
> I will be thought, Being wholly thought. - Amen.
> I will be washed,
> And I will wash. - Amen....
> I will flee,
> And I will remain. - Amen.
> I will adorn,
> And I will be adorned. - Amen.
> I will be united,
> And I will unite. - Amen.[103]

Through these self references to the polarities of human existence, he encompasses all of life. Christ integrates these paradoxes through his final "I will" statement as the supreme expression of unity.

The round dance also symbolizes the wholeness of the archetypal Self. As the disciples turn toward Christ in the center of the circle, so they turn inward toward the center within themselves.[104] It is this inward turning toward the still point at the center of one's being that leads to the wisdom of the heart. Christ who stands at the center of the circle reveals the way to the attainment of gnosis. For he also sings,

> I am a lamp to you who see me - Amen.
> I am a mirror to you who know me - Amen.
> I am a door to you who knock on me - Amen.
> I am a way to you the traveler - Amen.[105]

The image of the dancers who flow as one organism, connected to each other and Christ in the center as they dance the beautiful patterns of divine harmony, also presents a vision of the unity of the Pleroma. The image expresses the paradox of the differentiated wholeness which is the essence of the pleromatic fullness and the individuated Self. Kurt Rudolph suggests that the round dance depicts "the joy and harmony of the redeemed universe."[106] Followers of Christ who participate in the dance can experience this joyful union of all creation which will come about in the fullness of time. The purpose of the ceremonial round dance appears to be similar to that of the ritual of the bridal chamber in helping to bring about this act of redemption by actualizing the fullness of the divine realm here on Earth. For the round dance of Christ unites the human and divine, the cyclical and the eternal, the outer and the inner, in a symbolic expression of the dance of life. For pilgrims on the feminine bypath, the gnostic round dance is the dance of love, the dance of wisdom, the dance of wholeness.

GNOSTIC CHRISTIANITY ON THE PATH OF CHRISTOSOPHIA

The goal of gnostic Christians was to become "spiritually mature,"[107] to attain the higher levels of spiritual consciousness which they termed gnosis. This has always been a bypath which has appealed to only the few. The spiritual explorers who continue to follow this bypath on the Path of ChristoSophia may also attain greater "spiritual maturity" because of the greater commitment and effort which inner spiritual development requires. Those today who are more concerned with the inner process of spiritual transformation rather than following a set of prescribed rules and rituals may continue to discover much of value on the gnostic bypath.

Because of the destruction of this bypath as the interstate highway of the Church was built, much work still needs to be done to reclaim the riches of gnostic Christianity. A major task in this work involves the discernment between those aspects of gnosticism which are valuable for our present age and those which are not. The dualistic elements of gnosticism which perceived an absolute separation between the spiritual and material worlds are antithetical to the Path of ChristoSophia and the source of great harm in our world today. It seems historically that Christianity has incorporated much of the worst aspects of the gnostic world view into its own foundation of the interstate Church. The negative attitudes toward the physical world and the human body which prevailed as the institution of the Church developed were derivatives of the gnostic dualism which had coexisted with holistic views in the early Christian community. While accepting many of the more unfavorable aspects of gnostic thought, the Church neglected many of its extremely valuable insights. The gnostic Christian emphasis on the cultivation of inner wisdom, the attainment of wholeness, personal responsibility for spiritual practice, and inclusion of the feminine element have often been sadly lacking in the institutional Church. On the gnostic bypath itself, many of these elements which are so valuable are only partially realized and need to be completed. This is especially true of gnostic attitudes toward the Divine Feminine; although she is a much greater presence on the gnostic bypath than on the interstate highway of the Church, the cultural norms of the time which devalued women also influenced the gnostic view of the feminine. But in our modern era especially there is great promise for recovering the treasures of the gnostic tradition and building upon them in the renewal of the Christian mythos. This can be done through bringing one's eros faculties of imaginative insight to the gnostic myths in order to glean the symbolic interpretations from the many levels of meaning which are appropriate and helpful for our time. This particular task is being accomplished today by Jungian psychologists who have turned the focus of depth psychology on gnostic symbolism and amplified many meanings which can serve as very helpful guideposts for the modern pilgrim who pursues the quest of individuation. In addition to reading and interpreting the newly discovered mythological texts of ancient gnosticism, the seeker today must also employ the intuitive methods used by the gnostics themselves and turn inward to search for illuminating gnosis. The spiritual symbols which are meaningful for our present world can be discovered by the modern gnostic who cultivates the inner wisdom through meditation, dreams, and visions.

In these ways the pilgrim on the Path of ChristoSophia can help to carry on the Great Work of the gnostics which has remained unfinished. In fact, there is great promise today for the continuation of this work, because of the current transformation from the dualistic, patriarchal world view which has prevailed in Western culture to an emerging paradigm of wholeness. As Jungian psychologists have shown, gnostic symbols can be interpreted with meaning for our day as referents to wholeness. Carl Jung in particular has emphasized the importance of humanity becoming increasingly conscious today. In a world which is poised on the brink between nuclear and ecological destruction, it is imperative that human beings attain the transformation of consciousness which is the essence of gnosis if we are to avoid disaster. It is especially important to integrate the dark or shadow side of the Christian archetype into consciousness in order to avoid its destructive projection into the world.[108] Thus the Great Work today appears to be more than the gnostic task of uniting the scattered sparks of divine light; it seems to also include bringing forth the darkness into consciousness and reconciling the dark and light sides of existence. Gnostic Christianity can provide valuable aid to this task by providing an alternative spiritual vision which recognizes the importance of integrating the light and dark within the human soul rather than projecting it into the outer world.

The return of the Divine Feminine is essential to this process, for it is she who integrates the dark and light sides of existence. Because the interstate Church has only recognized the light side of the Divine, it is imperative for Sophia to re-emerge from her hiding places on the feminine bypath to bring forth the dark side into the consciousness of western Christian culture. Today we are seeing Sophia's emergence from her hiding places within gnostic Christian tradition and from the hidden depths of the soul of the contemporary seeker of gnosis. She is assuming the savior role along with Christ in aiding modern human beings in their quest for wholeness.

Symbolic images which unite the masculine and feminine are also necessary to guide us toward wholeness within the Self and partnership in our relationships. Many images of the union of masculine and feminine can be found on the gnostic bypath. The "divine syzygy" is a central element of gnostic mythology; the union of the divine couple is represented in the supernal Father and Mother God, Christ and Sophia, and Jesus and Mary Magdalene. This archetypal "divine syzygy" can be found today on the bypaths in the form of ChristoSophia. The union of Christ and Sophia in the bridal chamber will restore the fullness of the Pleroma; the union of ChristoSophia within the human soul restores the fullness of life.

As Elaine Pagels tells us, "Gnosis involves recognizing, finally, the limits of human knowledge."[109] The ultimate wisdom of the gnostics lies in the recognition of the Mystery. This is the hidden wisdom of Sophia which is found along the bypaths. The pilgrim who truly experiences the Mystery of ChristoSophia - the Love and Wisdom within the heart - receives the blessing of gnosis.

The Nature Bypath

"Thus says the Lord:
'Stand at the crossroads and look,
and ask for the ancient paths,
where the good way is; and walk in it,
and find rest for your souls.'"

Jeremiah 6:16

CHAPTER V: EXPLORING THE NATURE BYPATH

The natural world is the larger
sacred community to which we belong...[1]

As the designers of the interstate highway system rearrange the natural landscape in order to provide smooth and efficient transportation, so the interstate Church has typically viewed nature as something to be manipulated and controlled. However, those who walk on the nature bypath follow the small, rugged trails through the woods where they directly encounter trees, flowers, streams, rocks, birds, insects, and other animals as part of their journey. This leads to a deep awareness of the "sacred community" which humans share with the rest of the natural world. It is this intimate experience of belonging to the natural world and in this way connecting with the Divine that is gained by walking along the nature bypath. This experience is the basis for an "ecological spirituality"[2] which refutes the view of the Earth as an object over which humans have complete domination, and instead embraces an older view of the Earth as a living being to be nurtured.

There is much to draw from within Christian tradition to support the further development of an ecological spirituality by those who follow the Path of ChristoSophia. Many critics of Christianity accuse it of promoting a hostile attitude toward the natural world, which is a primary cause of our Western cultural practices of exploitation of the Earth and the source of our current ecological crisis. Although this criticism is often true of the institutional Church, in its separation of the "holy" world of the spirit from the "fallen" world of nature, this anti-nature prejudice against Christianity is too simplistic. There have been many other forces operating in Western culture besides Christianity which have led to the belief that humans have the right to dominate and use nature for their own benefit. Ultimately the basis for our Western culture's obsession with controlling the natural world lies in our anxiety regarding the eros side of human nature. Our fear of eros is linked to a fear of the wild, nonrational, uncivilized nature. Western culture has typically viewed the logos qualities of rationality, order and control as positive, and the eros qualities of instinct, disorder and chaos as negative. Thus, just as the Western mindset believes that eros must be suppressed by logos, so nature must be controlled by rational human beings and wilderness must be tamed by the forces of civilization. The Christian Church has generally been a major proponent of this view, to the point of equating many eros qualities with the "sinful" and "demonic," and therefore has played a decisive role in developing those attitudes toward nature which have led to widespread environmental destruction. Pagan practices which honored the Earth Mysteries in ancient cultures were often condemned and eradicated as the interstate highway of Christianity was built. Yet, attitudes toward the natural world within Christian tradition are quite varied and ambiguous.[3] On the nature bypath seekers can find the wisdom of the Earth which is also an important part of Christian tradition. Those who walk the Path of ChristoSophia can help avert ecological disaster, caused in part by the anthropocentric arrogance of the Church, by bringing back this wisdom gained on the nature bypath.

ATTITUDES TOWARD NATURE WITHIN CHRISTIAN TRADITION

In order to find the sources of the Earth wisdom which is to be found on the nature bypath, we will first take a look at how various attitudes toward nature developed historically within Christianity. We will see that Christianity's view of nature is an ambiguous one, filled with many contrasts and contradictions. This will give us the basis for understanding Christianity's negative attitudes toward the natural world as well as its possibilities for a truly ecological spirituality.

The Hebrew Scriptures

A careful reading of Scriptures reveals that there is much in the Bible which can help restore our connection with the Divine through the natural world. We will begin our examination with the Hebrew Scriptures since this is where the roots of much of Christian theology are found. Modern Biblical scholars have pointed out that the Hebrew world view did not contain the dualistic split between spirit and nature which developed in Western culture. As Rosemary Radford Ruether says, "The Hebraic understanding of the God of Israel...experienced God as Lord of heaven and earth."[4] In their view the Divine was to found on Earth as readily as in the transcendent realm. This can be seen in the Biblical creation story, when God stated emphatically that the natural world "was very good." (Genesis 1:31) The entire cosmos - from the Earth and all its inhabitants to the sun, moon and stars - was blessed as the creation of God. Human beings were indeed singled out by God and instructed to "have dominion over...every living thing that moves upon the earth." (Genesis 1:28) However, in the Hebrew view "dominion" does not refer to domination of other forms of life but instead to humans' role as **caretakers** of the Earth. Human dominion means that humanity has the task of stewardship as God's agents on Earth.[5] Thus, humans are not to abuse or exploit the Earth, but to care for the natural world which is ultimately God's creation and under God's rulership.

Many Biblical passages extol the Hebrew view that the cosmos belongs to God and manifests his glory and goodness. For example:

> The earth is the Lord's and all that is in it,
> the world, and those who live in it,
> for he has founded it on the seas, and established it on the rivers.

Psalm 24:1

119

> The heavens are telling the glory of God;
> and the firmament proclaims his handiwork.

Psalm 19: 1

The fertile, life-giving qualities of the Divine were seen by the Hebrews in God's care for the Earth and abundant blessings:

> You visit the earth and water it, you greatly enrich it;
> the river of God is full of water;
> you provide the people with grain, for so you have prepared it.
> You water its furrows abundantly, settling its ridges,
> softening it with showers, and blessing its growth.
> You crown the year with your bounty;
> your wagon tracks overflow with richness.
> The pastures of the wilderness overflow,
> the hills gird themselves with joy,
> the meadows clothe themselves with flocks,
> the valleys deck themselves with grain,
> they shout and sing together for joy.

Psalm 65: 9-13

The final verses of the psalm above present a beautiful image of the joy inherent in God's creation. This theme is developed further in the following psalm, as the whole created world joins in joyful praise of God. Hills, meadows, seas, and trees are personified as they "sing for joy" in these passages. Thus the creations of God in the natural world appear to the Hebrews as ensouled rather than as the lifeless material objects that they appear to most in modern Western culture.

> Let the heavens be glad, and let the earth rejoice;
> let the sea roar, and all that fills it;
> let the field exult, and everything in it.
> Then shall all the trees of the forest sing for joy
> before the Lord...

Psalm 96: 11-13

Other Biblical passages sing hymns to the Lord of the Elements, specifying God's creation and rulership over the four elements of water, air, fire, and earth.

> Bless the Lord, O my soul.
> O lord my God, you are very great.
> You are clothed with honor and majesty,
> wrapped in light as with a garment.
> You stretch out the heavens like a tent,
> you set the beams of your chambers on the waters,
> you make the clouds your chariot,
> you ride on the wings of the wind,
> you make the winds your messengers,
> fire and flame your ministers.
> You set the earth on its foundations,
> so that it shall never be shaken.

> Psalm 104: 1-5

These examples point to the rich resources which can be found in the Hebrew Scriptures for an ecological spirituality which recognizes God's presence in the natural world which He created, blessed, and continues to sustain and nurture.

The Gospels

The theme of the goodness of creation which was developed in the Hebrew Scriptures was echoed in the Gospel accounts of the life and teachings of Jesus. Since Jesus was a Jew, it is not surprising that he recognized and honored God's presence in the natural world. Jesus apparently felt at home in the wild places, close to nature. He often sought the solitude of desert, mountain or sea for communion with the Divine through prayer. His intimacy with the natural world is shown in many of his parables which refer to the processes of nature. For example, he says, "The kingdom of heaven is like a mustard seed that someone took and sowed in his field; it is the smallest of all the seeds, but when it has grown it is the greatest of shrubs and becomes a tree, so that the birds of the air come and make nests in its branches." (Matt. 13: 31-32) In this parable he compares the creative power of spiritual life, "the kingdom of heaven," with the germinating life force of the tiniest seed which grows into the great tree. There is no separation between the spiritual and earthly realms; rather the divine mystery of the spiritual world is mirrored in the natural world.

In another teaching Jesus says, "...do not worry about your life, what you will eat or what you will drink, or about your body, what you will wear. Is not life more than food, and the body more than clothing? Look at the birds of the air; they neither sow nor reap nor gather into barns, and yet your heavenly Father feeds them... Consider the lilies of the field, how they grow; they neither toil nor spin, yet I tell you, even Solomon in all his glory was not clothed like one of these." (Matt. 6: 25-29) In this passage he affirms the value of physical life and the earthly body, and reminds us that God provides abundantly for his creation. Jesus points to the awesome beauty of the flowers as evidence of the glory and goodness of God's creation.

It is also apparent that Jesus celebrated the joy of God's creation. Although he lived simply, he was not an ascetic like many later Christian saints. He is often reported as eating and drinking with his followers in the Gospel accounts. In fact, many of his miracles involved providing sustenance for the earthly body, such as turning water into wine (John 2: 7-9) and feeding the multitudes. (Matt. 14: 19-21) These activities parallel the "miracle" of God's providing the creative abundance of the world to sustain all living things.

The central sacrament of the Christian faith, the Eucharist, recognizes the spiritual, transformative aspect of common food - bread and wine created by human labor from grain and grape. Once again, Jesus does not separate the spiritual and physical as did many later Christians. He uses the food and drink of an everyday meal to convey the most sacred act of Christian tradition. The deep mystery of the Eucharist is found in the essential unity of the material and spiritual realm as bread and wine are transformed into the body and blood of Christ.

The miracles of healing which figure so predominantly in Jesus' ministry also reveal that the human body had value for him. He was not hostile towards the physical body, as were so many Christians at a later time. Jesus lived a fully embodied life and the Gospels emphasize that even his resurrection was in the body as well as the spirit. When he appears to his disciples, he emphatically tells them that he has "flesh and bones" and is not a "ghost." (Luke 24: 34) He eats fish (Luke 24: 42-43) and instructs Thomas to put his fingers in the nail marks of his hands. (John 20: 27) It is clearly important that the disciples recognize the importance of the earthly body which will be transformed in the resurrected life.

All of these resurrection accounts in which Jesus appears in bodily form show that he is master of the material world. This is the culmination of a number of instances where he takes on God's role in the Hebrew Bible as the "Lord of the Elements." His mastery of the air is shown in his calming of the storm winds (Mark 4: 39) and his mastery over water is shown by his walking on the sea. (Matt. 14: 25) His mastery of the element of earth is shown in the splitting of rocks and earthquakes which occurred in response to his crucifixion. (Matt. 27: 51) His mastery over fire is revealed in his act of baptizing "with the Holy Spirit and fire" (Matt. 3: 11), as demonstrated in the tongues of flame which appear at Pentecost. Through his bodily resurrection, master of both life and death, Jesus shows that he is Lord of both the physical and the spiritual worlds.

The Early Christian Church

The earliest Christians continued the traditional Hebrew view of the goodness and glory of creation which also was proclaimed by Jesus and manifested through him. That "the Word became flesh" (John 1: 14) was the basic premise of the early Christian community, meaning that the creative power of God became embodied in the human form of Jesus of Nazareth. Thus Christianity began with an affirmation of the sacredness of the physical body and the natural world.

The Wisdom Christology which developed among many of the early Christians was based on this assertion that the pre-existent divine creative force, called "Sophia" in the Hebrew Wisdom literature, had incarnated in Jesus Christ. As discussed in an earlier chapter, Sophia existed in the beginning with God, creation took place through her, and she is divinity which is immanent within the created world. In the Wisdom Christology of the early Christian community, "the crucified and risen Jesus is in his transformed humanity hypostatically united to divine Wisdom at the heart of all cosmic processes."[6] It is in his Sophianic aspect that Jesus Christ can be seen as the "Lord of the Elements," creator of the cosmos which he sustains by his divine presence within it. This Wisdom Christology of the early Christians provided a basis for perceiving an essential unity between the material and the spiritual realms. It was consistent with the life and teachings of Jesus as recorded in the Gospels which revealed the holiness of the human body and the sacredness of the natural world. The belief that Jesus Christ was the incarnation of Sophia laid the foundation for a Christian tradition which could revere the natural world for its divine creation, honor the divine presence within every created thing, and accept the responsibility of caring for the world and all living creatures as a spiritual act.

The Sophianic role of Jesus in the creation of the cosmos is most clearly shown in a passage contained in the letter to the Colossians, which most Biblical scholars believe is based on a hymn of the earliest Christians.[7]

> He is the image of the invisible God,
> the firstborn of all creation;
> for in him all things in heaven and on earth were
> created, things visible and invisible,
> whether thrones or dominions or rulers or powers-
> all things have been created through him and for him.
> He himself is before all things,
> and in him all things hold together.
> He is the head of the body the church;
> he is the beginning, the firstborn from the dead,
> so that he might come to have first place in everything.
> For in him all the fullness of God was pleased to dwell,
> and through him God was pleased to reconcile to himself all
> things,
> whether on earth or in heaven, by making peace through the blood
> of the cross.

> Colossians 1: 15-20

Here we see that the earliest Christians celebrated the Sophia aspect of Jesus Christ as the "firstborn of all creation" and the one "in" whom the entire cosmos was created. He is the sustaining power of the universe that "holds all things together" in the vast interconnected web of life. And ultimately it is through the Sophia in Christ that the reconciliation of "all things" in the cosmos is accomplished. As Denis Edwards says of this remarkable statement, "The Colossians hymn insists that the whole universe is caught up in the Christ event."[8]

The reconciliation of God with the entire creation, not just human beings, is a central theme of Wisdom Christology. This transformation of all of nature is accomplished in Jesus Christ as Sophia, the Divine Love and Wisdom which is the source of continuous creation. The love of God which is at the heart of the universe, the love which moves the sun and the stars, is the same love which Christ so dramatically revealed through his crucifixion. God's boundless outpouring of compassionate love for human beings and for the entire creation is the ultimate meaning of the cross of Christ.[9] Thus the Wisdom Christology of the early Christian community provides a "cosmological understanding of Christ as both creator and redeemer of the cosmos, and not just of human beings separated from the cosmos."[10] This cosmological view, which connects humans with the entire universe, is necessary in order to experience reverence towards the natural world.

The cosmological views held by the majority of Christians during the first few centuries seems to contrast sharply with the views which later developed as the interstate highway of the institutional Church was built. The early Christian community's emphasis on the basic goodness of creation, the sacredness of the natural world and the human body, and the cross of Christ as an expression of God's love for all of creation rather than as a sacrifice for human sin, often seems shocking to the interstate Christian traveler today. The repudiation of this cosmological view which later became dominant in the institutional Church had its seed within even the earliest Christian community. The greatest spokesperson for the early Christians, the Apostle Paul, demonstrates the ambiguity which was present from the beginning in Christianity's attitudes toward nature. We have already examined the aspects of Wisdom Christology in many of Paul's letters, such as his identification of Christ as "Wisdom" in the first two chapters of I Corinthians and the cosmological hymn in the first chapter of Colossians. However, Paul is probably better known to most Christians today for his statements which reveal a profound dualism between God and nature, spirit and body, man and woman. For example, in his letter to the Romans he says, "For those who live according to the flesh set their minds on the things of the flesh, but those who live according to the Spirit set their minds on the things of the Spirit." (Romans 8: 5) This attitude is due in part to the influence of the Neoplatonic philosophy of the Hellenistic Greeks on early Christian thought. This philosophy extolled the "higher world" of the soul which is superior to bodily and earthly existence. The early Christian community, which developed within the Hellenistic world, began to adopt some of these Neoplatonic ideas which eventually led to distortions in its originally positive attitudes toward nature, the body, and women.[11] So we also find in Paul's thought, as a Hellenistic Jew, the distinction between the life of "the flesh," which brings with it sin and death, and the life of "the spirit," which results in freedom and immortality. As he also says in his letter to the Romans, "with my flesh I am a slave to the law of sin... the law of the Spirit of life in Christ Jesus has set you free from the law of sin and of death." (Romans 7:25-8:2) As Rosemary Radford Ruether points out, "The problem in Paul's thought lies in the extent to which he identifies this evil condition with natural or created life, and thus sees redeemed life as something fundamentally transcendent to our original, created potential."[12]

It is also Paul who creates the basis for the theological concept of "original sin" in his identifying the life of the body with the "fallen Adam" and the life of the spirit with Christ. He says in the letter to the Romans, "Therefore just as one man's trespass led to condemnation for all, so one man's act of righteousness leads to justification and life for all." (Romans 5: 18) In this view the purpose of Christ's crucifixion and resurrection was to redeem the "fallen Adam." However, despite Paul's major influence, it appears that the majority of Christians did not accept his dualistic views. The concept that sin is the result of "Adam's fall" was not accepted by most early Christians, who instead believed that humans have been given free will and sin results from the choice to "turn away" from "the power of God that is our true nature."[13]

It took the work of Augustine approximately four hundred years later to finally complete the doctrine of "original sin" which was initiated by Paul and to establish this minority position as the dominant view within Christian thought. In the fifth century, the theological battle between Augustine and the British monk Pelagius defined the two major competing attitudes toward nature within Christian tradition. Pelagius was the spokesman for the traditional Christian view that the natural world was created by God and therefore had to be good, and that human beings were made in the image of God and therefore possessed free will. This was the view which had been supported by many of the Church Fathers, including Justin, Irenaeus, Tertullian, and Clement of Alexandria in the second century, and John Chrysostom in the fourth century. In an extension of Pelagius' ideas after his death, Julian of Eclanum insisted that the human body and sexual instincts were created by God and therefore could not be evil. He claimed that the "death" which is due to Adam's sin in the Genesis account must refer to moral and spiritual death because physical death is simply a part of the natural cycle. Every human being has the same choice that Adam did, to choose a sinful or spiritual life. Augustine held the totally opposite point of view, insisting that all of nature, including human nature, was corrupted by the sin of the first human beings, Adam and Eve. This "original sin" resulted in suffering and physical death, which was not "natural" as the Pelagians believed. Human beings since the time of Adam and Eve have been born with "original sin" and therefore have no free will. It is only through God's gift of grace that humans can hope to be redeemed through Jesus Christ.[14] This "fall and redemption" version of Christianity emphasized the guilt of human beings which had to be atoned for by the sacrificial suffering of Jesus on the cross, rather than the compassionate love of God which was revealed in the crucifixion as divine participation in the suffering of humanity. Although the Pelagian view was consistent with the Wisdom Christology of the early Christian community and was the dominant view of the Church during its first few centuries, the bitter political power struggle within the church hierarchy in the fifth century resulted in the condemnation of Pelagius as a heretic and the acceptance of Augustine's views as official church doctrine. Thus the dogmas of "original sin" and "the fall" were developed as major signposts for the traveler on the interstate highway of the Christian Church. Since they are such dominant directional markers for the interstate Church, it is often assumed that Christian tradition has always had a negative view of the natural world and the human body. We can only conjecture how differently Christianity would appear today if the views of Wisdom Christology and the Pelagians had been accepted as the primary signposts on the highway of the institutional Church. As Rosemary Radford Ruether says, "the evaluation of mortal life as evil and the fruit of sin has lent itself to an earth-fleeing ethic and spirituality, which has undoubtedly contributed very centrally to the neglect of the earth, to the denial of our commonality with plants and animals, and to the despising of the work of sustaining the day-to-day processes of finite but renewable life."[15] Today we must look on the bypaths to find the positive views of nature and bodily existence which were intrinsic to the message of Jesus and his early followers.

The Medieval Christian Church

During the Middle Ages the mystical tradition carried on much of the early Christian view of creation as a revelation of God's goodness and glory. Christian mystics from the twelfth to the fifteenth century such as Hildegaard of Bingen, Francis of Assisi, Thomas Aquinas, Mechtild of Magdeburg, Dante Alghieri, Meister Eckhart, Julian of Norwich, and Nicholas of Cusa affirmed a cosmological understanding of Christian faith.[16] They were greatly influenced by the Wisdom literature of the Bible, which was much more popular in the Middle Ages than it was after the Reformation. In particular, medieval theologians were intrigued by the texts which revealed Sophia as the Divine Feminine consort and co-creator with the Father God. Through her role in creation she was identified with Christ, thus continuing the tradition of the Wisdom Christology which was dominant with the early Fathers of the Church.[17]

However, Christianity's conflicting attitudes toward nature are readily seen in the work of medieval mystics. Their cosmological emphasis was due in part to the organic world view held by people in the Middle Ages, who saw themselves as inhabitants of a living universe in which the material and spiritual were inextricably interconnected.[18] All of creation was perceived as an orderly Great Chain of Being in which a "ladder of ascent" extended from rocks and rivers to plants, animals, humans, angels, and finally God.[19] This medieval paradigm contained possibilities for both positive and negative attitudes toward the natural world, which is why we often find such ambiguity in the spiritual writings of this period. On one hand, this hierarchical, linear view of creation in which the Earth and its creatures exist at the bottom of the ladder emphasized that the goal of the human being is to ascend from the earthly to the "higher" spiritual life. This viewpoint reinforced the dualism between matter and spirit which had already become dominant with Augustine's interpretation of "the fall." On the other hand, the concept of the Great Chain of Being revealed the inherent connection between the lowest and highest creations of God, just as the rungs on a ladder are intrinsically linked. The smallest ant or grain of sand was connected to the Divine through the Great Chain of Being.

To further understand these paradoxes within medieval Christianity, we will examine two of the mystics who are best known for their affirmations of the created world, Hildegard of Bingen and Francis of Assisi.

Hildegard of Bingen

Hildegard, a mystic of the twelfth century who founded a Benedictine community in the German Rhineland of Bingen, was often referred to as "the Sibyl of the Rhine."[20] Thus her visionary and prophetic powers were compared to those of the ancient feminine oracles. However, her talents spanned a broad range of activities; she was an abbess, herbalist, physician, preacher, prophet, musician, and writer of both spiritual and scientific works. But most of all, this complex and many-sided woman was a visionary who saw the "Living Light."[21] This direct experience of the Divine was the foundation for all of her other work.

As Barbara Newman points out, Hildegard reflected the characteristic ambivalence toward nature of medieval Christianity as she "oscillated between a joyful affirmation of the world and the body, and a melancholy horror of the flesh and its master, the devil."[22] Her writings reveal the paradoxical juxtaposition of the cosmological view of the early Christians with the dualistic, Augustinian interpretation of Christianity. As pilgrims on the nature bypath we can realize the complexity of Hildegard's spiritual vision and yet discover the insights and inspirations she offers which can aid us in developing a truly ecological spirituality today.

Hildegard's intimacy with the natural world and reverence for creation is shown throughout the wide variety of her books. The *Book of Simple Medicine* (or *Nine Books on the Subtleties of Different Kinds of Creatures*) is a summary of the natural science of her day, containing information on animals, herbs, trees, gems and metals.[23] Her scientific work reveals an astute observation of the natural world and the value that she placed on understanding it. Her other scientific writings, the *Book of Composite Medicine* (or *Causes and Cures*) was used as an aid in her activities as a healer.[24] This book also indicates that she was intensely interested in the human body and recognized the importance of physical life.

It is in her spiritual writings that Hildegard expresses her uniquely powerful images of creativity and creation that underlie her scientific work. In *De Operatione Dei* (*On the Activity of God*), Hildegard portrays the cosmological view in her depiction of goddess-like feminine images. As Barbara Newman says, "at the heart of her spiritual world there stands the numinous figure she called Sapientia or Caritas: holy Wisdom and Love divine..."[25] Her use of such feminine imagery is consistent with the figure of Sophia in the Wisdom literature of the Hebrew Bible. In the following, Caritas appears in Hildegard's vision as though she is the divine Sophia speaking: "I am the fiery life of the essence of God: I flame above the beauty of the fields; I shine in the waters; I burn in the sun, the moon, and stars. And, with the airy wind, I quicken all things vitally by an unseen, all-sustaining life."[26]

As in the Wisdom tradition, this feminine portrait of the Divine emphasizes the presence of God within the natural world. According to Barbara Newman, "Hildegard's keen sense of divine immanence led her to envisage the creative power not as a force propelling the world from without but as an ambience enfolding it and quickening it from within."[27] In her interpretation of "the Word made flesh" in the Gospel of John, Hildegard identifies this creative power of God, represented in the feminine figure of Caritas, with Christ who is incarnate Love.[28] In this interpretation she adheres to the Wisdom Christology of the early Christians with its emphasis on the divine love at the center of creation.

These cosmological themes are also developed in her book *Scivias* (*Know the Ways*), which is the amazing record of her visionary experiences and interpretations of their meaning. Here Hildegard truly seems to be the voice of the feminine aspect of God as mother, creator, and energizer of the cosmos. Because visions arise as an activity of our eros nature, they often reveal truths which are not accessible to our conscious mind. Hildegard's interpretation of her visions is an attempt by her logos nature to analyze the meaning of them through the use of words and concepts. Her rational attempts at verbal explanation are necessarily set within the framework of the cultural and religious paradigm of her day. This is why we often find Hildegard interpreting her visions within the dualistic viewpoint based on "the fall of man." However we can use these incredible breakthroughs of eros which occurred in Hildegard's visions to seek the deeper cosmological meanings which are consistent with an ecological spirituality today.

One of her visions which beautifully portrays the organic cosmology of the Middle Ages is the image of the universe as an egg.[29] This is Hildegard's representation of the "cosmic egg," which is a universal mythological symbol of the Divine Feminine as creatress and container of the universe.[30] The mystery of life is symbolized here as the egg which is enfolded in the womb of the Great Mother. This is an image of the cosmos which is alive and transforming. As Matthew Fox points out, the egg symbolizes the "beginning of...a new creation," so "Hildegard is celebrating the potential of our cosmos."[31] The egg is one of many of Hildegard's circular images of the Divine, which symbolizes the wholeness of the universe in which all parts are related.[32]

In Hildegard's cosmic egg imagery we can also discern the integration of the opposites which is a hallmark of the cosmological view based on the creative role of the Divine Feminine. She claims that "the visible and temporal is a manifestation of the invisible and eternal,"[33] which points out the interconnectedness of the earthly and the spiritual worlds. The dark and light aspects of creation are represented in images of "shadowy" and "white zones," "dark" and "white fires."[34] Hildegard interprets the presence of the sun in her cosmological image as representing Christ and the moon as representing the Church,[35] which in a broader sense can be seen as symbolizing the masculine and feminine aspects of divine creation. Thus her image of the cosmos is a holistic vision which synthesizes the polarities of spirit and nature, light and dark, and masculine and feminine.

The feminine aspect in Hildegard's symbolism of the Creator is also shown in her concept of "viriditas," or "greening power."[36] The green color that appears in many of her visions represents the fertile, fructifying power of the Divine that is found in nature. It is the creative energy of the life force which causes trees to leaf, flowers to blossom, and plants to bear fruit. Viriditas is the essence of life and growth which has always been associated with Mother Earth, and throughout human history celebrated in rites of Spring which honored the Goddess as she poured forth her blessings in the greening of the land. For Hildegard, viriditas also refers to the greening power found within the human soul when God is present. Then the soul experiences the moisture and juiciness which comes from spiritual life rather than the aridity which characterizes spiritual death.[37] Cultivation of this greening power leads to a joyful vitality and creativity; neglect of it leads to a despairing sickness and stagnation. Lauren Artress refers to this concept of viriditas when she says, "Just as plants are greened, so are we as well. As we grow up, our spark of life continually shines forth. If we ignore this spark, this greening power, we become thirsty and shriveled. And if we respond to the spark, we flower."[38]

The final cosmological image which we will examine is Hildegard's vision of Wisdom herself, who she describes as "a very beautiful figure...her head shines like lightning, with so much brilliance that you cannot look directly at it...she has on her head a circlet like a crown, which shines with great splendor...she is clad in a gold tunic...it has a stripe on it from the breast to the feet, which is ornamented with precious gems; they glitter in green, white, red and brilliant sky-blue."[39] In this powerfully numinous vision, Wisdom who appears in the form of Goddess joins with the Father God "in sweet embrace in a dance of ardent love."[40] As Barbara Newman points out, Hildegard's vision is the ancient symbol of the "hieros gamos, or marriage of the gods" which signifies "the oneness of the hidden God with his self-revelation."[41] This image proclaims the union of the transcendent and immanent aspects of the Divine. God and the created world are joined as in a nuptial embrace. Viriditas, the greening power which is the essence of all created life, is the fertility that results from this uniting of the masculine and feminine elements of the Divine. It is the divine dance of love which is the flow of energy that creates and sustains the cosmos. Here again Hildegard's vision points to divine love as the heart of the universe.

Francis of Assisi

Francis, a mystic who lived in the thirteenth century in the northern Italian town of Assisi, also experienced divine love as it is expressed in the natural world. After a youth spent in decadence, Francis turned to a life of extreme simplicity and service to the poor. He founded the Friars Minor, the "Lesser Brothers," whose goal was to serve "Lady Poverty." Although the ascetic qualities seen in his life and some of his writings seem to reflect the Augustinian hatred for the flesh and its evils, the humility and compassion that he developed through a life of poverty allowed him to recognize the Divine within all creatures. His love for the poor and the sick that he served, as well as the plants and animals of the countryside, was based on his ability to perceive the image of Christ within each one of them.

His Franciscan brother and biographer, Thomas of Celano, describes "the sweetness he enjoyed while contemplating in creatures the wisdom of their Creator, his power and his goodness."[42] Francis viewed all aspects of the natural world as symbols of Christ. He felt a special tenderness for the lamb because it is a major image for Christ in the Gospels, and he loved even the worm because of Christ's reference to himself as a worm. He glorified the flower as a symbol of the beauty of Christ, revered the rocks upon which he walked because Christ was called the Rock, and did not extinguish candles because they symbolized the Eternal Light.[43]

The many legendary tales of St. Francis's care for flowers, trees and all variety of animals is a major reason for his popularity today. It is said that he put out wine and honey for the bees to help them live through the winter, and picked up worms to put them in a safe place where they would not be crushed by human feet. He saved rabbits who had been trapped and threw fish back into the water, admonishing them not to get caught again. And he traded his own clothing to save lambs from slaughter. He would not allow a whole tree to be cut down in order that it could sprout again, and left the border of the garden undug so that the grass and flowers would have a place to grow.[44] Perhaps the best known example of the love that he bore toward all creatures is found in the stories of his preaching to the birds, who he exhorted to praise and serve God for His blessings to them. Seeing the reverent response of the birds to his teaching, Francis spent the rest of his life preaching to all God's creatures - the flowers and plants, fields and forests, stones and water, and even the elements of air, earth, wind, and fire.[45] Since "he discerned the hidden things of nature with his sensitive heart..."[46] he was able to perceive the soul inherent in all of nature, and thus overcome the anthropocentric arrogance which has plagued Western humanity.

Creatures responded to the devotion of Francis by freely giving him their love in return. Stories abound which tell of all manner of animals - birds, rabbits, fish and crickets - attaching themselves to him and obeying his requests. On the night of his death, his companions were filled with wonder at the sight of a flock of larks who appeared on the roof, remaining for a long time and noisily singing a song of "tearful rejoicing and joyful sorrow" in response to their beloved companion's departure from the earthly realm.[47]

This sense of brotherhood that St. Francis felt with all creation is given sublime expression in his well known prayer, "The Canticle of Brother Sun":

Praised be You, my Lord, with all your creatures,
especially Sir Brother Sun,
Who is the day and through whom You give us light.
And he is beautiful and radiant with great splendor;
and bears a likeness of You, Most High One.
Praised be You, my Lord, through Sister Moon and the stars,
in heaven You formed them clear and precious and beautiful.
Praised be You, my Lord, through Brother Wind,
and through the air, cloudy and serene, and every kind of
weather through which You give sustenance to Your creatures.
Praised be You, my Lord, through Sister Water,
which is very useful and humble and precious and chaste.
Praised be You, my Lord, through Brother Fire,
through whom You light the night
and he is beautiful and playful and robust and strong.
Praised be You, my Lord, through our Sister Mother Earth,
who sustains and governs us,
and who produces varied fruits with colored flowers and
herbs.[48]

In St. Francis's cosmological view, Christ as "the divine light" exists in all creatures and therefore connects the entire cosmos in one great family.[49] He continues the theme found in the Hebrew Scriptures which presents God as Lord of the Elements. Wind, Water, Fire and Earth are the four elements which show forth the glory of creation in their praise of the Lord. As Thomas of Celano says, "that original goodness which will one day be **all things in all** already shown forth in the saint **all things in all**."[50] Francis perceived the world as blessed in its origin, and it was this realization of divine grace which underlay the depth of his love for all of God's creation.

Francis also shows a balance of the masculine and feminine elements in creation as he praises his "brothers" Sun, Wind, and Fire as well as his "sisters" Moon, Water, and Earth. The moon, water, and earth have been symbolic expressions of the feminine since ancient times. In his exhortation to "Mother Earth" he alludes to the Divine Feminine immanent in nature. It is not surprising that Francis was profoundly devoted to the Virgin Mary as Mother of God, who was his model for spiritual development.[51] His life and his views expressed in the Canticle reveal a strong influence of the Sophianic aspect of the Divine.

St. Francis is especially known today as the patron saint of ecologists. We can look to him as a model for developing the Sophianic perception which sees God within every aspect of creation. It is this love that flows from a recognition of our kinship with all living creatures which forms the basis for a truly ecological spirituality.

The Reformation and the Age of Reason

We have seen that as the interstate highway of Christianity developed through the Middle Ages, attitudes oscillated between condemnation of the natural world and reverence for nature as a revelation of God's wisdom and love. Most medieval Christians experienced a distrust of instinctive nature while at the same time they felt a deep connection to the world around them. However, in the sixteenth and seventeenth centuries several developments took place which caused a radical shift toward the negative view of nature which has had such a major impact on our modern world. Western civilization's desacralization of nature was due primarily to the influence of the Protestant Reformation and the subsequent Age of Reason.

In the sixteenth century, the Reformation brought an emphasis on Scripture as the revelation of God. The cosmological view which saw "the Word" as Christ manifest in all of creation was generally supplanted in Protestantism by the belief that "the Word" was to be found in the Bible. Calvinist Protestantism in particular renewed an extreme vision of Augustinian dualism. Because nature exists in a "fallen" state it is under the Devil's influence, therefore Calvinist preachers railed against the corruption of nature and the evils of the flesh.[52] As the divine presence was no longer recognized in the natural world, sacred places on the land which had been respected by pagan and Christian alike were destroyed. Practices which honored the sacredness of the landscape were denounced as "superstitious."[53]

The seventeenth century brought the "Age of Reason" which elevated the logos qualities of rational thought and control to supreme importance. Correspondingly, those eros qualities of untamed, instinctual nature were met with even greater fear and disdain. A major consequence of the emphasis on human reason was the rise of science and the revolutionary paradigm change which accompanied it. The major components of our modern world view, especially our attitudes toward nature, were shaped during this period of scientific and technological revolution.[54]

Francis Bacon initiated the scientific method by advocating that knowledge should be gained through the empirical observation of nature. Bacon's actual role in the development of the scientific worldview has been hotly debated in recent years. Many commentators have traced the hostile, aggressive attitude toward nature that is so prevalent in Western culture to statements attributed to Bacon that advocate the enslavement and torture of nature by the mechanical devices of science in order to extract her secrets. But others have pointed out that Bacon himself never actually said these things, and that his dream of man's increasing dominion over nature through the application of the newly emerging scientific method was a benevolent one.[55] In the ensuing years, however, the belief that human dominion over nature refers to stewardship and caretaking, as in the Hebrew Scriptures, shifted to an emphasis on the manipulation and control of nature which remains the dominant view today. It is this transformation of humanity's relationship to nature that is creating such ecological problems in our modern world.

The second major figure of the Age of Reason who has exerted a profound influence on modern thought was Rene Descartes. His famous statement, "I think, therefore I am,"[56] laid the foundation for a philosophy based on the separation of mind and matter. This view further augmented the dualism of Augustine which split soul from body and spirit from nature. After Descartes this dualistic perception became the dominant, mostly unquestioned, view of reality in Western culture. Although Descartes was a religious person who believed that both mind and matter were creations of God, his thought enabled later scientists to study the material world without any reference to God.[57] Science and religion became divorced from each other and in the following centuries were often engaged in fierce combat.

Descartes promoted the mechanistic view of the universe, which also became a major component of the scientific paradigm. For him the material world, including the human body, was a machine governed by mechanical laws. The new, scientific image of the universe became the mechanistic "clock," rather than the cosmological image of divine immanence such as Hildegard's "world egg." And while Descartes claimed that human beings possessed a non-material soul, other living organisms did not.[58] This idea destroyed the sense of spiritual kinship with all living beings such as that experienced by St. Francis, which was based on a recognition of the divine presence in all creation. Most modern human beings have thus become alienated from our fellow creatures with which we share the planet. And without a "soul," plants and animals have no intrinsic value. This view has contributed greatly to the human arrogance that perceives other creatures as merely objects to be exploited for our own use. Thus Descartes' ideas served to support Bacon's in the use of science as a means to manipulate nature.

Isaac Newton furthered the scientific work of Bacon and Descartes by providing a mathematical model for the mechanistic universe. He was also a religious man, who believed that the efficient running of the "cosmic machine" was due to the work of the Creator. For Newton, God ruled the universe from the outside by setting up the laws of nature which could be understood through math and science. Thus God was seen as totally transcendent, and the immanent nature of deity was subsequently disregarded in Western culture. In later times when many scientists could no longer believe in a God in heaven who created the cosmos in the manner of a clockmaker who builds the clock, the Divine was eventually expelled from the scientific world view. This has resulted in the current common image of the universe as simply a lifeless material object with no meaning or purpose.[59] It is no wonder that modern human beings who in general unconsciously accept this mechanistic model of the cosmos commonly experience spiritual aridity, futility and despair as inhabitants of a world which appears to be meaningless.

Most people in Western culture today either accept this image of the cosmos with its sense of alienation because they believe it is based on "science" and therefore **must** be true, or else they combat the scientific knowledge of the past few centuries in the name of "religion" and turn back to an image of the cosmos as the creation of a transcendent Father God. Thus the legacy of Cartesian dualism which separates the physical from the spiritual, and science from religion, is still very much with us today. Neither of these approaches is adequate for the time in which we live, which demands that humanity restore an ecological harmony with the planet and all other creatures. What we urgently need today is a new mythos which celebrates and honors the natural world and is also consistent with modern scientific discoveries. In order to do this, we must go beyond the confines of Cartesian dualism to develop a synthesis of scientific and religious thought. Rather than retreating to a pre-scientific version of the nature of the universe or remaining stuck in a nineteenth century image, today's seekers must strike out in new directions on the nature bypath to develop an ecological spirituality which is appropriate and helpful for our time.

DIRECTIONS TOWARD AN ECOLOGICAL SPIRITUALITY

Pilgrims walking on the Path of ChristoSophia must reclaim the cosmological view in Christian tradition to aid the emergence of the new mythos which will underlie an ecological spirituality. We have seen that the influence of the cultural developments of the past several centuries, particularly the rise of the scientific world view, resulted in a virtual loss of the cosmological tradition within the Christian Church. However, we find ourselves today again in a time of transformation when cultural values, attitudes and beliefs are undergoing major upheavals. This paradigm shift that we are currently experiencing is fueled to a great degree by profound changes that are taking place within contemporary science, for most modern human beings still look to science for an understanding of "reality." The insights that are emerging from current investigations in fields such as physics, astronomy, and biology provide great possibilities for the recovery of a cosmological world view within the framework of contemporary scientific paradigms. As Thomas Berry says, "A new intimacy with the universe has begun within the context of our scientific traditions...Science is providing some of our most powerful poetic references and metaphoric expressions. Scientists suddenly have become aware of the magic quality of the earth and of the universe entire."[60] We are now in a period of great cultural transformation where science and religion need no longer be split from each other. Indeed, it is the new images and metaphors that science is providing today which can be used in the development of an ecological spirituality. We will first examine some of the most significant ideas of modern science which are consistent with the cosmological tradition, and then take a look at the work of some contemporary seekers who are aiding the birth of the new mythos through their integration of scientific knowledge with spiritual wisdom.

The New Science

The new vision of reality which is transforming our culture has been most influenced by the revolutionary discoveries of modern physics. As physicist and social activist Fritjof Capra points out, the "holistic and ecological" view of the world which emerges from the "new physics" is very similar to the vision expressed by many mystics.[61] This profound transformation in our perception of reality began with Albert Einstein's special theory of relativity and quantum theory, which drastically altered the Cartesian-Newtonian model of the universe. While the laws of classical physics as defined by Newton continue to apply to the world of ordinary sense perception, they are no longer viable in the quantum world of subatomic particles.

When the world of matter is penetrated to its smallest components accessible to modern technology, the physicist does not find the smaller and smaller material objects which had been expected, but instead "a network of dynamic relationships that...appears as a harmonious indivisible whole."[62] Twentieth century physics replaced the earlier scientific metaphor of the universe as a mechanistic clock with the metaphor of the cosmos as a creative dance of energy. As Albert Einstien poetically expressed it, "Human beings, vegetables, cosmic dust, we all dance to a mysterious tune, intoned in the distance by an invisible player."[63] The patterns of this dance, the "probability waves" of the scientists, create the phenomenal world that we experience. As Rosemary Radford Ruether points out, "This matrix of dancing energy operates with a 'rationality,' predictable patterns that result in a fixed number of possibilities. Thus what we have traditionally called 'God,' the 'mind,' or rational pattern holding all things together, and what we have called 'matter,' the 'ground' of physical objects, come together."[64] The Cartesian separation of mind and matter is overcome in this vision of the quantum world. There no longer appears to be any primal material "things" from which the universe is made; instead mind or consciousness seems to be the central feature of all cosmic processes. And human consciousness is an integral part of this new picture of the cosmos, for modern physics has demonstrated that the human observer plays an essential role in the processes of the quantum world.[65]

Based on these discoveries of modern physics, religious and philosophical paradigms based on the earlier mechanistic view of the universe can no longer be accepted. The portrayal of God as the designer and builder of a machine-like world, who remains outside of his creation, is outdated. Likewise the more skeptical mechanistic view which dispensed with God's role entirely and saw the cosmos arising simply through chance occurrences now appears to be questionable. As Fritjof Capra points out, a number of twentieth century scientists such as Julius Oppenheimer, Niels Bohr, and Werner Heisenberg recognized that the language of quantum physics expresses the insights which have been conveyed through religious symbolism and metaphor by mystics throughout the centuries.[66] The physicist Freeman Dyson has made strong arguments against the perception based on earlier science that the universe is devoid of life, meaning, or purpose. Although he acknowledges that science cannot prove the existence of God, which is ultimately a religious question, nevertheless he maintains that the structure of the universe as understood by contemporary science is consistent with "the hypothesis that there exists a universal mind or world soul which underlies the manifestations of mind that we observe."[67]

The emerging scientific paradigm of the twenty-first century gives strong support to the cosmological tradition within Christianity. The belief that the Divine is immanent within the created world is consistent with the scientific view of quantum physics which reveals the ultimate unity of mind and matter; or, in religious terminology, spirit and nature. All aspects of creation from the subatomic "quark" to the huge galactic clusters, as well as the plants, animals and human beings that inhabit the planet Earth are manifestations of the "mind" of the universe, which may be expressed in scientific terms as "patterns of quantum energy" or in religious terms as "God/Goddess." From the perspective of Wisdom Christology, the "universal mind" or "world soul" which Freeman Dyson refers to is seen as Sophia. She is an "emanation" of God (Wisdom of Solomon 7: 25), the continual stream of quantum energy which gives rise to the immensity of the cosmos. She is a "master worker," (Proverbs 8: 30), providing the patterns of energy which manifest in creation. Jesus Christ as the incarnation of Sophia was seen by many early Christians as this Divine Mind which is at the center of the cosmos. In the light of modern physics, we can interpret the Sophianic aspect of Christ as the primal source of the energy of creation as well as the underlying cosmic pattern in which all things are held together in an interconnected web of relationship.

The awareness of the interconnectedness of all creation which lies at the heart of the Wisdom tradition has been rediscovered by modern science as it probes the deepest secrets of life. This insight has led to the formulation of a "systems view" of life, which "is based on awareness of the essential interrelatedness and interdependence of all phenomena."[68] Mechanistic science attempts to understand phenomena by breaking things down into their smallest parts. For example, physicists look for smaller and smaller subatomic particles in order to understand matter, and biologists analyze a cell in terms of its smallest components in order to understand life. Science based on a systems view, however, is concerned with the connections between various aspects of the phenomena under study. Physicists focus on the patterns of relationship among subatomic energy events and biologists emphasize the interconnections between different parts of the body, the mind and the environment.

The scientific paradigm that emerged during the late twentieth century to analyze the organizing structures that underlie complex systems from snowflakes to galaxies came to be known as "chaos" or "complexity theory."[69] Today most people are familiar with chaos theory through its depiction of "fractal images" – those fascinating and hauntingly beautiful pictures that reveal the hidden patterns underlying the complex systems of the natural world. The holistic perceptions of chaos theory also provide a scientific source for the development of an ecological spirituality as it emphasizes our intrinsic connectedness to the entire cosmos.

A corollary to the science of complexity that has significant implications for an ecological spirituality is the view of our planet Earth as a living being, called the "Gaia hypothesis" by the scientists James Lovelock and Lynn Margulis. They base their hypothesis on the realization that the Earth is a self-organizing system whose processes are similar in many ways to those of the human organism. The planet is remarkably able to regulate its environment in order to maintain conditions which are conducive to the evolution of life. All parts of the planetary being, including the air, water, soil, and living creatures, are connected to each other in a dynamic, complex system of interdependence.[70] This image of "Gaia" also links modern scientific understanding of the geological and biological planetary processes with the spiritual insights of much earlier peoples. The perception of the Earth itself as a living organism is a scientific expression of the fundamental spiritual awareness of the sacredness of the Earth which was often expressed in spiritual terms as the "Goddess of the Earth," "Earth Mother," or "Mother Nature." In fact, the name "Gaia" was chosen by the scientists in reference to the Earth Goddess of the ancient Greeks. Within Christian tradition, "Gaia" as a planetary being has connections with Sophia in her aspect of World-Soul. She is the Divine Mind at work in the creation of the natural world and the regulation of the planetary processes. She is the divine presence which inhabits every aspect of the planet Earth - the molten rocks of the depths, the vast continents of land, the streams and the oceans, the rainforests and the deserts, the crawling insects and the soaring eagles, and all of diverse humanity. Instead of the earlier scientific view of Earth as an inanimate ball of inert matter, this new scientific perception of the Earth as "Gaia" leads to a feeling of incredible awe at the ability of our planet to give birth and to maintain life. Images of the Earth as seen from outer space have impressed upon our modern consciousness the unique beauty of our planet as the living Gaia, the Mother of all. Experiencing the mystery of our Mother Earth in this way can lead to relationship with her instead of the manipulation and exploitation which has been the norm for the last few centuries. Thus the Gaia hypothesis with its ecological view of the interrelated, interdependent processes of the living planet provides a very helpful scientific model for a spirituality which honors the sacredness of the Earth.

Images of wholeness emerging from modern science – the fractal image of chaos theory and the planetary image of space travel – evoke our deepest feelings as they symbolize the beauty and the mystery at the heart of creation. These are examples of the new images that are needed on the nature bypath as they bring together the scientific and the mystical approaches to understanding and responding to life.

MODERN CHRISTIAN VISIONARIES

As the scientific paradigm has undergone profound change during recent times, so have many contemporary seekers glimpsed a radically new spiritual vision. And as the new science is much more consistent with the cosmological tradition than the science of Descartes and Newton, so does this emerging spirituality provide much greater support for an ecological world view than did the theology of Augustine or Calvin. A number of contemporary Christian visionaries are helping to birth the new mythos which is consistent with Christian tradition, the modern scientific world view, and the needs of our planetary community for harmony and wholeness. Three of the most significant of these visionaries whose major ideas we will examine are Pierre Teilhard de Chardin, Thomas Berry and Matthew Fox.

Pierre Teilhard de Chardin

Teilhard integrated the spiritual and scientific quests in his life as a Jesuit priest, geologist and paleontologist. His major work was an attempt to integrate the spiritual and material worlds, particularly through a reconciliation of Christianity with the scientific theory of evolution. He presented his intriguing visionary ideas in *The Phenomenon of Man*, which was only published after his death in 1955 due to censorship by the Church.

As a scientist Teilhard accepted the theory of evolution, which has been so problematical for many modern Christians. However, he rejected the dominant view of evolution which excludes the role of God in creation by claiming that variations in species are due simply to chance random mutations which promote survival. Instead, Teilhard's understanding of evolution is much closer to a systems view than it is to the classical Darwinian theory.[71] He emphasizes that the universe is a **process** of becoming. To him, the evolution of the universe does not lack purpose or meaning, but is directed toward achieving ever greater complexity. As the nervous systems of living organisms become more and more complex, consciousness correspondingly increases, until finally the level of human consciousness and spirituality is attained. Therefore Teilhard claims that the purpose of evolution is "an ascent toward consciousness."[72]

Teilhard's thinking is consistent with the discoveries of modern physics in the primacy he places upon mind or consciousness. He poetically states that "the living world is constituted by consciousness clothed in flesh and bone."[73] Through the evolutionary process the mind manifests in larger systems until it finally culminates in human evolution with the development of a "noosphere," or "mind-layer" which covers the planet above the biosphere.[74] Today this idea may seem prophetic when we consider the rapid rise in global communication systems and computer technology such as the Internet and World Wide Web. The "noosphere" that Teilhard postulates appears to be evolving toward ever greater complexity and global unification.

The continued evolutionary progress of human beings, which Teilhard claims must now be spiritual rather than physical, is directed toward the goal of the "Omega point," a higher order center of global consciousness as individual minds converge together.[75] At this point humanity and all of creation will be united with God. It is Christ, through his "redeeming incarnation" into the evolutionary process, who animates and directs the ascent of consciousness to its final unification in Omega.[76]

Teilhard's proposal is a restatement of the cosmological vision of early Christianity in scientific terms. The view that evolution is directed toward a transformation of the entire universe as it unites in Omega is a modern interpretation of the eschatological belief of early Christians that all of creation would be ultimately reconciled through the Sophia in Jesus Christ. Teilhard also echoes the early Christian community's proclamation that it is the love of God, as revealed in Christ, which is at the center of the universe - creating, sustaining, and fulfilling the world. For him it is the force of divine love which propels the evolutionary ascent. Initially it is through the power of love that "the fragments of the world seek each other so that the world may come into being."[77] Ultimately it will be the power of Christ's love that will bring about the final union of the entire cosmos in God. The evolving spiritual consciousness of humanity is also based on our development of this love, to the point where we will be able to love God "with every fiber of the unifying universe."[78]

Teilhard strongly believed that Christianity is even more important today than in the past in order for humanity to achieve a sense of meaning in a world which has been transformed by modern scientific thought. He provided a new mythic image of the universe and humanity's purpose in it through his concept of noogenesis toward the Omega point. This is a very valuable image for us today because it is consistent with Christianity's emphasis on the redeeming power of Christ as well as the scientific theories of evolution and complexity.

Thomas Berry

Thomas Berry is a Catholic monk whose work also provides a means for perceiving the sacred in nature in the context of modern scientific discoveries. He contributes to the creation of a new mythos through his beautiful narrative of *The Universe Story*, which is co-authored with scientist Brian Swimme. Berry acknowledges that the transformation of our present age requires a "new story" to provide meaning and guidance for our lives today, the basis for which is the story of the "emergent universe." He believes that the major change in the consciousness of modern humans is the shift from a cyclical sense of time to an evolutionary viewpoint.[79] *The Universe Story* traces the evolution of the cosmos from the "primordial flaring forth" to the creation of galaxies, our solar system, and the planet Earth, to the birth of the first forms of life and its evolution to human beings, and finally the historical and cultural development of humanity. This story provides a sense of the sacred mystery of the creation of the cosmos as well as our intimate connection to the entire universe. For through this story we learn that we are related to the smallest subatomic particle as well as the furthest star in the cosmos by our common origin in the great "flaring forth" of the primordial energies of the universe. Likewise we are kin to every other living being on Earth through our common genetic inheritance.[80] We are truly, as St. Francis pointed out, "brother" and "sister" to all the elements and living creatures of the world. Thus understanding the meaning of "the story of the universe" provides a scientific basis for the experience of a mystical identification with the entire cosmos.

Berry claims that the most important need for humans today is to recognize the sacredness of the natural world as "our primary revelation of the divine."[81] Our second most important need is to shift our emphasis from the processes of redemption to those of creation. He explains that, "Creation, however, must be experienced as the emergence of the universe as a psychic-spiritual as well as a material-physical reality from the beginning. We need to see ourselves as integral with the emergent process, as the being in whom the universe reflects on and celebrates itself."[82] Berry thus seems to agree with Teilhard's view of the primacy of mind-spirit in the evolutionary process. The emerging powers of human consciousness, "noogenesis" in Teilhard's terms, are central to this process. The purpose for this evolution of consciousness is for human beings to recognize the awesome majesty of the universe and to celebrate the joy of life.

We are now at the stage in the development of human consciousness where we have the possibility of entering what Berry calls the "Ecozoic age." This will be based on our turning away from the view that the Earth is an object to be exploited for our benefit and returning to the ancient awareness that the Earth is a living being that we can commune with. The recognition of the emergent universe provides the modern context for experiencing our oneness with the natural world and developing a new relationship with the

Earth in which our primary concern will be for the welfare of the entire planet.[83] When we perceive the Earth as a living organism, we experience a "reenchantment with the Earth"[84] which forms the basis for the ecological spirituality that will be necessary if we are to enter the Ecozoic age.

In order to accomplish this "reenchantment" with the natural world and recover the sense of mystery and awe in the presence of creation, we can re-interpret scientific insights into mythological concepts. Berry does this when he translates the mathematical and scientific understanding of the curvature of the universe as "the vast embrace bonding all things together" and relates this image to the symbol of the Great Mother.[85] In spiritual terminology it is the Divine Feminine, as the cosmic "embrace," which is the source of the connectedness of all things. This scientific concept of the curvature of space can also be related to Hildegard of Bingen's vision of the universe as a "cosmic egg" in which all of creation is enfolded within the Great Mother. Her organic image for the totality of the universe expresses the feminine theme of interconnectedness which is at the heart of modern scientific insights into the cosmos. In Christian tradition the primary symbol for the Divine Feminine who upholds the universe in her "vast embrace" is Sophia. As Thomas Berry implies, the new mythos must recognize the Divine Feminine at the center of the cosmos in her birth-giving and nurturing roles. The story of the emergent universe can be seen as a revelation of the Sophianic process; our recognition of the sacredness of the transforming universe corresponds to the re-emergence of Sophia within human consciousness today.

Matthew Fox

Matthew Fox is another contemporary priest who is aiding the birth of a new mythos through his advocacy of a "creation-centered spirituality." He agrees with Thomas Berry that we must de-emphasize the fall/redemption approach to religion which has dominated Christianity since the time of Augustine. For this is a "dualistic...and patriarchal" model which "fails to teach love of the earth or care for the cosmos...it is not only silent toward science but hostile to it."[86] Creation-centered spirituality on the other hand

148

reclaims the cosmological view of the Hebrew Scriptures, the early Christian community and the medieval nature mystics. Fox believes that the integration of the two powerful sources of wisdom regarding nature which are available to us today -- the Christian cosmological tradition and modern science -- can bring about a profound transformation in our culture.[87]

According to Fox, a creation-centered spirituality must begin with an emphasis on "original blessing" rather than "original sin." The creative energy of God, the "Dabhar" in Hebrew which is translated as "Word and Wisdom," poured forth in the creation of the cosmos which was therefore blessed in its origin. The universe was born through divine love, and God loves the created world unconditionally as a parent loves a child. Fox echoes the themes in the Hebrew psalms that creation is good and the world is filled with the abundance of God's blessings. Western Christianity's emphasis on "original sin" however has perverted the truth about creation and poisoned our attitudes toward the natural world. This has actually had the effect of leading us to sin in our destruction of the Earth and her creatures. For Fox the most basic sin is dualism, the separation of subject and object which allows us to manipulate and exploit that which we perceive to be outside of ourselves. This has been the great sin which Western civilization has perpetrated against oppressed people, other species, and the Earth herself.[88]

The antidote to this destructive, dualistic perception is the panentheistic view which sees God in everything and realizes that everything is in God. Fox says, "Panentheism is a way of seeing the world sacramentally."[89] It involves the awareness that the original blessing, God's Word and Wisdom, is contained within every aspect of creation. Fox says, "The Western term for this image of God present in all things is 'the Cosmic Christ.'"[90] This experience of the Cosmic Christ in all creatures was the essential feature of the spirituality of St. Francis. When we also are able to recognize the presence of Christ in all aspects of creation, we too will be able to call the heavenly bodies, the elements, and all living creatures our "sisters" and "brothers."

Fox updates the major insight of Wisdom Christology, that it is the Sophianic Christ who holds all of creation together, in a scientific context when he describes the Cosmic Christ as " 'the pattern that connects' all the atoms and galaxies of the universe, a pattern of divine love and justice that all creatures and humans bear within them."[91] He believes that the changing scientific paradigm will facilitate the re-emergence of the Cosmic Christ, along with a renewed mystical appreciation of the universe. The paradigm shift in Christianity for the third millennium must be based on this increased emphasis on the Cosmic Christ. The historical Jesus, which has been the major focus of Christianity since the Enlightenment, must be integrated with the cosmological role of Christ to provide the basis for a creation spirituality. As Fox indicates, this is essentially a feminist spirituality, which emphasizes eros and wisdom.[92] Thus the Cosmic Christ is also identified with the Sophia of Wisdom Christology as Fox points to the need in our time for recognizing and honoring the Divine Feminine within creation.

He especially emphasizes the feminine face of the Divine when he suggests that the most appropriate symbol for the Cosmic Christ today is that of Mother Earth, who is crucified by the destructive acts of humans, and yet is resurrected daily.[93] In this image we can also see the suffering of Sophia in her aspect as World-Soul. Whenever we do harm to the Earth we cause her pain, just as though we were driving the nails through the hands and feet of Christ. Matthew Fox makes a powerful contribution to the creation of the new mythos through his vision of the passion of the Christ who is present in Mother Earth and experiences her death and resurrection. This image can contribute greatly to an ecological spirituality as it compels us to demonstrate our love for Christ, as the Sophianic aspect of Mother Earth, through our compassion toward the Earth and all of her creatures.

The new spiritual visions which we have examined -- Teilhard de Chardin's concept of noogenesis toward the Omega point, Thomas Berry's narrative of the emergent transformative universe, and Matthew Fox's re-interpretation of the Paschal mystery as the passion of Mother Earth - are all examples of the new mythos which is being born today, as ancient cosmological themes are blended with modern scientific thought. The emergence of this new mythos, through its recognition of the Divine Feminine and our oneness with all of creation, will provide us with the sense of meaning and the guidance which we so desperately need today. Humanity's purpose, the ascent of consciousness as described by Teilhard, must include a heightened moral awareness which leads to ecological responsibility and care for Mother Earth. The healing of our dualistic perception, the basic sin according to Matthew Fox, is the basis for this heightened spiritual and moral consciousness. Then we will eventually attain the consciousness of great spiritual masters such as Hildegard of Bingen and Francis of Assisi in our recognition and celebration of the divine presence in all of creation.

Contemporary spiritual visionaries such as Thomas Berry and Matthew Fox proclaim the need for new forms of worship which are grounded in the emerging mythos to help in this transformation of consciousness. Rituals and liturgies corresponding to new spiritual visions are needed to help us experience the mystery of creation and express our wonder and awe, celebrate our communion with the natural world, and acknowledge our participation in the joy and suffering of our Mother Earth. Perhaps most important in this time of ecological crisis, these new forms of worship will help energize us to care for the Earth and all of her creatures. The new mythos, with its accompanying transformation of religious ritual, will lead toward a spirituality in which we truly experience the natural world as our "sacred community." The entire cosmos then becomes our cathedral, in which we praise God who is present in all creation.

THE NATURE BYPATH

It is apparent that the interstate highway of the Christian Church, which was built over many centuries on the foundation of Augustinian dualism, still considers much of the emerging spiritual paradigm to be dangerously radical and even heretical. We have only to consider how Teilhard de Chardin's work was censored and Matthew Fox was officially "silenced" by the Catholic Church to see that our quest to restore the cosmological tradition in Christianity must still take place largely on the bypaths. Like the modern Christian visionaries, we must search on the nature bypath to discover those hidden traditions which can provide us with the Earth wisdom which we need to develop an ecological spirituality.

The Sophia of Wisdom Christology

The most significant marker on the nature bypath which directs us toward a restoration of the cosmological view to Christianity is the Wisdom Christology of the early Christian community. The belief that Jesus of Nazareth was the incarnation of the divine Sophia provided the basis for his cosmological role as Christ, often referred to as the "Cosmic Christ." As we have seen, early Christians as well as many Christian mystics throughout the centuries have recognized Jesus Christ in this Sophianic aspect as the source of creation as well as the divine presence within it. Modern physics has provided an intriguing perspective on this traditional cosmological view by recognizing the primary role of mind or consciousness as the substrata of the material universe. A spiritual image which emphasizes the primacy of mind is expressed by Anthony Duncan as: "The whole universe, and everything in it, is a thought in the Mind of God; and the patterns, and shapes and forms of creation are the thought-patterns of the Almighty."[94] Sophia as Divine Wisdom may be seen as the "patterns of thought" in the "Mind of God." This is how she performs those functions ascribed to her in the Wisdom literature of the Bible: co-creator of the universe, artisan of creation, and emanation of God. For the entire cosmos is a manifestation of these patterns of quantum energy, Divine Mind or Cosmic Consciousness, the holy Wisdom of Sophia.

In this way modern science is combining with the new spiritual mythos to help us realize again the ancient truth that it is Divine Mind which expresses itself in all the patterns of physical life as well as the archetypes of the unconscious, in synchronistic occurrences and oracular divinations. Looking for these patterns and listening to their harmonics seems to have always been a part of human understanding until relatively recent times with the advent of materialist science. Sophia's return will bring about the "re-enchantment of the world," the recognition of an immanent deity which communicates with us through the sights and sounds of the natural world.

These "thought patterns" of divine creativity have also been expressed by modern scientists using the metaphor of the "dance of energy." In an ancient cosmological symbol the Divine Feminine dances, and the patterns of her dance give rise to all the manifestations of the phenomenal world. Sophia dances, and the emanation of the thought patterns of the Divine brings into being the multiplicity of forms of the created world just as light passing through a crystal produces all the dancing colors of the rainbow. Thus the divine dance is what creates and sustains all life. As the Wisdom literature tells us, Sophia plays and rejoices in her creativity. She celebrates creation as she playfully dances the cosmos into existence; the world which is the creative expression of her joy and wisdom is therefore blessed from its origin. All of creation joins Sophia in her cosmic dance through the cycles of birth, growth, death and rebirth. As Sophia spins and twirls in her dance of rainbow colors, atomic particles appear and disappear, solar systems form, supernovas explode, babies are born, plants and animals die. Thus we experience the light and the dark aspects of the Divine Feminine as we dance with her through the patterns of creation and dissolution in the rhythmic cycle of life. Yet at the center of the dance, from which all movement proceeds, is divine love. Thus, as we experience both the joy and the suffering which accompany our steps in the dance of life, we know that our partner in the dance is love.

This is the essence of Hildegard of Bingen's numinous vision of Divine Wisdom joining with God in a dance of love. This image symbolizes the union of Love and Wisdom which can be interpreted as the integration of Christ and Sophia or ChristoSophia. The joyful dance of energy which underlies the cosmos is the dance of love, uniting Christ and Sophia, God and the world, the spiritual and the material. The ancient symbol of the round dance, an image that expresses the cosmological wisdom of early Christians, is returning to modern consciousness. Today we join with all of creation in dancing together in an unbroken circle of wholeness around the center of Love and Wisdom. This is the dance of life, and our task on Earth is to recognize and honor this dance in every aspect of creation. As we walk on the nature bypath we encounter many of the hidden traditions within Christianity which have recognized this divine dance of creation. Two of these which are especially significant for helping us to develop an ecological spirituality today are Celtic Christianity and the Green Man of medieval Christianity. It is these aspects of the nature bypath that we will explore in the following chapters.

CHAPTER VI: CELTIC CHRISTIANITY

I wish, O son of the living God, O ancient
Eternal King,
For a hidden little hut in the wilderness
that it may be my dwelling.

An all-gray little lake to be by its side.
A clear pool to wash away sins through
the grace of the Holy Spirit.

Quite near, a beautiful wood around it
on every side,
To nurse many-voiced birds, hiding them
with its shelter.

A southern aspect for warmth, a little brook
across its floor,
A choice land with many gracious gifts
such as be good for every plant. . .

A pleasant church with linen altar-cloth,
a dwelling for God of Heaven;
Then shining candles above the pure white
Scriptures. . .

This is the husbandry I would take, I would
choose, and will not hide it;
Fragrant leek, hens, speckled salmon, trout,
bees.

Raiment and food enough for me from the King
of fair fame,
And I to be sitting for a while praying to God
in every place.[1]

In our contemporary, complex culture, where there is never enough time to accomplish all that must be done, the above verses seem to be far removed from our view of reality. They express the very heart and soul of the nature bypath that has been almost totally lost in the building of the interstate Church. Many of us may yearn for the simple, pastoral lifestyle embodied in the poem, but we don't feel capable of experiencing it. Very few of us today would be willing to give up our job, our home, our family, and our friends (not to mention our modern technology!) to go off into the wilderness and commune with nature and the Divine. Yet, all of us in some way seek to relate to nature; it may be by taking a walk in a city park during lunch hour, or by looking at a sunset from the balcony in an urban apartment complex, or by any number of little ways that nature impinges herself upon our consciousness in our busy lives. But we need more than an infrequent "impinging" of nature—our culture needs to relearn how to live in harmony with nature and to reestablish the practice of walking the nature bypath. This is where the unknown monk from over fourteen hundred years ago who penned the above verses can be of invaluable aid to our times. He was a member of the Celtic community of Christians. His poem represents a pious love of all nature and the Divine that was the foundation of the Celtic worldview. All of creation was seen as a manifestation of the Divine by Celtic Christians. The Divine was not only transcendent but was also immanent in the natural order; therefore, Celtic Christians developed many prayers and rituals that honored the Earth. They recognized the importance of blessing the land, honoring sacred places such as wells, springs, streams, and mountains, and practicing religious observances which were closely related to the cycles of the sun and moon. They encouraged the faithful to cooperate with the nature spirits in their environment. Religious practice was tied to every intimate aspect of living in close harmony with nature. The Celtic Christians blazed the nature bypath more than any other branch of the early Church. Thus, in a culture that has basically ignored the immanence of the Divine and therefore now lives alienated from nature, we can turn to the saints of the Celtic Christian community for inspiration and spiritual renewal.

ORIGINS OF CELTIC CHRISTIANITY

In order to understand the role of Celtic Christianity in the development of the nature bypath, we must first examine the origins of the Christian Church in the British Isles. It is difficult to determine exactly when Christianity first appeared among the Celtic clans of Britain and Ireland. There is an ancient legend stating that the pagan Celtic druids were completely aware of Christ's ministry, crucifixion, and resurrection. Whether this was in a physical sense or through contacts within the Otherworld is impossible to say, but, nevertheless, some people believe that Christianity has been in the British Isles from its very beginnings. The famous poet, W. B. Yeats, refers to this legend when he recounts the story of King Conchubar's conversation with Buchrach, the Chief Druid of Leinster: "Conchubar notices 'that unusual changes of the creation and the eclipse of the sun and the moon at its full'; he asks the Druid the cause of these signs and Buchrach replies, 'Jesus Christ, the Son of God, who is now being crucified by the Jews.'"[2] According to the monk Gildas in the sixth century, Christians first arrived in Britain during the reign of the Emperor Tiberius who died in 37 C.E. He wrote, "These islands received the beams of light. . .in the latter part of the reign of Tiberius Caesar, in whose time this religion was propagated without impediment or death."[3] While there is no way to document this other than by the words of Gildas, the early presence of Christianity in Britain is certainly possible since there were Celtic mercenaries in the Roman legions during the time of Christ.[4] Many Christians to this day believe that Christ himself came to Celtic Britain during the so-called "lost years" between his childhood and ministry. According to legend, Joseph of Arimathea was a trader in tin who came to southwest Britain regularly to obtain the valuable tin needed to make bronze. The legend says that Jesus worked with Joseph and traveled with him for the tin trade. After the resurrection of Jesus, Joseph left Jerusalem with members of his family and friends and came to Glastonbury bearing the Holy Grail with the blood and sweat of Christ and the spear of the centurion Longinus which had pierced Christ's side at the crucifixion. According to the same legend, it was at Glastonbury that Joseph established the first Christian church. As a possible corroboration of the legend, archeologists have found the remains of two villages from the early Christian era in Glastonbury which contain artifacts with many Christian as well as pagan themes.[5] This discovery certainly lends plausibility to the belief that there were Christians residing in Britain from the earliest times. If the legend is indeed based upon factual history, Joseph of Arimathea's settlement in Glastonbury was established before the time of the ministry of St. Paul. Believers of this story claim that Britain is the land of the very first Christian church.

The first documentation of a Christian in Britain was Sergia Paula who was the wife of Gaius Frontu, the Roman commander at Eburacum (York) in 79 C.E. She was the daughter of Sergius Paulus of Cyprus who heard Paul and Barnabas preach as recorded in Acts 13:7,12.[6] Further documentation of the presence of Christians in early Britain is made by two Church Fathers, Tertullian and Origen, who refer to the Christian Church as active in Britain in the late second and early third centuries. By the early fourth century, Christianity appears to have been well established in Britain. Bishoprics existed in York, London, and Colchester, from which delegates attended the Council of Arles in 314. In 325, St. Athanasias indicates that the Church of Britain had accepted the edicts of the First Council of Nicaea. Thus, there appears to have been an active Church of Britain during the Roman occupation from some time in the third century up until the departure of the legions in 407.[7]

From these early beginnings, Christianity spread among the native Celtic Britons who quite readily embraced the spirituality of the new religion. While Roman influence in Britain was strong in the larger trading centers, the more remote areas of Northumbria, Scotland, Wales, and Cornwall were not assimilated into the mainstream of Roman culture. Many of these non-Romanized Celtic clans, some of which were probably Christian, would have been able to develop their religious practices and teachings isolated from the influence of the hierarchical, urban Roman Church. Therefore Celtic Christianity in Britain developed in a rural setting where the new religion was adapted to the existing pagan practices. Ireland was even more isolated from Roman influence as it was never a part of the Roman Empire. The Roman general Agricola, who commanded the legions in Britain in the first century, intended to invade Ireland but changed his plans. By the beginning of the second century no other Roman general or emperor considered Ireland worth the effort to control. This left Ireland with only indirect Roman influence during the Roman occupation of Britain. There is archeological evidence of Romano-British trade with Ireland in the first four centuries and even more evidence of Roman artifacts as the result of fourth and fifth century Irish raids on Roman Britain. But Ireland remained firmly pagan and Celtic until the fifth century. Christianity may have come to Ireland in the earliest centuries through trade with merchants from Britain and Gaul. St. Martin of Gaul who established the first major Western monastery in 361 was venerated by early Irish Christian monks, so it is possible that he had direct contact with Irish Christians in the fourth century. It was not until they began to flee the Anglo-Saxon raids in Britain in the fifth century that Christians began arriving in Ireland in significantly large numbers according to St. Patrick.[8] St. Patrick, the "patron saint of Ireland," is popularly believed to have brought Christianity to Ireland. However, it is known that there were native Celtic Christian communities already in Ireland when Patrick arrived. In all probability Patrick and Palladius, who preceded Patrick to Ireland by a year, were either requested by Christian communities in Ireland or sent to Ireland to protect the Christian communities from the prospective influence of Pelagianism which was then receiving widespread acceptance among British Christians.[9] In any event, the Ireland to which Patrick and Palladius came was predominantly an Iron Age culture divided into many clans lead by minor "kings," with no central authority or institutions, and no written language other than the Ogham alphabet used by the druids.

The tribal spiritual leaders of the pagan Celts were the druids. It is difficult to define the term "druid" as much of what is known of them comes from Roman writers who were prejudiced against their beliefs and practices. Caitlin Matthews signifies their importance within the clan when she describes the druid as a "seer of great knowledge, whose closeness to the natural world put him or her in the position of a walker between the worlds of humankind and the unseen worlds."[10] When the Celtic tribes in their rural environment first encountered Christianity, they found that the role of the Christian priests coincided in many ways with that of their druids.[11] Both the druids and priests advised their people in dealing with the problems of everyday life. They were both usually married with families so they were a part of the past and future of the clan. Priests and druids frequently practiced some craft which helped to support the community. They were responsible for the organization and celebration of the festivals and for judging and administering the laws. Thus, the Celtic druids and Christian priests were integral members of the communities in which they served. It is probable that for generations there were both Christian and pagan Celtic communities in close proximity. Christian priests would have borrowed and translated much of the druidic tradition into Christian forms. The Celts were rural people who lived in close contact with nature. Since the druidic tradition involved relating closely to nature spirits, the early rural Christian priests assimilated these spirits, especially those associated with wells and springs, into Christian tradition. It is likewise probable that many druids became Christians at this early time and because of their special gifts became Christian priests. These converted druids who became priests could be the source of the controversial Celtic Christian tonsure. This was the shaving of the head of the clergy from ear to ear rather than the Roman tonsure of a shaved circle on the top of the head. The pagan druids had used this tonsure as a sign of their office for centuries before the time of Christ and it is probable that native Celts would continue the tradition of their tonsure as Christian priests. In any event, there is little doubt that there was a close affinity between the early Celtic priests and their druid forebears. This can be seen in the statement attributed to the sixth century Welsh bard Taliesin, "Christ, the Word from the beginning, was from the beginning our Teacher, and we never lost his teaching. Christianity was in Asia a new thing: but there was never a time when the Druids of Britain held not its doctrine."[12] This passage underscores the affinity that the native Celtic druids had for the doctrines taught by the Christian clergy. It can be said in this sense that Christianity was the fulfillment of pagan Celtic beliefs.

It is important to realize that there was never an autonomous Celtic Church which existed separately from the Roman Church. In fact, Celtic Christians considered themselves to be an integral part of one universal Christian Church. However, theirs' was a Christianity which developed independently of the Roman form of Christianity and was therefore able to retain the eros aspects of the Celtic spirit. Celtic Christianity possessed the intuitive, holistic vision inspired by eros which was suppressed in Roman Christianity due to its emphasis on the logos characteristics of organization and law. Because Celtic Christianity was not as influenced by Greco-Roman cultural and political norms, it did not experience the extreme dualistic split between the physical and spiritual worlds which developed in the Roman Church. Thus the Celtic Christians were able to maintain their sense of connection to nature and integrate earlier pagan elements of the Earth Mysteries into the new religion. If the monk Pelagius is representative of the early Church in Britain, it would appear that the created world was perceived as "good" and pagan practices which honored nature were not considered evil or sinful as was usually the case in Roman Christianity. Celtic Christianity's greater expression of the eros aspect of human nature also can be seen in its emphasis on mythic consciousness. The Celts have always been known for their gift of storytelling, which is seen even today in the concept of the Irish "blarney." In the telling of the great Celtic heroic legends and sagas, the archetypal aspects of human experience found their expression. The Celtic Christian monks and scribes followed the long tradition of the bards and druids in retelling the ancient myths in their new form in the light of Christ's life, death, and resurrection. The Celtic people could substitute the figures of the

Old and New Testament for the pagan heroes and heroines that they had previously venerated. For the Celts, the biblical stories were perceived primarily as mythic expressions of the human soul rather than as literal historical documents or moral lessons. Thus, Celtic Christianity incorporated the mythological significance of its pagan past, including the reverence for nature, into Christian tradition.

These essential differences between the Celtic and Roman approaches to Christianity can also be seen in the outward form of their ecclesiastical structures. Celtic Christianity was based on a monastic model which followed the traditional pagan pattern of governance as well as the mystical practices of the Christians in the Eastern church. In Gaul, St. Martin and his followers were the first to establish monasteries based upon the Eastern practice. From Gaul and Britain, monks were sent to Ireland as missionaries of the new Eastern ascetic model. They and their converts, like the Eastern desert monks, sought remote places to found their cells and hermitages. A number of disciples seeking solitude began to gather around the original founder, each having his own cell. These groups of Christians gradually became like the traditional Celtic clans—a family dependent upon one another for their basic survival needs. Moreover, the monastic community was a family of pious people seeking the Divine through prayer, contemplation, ascetic discipline, and mystical vision. The Celtic monasteries grew up in rural areas and were geographically isolated from each other. Because of their relative autonomy and lack of a central organizing authority, the Celtic monastic communities never developed the hierarchical, institutional structure which characterized the interstate Church of Roman Christianity. Celtic Christianity remained as a distinctly viable bypath within Christian tradition until suppressed by the greater political power of the Roman Church.

THE ECOLOGICAL SPIRITUALITY OF CELTIC CHRISTIANITY

The nature bypath was easily accessed through the ecological spirituality of the early Celtic Christians. These Christians who were not far removed from their pagan roots still believed in the existence of the nature spirits that inhabited sacred springs and wells, although now these spirits were given the names and attributes of Christian saints. The Christian priest was able to commune directly with these spirits of nature, now in the form of saints, as had the druids before him. Thus, in the Celtic worldview, there was still a widely held belief in magic. Was not the transubstantiation of the bread and wine into the body and blood of Christ a form of magic? Were not the biblical stories of the miracles of Jesus, the Apostles and the saints also examples of magic to the Celtic mind? Magic is relegated to the realm of superstition by educated persons today; therefore, we can see how incredibly difficult it is to experience the spirituality of the ancient Celtic Christians. This spirituality was based upon the magical practice and mythology of the pagan Celts. As the Celtic pagans became Christians, they were still ultimately Celts with all of the heritage of magic and myth deeply ingrained within them. In becoming Christians they did not deny that heritage but rather built the Church of the new Celtic hero, Christ, upon the strong foundation of the polytheistic pagan past. The Celtic Christians believed in natural magic, a magic based on their intimate relationship with the natural world. Christ, the archetypal magician or "Lord of the Elements,"[13] became for them the embodiment of nature. In this sense the Celtic Christian reverence for nature can also be seen to reflect their reverence for the Sophianic essence of Christ, the Divine, which is immanent in all creation. We can see this association of Christ with nature in many of the hymns and poems of the early Celtic Christian saints. Perhaps the most famous early prayer that has come down to the present is St. Patrick's *Lorica*, a prayer of protection called "The Deer's Cry" which includes the following lines:

> I arise today through the strength of Heaven:
> light of Sun, brilliance of Moon,
> splendour of Fire, speed of Lightning,
> swiftness of Wind, depth of Sea,
> stability of Earth, firmness of Rock.[14]

St. Patrick addresses the four ancient basic elements of all creation: fire, air, water, earth. Mastery of the four elements was the mark of the magician. To St. Patrick, Christ had become the Divine Magician, the Lord of the Elements, who would control the elements to protect the faithful. These verses from the *Lorica* do not seek protection from the natural world; instead they are an expression of St. Patrick's reverential attitude toward nature.

By the sixth century, the most prevalent expression of Celtic Christianity was found in the monastic communities of hermits and anchorites. Most of these communities were very small and isolated and, by necessity, very much part of their natural environment. Monasteries were generally built on sites which had been sacred to the pagan Celts. Although this practice is often interpreted by historians as a political move in which the new religion appropriated the old pagan site and "Christianized" it, it is also very likely that the early Celtic monks actually experienced the spiritual energy of these sacred places. Sharing the sensitivity to the land which was characteristic of their druid kinsmen, the Celtic monks may have chosen sites for their churches and communities based on the presence of the Earth energies. Even today the power of the Earth can be experienced very strongly at these Celtic monastic sites, though they now lie in ruins. They are often located in wild and remote areas, where the Celtic monks could not help but experience the embeddedness of human life within the natural world. For example, the monastery of Skellig Michael was built in the sixth century on a small island of rock in the Atlantic Ocean ten miles from the coast of County Kerry. For the modern pilgrim, the journey by small boat across the churning seas and the 700 foot climb up the rocky crags to the site of the monastic ruins is an awe-inspiring experience. While hearing the constant song of the soaring sea birds who inhabit this rocky outpost, feeling the strong gusts of wind blowing off the north Atlantic, seeing the grey sea mist rolling in and enveloping all of the familiar landscape, it is evident that in this place the Celtic monks would have experienced the primal power of nature - her danger as well as her beauty - the dark and light sides of existence. After climbing the great height to the monastery and entering the well-preserved "beehive huts," one may have the incredible experience of entering the womb of the Earth Mother. At Skellig Michael, certainly, the unity of Heaven and Earth has been achieved.

The effect that such a spirituality anchored in the natural world had on the Celtic monks is described by Robin Flower: "It was not only that these scribes and anchorites lived by the destiny of their dedication in an environment of wood and sea; it was because they brought into that environment an eye washed miraculously clear by a continual spiritual exercise that they, first in Europe, had that strange vision of natural things in an almost unnatural purity."[15] Some examples of anchorite nature poetry will help us to understand that vision:

> Learned in music sings the lark,
> I leave my cell to listen; His open beak spills music, hark!
> Where Heaven's bright cloudlets glisten.
> And so I'll sing my morning psalm
> That God bright Heaven may give me
> And keep me in eternal calm
> And from all sin relieve me.[16]

To this Celtic Christian monk, songbirds were considered oracles of the divine songs of Heaven. He is inspired by the song of the lark to praise God by singing his own psalm. The anchorite, alone in his cell, is never truly alone because he is surrounded by the spirit of the Divine in nature. If we recall the sound of songbirds at dawn on a soft spring morning, we can share in the joy that this Celtic monk/ poet feels for the twittering of the songbirds around his hermitage and understand how, to him, the song of the birds is the music of God.

> He whistles in the willow tree,
> Descanting from his yellow bill,
> Gold-beaked, black-coated, that is he,
> Stout ousel and his trembling trill.[17]

We can hear in the song of the ousel the glory of God and all creation. In medieval music, descanting was the art of improvising a melody above the original plainchant—an outpouring of the creative response of the singer to the inherent beauty and sacredness of the chant itself. Such a beautiful analogy our anonymous monk makes! The colorful ousel, as a devout creature of God, is trilling forth his joy above the underlying chant of God's love. Another ode to the ousel is more contemplative:

> Sweet ousel chanting blithely there,
> Where in the bushes hides thy nest?
> Thou hermit no bell calls to prayer!
> Thy soft sweet music speaks of rest.[18]

We can see here an allusion to the unseen angelic choirs. The ousel can be heard but not seen. In early Byzantine churches, the choir was placed behind an intricately carved screen so that the congregation could not see them, thus the human choir became a graphic symbol of the angelic choir. Our unknown monk appears to be rather jealous of the ousel's freedom from the constraints of time; the ousel has no bell from the oratory calling him to leave his private devotion and join in the structured prayers of the community. The hermit's day is tightly structured around the canonical hours such as matins and vespers. The last line is rather like a lullaby; the hermit is tired and contemplative, yet he must continue the organized rounds of the monastic order.

The songs of birds are not only beautiful but they are also filled with healing grace as can be seen in the next example:

> The singing birds of Heaven greet
> The Virgin's son with music sweet;
> One whisper of their song would heal
> The agonies damned spirits feel.[19]

In this short, delightful hymn, the monk rejoices in yet another aspect of birdsong - its power to heal. The heavenly birds' song can heal even the damned but the song of birds in the natural world can likewise heal. We need to be healed when we are troubled about everyday affairs; we are cut off from the vitality of the natural world and everything appears bleak. But if we open ourselves to hear the music of nature surrounding us, we are immediately healed and put in touch once again with the wellsprings of life. We can awaken before dawn and begin to ruminate about a problem that needs to be dealt with and go out to get the newspaper and suddenly be transformed into a state of tranquility by the sound of a multitude of birds singing. Our problems shrink to insignificance as we are filled with the sense of the divine eternal essence pouring forth all around us. We can become united in spirit with the early medieval monk and be healed by the oracles of God's divine music. Even if we listen soulfully for only a few moments, we may become conscious that all problems have their solution through the divine presence and we can go forth into the mundane world with renewed vigor.

As the oracles of the Divine, birds were perceived by the Celts as mediators between the earthly world and the Otherworld. They were the spiritual messengers from an unseen realm that lay just beneath the surface of our everyday reality. The concept of the pagan Celtic Otherworld differed greatly from the modern Christian view of Heaven. Celts believed that the Otherworld was not "up there" but was tangential to the temporal world and that one could move between the worlds while alive in the body. This view that the spiritual realm overlay and interpenetrated the earthly realm imparted a sense of sacredness and mystery to everyday life. Modern science has provided new metaphors for this invisible world which lies just beyond the sensory realm -- the unconscious, archetypes, quantum particles -- but the mystery of this Otherworld remains. One way to envision the Celtic Otherworld is as a deep reflection of our natural world. Since we can never truly be apart from nature, when we consciously "reflect" upon our actions in the natural environment, we can be said to be more "in tune" with the Otherworld. We can commute to work every day totally oblivious to the spectacular sunrise, but if we stop and take the time to notice the rising of the sun, we can be filled with awe at its beauty. The beauty is always there but we are usually unconscious of it. The same is true of the Otherworld -- we can experience it by reflecting upon the wonders of the natural world. Since birds are creatures which mediate between the worlds, they especially provide access to this other reality. By following the example of the Celtic hermits and listening soulfully to the songs of the larks, ousels, and warblers, we too may make contact with the Otherworld.

It is unfortunate that in the English language the word "other" connotes "separate" or "apart from." We have come to believe that the Otherworld is a place that is therefore apart from us. A more accurate term for the Otherworld might be "Essenceworld." The Otherworld is really the divine essence which permeates the natural world. As in the example of the unnoticed beauty of the sunrise, just because we are unconscious of the spiritual essence of nature doesn't mean that this essence doesn't exist or that it exists only in a separate dimension. The word "essence" is also related to the word "essential." To be aware of the divine essence of things is essential if we are to stop the wholesale destruction of the natural world. Even environmentalists talk about saving our "natural resources" as if somehow the natural world was a "resource" for humanity. The true resource of nature is the Otherworld -- the essence of nature. The view of the Otherworld as permeating our earthly world also points to Sophia -- the integration of her divine, spiritual aspect with her Earth Mother aspect. The Celtic people intuited Sophia in their realization of the Otherworld.

The Celtic Christian view of Heaven was influenced by the pagan concept of the Otherworld. The essence of nature which pervades the Celtic Otherworld is seen in this description of Heaven by a Celtic monk:

> The Tree of Life with bloom unchanged
> Round it the goodly hosts are ranged,
> Its leafy crest showers dewdrops round
> All Heaven's spreading garden-ground.
>
> There flock bright birds, a shining throng,
> And sing their grace-perfected song
> While boundless mercy round them weaves
> Undying fruit, unfading leaves.
>
> A lovely flock! bright like the sun,
> A hundred feathers clothe each one,
> And pure and clear they chant together
> A hundred songs for every feather.[20]

In this joyous hymn, Heaven is described as a celestial Garden of Eden – the spiritual essence of nature's garden. The Tree of Life is not just an abstract symbol for the contemplation of the Divine, but is analogous to a living tree filled with songbirds in the monastery garden. The ecstatic never-ending songs of the heavenly birds enhance the everlasting leaves, flowers and fruit of the Tree of Life. In this hymn, the Tree of Life could be said to symbolize God who is at the center of Heaven around which all the heavenly hosts are gathered. The dewdrops could symbolize the unending grace of God as the Tree of Life which shelters and sustains all the heavenly host - the bright birds. The colorful plumage of the natural songbirds is but a pale reflection of the brilliance of the celestial birds, but the pure sound of their divine chant is far greater than their visual beauty. Even in the mundane world, some of the most beautiful songs come from very dull-colored birds such as skylarks and warblers. This is simply another reminder that the divine essence of the Otherworld is present in even the most ordinary aspects of the earthly realm. This perception is the source of the Celtic Christians' belief that the "heavenly hosts" surrounded them throughout all the daily activities of waking and sleeping. The Trinity, the Virgin Mary, the angelic powers, disciples, and saints who inhabited the realms of Heaven were also intimately present in the everyday world. Celtic Christians invoked the blessings of this great company of heaven on all the tasks of daily life, from the first kindling of the fire in the morning through the daily round which included sowing, reaping, milking, herding, weaving, to the final banking of the fire at night. For example, a typical milking song begins:

> Come, Mary, and milk my cow,
> Come, Bride, and encompass her,
> Come, Columba, the benign,
> And twine thine arms around my cow...[21]

These rituals and incantations for the living of everyday life were adapted by the Celtic Christians from pagan practices which invoked the power of the gods and goddesses. Like their predecessors who perceived the divine presence in all aspects of life, the Celtic Christians recognized a spiritual purpose in ordinary activities and their daily life was an offering to God.

These practices also reflect the strong elements of panentheism in Celtic Christianity. The hierarchical Roman Church emphasized the role of the transcendent God; once Christ had ascended, He was "beyond" the natural, temporal world. With the Celtic emphasis on the Divine "within" and "through" the natural world, we can see one of the most basic differences between the worldviews of Roman and Celtic Christianity. The Celts placed more emphasis on the view of Christ expressed in Acts 17:28: "For in him we live, and move, and have our being..." and in Colossians 1:16-17: "For by him were all things created . . . He is before all things and in him all things hold together." In the Roman Church, the emphasis on the transcendence of God led to the dualistic separation of society into sacred and secular. In the Celtic mind, there was no false separation into sacred and secular—all is blessed because the Divine is All. When St. Patrick was trying to convert the daughters of the High King at Tara, he was questioned about the attributes of his 'new' God. He answered:

> Our God is the God of all men
> the God of Heaven and Earth, of sea
> and river, of sun and moon and stars,
> of the lofty mountain and the lowly valley,
> The God above Heaven, the God in Heaven,
> The God under Heaven;
> He has his dwelling round Heaven and Earth
> and sea and all that is.
> He inspires all, he quickens all,
> He dominates all, he sustains all.
> He lights the light of the sun;
> He furnishes the light of the light;
> He has put springs in the dry land
> and has set stars to minister to the greater lights. . . .[22]

If we examine his words carefully we can recognize the spirit of panentheism in them. He is referring not to God as transcendent only, but to an immanent God: God "of sea and river," God "of the lofty mountain and the lowly valley." We see a personal expression of St. Patrick's panentheism in his famous *lorica*:

> Christ with me, Christ before me,
> Christ behind me;

Christ within me, Christ beneath me,
Christ above me; Christ to right of me,
Christ to left of me;
Christ in my lying, Christ in my sitting, Christ in my rising;
Christ in the heart of all who think of me,
Christ on the tongue of all who speak to me,
Christ in the eye of all who see me,
Christ in the ear of all who hear me.[23]

This panentheistic attitude was to remain central to Celtic Christianity. Christ is "sitting at the right hand of the Father," but He is also within every creature and every "where" and every "thing." He is the "Cosmic Christ" who provides the divine pattern of interconnectedness.

John Scotus Eriugena, the great ninth century theologian, continued in the Celtic Christian tradition by expressing panentheistic views, for which his work was later condemned by the Pope. The following passage from Eriugena's *Homily on the Prologue to the Gospel of John* discusses how the "Word" of God (Christ) is found in nature:

Observe the forms and beauties of sensible
things, and comprehend the Word of God in them.
If you do so, the truth will reveal to you
in all such things only he who made them,
outside of whom you have nothing to contemplate,
for he himself is all things. For whatever truly is,
in all things which are, is he.
Indeed, just as no substantial good exists
outside of him, so no essence or substance
exists that is not he.[24]

In this passage, Eriugena asks us to observe the essence of the natural world around us; this essence is the immanent Christ. Eriugena does not refer to observation in the sense of being a passive spectator. Rather, by actively and consciously attuning ourselves to the natural world, we will experience the creator of all things. We don't have to contemplate anything else since God, who is beyond all, is also in all.

Perhaps Eriugena's greatest work was *Periphyseon: On the Division of Nature* which presents a pantheistic approach to understanding the nature of God. This is expressed through his interpretation of the doctrine of "theophany":

> He will appear in his *theophanies*, that is,
> in divine apparitions in which, according to
> the purity and virtue of each, he will appear.
> In the same way perfectly purified souls and
> intelligences are theophanies; in them God
> manifests himself to those who seek and love
> him; in them, as in clouds, the saints are caught up.[25]

Eriugena recognizes that the ultimate nature of God is beyond mind; even the saints themselves cannot "see" the fullness of the Godhead. Yet the Divine manifests to us through the created world if we strive to apprehend it. Thus theophany involves a two-way process - God's outward pouring forth through nature, the manifest universe, and our striving to apprehend the mystery of God. This two-way relatedness between Creator and created we call love. As Eriugena says, "This is the cause and substance of all virtues. Every theophany, every virtue, both in this life and in the future life, is produced not outside a human being but in him or her and arises both from God and from human beings themselves."[26] The Celtic saints time and again show this pantheistic awareness of theophany through their deep love for, and companionship with, nature as an expression of the Divine:

> Over my head the woodland wall
> Rises; the ousel sings to me;
> Above my booklet lined for words
> The woodland birds shake out their glee.
> That's the blithe cuckoo chanting clear
> In mantle grey from burgh to burgh!
> God keep me still! for here I write
> A scripture bright in great woods now.[27]

This anonymous ninth century saint has captured the essence of Celtic spirituality—the oneness of the Divine with nature. The act of writing out the scripture while surrounded by the beauty of creation is far different from the usual image of a monk bent over a table in a cold stone cell writing by a flickering tallow lamp. There is gentle humor here, too: the monk writing this verse is being distracted by the natural beauty and birdsongs and has to ask the Creator to keep him still, focused on the task at hand. We can find countless examples of the love of nature in Celtic spirituality. There is a kinship with the animal kingdom that pervades the stories of the saints. One famous example concerns St. Kevin who lived during the sixth century. He would spend the Lenten season in a small woodland hut with a gray flagstone for his bed. One Lent, a blackbird came and rested on his outstretched hand while he was lying on the bed and proceeded to build her nest there. Kevin, not wanting to disturb her, remained in that position until she had safely hatched her young. That this compassion was reciprocal between the animals and humans is seen in the many stories which tell of the "animal helpers" of the saints. St. Cuthbert during the seventh century was the great spiritual leader of the Lindisfarne monastery in Northumbria. On one occasion he felt moved to pray all night while standing up to his neck in the icy water of the sea. In the morning he went back to the beach when two otters came out of the water and warmed his feet by blowing on them and warmed his body with their fur. While we can look at such legendary accounts of St. Kevin and St. Cuthbert with a skeptical eye, it is their kinship with birds and animals that gives a lasting impression of the gentle spirit of these pious people.

Such stories also reveal another aspect of Celtic Christian spirituality—the ability to communicate and identify with creatures. Perhaps the legendary ability of St. Francis to communicate with animals indicates that he was influenced by the saints of Celtic Christianity. This kinship with other creatures might be a remnant of the ancient shamanism practiced by the druids whereby they reputedly could take the form of animals and birds to explore the natural world with an affinity that no one in human form could do. In our modern world, we take the opposite view; we attempt to domesticate or tame wild creatures so they will have more human qualities. It is another example of how the modern culture seeks to control nature and improve upon it. It is interesting to note that there are many people today seeking to return to these earlier modes of identification with the animal kingdom through shamanistic practices. We can find such inspiration for experiencing a greater kinship with the other creatures of Earth from the stories of the Celtic saints.

CELTIC SAINTS AND THE NATURE BYPATH

The term "saint" was used in the early Church as a synonymous term for "ecclesiastic," a learned, literate person. The term "saint" can also be used in a psychological sense as an embodiment of a universal, underlying archetype wherein the historical person becomes identified with the archetype, i.e., the saint takes on the qualities of the god or goddess of the older faith. Through this process the Celtic saints appropriated the attributes of the ancient pagan heroes, heroines, and deities. Furthermore, there were many Celts who were considered "saints" in the more usual sense—people who received a special blessing from God and who were known to perform miracles. The four major saints of Celtic Christianity in Ireland are Saint Columba (also known as Columcille), Saint Brendan, Saint Patrick and Saint Brigit (also called Saint Bride). What we know of them comes primarily from the *vitae* or "lives of the saints" which were first written in the Middle Ages. They are not historical biographies as we would expect today, but were primarily used to aid the faithful in prayer and devotional activities. As such, the *vitae* embody the spirit of the saints, not the actual details of their lives. They are meant to be read as mythological expressions of Celtic Christianity rather than literal, historical documents. Their *vitae* reveal that these saints were trailblazers on the nature bypath. Many of their experiences, which showed their deep relationship to the natural world, obviously derived from pagan tradition. The supernatural aspects of the saints' lives were enhanced as they took over the role that the Celtic heroes and heroines played within the culture. For example, shape-changing was reported to be an ability of the ancient druids who commonly took the form of an animal to obtain the experience of that animal's spirit. St. Patrick (c. 390-461) supposedly had this ability, too. In one instance when he and a number of his companions were about to be killed treacherously by King Loiguire, Patrick exhibited the ancient druidic practice of shape-changing by turning himself and his companions into deer and escaping into the wilderness. This story is the origin of "The Deer's Cry" *lorica* quoted earlier. A lorica is a Roman breast-plate used for protection in battle, hence it becomes an invocation for protection. We can assume that Patrick became a stag, an ancient symbol for the "natural man" (e.g., Cernunnos, god of fertility, abundance, and regeneration) and thus a synthesis figure uniting pagan tradition with Christianity.

St. Brendan (c. 486-578) is mostly known for his sea voyage. This story was one of the most popular stories of the Middle Ages throughout Europe and is found in many languages in over a hundred medieval manuscripts that have survived to the present. The Irish, British, and Welsh Celts have always had a close affinity for the sea and so it not surprising that many of their legends and stories, both pagan and Christian, involve the sea. St. Brendan's voyages were filled with the dangers of the open ocean and the pious faith that allowed him and his men to overcome these dangers. One episode tells of their meeting with a sea monster who was about to swallow their boat with all on board. After fervently praying for protection, St. Brendan and his companions were saved by the appearance of a second sea monster that destroyed the first. He said, "'Do you see, dear monks, the marvels of the Lord, and the obedience which the creature renders to the Creator?'"[28] Most of St. Brendan's adventures occurred on islands much like a Celtic Odysseus, and throughout both voyages he called upon God and performed the appropriate rituals to God very much in the same manner as Odysseus did to his gods. The message is clear—a faithful person who lives in harmony with the environment and the Divine will experience the fullness of life.

St. Columba (c. 521-597) is known for establishing many monasteries in Ireland as well as the monastery at Iona in Scotland and for converting the Picts to Christianity. His name in Latin means 'dove' and its symbolic association with the Holy Spirit and the bird of peace was not lost on his followers. Like the other Celtic saints, St. Columba was deeply connected to nature through his faith. In *The Life*

of St. Columba, written by Adamnan, one of his successors at Iona
in the late seventh century, St. Columba encountered the infamous
Loch Ness monster. The story recounts that after missionizing
among the Picts in the Scottish highlands, he came to the river Ness
and found the people burying the remains of a man who had been
killed by the monster. Since there was no bridge and he had to cross
the river, St. Columba told one of his faithful servants to swim over
and fetch a small boat from the other side. As his companion swam
across, the monster rose up from the depths with a fearful roar and
opened its mouth to devour the poor man. St. Columba immediately
made the sign of the cross and commanded the monster: "Think
not to go further, nor touch thou the man. Quick! go back!"[29] The
monster instantly retreated in great fear and the companion was able
to come with the boat. Such faith in the power of God to stand up to
such a monster! St. Columba was a man who found the power of the
Divine everywhere in the natural world and he had no hesitation to
invoke it. His love of the natural world is probably best expressed in
his famous psalm composed while he was abbot of Iona:

> Delightful I think it to be in the bosom
> of an isle, on the peak of a rock,
> that I might often see there
> the calm of the sea.
>
> That I might see its heavy waves over the
> glittering ocean, as they chant
> a melody to their Father
> on their eternal course.
>
> That I might see its smooth strand of
> clear headlands, no gloomy thing;
> that I might hear the voice of the
> wondrous birds, a joyful tune.
>
> That I might hear the sound of the
> shallow waves against the rocks,
> that I might hear the cry by the
> graveyard, the noise of the sea.

That I might see its splendid flocks of
birds over the fullwatered ocean;
that I might see its mighty whales,
greatest of wonders.

That I might see its ebb and its floodtide
in their flow; that this might be
my name, a secret I tell, "He who
turned his back on Ireland."

That contrition of heart should come
upon me as I watch it;
that I might bewail my many sins,
difficult to declare.

That I might bless the Lord
who has power over all,
Heaven with its pure host of
angels, earth, ebb, flood-tide.

That I might pore on one of my books,
good for my soul;
A while kneeling for beloved Heaven,
a while at psalms.

A while gathering dulse from the rocks,
a while fishing,
A while giving food to the poor,
a while in my cell.

A while meditating upon the Kingdom of
Heaven, holy is the redemption;
A while at labor not too heavy;
it would be delightful![30]

The last three verses give us an intimate glimpse into the daily
activities of one of Celtic Christianity's greatest saints. The fervent,
almost whimsical, wish of the last line speaks deeply to those of us
who are caught up in the stresses of modern life.

St. Brigit (c. 452-524) is more closely associated with nature than any other Celtic saint. As the primary female saint of the Celtic Christians, this fifth century quasi-legendary figure has many of the attributes of the pagan goddess with whom she shares her name. The triple-goddess Brigit had been the most popular of the pagan Celtic deities, therefore it is not surprising that she was assimilated into the Christian faith as St. Brigit of Kildare who to this day is the most popular saint in Ireland after St. Patrick. The connection between the two Brigits is seen in that the date of the pagan Celtic feast of Imbolc, which honored the goddess Brigit on February 1, was retained as the Christian feast day of St. Brigit. The feast of Imbolc celebrated the birth of the new lambs and the lactation of the ewes, and Brigit was venerated as a fertility goddess who was especially concerned with the welfare of livestock. In her role as saint, Brigit is also regarded as a protectress of livestock, particularly cattle. Legend claims that she was nourished by a sacred cow in infancy, and she is often pictured with a cow by her side. The earlier substrate of pagan goddess worship is also seen in the symbolism of sacred fire which has accrued to St. Brigit. Her monastery at Kildare kept a sacred fire continually burning which was attended by twelve nuns in a manner similar to the priestesses of temples dedicated to sacred goddesses. Brigit as mother-goddess was also associated with the hearth fire like the Roman goddess Vesta. As the Christian St. Brigit, her symbol became the fiery solar cross made from corn husks or reeds which today is found in every tourist shop in Ireland.[31] As a saint, Brigit is primarily remembered as the embodiment of Christian virtues: loving, prayerful, innocent, forgiving, humble, pious, modest, gentle, wise, firm, and abstinent. Yet, we can see another side of the humble saint—righteous indignation. Once a woman brought a basket of apples to St. Brigit as an offering. While the woman was still there, a group of lepers came begging and St. Brigit gave the apples to the lepers. The woman became angry, telling St. Brigit that the apples were for her alone and certainly not for lepers. St. Brigit, indignant that the woman forbade her giving the apples as alms, cursed the woman's apple trees. When the woman returned home all of the apples were gone and her trees were barren from that time on.[32] Apples are sacred to the Mother Goddess and the woman was guilty of profaning the Goddess by denying her bounty and their healing energy for the lepers. Therefore, St. Brigit, as the Earth Goddess, withdrew her bounty from the woman. In this tale, the dark side of the goddess emerges. St. Brigit, like the earlier pagan goddess, wields the power of both life and death. Thus, St. Brigit is not only closely associated with nature, but in a way it can be said that she **is** nature in both its creative and destructive aspects.

The prominence of St. Brigit among the Celtic saints attests to the strength of the manifestation of the Divine Feminine within Celtic Christianity. In the medieval *Book of Lismore* she is accorded such titles as "The Prophetess of Christ," "The Queen of the South," and "The Mary of the Gael."[33] Her spiritual power is mirrored in her temporal authority. According to legend, Brigid was consecrated as bishop in addition to presiding as abbess over a double monastery, which contained both men and women, at Kildare. The great reverence for the feminine Brigit appears to be reflected in a greater acceptance of women's roles within Celtic Christianity. Although there is much debate among scholars regarding the true position of women in the Celtic Christian communities, there is evidence that women had more opportunities for leadership than they did in Roman Christianity. The holistic view of creation held by the Celts did not draw the sharp distinctions between masculine and feminine as was the case with the more patriarchal Romans. For the Celtic Christians who walked on the nature bypath, acceptance of the Divine Feminine in all her aspects was a corollary to their reverence for the sacredness of the Earth.

CELTIC CHRISTIAN ART

For the Celtic Christians art had a spiritual function, as is seen in many superb examples of sculpture, metalwork and manuscript illumination which were created to glorify God. This art reflected the perceptions of Celtic society in its holistic view of life, in which the natural and spiritual worlds, plant and animal kingdoms, and divine and human life are inextricably connected. It clearly shows the synthesis of earlier pagan elements and Celtic Christianity. One of the greatest contributions to Christian sacred art is the Celtic high cross. Stone crosses, sculpted from the ninth through twelfth centuries, are found throughout Ireland and in many areas of England, Scotland, and Wales. These high crosses are the remnants of a faith almost forgotten. They are weathered, with mostly indecipherable inscriptions, usually found in out-of-the-way places. Although there are over a hundred ancient high crosses still to be found in Great Britain and Ireland, many hundreds must have once existed before the ravages of time and the fanaticism of "reformers" destroyed them. For the spiritual seeker who travels the bypaths, these high crosses are not only signposts of sacred places, but they point to a form of worship and adoration that is sadly lacking in the modern world. The Celtic Christians honored the Divine in nature as they gathered outdoors around the high crosses, many of which had originally been placed within ancient pagan sacred precincts. The Celtic cross, with its intersecting circle, symbolizes the transcendent and immanent divinity, not only the crucifixion of Christ. In fact, most of the early crosses do not emphasize the crucifixion; they graphically depict biblical scenes in a simple and vigorous manner. Daniel in the lions' den, the slaying of Abel by Cain, the loaves and fishes feeding the multitudes, Adam and Eve covering their genitals, and the sacrifice of Isaac are the most common themes found on the crosses of the 9th and 10th centuries. Their sculpted panels spoke strongly to a simple people who were for the most part illiterate and worked with their hands, not their heads. The rural Celts would not have been impressed by the intricacies of subtle theological logic debating the "procession of the Holy Spirit" or whether or not laity should receive "both species" at communion. Instead they responded to the biblical stories which are so beautifully depicted on the high crosses. We can assume that the worshippers would gather around the high crosses and celebrate the deity who is found in Heaven and all creation by singing songs of praise, chanting prayers, performing dances of devotion, acting out favorite biblical stories, and listening to words of scripture and the lives of the saints. These celebrations would not have been limited to Sundays and major feasts like Easter and Christmas, but also would have occurred on the "pattern day" of the local patron ("pattern") saint. Many festivals held around the high crosses would have corresponded to the ancient pagan calendar which was based on the cycles of sun, moon, and the seasons.

We can imagine individuals, families, and clans on the pattern day following the ancient traditions of their pagan ancestors by offering libations at the foot of the high cross and gifts of food or craft goods to honor the Divine as expressed through the life and legend of the local saint. We likewise can imagine processionals from the homes to the high cross and even pilgrimages to other high crosses in nearby villages, thereby honoring the interconnectedness of sacred time and place. Undoubtedly, the high crosses were much more than monuments to the historical event of Christ's crucifixion; they were the sacred centers in the daily lives of the Celtic Christians.

Many high crosses depict a cross-fertilization of pagan and Christian symbols. For example, the so-called "Pictish" stone crosses found at Aberlemno and Glamis in Scotland are filled with fascinating pagan or pagan-derived symbols. Often the front of the cross exhibits traditional Christian motifs while its back displays mysterious symbols of a dim past which we can no longer interpret. However, it can be inferred that these symbols were consciously integrated with the Christian cross to inspire adoration of the Divine.

Aberlemno "Pictish" Cross Slab   **Glamis "Pictish" Cross Slab**

The unity of the physical and spiritual realms is also expressed in the art of the Celtic high cross in the intermingling of plants and animals with the biblical scenes. It appears that religious themes could not be conceived apart from the world of nature. A particularly intriguing feature of the high crosses is the prevalence of serpents carved upon them. Especially fascinating is the symbol of three heads surrounded by intertwined serpents which is found on many of the Irish high crosses. The cult of the head was a common theme in pagan Celtic mythology. By making the heads those of saints, the Church cleverly transformed the symbol into a Christian context. The underlying meaning of the serpents remains unclear, however. Although traditional Christian interpretations regard the snake as an evil tempter, it seems possible that the combination of the snake and head imagery might hearken back to earlier pagan associations of the serpent with wisdom, illumination, and resurrection.

Section from Muiredach's Cross at Monasterboice Abbey, Ireland

Celtic high crosses are especially known for their intricately carved interlacing which is astonishing in its complexity. The various patterns which are found on the crosses are derived from earlier pagan designs of Celtic spirals and knotwork. It may be inferred that the Celtic Christian monks adopted these complex interlacing designs to symbolize their panentheistic view of the interconnectedness of God with creation. On many crosses, one side depicts images of the crucifixion and resurrection and the other side portrays the "cosmic design" through the pattern of interlinking spirals and knotwork. In contemplating these swirling patterns which continually flow into each other, one can truly experience the joyful energy of the divine dance of creation.

The great manuscript illuminations of the Book of Durrow, the Lindisfarne Gospels, and the superlative Book of Kells all express a Celtic love for a similar florid interlacing. Spiral designs are mirrored in the interlinking of human limbs and the interconnected patterns of animals, plants, and birds which decorate the manuscripts. The interdependence of the kingdoms of creation which is abstractly symbolized in the spiral patterns is expressed in the concrete imagery of plant, animal, and human forms which flow into each other. Just as nature and spirit merged in the art of the high cross with the juxtaposition of earthly creatures and biblical scenes, so are animals and plants integrally connected to the letters of the manuscript. It can even be conjectured whether the zoomorphic shapes which are so prevalent were perhaps derived from the pagan druid tradition of shape-changing, since human and animal forms are so closely connected throughout the manuscripts. Many of the figures appear quite playful, such as one in which two monks sit with their limbs intertwined and their hands pulling each others' beards. Whimsical images such as these are a tribute to the Celtic imagination. The incredibly vibrant colors of the manuscripts which survive to this day reveal the rich vitality and beauty which formed the perception of the Celtic monks. Their art deeply expresses the joy of life and the goodness of creation which are central to Celtic Christianity. The illuminated manuscripts as well as the high crosses are ultimately a profound celebration of cosmic harmony and unity.

Interlacing border from the Book of Durrow

SACRED SHRINES

A major expression of Celtic Christian spirituality which honored the Earth involved devotional practices at sacred shrines in nature. In these spiritual activities we can especially see the influence of earlier pagan Celtic belief that the land was sacred. This has also been an avenue through which the Divine Feminine was able to manifest in Celtic Christianity, for pagan Celtic goddesses such as Macha, Etain, and Anu were associated with the land itself. For example, the "Paps of Anu" are mountains in County Kerry, Ireland, that were once thought to be sacred to Anu, perhaps even embodying the goddess in her form of Earth Mother. There are literally hundreds of mountains, rivers, lakes, springs and other places that were once sacred to goddesses throughout Ireland and Great Britain. Ancient pagan Celts had looked upon the Earth as the Mother, the Birth-Giver, the Source of All. The spirit of the Divine Mother pervaded everything in the natural world. Sources of water especially became associated with the Goddess because water came up from the Great Mother Earth and was necessary for maintaining life. Among the pagan Celts, each spring and well was named for a local goddess. This goddess served as a protectress, a source for inspiration, a healer, and an oracle. Thus, the area of the spring or well became a place of communion and reverence by the clan. Pagan Celts believed that the human spirit resided in the head and so triumphant warriors would decapitate their enemies and bring the heads back to the clan. If the head was that of a chief or other powerful person, it would be placed in the well so that the water would henceforth have the spirit and power of that person within it. When Celtic Christianity was well established, sacred springs and wells honored by Celtic pagans were given Christian associations and named for angels or saints with similar attributes to the pagan spirits or gods. Since the early Celts had viewed the spring as the source of the "living water" which flows from the Earth Mother, the Divine Feminine continued to be honored in the Celtic Christian shrines at holy wells. For example, many wells and springs had been dedicated to the Mother Goddess Anu by the pagan Celts. Christian clergy simply changed Anu to St. Anne, the mother of Mary, and appropriated Anu's attributes and gave them to Anne.[34] Christian clergy also on occasion even continued the practice of placing heads in the wells. Instead of the heads of enemies from the battlefield, these were the heads of saints! If the saint's head was placed in a well that had been a pagan oracle, it was believed by the Christian faithful that the water from the well would enable the drinker to receive the saint's prophecy.[35]

Many sacred wells were used for baptism by the Celtic Christians. This continued a practice common to the pagan Celts as Alexander Carmichael explains: "It is known that a form of baptism prevailed among the Celts previous to the introduction of Christianity. Whenever possible the Celtic Church 'Christianized' existing ceremonies and days of special observance, grafting the new on the old."[36] In a practice reminiscent of earlier pagan customs, the midwife performed a Christian birth baptism as soon as the baby was delivered in order to protect the soul of the infant from being taken away by the sidhe or fairies. This was accomplished by sprinkling three drops of water on the forehead of the infant while saying this prayer:

> . . .The little drop of the Father
> On thy little forehead, beloved one.
> The little drop of the Son
> On thy little forehead, beloved one.
> The little drop of the Spirit
> On thy little forehead, beloved one.
> To aid thee, to guard thee,
> To shield thee , to surround thee.
> To keep thee from the fays,
> To shield thee from the host.
> To sain thee from the gnome,
> To deliver thee from the spectre.
> The little drop of the Three

To shield thee from the sorrow.
The little drop of the Three
To fill thee with Their pleasantness.
The little drop of the Three,
To fill thee with Their virtue.
O the little drop of the Three
To fill thee with Their virtue.[37]

While in this baptism prayer the three drops symbolize the Holy Trinity of Father, Son and Spirit, in pagan times they would have signified the three aspects of the Mother Goddess. Christian and pagan elements are closely interwoven throughout the prayer. The church baptism then took place at the eighth day after birth and if a sacred well was available, the water for the baptism came from the well. Many of these wells were dedicated to St. Brigit as the protector of infants, holy midwife, wet nurse, and guardian of women in labor.[38] Celtic Christians continued to revere ancient wells even after attempts by the Roman Church officials to forbid worshipping at them during the fifth and sixth centuries. However, Pope Gregory the Great, at the beginning of the seventh century, issued an edict stating that "objects of pagan worship should be dedicated to Christ."[39] He also indicated that all wells should be named for saints and encouraged the annual "glorification of a well" in the local parishes.[40] To this day, "rounds" are made to many of the ancient wells. Devout Christians in Ireland still travel to sacred wells such as those associated with St. Gobnet in Ballyvourney and St. Brigit in Kildare where Christian prayers honor the Divine Feminine in the form of the female saint.

St. Brigit's Well, Kildare, Ireland

Another essential aspect of Celtic Christianity which is still practiced today, especially in Ireland, is the pilgrimage or making the "rounds." The traditional Christian pilgrimage derived from pagan practices which honored the spirits of nature and the sacred landscape. Human beings who lived in close contact with the natural world recognized a reciprocal relationship between human consciousness and the "soul" of nature. Ancient practices of pilgrimage to sacred shrines were a form of communion with the goddess of Mother Earth. Although the penitential aspect of Christian pilgrimage is emphasized today, one wonders whether this is a later overlay of Roman Catholicism based on the belief of "original sin" which requires atonement. If instead earlier Celtic Christian pilgrimage practices had a closer affinity to their pagan predecessors, the purpose of the pilgrimage might have emphasized attuning one's soul to the power of the divine which resides in the natural world. It is in this sense that Christian pilgrimage can involve communion with Sophia in her aspect as World Soul.

Many pagan elements were incorporated into the Christian practice of "rounds," including a recognition of the power of the elements and a reverence for the forces of nature. Many "stations" are found at megalithic tombs which are made up of huge cairns of stones. The Christian pilgrim acknowledges the sacred power found in the stones in a manner similar to the statement of Jesus in the Gospel of Thomas: "Lift up the stone and you will find me there."[41] At some stations, Christian prayer is combined with the sacred practice of touching one's hand to the stone and then to the head, thus assimilating the power in the stone within oneself. At other stations, special stones may be present which contain special properties of healing. One may pass the stone around one's body in a prescribed way in order to bring the healing power within oneself. Sometimes these stones are even "loaned out" to people in the community who are in need of healing and not able to make the rounds. A number of traditional pilgrimages to Celtic holy places are still conducted today. One of these is the "an Turas," Irish for "the Journey," which is still performed at Glencolumcille (the "valley of Columcille") on June 9, the feast day of Columcille or Columba.[42] When Columcille established his monastery in this beautiful glen in the mountainous land of northwestern Ireland in the sixth century, he found numerous pagan standing stones already present as well as megalithic tombs which were the legendary beds of the lovers Diarmuid and Gráinne of the Irish pagan sagas. According to tradition, the saint had Christian symbols engraved on the standing stones and instituted the practice of performing "turas" or "stations" around them. This was an ingenious way of incorporating the people's earlier pagan beliefs and practices into Christian devotion.

Standing Stone with Cross
Glen Columcille, Ireland

The contemporary Glencolumcille pilgrimage is a three-mile circular route through the valley which consists of fifteen stations that incorporate Christianized standing stones, megalithic tombs and cairns, and a holy well. The pilgrim normally circles each station three times clockwise, performing specific spiritual acts and prayers at each station.[43]

Another important site of pilgrimage for contemporary Christians is the summit of Croagh Patrick or The Reek, known as the sacred mountain Cruachán Aigle to the pre-Christian Celts. This conical mountain, its slopes covered with scree and topped with white quartz, rises like a dark brooding presence over the landscape of County Mayo in western Ireland. The summit of Croagh Patrick is usually hidden in the clouds, which further adds to the mystical aura surrounding the mountain. Upon viewing Croagh Patrick, it

189

is no wonder that the pagan Celts considered this to be a mountain of special holiness, and that it is still the most sacred mountain in Ireland for Christians today.

For the pagan Celts, Cruachán Aigle was associated with the goddess of fertility. Women who desired to bear children slept in the "bed" of the goddess on the summit on the eve of Lughnasa, the Celtic feast day on August 1 which celebrated the first fruits of the harvest. Cruachán Aigle was also traditionally associated with the Celtic god of the harvest, Crom Dubh, whose feast was celebrated at the end of July. These associations are retained even today in the date of the contemporary Christian pilgrimage, Reek Sunday, which is the last Sunday of July.[44] St. Patrick made the journey up the mountain in the fifth century and fasted for forty days and nights during Lent. He then instituted the practice of Christian pilgrimage to the summit of the mountain which then came to bear his name.[45] The modern pilgrim thus follows in the footsteps of other pilgrims who have trod this path for 1500 years. He or she walks up the steep ascent of 2510 feet, stopping at several "stations" for devotional acts, until reaching the summit where a modern chapel now stands. The Christian mass pilgrimages up Croagh Patrick typically ended with earthy festivities when the exhilaration of the ascent and descent was accomplished, another practice which harkens back to pagan times. In fact, the subsequent drinking and sexual activities brought condemnation of the pilgrimage activities by the Roman Catholic Church in the nineteenth century. However, the merrymaking at the end of the pilgrimage would seem to be consistent with the Celtic Christian integration of the physical and spiritual worlds. It seems only natural that the joy and ecstasy to be found in the earthly delights of food, drink, and love-making would accompany the adoration of the Creator.

View of the Pilgrim's Path from near the summit of Croagh Patrick, Ireland

THE SIGNIFICANCE OF CELTIC CHRISTIANITY FOR THE NATURE BYPATH

The recovery of the vital elements of Celtic Christianity is immensely valuable to the development of an ecological spirituality which is firmly rooted in Christian tradition. By getting in touch with the perceptions and practices of these early Christians who walked firmly on the nature bypath, we can help restore the necessary eros to contemporary Christianity. If we follow the examples of the Celtic monks by attuning ourselves to the natural world, we too may perceive the close connection between the earthly and spiritual worlds. Through cultivating the intuitive, imaginative faculties of our eros nature, we can experience the divine essence within all aspects of creation and recognize the interconnectedness of all life. Through the Celtic heritage, which is open to all Christians, we can rediscover spiritual practices which honor the Earth as a manifestation of the Divine.

Many elements of Celtic spirituality are still alive in the Celtic lands today, especially in Ireland. Many modern Irish Christians still pray for blessings at holy wells dedicated to the local saint, and

191

practice the devotion of pilgrimage to sacred sites as their ancestors have done for thousands of years. In many places in Britain and Ireland, small groups of Christians have committed themselves to restoring and maintaining their Celtic heritage. An especially beautiful synthesis of the ancient Celtic traditions and Christianity is found at Ballintubber Abbey in County Mayo. Here the people of the community have restored the old abbey which marks the start of the "Tochair Padraig," the pilgrimage route to Croagh Patrick. They are preserving the ancient practice of pilgrimage to the holy mountain as a spiritually meaningful act for modern Christians. The Abbey is the center at which three pathways converge; in addition to St. Patrick's track way, pilgrims may also travel the Way of the Cross and the Way of Mary. This latter pathway, also called the Rosary Way, is a unique depiction of Mary's pilgrimage through life as expressed through Celtic spirituality. Celtic traditional symbols, standing stones, dolmens, and stone circles are incorporated into the devotional "stations" which represent the significant markers of the life of Mary. The Divine Feminine is symbolically expressed through the profusion of flowers and water which are present everywhere along the Rosary Way, and its culmination in the beautiful natural setting of a holy well. In walking the Way of Mary at Ballintubber, the modern pilgrim can truly experience the heart of Celtic Christianity in its interweaving of the feminine and nature bypaths.

Similar dedication to blazing the trail of the nature bypath through restoring the treasures of Celtic Christianity is found throughout the British Isles. Another center for this work is at Holy Island, off the coast of Northumberland, England, the ancient monastic site of Lindisfarne which was founded by St. Aiden in the seventh century. This became a major pilgrimage site in England as the shrine of St. Cuthbert, and the place where the famous Lindisfarne Gospels were created. David Adam, recent vicar of the parish church of St. Mary on Holy Island, is committed to the preservation of the Celtic Christian tradition as shown in his many books such as *The Edge of Glory: Prayers in the Celtic Tradition.* The small church of St. Mary recognizes its mission in educating people about the Celtic heritage within Christianity which is still alive today. Traditional Celtic symbolism is found throughout the Church, including a carpet woven by the women of the island which is based on the Celtic designs from the Lindisfarne Gospels.

A similar commitment to the Celtic tradition may be seen at St. Fergus Kirk in Glamis, Scotland, named for the saint of the early eighth century. The kirk (church) was built next to Glamis Den, a wooded area which is the site of the cave and well of St. Fergus. A minister of the church in the early part of the 20th century recognized the importance of the Celtic heritage of this place and the congregation appears to be actively preserving it. They have restored the holy well and use its water for baptisms. A walkway was built to make the sacred site of Glamis Den accessible and beautiful flowers are planted throughout the area. The physical renewal of this ancient site has also restored the "spirit" of the place. When one sits quietly by the well and gazes upon the water and the flowers, there is a palpable feeling of peace and love. The appreciation of these modern Christians for their Celtic heritage which perceived God in the beauty of the natural world is being shared with today's pilgrims who come to visit this sacred site.

The small isle of Iona in the Scottish Hebrides, founded by St. Columba (Columcille) in the sixth century, remains true to its ancient heritage as a major place of pilgrimage today. Despite the lengthy journey to this small outpost of Celtic Christianity, Iona draws thousands of people each year from all around the world who are seeking a deeper spiritual experience in the manner of the Celtic saints. The wild, primitive beauty of this land of rock, moor, and sea makes it very easy to connect with elemental nature as did the Celtic monks of long ago. The Iona Community, an ecumenical group with worldwide membership which maintains a residence on Iona, provides an excellent model for the restoration of a Celtic spirituality which is open to all regardless of geographical locality. The worship services of the Community, which are held in the restored medieval Abbey, are imbued with the spirit of Celtic Christianity as they emphasize wholeness, the integration of the spiritual and the secular, and the celebration of the Divine in all creation. Traditional Celtic Christian prayers are updated into a modern form and incorporated into contemporary rites of worship where men and women participate equally in the services.

Places such as Ballintubber Abbey, St. Mary's parish church of Holy Island, St. Fergus Kirk, and the Iona Community demonstrate what a small group of loving and dedicated people can accomplish in integrating Celtic Christianity into modern times. These places emit a spark of light - small but powerful - reaching out to connect with other sacred places on the Earth and helping to rekindle the Light of the World which is found in all creation. Pilgrims who walk on the nature bypath, regardless of nationality, can be inspired by these trailblazers in their quest to develop an ecological spirituality. For the essential aspect of Celtic spirituality which must be renewed today is the recognition of the Divine within the natural world and respect for the sacredness of Mother Earth and all her creatures.

CHAPTER VII: THE GREEN MAN

God is my sap: the leaves and buds I show,
They are his Holy Ghost, by whom I grow.[1]

In the preceding quote that appears in a 17th century alchemical text, God is equated with the "sap" of the archetypal Tree – the vital energy that nourishes the growth of the green world of nature. This divine fructifying principle of life has also been known throughout the ages as the Green Man. It is the Green Man who accompanies us when we walk on the nature bypath and open ourselves to our surroundings. If we allow him to guide us, he can help us become vital citizens of the sacred community that we share with the natural world. His return to human consciousness is the power behind the emergence of ecological spirituality.

As we travel along the bypath, we realize that the Green Man is the embodiment of Hildegard's *veriditas*; he is the divine essence in the overarching trees, in the myriad plants at our feet, in the mosses on the rocks, in the verdant air we breathe. He is the juiciness of the sap that rises and renews life each spring; he is the "blood" of the plant kingdom that sustains all animal life. We usually see images of the Green Man as a figure dressed in green leafy attire, or as a head surrounded by leaves, and even with leaves sprouting from his mouth, brow, ears, eyes, cheeks, chin or nose. This synthesis of the human and plant kingdoms is a powerful lesson for modern humanity of the symbiotic relationship we have with nature and the need to nurture that relationship.

In his book *Green Man*, William Anderson gives a beautiful description of the vitality of this archetype:

> As the disgorger or devourer of vegetation he speaks of
> the mysteries of creation in time, of the hidden sources of
> inspiration, and of the dark nothingness out of which we
> come and to which we return. As the fruit of vegetation, he
> signifies the mystery of law and intelligence in natural forms
> and expresses our own instinctive desire to anthropomorphize
> everything that is beautiful, touching or powerful in the world
> about us. In all his forms he is the Poet who in revealing
> mysteries opens up even more wonderful and enticing
> mysteries beyond the words he speaks.[2]

The "mysteries of creation in time" refer to the most basic aspect of the archetype of the Green Man: the cycle of decay and renewal. The Green Man disgorges vegetation in the spring and devours it in the fall. All of creation in time is cyclical; all natural life exhibits the process of birth and death and rebirth - the central mystery of Christ's incarnation, crucifixion and resurrection. In this light, we can see why the Green Man is such a significant aspect of the nature bypath. For the Green Man forges a connection between the hidden tradition of Christian spirituality and the ancient Earth mysteries. By dancing with the Green Man, we enter into the deepest mysteries of life itself. By acknowledging the presence of the Green Man, we join the multitudes of humans who have celebrated the divine dance of creation with him from the beginnings of human existence.

THE ARCHETYPAL SIGNIFICANCE OF THE GREEN MAN

The Green Man is a very ancient archetype, first appearing in prehistoric times in cultures all over the world as evidenced by the numerous fertility statues and cave-paintings of phallic beings and creatures. Like Sophia, he represents one of the most fundamental archetypes and has worn many symbolic masks throughout history. His earliest historical appearances are in Egypt as the god Min, who bestowed sexual vigor to humanity, and Osiris, the god of grain and vegetation who was usually depicted with a green body. To the Sumerians he was known as the fertility god Dumuzi; to the Akkadians, he was Tammuz, the consort of Ishtar. In Palestine, the Green Man appeared as Baal, the lord of the furrows of the field, and to the Hittites he was the god of agriculture, Telipinu. The Greeks knew him as Dionysus, god of the vine and intoxication and Pan, god of shepherds and unbridled procreation; and the Phrygians as Attis, the self-mutilated god of Spring, and Priapos, the satyr-like fertility god. Saturnus, the Roman god of sowing and seed-corn; Silvanus, the god of gardens and the fertile countryside; and Bacchus, the Roman equivalent of Dionysus, embodied the archetype of the Green Man.

The Green Man and Sacred Trees

The Green Man with his leafy attributes is closely associated with trees, especially the ash and the oak. Trees have always had special significance to humans for their life-giving qualities, and we find allusions to the sacredness of trees in most cultures. Among animistic societies, trees were considered to be ensouled by spirits; they could be the dwelling places of the souls of departed ancestors. According to John and Caitlin Matthews, "An oak-tree was a tree, but also the indwelling god of the forest, a totem of the Green Man. When the tribal ruler dressed himself in oak leaves, he became the living embodiment of the god himself."[3] Thus the shaman became the oracle of the god by participating in the archetype of the Green Man and performing rituals at the sacred oak.

The Tree of Life, a central image associated with the Green Man, appears as a motif in many religions. To the Nordic peoples there is the gigantic ash tree, Yggdrasil, which spreads over the entire world and binds earth, heaven, and hell together. It was on this tree that their father god Odin suffered for nine days. Groves of trees, termed *nemeton* by the Romans, were sacred to the Iron-Age Celts. Roman historians such as Lucan wrote about the Celts of Gaul who worshipped in groves of trees. Some of their shrines may have stood within these sacred groves.[4] Along the Rhine River, there are ancient Celtic altars to the Great Mother which have sacred trees as their focus. In Celtic lore, the symbol for the Otherworld was the apple tree in which lived the goddess Cliodna's magical birds whose song healed all those who heard them. In the Celtic Fionn Cycle the Tree of Immortality exists at the center of the Forest of Duvnos, guarded by a fierce one-eyed monster named Sharvan the Surly.

The Tree of Life is also a major symbol within the Bible, appearing in the beginning in the Garden of Eden in Genesis and at the end in the Heavenly City in the Book of Revelation. The sacred tree is the tree of immortality (Gen. 3:22) and healing (Rev. 22:2). As we have seen, in Biblical tradition the Tree of Life is associated with the Divine Feminine for Proverbs 3:18 refers to Sophia: "She is a tree of life to those who lay hold of her..." The importance of trees in our Judeo-Christian culture is seen in the fact that the Garden of Eden is actually a garden of trees - plants and bushes are not mentioned. "And the Lord God planted a garden in Eden...And out of the ground the Lord God made to grow every tree that is pleasant to the sight and good for food, the tree of life also in the midst of the garden, and the tree of the knowledge of good and evil." (Gen. 2:8-9) Perhaps the Garden of Eden would be better named the Grove of Eden!

Trees were so closely associated with sacred symbolism in ancient cultures that when one religion sought to overthrow the deities of another, one of the best ways to destroy the power of the old gods was by cutting down their sacred groves. While Christian theologians honored the Tree of Life and even associated it with the Cross of Calvary, they zealously cut down the pagan sacred groves. For some reason, these fanatic theologians had no trouble assigning saints to replace the pagan deities of the sacred springs and wells, yet they would not do so in the case of the sacred trees and groves. There are many accounts of their destruction under the careful scrutiny of pious bishops.[5] Yet the great Celtic Christian saint, Columba, the founder of Iona, "deplored the destruction of an oak-grove at Derry and forbade the felling of oaks."[6] Having been raised as an Irish pagan, he was doubtless aware that it was a serious offense to cut down an oak tree. Thus, Columba helped to stop the wanton destruction of the ancient groves.

In our modern world we have strayed far from our ancestors who firmly believed in the spirits of the trees, their sacredness with the Earth, and their central place in all of the natural landscape. Today, much of the industrialized world talks about "harvesting" trees, creating tree "farms" where genetically engineered trees will grow fast and straight and resistant to insects and other "natural" predators, and managing the forests to create an environmental balance between recreation and sustainability. If there is a symbolic representation of the dissociation modern humanity has with the natural world it is the deteriorating condition of the world's forests. By exploring the nature bypath, we can once again experience the sacredness of trees as we rediscover our sylvan heritage within Christian tradition. It is the Green Man, the spiritual essence of the trees, which we need to contact to help us once again be caretakers of the Earth rather than exploiters of it.

The Vegetation God

The archetype of the Green Man in his myriad guises also represents the death and renewal of the seasons including the sowing and reaping cycle upon which early agricultural societies were dependent. We have lost that dependence in the modern technological world due to efficient methods of long-term storage, refrigeration, and transportation. Most people in Western civilization today have never sown nor reaped any crop, so we are blissfully unaware of any climatic effects of nature on our food supply. We might complain about the price of tomatoes after a drought, but we expect to have tomatoes any time of year. But in earlier societies in which physical survival was much more precarious, people were deeply aware of their dependence upon Mother Earth who could give or withhold her bounty. Especially in northern climates which have four distinct seasons, the rebirth of plant life (the "greening" or "springing forth") after the "death" of the winter season was cause for great rejoicing. So the Green Man evolved from the ancient "agri-cultures" as a figure of vibrant energy closely associated with Mother Nature.

The Green Man as the god of vegetation was personified in many different forms throughout the ancient world. The myth of the Sumerian god Dumuzi, known as Tammuz to the Akkadians and Adonis to the Greeks, recounted his annual sojourn in the lower world for half the year and his subsequent return in Spring to the upper world. The Phrygian god Attis, who was often identified with corn as well as the pine tree, followed a similar cyclical pattern. This mythic death and rebirth of the god clearly represents the cycle of vegetative life, which is buried in the earth for half a year before it rises above ground. As Sir James Frazer has shown, it was natural for agricultural peoples to interpret "the dying and reviving god as the reaped and sprouting grain."[7]

The Egyptian god Osiris, who was revered for introducing agriculture to Egypt, followed the same archetypal pattern. Stories of the death, dismemberment, and scattering of the body parts of this vegetation god across the land are mythic representations of the sowing of the grain. The rebirth of Osiris in the Spring brought the promise of eternal life and provided the basis for the elaborate death rituals to insure immortality which were a hallmark of Egyptian culture.[8] The Greek god Dionysius, known as Bacchus in Rome, who is best known for his association with the vine and the intoxication which comes from the juice of its grapes, also participated in the mythic pattern of the vegetation gods in his violent death and resurrection. Other references to his role as a vegetation god include his work in plowing and scattering seeds and his emblem of the winnowing-fan which was used to separate grain from the chaff. Dionysius' similarity to many other vegetation gods is also shown in his connection with trees, especially the pine and fruit trees.[9]

As we have seen, the vegetation god embodied the power inherent to the grain crops upon which agricultural societies depended. But he also was associated with trees and forests, vines and shrubs, nuts and fruits - all unruly vegetation in a natural state. In both his cultivated and his wild condition, the seasonal cycle of the vegetation god was crucial for the life and death of early agricultural peoples.

The Green Man and the Divine Feminine

Whenever the archetype of the Green Man appears, we also inevitably find the presence of the Divine Feminine. For the Green Man and the Goddess represent the archetypal masculine and feminine polarities which are the source of created life. In ancient cultures the Green Man often took the form of the son/lover of the Goddess. For example, the vegetation gods Dumuzi, Tammuz, and Attis who were referred to as "the Green One,"[10] were both the son and lover of the Goddess in her forms as Inanna, Ishtar, and Kybele.

Anne Baring and Jules Cashford explain the archetypal significance of this myth of the son-god in this way:

> The Goddess may be understood as the eternal cycle of the whole: the unity of life and death as a single process. The young...god is her mortal form in time, as manifested life... subject to a cyclical process of birth, flowering, decay, death and rebirth.[11]

Thus the Goddess as the infinite, timeless, unchanging aspect of life gives birth to her son as the finite, temporal, changing mode of life that we are so familiar with as we view the natural world, the change of the seasons, and our own short human life spans. It is this tragic sense of the decay and death that is inherent to natural life that the Green Man personifies but also transcends in the ancient myths. For the young god is sacrificed, descends into the darkness of the underworld where the Goddess as his mother/lover must search for him, and is subsequently reborn. It is easy to see the connection between this myth and the seasonal cycles of the sacrifice of the crops at harvest time, the death of vegetation during the dark, cold winter, and the rebirth of plant life in the Spring. For the return of the young god in the greening of the Earth, embraced by the warmth of the Spring, heralds the joyful news that life is reborn from death. This yearly cycle of the vegetation god was the mythic basis for the death and resurrection drama which was ritually celebrated throughout the ancient Near East and Mediterranean cultures. In some cases this ritual may have been literally enacted in the death of the year king and his rebirth in the crowning of the new king.[12]

The celebration in Spring of the resurrection of the God from his sojourn in the underworld culminated in his union with the Goddess in the sacred marriage or *hieros gamos*. The ritual enactment of this union was accomplished by the king or high priest of the city, in the role of the resurrected vegetation god, and the priestess who represented the Goddess. It was this rite of the sacred marriage, the union of the Goddess and Green Man, which was critical for insuring the fertility of the Earth.[13] The celebration of the sacred marriage honored not only the fecundity of the plant and animal kingdoms, but also the sexuality of men and women. For the Green Man in his totality embodies the life force; he is the instinctual energy which causes the rising of the tree sap as well as the human phallus.

In Celtic lands, the sacred marriage was mirrored in the union of the King with Sovereignty, the Goddess of the Land. As the divine embodiment of the natural world, the Celtic goddess Sovereignty is linked to the Biblical figure of Sophia. Sovereignty takes the forms of earthly Queen as well as Otherworldly woman in Celtic mythology. But in all of her guises Sovereignty represents the land itself. The fruitfulness of the land, and the wellbeing of its people, depends upon the true union of a worthy King and Sovereignty. Thus in the Arthurian myths, the Wasteland is caused by the breakdown of the relationship between King Arthur and Sovereignty.[14]

These ancient fertility rituals appeared in more recent times in the European festivals of May Day which to this day celebrate the renewal of life in the Spring. The honoring of the flower-bedecked May Queen, who is Sovereignty in her Flower Maiden aspect,[15] and her consort the May King are reminiscent of the sacred marriage ritual enacted in earlier times. Although the rites of the sacrifice of the God and the sacred marriage are no longer literally enacted, the archetypal meanings of these ritual dramas are still present today. As Baring and Cashford explain:

> The sacred marriage in which the Mother Goddess as bride is united with her son as lover, reconnects symbolically the two "worlds" of *zoe* – eternal and infinite life - and *bios* - finite and individual life - and it is this union that regenerates the earth.[16]

The sacred marriage of the Divine Feminine with her consort, the Green Man, reunites the eternal with the temporal, the invisible with the visible, and the spiritual realm with its manifestation in the natural world.

The Wild Man

The Green Man is closely connected to the archetype of the Wild Man and they appear, disappear, and reappear together throughout recorded history. The Wild Man, who is frequently called Wodewose (a creature living in the woods), is always a creature of the wild woods - the domain of the Green Man. The symbols of Pan, Herne the Hunter, King of the Wood, and Merlin, to name a few, indicate the primitive, instinctual wild man who has little or no civilized attributes. In the medieval concept of the chain of being of God's creation, the Green Man represented the highest level that the plant kingdom could attain - the humanized plant, and the Wild Man represented the lowest level of the human - the "animalized" human. Thus, the two archetypes stood next to each other on the chain of being.

Some of the more famous appearances of the Wild Man archetype in history are as Enkidu in the *Epic of Gilgamesh*, as the prophet Elijah in the Old Testament, as Polyphemus the Cyclopes in Homer's *The Odyssey*, as Merlin in the Caledonian Forest in the medieval *Vita Merlini,* as Caliban in Shakespeare's *The Tempest* and as "Tarzan of the Apes" in the 20th century. The Wild Man often appears in medieval art as a giant or as an exceptionally hairy normal-sized man and even sometimes as an ugly dwarf. He is usually depicted as extremely stupid, incapable of speech, and prone to violent outbursts of temper with resulting death and destruction of any creature or property in his vicinity. The Wild Man symbolizes the reckless, impulsive, physically self-assertive, primitive nature of mankind which is totally antithetical to civilized society. The Wild Man is frequently described as "lunatic" and while in this state, can be prophetic. This trait indicates the Wild Man's relationship with the Goddess since the very term lunatic means to be moon-struck, i.e., to be filled with the eros wisdom of Sophia rather than the logos reason of the solar God. An interesting example is the prophet Elijah, who is described as a "hairy man with a leather belt around his waist" (2Kings 1:8) When in his prophetic state he talks with Yahweh, but in his everyday state he is considered lunatic. In Islam, Elijah's name is Khidir, which means "Green One." So Elijah exhibits both the Wild Man and Green Man aspects of the archetype.

The lunatic Wild Man can be tamed and turned into a civilized human being since the logos attributes are always latent and only have to be stimulated in order to manifest. Since the Church was primarily concerned with leading souls to Christ, the concept of curing or redeeming the Wild Man from his lunacy and wildness became a potent symbol for redemption of pagans who had followed the Old Religion of the Goddess.

Notwithstanding the prophet Elijah, from the medieval point of view the Wild Man, as a bestial sub-human creature, is incapable of ever knowing God. However, he is also incapable of knowing **any** form of God so he could not represent heresy or idolatry. The Wild Man lives in a state of primordial innocence - without guile, deceit, or treachery. He can symbolically represent the lost golden age of Paradise wherein humanity lived a simple, bucolic life, undisturbed by the complexity and artificiality of modern civilization with its arts of technology, mining, metallurgy, and war. Of course, the Hellenic Greeks of Plato's era also considered themselves to be a modern civilization and yearned for the simple life of Arcadia lost in the mists of time. Every civilization and every generation continues the myth about the golden age of the distant past where life was simpler and more secure and predictable. From this myth the Wild Man appears as the Noble Savage who can help the modern civilized generation rediscover what was lost by becoming civilized. The Green Man also participates in this myth since the lost Paradise is always a garden or grove which supplies all of the needs of its inhabitants.

We have seen that the Green Man appears in many guises with unique qualities and aspects; nevertheless, he manifests through them all. Like all archetypes, he has a complex nature with attributes as diverse as fertility, prophecy, vitality, trickiness, sexuality, healing, inspiration, drunkenness, playfulness, wildness, creativity, and love. Because it is these characteristics of the Green Man which can restore the necessary eros to Christianity, it is imperative that we discover his significance in Christian symbolism. However, we must first understand his role in the Earth mysteries of pagan mythology in order to discern his presence, which was usually disguised, within later Christian tradition.

THE GREEN MAN IN PAGAN MYTHOLOGY

As we have seen, the archetype of the Green Man appeared in the earliest civilizations long before the appearance of Christianity. In ancient agricultural societies, the Green Man was the vegetation god that was sacrificed as an offering to the Great Mother who was the vital spirit of the fruitful Earth. As E. O. James explains, the purpose for this sacrifice was to ensure "the continuance of the crops through the potency of the mother symbol, the newly reaped cereals transmitting to the earth and the crops renewed energy to produce their fruits by virtue of the life-giving qualities with which they are charged."[17] The Green Man was thus the "newly reaped cereals," the vegetative sacrifice by which the Great Mother was honored.

Once the sacrifice had been made, the sacred marriage could occur that united the old with the new. For example, in Babylon the marriage took place between the water and the land since the fertility of the land was dependent upon the annual flooding of the Tigris and Euphrates. Tammuz, whose name means "lord of the flood," was directly responsible for the greening of the land. Tammuz was the living water which was born in the winter rains, died by drying up during the summer drought, and was reborn in the following winter rains. E. O. James says, "As the personification of the fertilizing waters which flooded the land in winter and which died away in summer, Tammuz was regarded as the source and controller of vegetation *par excellence*, and, therefore, the corn-spirit who dies and comes to life again every year."[18] Ishtar, the goddess symbolizing the land fertilized by the living water of Tammuz, was the *mater dolorosa*, grieving mother, in the summer when she went about looking for her son who had been sacrificed for the vegetation. A similar relationship existed between Isis and Osiris in Egypt. Isis was the goddess symbolizing the earth of the floodplain while Osiris was the god symbolizing the flooding waters of the Nile. However, Isis was called the "creatrix of the Nile flood"[19] so she can be considered the primal desire or need of the land that instigated the fertilizing flood. As E. O. James so aptly put it: ". . .the sacrificial ritual has emerged as a means of controlling the processes of vegetation... When this system of offerings is brought into relation with the death and resurrection drama, it assumes a mystery significance as part of the culture pattern centering in the divine kingship and its relations to the natural order. . ."[20] The Green Man as the divine Corn-King or Life-giving Water had to be killed so that his sacrifice would vitalize nature through the process of rebirth.

The representation of the Green Man as a foliate head or leaf mask also appeared first in pagan cultures. One of the earliest examples is found in a temple dedicated to Bacchus at Baalbek, Lebanon, which was built during the reign of the Roman Emperor Antonius Pius (138-161 C. E.).[21] Since the cult of Dionysius was the origin of classical Greek tragedy, and we know that tragic actors always wore a mask, it is not too big a risk to assume that the appearance of the Green Man as a leaf mask of Bacchus at Baalbek was a direct result of the practice of the Dionysian/Bacchan cult. Of course, Baal was a primary vegetation deity in the Middle East so the leaf mask may also be derived from his worship.

A contemporaneous Green Man, only partially visible due to deterioration, appears on the façade of a mid-second century temple at Al Hadr, Iraq.[22] In addition to leaves sprouting from the cheeks, chin and mouth, snakes appear to be issuing from his hair or from behind his head. The serpents on or by his head could be an example of his role as consort to the Great Goddess as evidenced in the famous statuette of the Minoan Snake-goddess from Knossos. The juxtaposition of serpents and leaves are an indication of the vitality of the *veriditas,* the union of the animal and plant kingdoms as well as the human and divine in the natural order.

In Celtic Europe, we find the pagan Green Man in the guises of Belenus, Robin of the Wood, Robin Goodfellow, Puck, Green Jack or Jack-in-the-Green, Green George, the Green Knight, Merlin, the King of the Wood, the King of May, Herne the Hunter, Cernunnos, John Barley-corn, among others. As the archetype of the Green Man was being gradually assimilated into Christianity, he still appeared prominently in many of the ancient pagan legends and festivals such as those found in the Arthurian cycle and the increasingly popular Robin Hood and Wild Man plays. These potent pagan figures fertilized the arid theology of the institutional medieval Church with the green earthiness found on the nature bypath.

The central Green Man figure of the Arthurian legends is Gawain. Originally a Celtic hero with the name of Gwalchmai, Gawain was Arthur's foremost champion in the earliest pagan versions of the story. His personification of the Green Man is seen in his association with the Divine Feminine, for Gawain was the Champion of the Goddess of the Land, Sovereignty.[23] However, by the 12th century, Gawain became superceded by the chivalric courtly Christian knights Lancelot, Perceval, and Galahad since he didn't represent the spiritual virtues of the institutional Church. Gawain was the purely natural man, the embodiment of the secular hero who was to be admired, but he was not a role model for attaining Heaven. Since Gawain was so strongly associated with Sovereignty, the Christian authorities who sought to eliminate any devotion to the pagan goddesses significantly downplayed his role in the Christianized medieval Arthurian romances. He was relegated to the bypaths by the Church and we now find him as a central figure on the nature bypath of Christianity: he is the Green Man as champion of Sophia in her guise as Sovereignty. Even though he was no longer the central hero of the medieval Arthurian tales, Gawain did become the protagonist in one of the most popular late medieval romances, the 14th century *Sir Gawain and the Green Knight.*

Sir Gawain and the Green Knight is a Christianized version of a common pagan legend usually referred to as the Beheading Game. In it, the king's greatest champion is challenged to behead an otherworldly larger-than-life figure with the understanding that the hero will allow himself to be beheaded a year hence - a theme that is reminiscent of the ancient sacrifice of the year-king. In this story, the Beheading Game begins in mid-winter at the Christmas Feast in King Arthur's Court. Gawain decapitates the Green Knight with the knight's own axe whereupon the Green Knight picks up his severed head and rides off, reminding Gawain that he has promised to receive a like blow at the Green Chapel in one year. The following year, as Gawain searches for the Green Chapel, he tarries for a few days at the castle of Sir Bercilak. Although the Lady Bercilak attempts to seduce him, he chivalrously accepts only her kiss and a green baldric. In his subsequent fateful meeting with the Green Knight, Gawain suffers only a slight blow of the axe to his neck, and learns that the Green Knight is actually the enchanted form of Sir Bercilak.

The characters of both Gawain and the Green Knight symbolize the Green Man who can be found on the nature bypath. Even through the thin veneer of Christianity in this tale which refers to the feast of Christmas, we can glimpse the pagan symbolism of the ancient solstice rites of Midwinter. For the Green Knight represents the ancient King of Winter, who is frequently depicted wearing holly and trimmed in evergreen boughs. Although at first he appears to be a figure of death, he is truly a figure of life. Even when all appears dead and barren, there is still the *veriditas* - the green life force waiting to be reborn. This meaning can still be seen in the prominent use of holly and evergreen in our celebrations of Christmas, which are still powerful symbols of new life as represented in the birth of Christ in the bleak darkness of Midwinter.

In this story which introduces earlier pagan themes into a Christian setting, Gawain appears to have forgotten his pagan heritage as the champion of the Goddess Sovereignty. He must go on a quest to reestablish his relationship to the Goddess and once again take on the mantle of the Green Man. Gawain can be seen as representing the human being of this time period who was losing contact with the inner Green Man. By the High Middle Ages of the 13th and 14th centuries, the Divine could no longer be worshiped in natural settings but only in huge cathedrals of stone and stained glass according to the institutional Church. The rise of cities, improvements in transportation, communication, and technology, and the building of the interstate Church all contributed to the repressing of the *veriditas* of the Green Man. The fact that Gawain accepts the challenge of the Green Knight and relates to the Lady Bercilak by accepting her gift indicates that the Green Man will no longer be repressed. The denouement takes place at the Green Chapel where the Green Knight passes the mantle of the Green Man to Gawain who once again becomes the Champion of Sovereignty.

Obviously, there are many levels of interpretation of this legend, but John Matthews' comments on the character of the Green Knight are worth noting: "The God (for to call him less is foolish) offers his life-blood for the sake of the people in return for *their* courage and self-sacrifice. . .As the guardian of the natural world (and, yes, the lover and son of the Goddess who is also the earth) he challenges all people to acknowledge his yearly sacrifice by offering their own love, trust and service to created things."[24] We could say in this instance, that the Green Man is telling us that we *must* be cognizant of the effects of our actions on the environment. We have the freedom to seemingly destroy the natural world through war, pollution, and technology, but, in the end, our actions will be repaid in kind. We must be like Gawain and face up to the terms of our commitments to the natural world. We too can get in touch with the *veriditas* of the Green Knight by participating in the rebirth of life through our self-sacrifice. We can sacrifice our right to choose from seventy different brands of cosmetics or fifty different models of cars or thirty different sizes of TV sets. We can sacrifice some of our freedom to commute alone in our personal cars, to treat land as a personal commodity, and to define progress in terms of personal convenience. Then we will join with Gawain as Champions of Sophia in her guise as Sovereignty.

By far the most popular symbol of the Green Man in the English-speaking world is Robin Hood. His guise as the outlaw of Sherwood Forest who robs the rich to help the poor is a late medieval reconstruction of the ancient Green Man. As John Matthews says, "Both Robin and the Green Man have fed each other, and it is at the centre of this interaction that the most powerful elements of the living Greenwood myth have their place."[25] His story, along with those who are closely related to him, is a wonderful way of accessing the nature bypath.

Robin Hood obviously is the Lord of the Greenwood and the Lord of the Hunt, both universal symbols of the Green Man. His ability to lose himself in the forest when threatened by civilized authority is indicative of his oneness with nature and his aversion to urban life. Robin Hood is the King of the May as Marian is the May Queen; he is Robin Goodfellow, the trickster who also goes by the name of Puck; he is Green Jack, or Jack-in-the-Green, a figure associated with chimney-sweeps who parades in the May Day festival.

Robin Hood represents the Green Man in his Spring aspect rather than the King of Winter as portrayed in *Sir Gawain and the Green*

Knight.[26] In his association with the greening of the land which is celebrated in the revels of May Day, Robin Hood is clearly a symbol of the pagan god of fertility who suffered death and was then reborn. In a medieval enactment of the ancient drama, Robin bled to death from an arrow wound but was healed by the love of Maid Marian. Here Robin Hood and Maid Marian represent the earlier Celtic figures of the Hero and Sovereignty, whose union is necessary to ensure fertility. As E. O. James remarks about the archetypal role of Robin Hood, "In the capacity of the Robin-of-the Wood, he was essentially a vegetation sacral hero rather than the leader of a robber band in the forest, or the highly skilled archer of the ballad and romance..."[27]

Both the Robin Hood and the Arthurian legends have recently experienced a renaissance in popular culture. Movies, television, comic strips and innumerable books are retelling the legends in fresh new ways. This rekindled interest appears to be a sign of the reappearance of the Green Man archetype as a central image in the emerging mythos.

THE GREEN MAN IN CHRISTIAN SYMBOLISM

Early Christianity

There are no direct references to the Green Man in the early Christian Church; however, as we shall see, his archetype appears in numerous guises. As the disciples of Christ began proselytizing among the Gentiles, they came into contact with a variety of sacred symbols that were different from those of Judaism. The mystery religions which honored Isis, Dionysus, Kybele, and Mithras developed many of the symbols associated with the Green Man archetype: the sacred trees and groves; seasonal festivals celebrating the sowing and harvest periods with songs and dances; and temples containing many images of vegetation in murals, columns, and mosaics in the interior and ornate statuary symbolizing the vegetation gods on the exterior. In the process of converting these pagans, many of their symbols and traditions were assimilated into the Church to aid in the transition from the old to the new faith. For example, Roman statues of Mithras were transformed into Christ, the "Good Shepherd," and statues of Isis with her son Horus became the Madonna and Child.

The earliest known example of an actual Green Man image in a Christian context appears on a sarcophagus from the late fourth century in Poitiers, France.[28] Since it is found on a Christian tomb, it may be assumed that the figure symbolizes rebirth or resurrection. It is interesting to note that the leaves on the Green Man appear to come out of his nostrils. This could be an allusion to the life breath or spirit (*ruach* in Hebrew) renewing life as does the appearance of green leaves in the Spring. Could this worn image be a symbol of Christ as the Green Man?

Other examples from the fifth and sixth centuries come from Constantinople where the Green Men appear as capitals of columns.[29] While these columns do not appear to have been in churches, the Byzantine Empire for all intents and purposes was a Christian theocracy. Therefore, any publicly displayed sculptures would have been under direct ecclesiastical authority; we may assume that they were not considered contrary to Orthodox doctrine. The Green Men in the capitals are magnificently carved with acanthus leaves sprouting from the nose, chin, brow and hair. The expressions range from wise to surprise and from weary to jolly. They are truly harbingers of the later medieval carvings in Western churches. It is possible that they served as sources of inspiration to the crusaders of the late eleventh century as it was not until the twelfth century that the Green Man motif became commonplace in Western churches.

Celtic Christianity

The archetype of the Green Man was expressed in the Celtic Christian tradition which was built on its pagan heritage. Since the pagan Celts were not literate, we are dependent on the accounts of Greek and Roman commentators and archeological evidence for any clues about their culture. One fascinating Celtic object from the fifth century B.C.E. which was found near Heidelberg, Germany, is a stone head with three leaves on the forehead and wearing what appears to be a leaf crown.[30] Obviously, we have no idea of the original purpose or meaning of this sculpture, but it does infer an association in the mind of the artist between humans and leaves. It is possible that it is some type of votive object since many hundreds of votive pieces have been found in ancient Celtic springs, wells, streambeds, and bogs. A similar head with leaves on the forehead and forming the beard is found on the St. Goar pillar at Pfalzfeld, Germany, also from the fifth century B.C.E. The pillar is phallic in shape and would appear to be representative of a fertility deity.[31] We can assume that both of these objects had a religious significance that in some way was associated with the Green Man archetype. The druids who performed religious functions in Celtic society could be considered Green Men themselves; in fact they were called "men of the oaks" by the Greeks and Romans of their times. The famous Gundestrup Cauldron from the first century B. C. E. portrays many figures which appear to have druidic attributes.[32] The antler-crowned figure (usually named as the Celtic god Cernunnos) appears to be in a ritualistic posture, perhaps shamanically relating to the surrounding animals. There are heads around the cauldron with hair and beards of leaves reminding us again of the Green Man.

By the time Celtic Christianity developed in the third century C. E., the pagan druids had a centuries-long tradition involving the Green Man for the Christian monks to assimilate. As Anderson says, "This may explain part of the attraction of the Green Man for the Church. Whether consciously or not, the missionary saints needed to bring the greatest source of living power on earth under the guidance of Christ: the power that is in grass and leaf and sap on which all living things depend."[33] We see this tradition especially in early Irish art. For example, on the North Cross at the Celtic monastery at Clonmacnois there is the figure of a horned man usually associated with Cernunnos, a pagan Celtic symbol of the Green Man.[34] The famous Book of Kells contains numerous examples of humans and beasts disgorging and devouring vegetation. This form of the Green Man seems to have first appeared in Celtic manuscript illuminations.[35]

The early Christian converts in Celtic lands were inhabitants of what has been called the Greenwood or Wildwood.[36] Large deciduous forests covered vast areas of Celtic Europe and there were no cities worthy of the name. Most people lived in settlements connected by cart tracks in clearings in thick woods of oak, ash and beech. As

Romanized Christian missionaries spread into Celtic lands from the Mediterranean, they encountered a green rural culture with a wild atmosphere and setting far removed from their sunny climate and busy cities. This was truly the domain of the Green Man. They found the Celtic Christ, who was not a remote figure worshipped in large cathedrals, but a Christ who appeared primarily through the green world of nature. And the Celtic Christian monks, who followed in the footsteps of the druids, could themselves be seen as the living embodiment of the Green Man.

One of the greatest Celtic Christian sages was John Scotus Eriugena. As mentioned in the preceding chapter, Eriugena developed a panentheistic viewpoint of God as both transcendent and immanent in nature. In his magnum opus, *On the Division of Nature*, he emphasizes that humans contain all of the kingdoms of creation within them. Therefore, we can say that our life contains the juiciness and vigor of the plant kingdom, the senses and mobility of the animal kingdom, the strength and steadfastness of the mineral kingdom, and the spirit and wisdom of the angelic kingdom. It is interesting to speculate that Eriugena may have been responding to the re-emergence of the archetype of the Green Man in a manner similar to the architects and sculptors of the Romanesque and early Gothic cathedrals because we see a proliferation of fantastic plant and animal images appearing in statues, stained glass, and manuscript illuminations at this time. It is certainly probable that the Green Man may have become so popular since he ideally expresses the plant kingdom contained within human nature.

Medieval Christianity

As the Middle Ages evolved, sacred trees became ever more deeply ingrained in the symbolism of the Christian Church. As the majestic Romanesque and Gothic cathedrals were built, their vaulting resembled the intertwined branches of sacred groves and the columns supporting the vaulting became the trunks of sacred trees. At the top of the columns frequently appeared the Green Man, peering out through the leaves or disgorging them from his mouth. As we shall see, there are many interpretations of his presence but no one can deny the importance of the Green Man for medieval Christians.

Green Man on column at St. Magnus Church, Kirkwall, Orkney Islands

The Green Man was evidently one of the favorite symbols of the Cluniac monasteries of the Romanesque period because his sculptured image appears in great profusion throughout their monastic empire. The Benedictine Abbey at Cluny had created the largest network of hospice monasteries on major pilgrimage routes during the tenth and eleventh centuries. They offered food, shelter, and spiritual guidance for pilgrims, both rich and poor, who were traveling to sites where sacred relics were located. Since pilgrims came from diverse areas, we can assume that widely recognized images would be typical along these routes. The Cluniac monastic network might have used the Green Man and other images much in the way of a modern trademark - something familiar to a wide variety of people that would make them feel at home. As pilgrims from different parts of Europe came together and shared their folk-tales and customs it is easy to see how a cross-fertilization of images and ideas could occur. A centrally powerful network like the Cluniacs could promote the interpretation of these images and ideas as they saw fit. The fact that the Green Man and other images with a pagan heritage were utilized so frequently along pilgrimage routes had to have been a conscious decision on the part of the Cluniac authorities.

Interpretations of the meaning of the Green Man for the medieval monks are varied. In the Cluniac churches the Green Man appeared in a great variety of images. He was frequently seen as a horned head disgorging vegetation, causing many observers to perceive him as a demonic form. In the late tenth century, a manuscript called the Codex Egberti shows heads which could be seen as demonic, from which birds and fish appear along with vegetation. According to Kathleen Basford, "even the leaves have become demonic."[37] However, these heads could equally be called whimsical. One of the more idiosyncratic theologians, Rabanus Maurus, a ninth century Benedictine, espoused the idea that "leaves represented the sins of the flesh or lustful and wicked men doomed to eternal damnation."[38] Since Rabanus was very influential, we can see why many of the Green Men might have been considered demonic. This negative view was consistent with the attitudes of many within the institutional Church who condemned the natural world, which the Green Man represented, as evil. But deeper meanings of the Green Man image could be found by those pilgrims who walked on the nature bypath.

The Gothic period of the late eleventh through fourteenth centuries brought the full flowering of the Green Man archetype, simultaneously with the growth of the Cult of the Virgin Mary. The ancient images of the Goddess and the Green Man renewed their appearance in the stone carvings of the soaring Gothic cathedrals. As the Cult of the Virgin gained in popularity, Mary "became an exalted personification of Nature, idealized as the Queen of Heaven and identified with Wisdom..."[39] At this time Mary's special association with leaves and flowers connects her to the Green Man, whose leafy image appears frequently in the Lady Chapels of English cathedrals.[40] A particularly intriguing expression of this archetype appears in the weird and wonderful Green Men that form the roof bosses in the Lady Chapel of Ely Cathedral. The Virgin Mary with Christ Child, surrounded by leaves, makes a surprising appearance in one of the roof bosses among the ubiquitous Green Men. Here she is called the

"Green Virgin," a clear reference to her association with the ancient nature goddesses.

Green Man, Lady Chapel, Ely Cathedral

Virgin Mary as Green Lady with Christ Child, Lady Chapel, Ely Cathedral, England

The archetypal matrix of the Green Man and the Divine Feminine is clearly seen at Chartres Cathedral, one of the earliest of the Gothic cathedrals, which contained the most important cathedral school in Europe in the twelfth century. Chartres has long been associated with the Divine Feminine. It exists on the site of an earlier druid shrine dedicated to a virgin goddess, and an ancient healing well - sacred to the pagan goddess - is found within the crypt. The sacred precinct of the goddess was transferred to the Virgin Mary when Chartres was appropriated by Christianity. The preeminence of the Divine Feminine is seen in the cathedral's famous relic, the veil of Mary, and its Black Virgin statue.[41]

Chartres became the principal center for the veneration of the Virgin Mary during the Gothic period. At the same time the Green Man made his earliest significant appearance as exterior statuary on the west facade of the cathedral. Forty-four heads personifying the Green Man arise from bands of foliage in the outermost arches that frame the three portals, with the apocalyptic Christ in the center. These heads seem to portray the Green Man "as the fruit or flower of vegetation, here flourishing in all the benefits of the universal knowledge radiating from Christ..."[42]

Green Man in archivolt of West Portal, Chartres Cathedral, France

The images of the Green Man at Chartres illustrate his transformation from the Romanesque era. In addition to his greater ubiquity throughout Christian art work, the Gothic Green Man is rarely shown in a demonic guise; rather, he shows a full range of human emotions dependent upon the context of his appearance. One of the greatest achievements of the Gothic artists was their ability to express the individuality of their subjects. Carvings of the Green Man were now much more precise in their depictions of the human face as well as the various forms of vegetation.[43] As William Anderson remarks of the artists at Chartres:

> In their portrayals of the Green Man as a benign and beaming
> image, they expressed a new attitude to Nature, one in which
> she is no longer the terrifying enemy of human existence
> of so much Romanesque sculpture but the kindly ally of
> man. Here, through the image of the Green Man, the moods
> of Nature become humanized; and the attitudes of man
> and woman are reflected back to them in the principle of
> awakening consciousness underlying all creation.[44]

The re-emergence of the Green Man and the Divine Feminine during the Gothic period also brought a resurgence of the folk fertility festivals that celebrated the sacred marriage as the source of nature's bounty. In the Roman Catholic Church, the Pope and all bishops, priests, deacons, and monks were prohibited from engaging in any type of sexual activity. Since the Green Man and the Wild Man were very potent fertility symbols, they had to be handled very deftly by the hierarchy who, on the one hand, wanted the laity to procreate in great numbers, and on the other hand, needed to strictly control the manner in which they did so. Obviously, the monks and clergy were supposed to live by their vow of celibacy; yet they could not deny or repress the sexual energy in the laity except through extreme moral posturing. The Church missionaries from very early on had used the power of celibacy to convert the pagans by inferring that their God was so powerful they didn't need or desire sex! This may have had an impact on some people, but the traditional pagan seasonal festivals of plowing and harvesting continued unabated. Exhibiting an "if you can't beat them, join them" attitude, the Church in the 11th and 12th centuries begrudgingly appropriated the fertility rites into Christian dogma by adapting them into religious dramas and festivals which became increasingly popular well into the 16th century.

Religious dramatic productions and festivals involving entire communities were known as miracle plays, mystery plays, Marian plays, Corpus Christi cycles, Wild Man plays, and Mummer's plays along with many types of folk plays. These productions were meant to take the place of pagan fertility festivals. Many of the stock characters came right out of the pagan heritage. The Feast of the Ass, the Feast of Fools, burlesques, and pastorales were all countenanced by the Church in the attempt to assimilate the pagan traditions into mainstream Christian dogma. The most popular times for these pagan adaptations were at Carnival at the beginning of Lent (of which Mardi Gras in New Orleans is a remnant), Twelfth Night, and Pentecost. There are literally hundreds of references in ecclesiastical records describing pageants, plays, festivals, and dances closely based on pagan rites of fertility. At these times the strict prohibitions against sexual license, nudity, suggestive dancing, and inebriation were relaxed.

The Green Man was a central character in the medieval pastorales. These folk plays, performed on the commons in front of the churches, featured Robin and Maid Marion. At first these characters were simple rustic folk celebrating the season of Spring, but later they came to represent the King and Queen of May celebrating the ancient Celtic *hieros gamos* between the Green Man with his phallic maypole decorated with greenery and Sophia as the May Queen crowned with garlands and escorted by young maidens. Thus Maid Marian, as consort to Robin Hood, appears to be another important symbol of the Divine Feminine which occurs in conjunction with the Green Man. Her role as the Flower Maiden in the medieval folk plays seems to mirror the more exalted image of the Virgin Mary, the *fleur de lis* of the Gothic cathedrals.

The inclusion of these elements of the ancient fertility festivals within a Church which preached sexual purity demonstrates the conflicting attitudes toward the characteristics of the Green Man which are found in Christian tradition. The popular celebrations which incorporated the instinctive qualities of the Green Man helped to overcome the dualistic split between body and spirit which was endemic to the institutional Church. The sacred marriage which was celebrated in the medieval pastorales reflected the union of the physical and spiritual aspects of humanity, and as such, were an antidote to the Church's "fall of man" doctrine which equated sexuality with sin. It was the archetypal Green Man and the Goddess in their myriad roles who were able to infuse the medieval Christian Church with the life-renewing energy that comes from this union.

CHRIST AS THE GREEN MAN

Perhaps the most hidden aspect of the nature bypath relates to the Green Man aspect of Christ. The mythological god-man, as the incarnation of the Divine – whether Osiris, Tammuz, Attis, or Dionysius – was always the Green Man, the dying and reborn vegetation god, the Spirit that manifests in the cycles of earthly life. Perhaps the Green Men found throughout the cathedrals of the Middle Ages were encoding the hidden truth that Christ is another representation of the archetypal vegetation god. The official Church doctrines may have interpreted the Green Man as demonic and a warning about the evils of sin, but the few initiates of the hidden tradition – many of whom were instrumental in building the magnificent medieval cathedrals – knew the deeper secrets of the

Green Man as a symbol for Christ, another form of the archetypal dying and resurrected god-man. As we walk on the nature bypath today, recognizing the mythic similarities between Christ and the Green Man can help us regain the wisdom of ancient cultures which honored the sacredness of the green world of nature.

Christ as the Lord of Vegetation

The many Gospel accounts which associate Jesus Christ with gardens reveal his symbolic role as "the gardener" who is the Lord of vegetation. Christ may be considered as the archetypal gardener of the primordial Garden of Eden for "all things were made through him." (John 1:3) As "the Word," or Logos, Christ provides the organizing patterns of nature which are reflected in the form of a well tended garden. The paradisal Garden symbolizes the all-giving, endless source of sustenance which Christ as the gardener provides for humankind. He continues this nurturing role through his mission to provide "abundance of life." (John 10:10)

Christ frequently teaches his disciples in the Garden of Gethsemane (John 18: 1 & 2), which is located at the foot of the Mount of Olives. The term "Gethsemane" comes from the Chaldean words *gath*, meaning a wine-press, and *shemen*, meaning perfumed olive oil. Wine and oil do not exist in nature but are the result of human activity which transforms the natural fruit. Thus, the Garden of Gethsemane represents a place where humanity unites with nature to produce wine, with its ancient association to the god such as Dionysius, and olive oil which is sacred to the goddess. Thus we might say that symbolically Christ unites his characteristics as Son of Man and Green Man to bring forth the sacred wisdom of the Goddess. It is in the Garden of Gethsemane that Christ, the nurturing gardener, imparts Sophia's divine wisdom to his disciples.

The garden is also related to the kingdom of heaven in Jesus' parable of the mustard seed (Luke 13:18-19):

> He said therefore, "What is the kingdom of God like?
> And to what should I compare it? It is like a mustard
> seed that someone took and sowed in the garden; it

grew and became a tree, and the birds of the air made nests in its branches.

Christ is the gardener who plants and nurtures the mustard seed, for he provides the way to the kingdom of God. The mustard seed becomes the sacred tree and is inhabited by the heavenly birds as alluded to by the Celtic monk in his beautiful poem *The Tree of Life with bloom unchanged.*[45] Paradoxically, Christ is not only the gardener but also the fruit of the garden. He is the vegetation, the olive which grows from the tree, and the smallest mustard seed.

The Biblical garden is also symbolic of the place of sacrifice since the living plants are sacrificed (picked and pressed) to provide nourishment for life. In the parable of the fig tree (Luke 13:6-9), the gardener is told to cut down the tree without fruit but the gardener asks to nurture it for another year so that it may bear fruit. If it is barren, there is no sacrifice since it is already dead. However, the gardener nurtures life by allowing the fruit to mature so that it may be picked (sacrificed) at its highest degree of life (ripeness) to provide life to the living. In this parable Christ may be seen as both the gardener who cultivates growth, as well as the fruit which must be sacrificed in order to give life to others.

The meaning of this parable is further shown in Christ's reference to himself as the vine: "I am the true vine, and my Father is the vine grower. He removes every branch in me that bears no fruit. Every branch that bears fruit he prunes to make it bear more fruit." (John 15:1-2) This statement clearly shows the relationship between Christ and the vegetation gods such as Dionysius and Bacchus. As the Green Man, he is a living vine which needs to be pruned (sacrificed) to bear more fruit. Jesus says further: ". . .Just as the branch cannot bear fruit by itself unless it abides in the vine, neither can you unless you abide in me. I am the vine, you are the branches. Those who abide in me and I in them bear much fruit, because apart from me you can do nothing." (John 15:4-5) Here is the *veriditas* of Christ, his essential greenness that he shares with the Green Man and that he imparts to his disciples.

The revelation of Christ as the archetypal Green Man, although hidden within the doctrines of the Church, is shown very clearly in certain Christian art works. The Antioch Chalice, thought by some to be the literal "Holy Grail," portrays a very Dionysian image of Christ surrounded by grapes and leaves.

The Antioch Chalice Metropolitan Museum of Art, New York

**Detail of Antioch Chalice showing Christ
as the Green Man surrounded by vegetation**

The Green Man symbolism of Christ is even more explicitly developed in Eastern Orthodox icons from Romania that depict Christ with grape vines growing out of his wounded side.

**Romanian Orthodox icon of Christ with grape vine growing
from his side squeezing the grapes into the communion chalice**

And a contemporary sculptured plaque at Rosslyn Chapel in
Scotland shows Christ hanging on a tree, surrounded by grapes and
leaves, with the "true vine" Biblical verse engraved at the base.

Christ as the True Vine sculpture at Rosslyn Chapel, Scotland

This image may provide a key to one of the mysteries that surround this small chapel, which was built by Knights Templar in the fifteenth century. One of its fascinating features is the presence of over one hundred Green Men that appear everywhere throughout the chapel. A long standing tradition has held that the Templars who built this chapel were encoding hidden secrets of Christianity within its stone walls, and perhaps the ubiquitous Green Man points to his connection with Christ, a truth that can be more explicitly revealed today.

Christ also possesses the life-giving water attributes of the Green Man, which we have already seen were characteristic of the vegetation gods Tammuz and Osiris. Christ refers to himself as the "living water" (John 4: 10-11) necessary for eternal life. As the living water for all humanity, Christ is the *veriditas* that inundates the aridness of our lives, bringing forth a soul-satisfying union with the natural world around us.

The connection between Christ and the god of the grain such as Adonis is shown in John 6:35, where he says to the multitude of people, "I am the bread of life." Just prior to this he had instructed them, "For the bread of God is that which comes down from heaven, and gives life to the world." (John 6:33) The grain must be sacrificed by threshing, grinding and kneading to make the bread which sustains life just as the grape must be plucked, pressed, and strained to make the wine that likewise nourishes life. The central event of the Christian liturgy -- the transubstantiation of the bread and wine into the mystical body and blood of Christ -- symbolizes the sacrifice of the god in images which again remind us of Dumuzi, the god of the grain, and Dionysius, the god of the grape. This central mystery shows the dual nature of Christ's sacrifice - the blood sacrifice of the crucifixion represented by the wine and the bloodless sacrifice of Christ as the Green Man represented by the bread.

The Sacrifice of Christ

Perhaps the greatest connection between Christ and the Green Man lies in this realm of sacrifice. From the earliest archeological artifacts we know that human beings have used sacrifice to propitiate the gods and to ensure bountiful hunts and harvests. There are two broad classes of sacrifice: blood sacrifice and vegetative (bloodless) sacrifice. In the story of Cain and Abel in the Old Testament, we find a graphic representation of the debate between the two forms of sacrifice. Cain, who tilled the ground and nurtured the crops, is allied with the Christ as Green Man, while Abel, who tended the sheep, is allied with Christ the Good Shepherd. Cain's offering to Yahweh was the first fruits of his harvest, the vegetative sacrifice, while Abel's was the blood sacrifice of the first-born lambs. Yahweh accepted the blood sacrifice but not the vegetative sacrifice (Gen. 4:4), telling Cain that his bloodless sacrifice was not adequate and that he would be accepted only if he did the sacrifice well. Cain, the harbinger of all human jealous rage, then made Abel his blood sacrifice, bequeathing to humanity in the West the idea that only blood sacrifice will invoke divine assistance to solve its problems. The three major religions of Abraham -- Judaism, Christianity, and Islam -- are religions of blood sacrifice. This is shown when Yahweh asked Abraham to offer his son Isaac as a sacrificial burnt offering. Although Yahweh at the last minute told Abraham to substitute a ram for Isaac, he nonetheless reaffirmed his preference for blood sacrifice.

On the other hand the vegetative or bloodless sacrifice, which was rejected by Yahweh, has been from the beginning associated primarily with the Great Mother. Only a woman can be a mother, the life-giver, the source of vitality for the human race. As agriculture developed, the Earth by analogy became the source of vitality and therefore, the feminine was honored as the Earth Goddess or Great Mother. The vegetation god in the form of grain was sacrificed to the Great Goddess in order to ensure her continued bounty. Thus the blood sacrifice has been associated with the masculine solar gods and the vegetative sacrifice with the feminine earth goddesses for many millennia. The sacrifice of Christ fulfilled both the blood and bloodless types of sacrifice. His crucifixion as the Lamb of God was the blood sacrifice for all of humanity. Through that sacrifice, Christ's logos nature is transferred to the faithful, who receive regenerated life -- the vitality of dedication, commitment, healing, and growth. Through the bloodless sacrifice of Christ, that of the Green Man, his eros nature is transferred to the faithful: love, nurturing, relatedness, and compassion. In the dual nature of Christ's sacrifice, we see the emergence of ChristoSophia, the totality of the divine nature.

Christ and the Divine Feminine

The central theme of the Christian mythos, the death and resurrection of Jesus Christ, closely corresponds to the ancient myths which celebrated the sacrifice and rebirth of the Green Man as the son-lover of the Goddess. But the Christian story is unique because Jesus willingly accepted his sacrifice and was able to explain its meaning to his disciples.[46] Thus, the archetypal sacrifice of the son-lover of the Goddess was enacted in historical time as the Passion of Christ, an event which marked the transformation of a higher level of consciousness for those who participated in its Mystery.

Within Christian tradition the figure of the Goddess associated with Jesus Christ has been split between the Virgin Mary, his mother, and Mary Magdalene, his lover as portrayed in some gnostic texts. Although the roles of these two Marys are often conflated, the archetypal Great Goddess has become fragmented in Christianity. Recognizing Christ in his Green Man aspect as the son and lover of the Goddess can help us reconnect with the images of the Divine Feminine which are hidden within Christian tradition.

The most obvious representation of the ancient Mother Goddess who mourns her sacrificed son is the Virgin Mary, mother of Christ. As the *Mater Dolorosa,* the grieving mother, Mary follows the archetypal pattern of goddesses such as Inanna, Ishtar, Isis, and Kybele in weeping for her crucified son.[47] During the Middle Ages this representation of the Virgin Mary became especially popular, and many representations of the *Pieta*, the Virgin Mary mourning the body of her dead son, appeared in art and sculpture.

Although the appearance of the mournful mother can be readily found on the interstate highway of Christianity, the figure of the grieving lover which is also central to this archetypal complex is not accessible on the surface. The institutional Church, in its typical condemnation of sexuality, especially repressed the Divine Feminine in her role as consort to the dying god. However, glimpses of her presence may be found even in the Gospels of the New Testament in references to Mary Magdalene, who grieved for Jesus after his crucifixion just as the ancient goddesses mourned the death of their beloveds.

The function of Mary Magdalene as the goddess-lover is also intimated in the Gospels in their description of the woman who anoints Jesus with precious oil, an act which he commends as preparation of his body for burial. This "woman with an alabaster jar," (Matthew 26:7) who is usually believed to be Mary Magdalene, is playing the role of the temple priestess who performed the ritual anointing of the god before his sacrifice. The Gospels also reveal the significance of Mary Magdalene as the first to see the resurrected Christ. Just as the ancient goddess sought her lover in the darkness of the Underworld, Mary Magdalene entered the darkness of the tomb in search of the body of her Lord. The image of Christ as the Green Man is strongly evoked in the Gospel of John where Mary Magdalene mistakes the newly risen Christ for the "gardener."

> Jesus said to her, "Woman, why are you weeping?
> Whom are you looking for?" Supposing him to be
> the gardener, she said to him, "Sir, if you have
> carried him away, tell me where you have laid him,
> and I will take him away." (John 20:15)

The work of the "gardener" is to nurture vegetation, a primary role of the Green Man. The risen Christ's association with the gardener resonates with the archetype of the Green Man, for the Sumerian god Dumuzi, who was mourned by the goddess Inanna, was also given the name of the gardener.[48]

Mary Magdalene's role as the grieving lover of the crucified Jesus is even more clearly indicated in scriptures which can be found when traveling on the bypaths. As discussed in an earlier chapter, gnostic gospels frequently depicted Mary Magdalene as the beloved of Jesus, a figure reminiscent of the goddesses of antiquity.

Allusions to the archetypal sacred marriage between the Green Man and the Goddess can thus be found in gnostic references to Mary Magdalene as the consort of Christ. But the *hieros gamos* is such a powerful archetype within the psyche that it makes its appearance even within the institutional Church. In the twelfth century, with the re-emergence of the Divine Feminine, images of the "Coronation of the Virgin" became prevalent in Christian art. As the Green Man motif appears prominently in the great Gothic cathedrals such as Chartres, so does Mary as the crowned Queen of Heaven appear in the portals of Chartres Cathedral. In these images of her coronation, Jesus and Mary seem to relate to each other as a bridal couple as he tenderly places the crown upon her beautiful head.[49] In medieval iconography, the Green Man as the son and lover of the Goddess makes his appearance in Jesus Christ as both the son and consort of Mary. These images which are found within the institutional Church that point to the sacred marriage of the god and goddess are more clearly delineated on the bypath of gnostic Christianity which emphasized the central importance of the union between Christ and Sophia. The Divine Feminine as the gnostic Sophia integrates the roles of mother and lover of the god which have been fragmented through the Church's depictions of the Virgin Mary and Mary Magdalene. Sophia, who is both the mother and the consort of Christ, provides the fullest archetypal complement to the Green Man aspect of Jesus Christ.

The Green Man as the oracle of the goddess reveals the secrets of Wisdom to humanity.[50] This aspect of the Green Man can be seen in the figure of Jesus Christ as the incarnation of Sophia. It is Christ as the Green Man in whom lies Sophia's secret of creation, the life-essence, the Soul of the World. In our patriarchal history, it has been the Green Man who has been able to keep the creative powers of the Goddess alive, but hidden in himself. Christ as the Green Man has mediated the creative power of the Divine Feminine to the world.

The Sophianic nature of Christ as Green Man is beautifully expressed in this 18th century New England song entitled *Jesus Christ the Apple Tree*:

> The tree of life my soul hath seen,
> Laden with fruit, and always green:
> The trees of nature fruitless be
> Compared with Christ the apple tree.[51]

In this simple yet profound verse, Christ as the evergreen "tree of life" can be clearly seen as the archetypal Green Man. But here the tree of life is "the apple tree," a tree which has ancient associations with the goddess. Christ's Tree of Life is Sophia's Tree of Wisdom which brings forth the apple of wholeness. Christ as the Green Man and Sophia as the Goddess are united in this lovely image - the apple tree which symbolizes ChristoSophia.

Christ Consciousness

One of the purposes of the Green Man in Christian churches was to represent the consciousness of God – the Divine as immanent in the life force – to those who realized the inner mysteries of the faith. For the Green Man symbolizes the synthesis of human consciousness and the consciousness of the vegetative kingdom, which is the closest that the limited human mind can approach to understanding the mind of God. It is not the leaves and flowers that typically accompany the figure of the Green Man that alone symbolize divine consciousness, but the human face that peeks out from behind the foliage that exemplifies the integration of self-consciousness and nondual awareness. Thus the Green Man symbolizes the consciousness of Christ, the archetypal god-man who is also the vegetation god. This is the Christ Consciousness attained by the mystic, who has an awareness of self but can transcend this to nondual awareness. On the nature bypath the Green Man can impart to us this Christ Consciousness that enables us to overcome the false sense of separation between ourselves and the natural world.

THE GREEN MAN TODAY

As the 21st century unfolds, the nature bypath is being explored by an ever-increasing number of visionaries who are led by the call of the Green Man. Not only religious leaders like Thomas Berry and Matthew Fox, but also open-minded thinkers from all walks of life including artists like Robert Rauschenberg and Jacques van der Heyden, and scientists like Fritjof Capra and James Lovelock, along with thousands of their colleagues and everyday citizens throughout the world, are stirred by the emerging mythos of the Green Man.

The Green Man is reawakening today because of our deep spiritual and ecological crisis. As surely as the sap rises in the spring, he is rising from the depths of the collective unconscious to rekindle our relatedness to the natural world. As in the past, sensitive people are the first to hear his call while many continue in the old traditional ways completely unaware of the transformations which are occurring. He walks the nature bypath, beckoning those who have turned off the interstate highway to seek the Divine through nature. The Green Man's voice is the language of nature and if we seek to learn that language we will understand him and hear his voice.

Most images of the Green Man show him to be quietly watching the outer world through a maze of leaves with an aura of expectancy - anticipating our joining him in the awakening of the vision of the interconnectedness of all creation. Anyone who is sensitive to the unitive spirit of interrelatedness that is slowly unfolding throughout the world is ready to participate with the archetype of the Green Man. We prepare ourselves to hear the Green Man's voice by the process called "psychic photosynthesis."[52] We are so accustomed to being active doers, constantly seeking to bring about change through the exercise of our individual wills, that we often fail to take the opportunity to observe the natural world around us, quietly witnessing the mystery of life and absorbing this mystery deep into our souls.

> . . .our universe came into existence in its particular
> form so that its glories could be seen and enjoyed
> and so that God could look on his works through our
> unclouded eyes. The Green Man, watcher and trans-
> mitter of life, is a perfect symbol of this process.[53]

If we reflect on the idea of psychic photosynthesis and the Green Man, we realize that it is an activity that does not require the exercise of the will. It is quiet, natural, and spontaneous just as is the process of photosynthesis in the plant kingdom. Photosynthesis involves all of the traditional elements (fire, air, water, earth) which are united in the plant; psychic photosynthesis unites the totality of existence within us. In another way, we could say that the process of psychic photosynthesis is the "greening" of our souls or psyches (Hildegard of Bingen's *veriditas),* wherein the water of eros and the light of logos combine to produce the creative manifestation rooted in the dark depths of the unconscious. Psychic photosynthesis draws on the energies of the instincts and unconscious as well as the transcendent and spiritual.

We can visualize the emerging presence of the Green Man by imagining ourselves walking along a forest path in midwinter. All around us is dead vegetation and Spring seems a long time away. Yet if we look beneath the dead leaves on the forest floor, we can find tiny green shoots hidden from our casual gaze. These sprigs of verdant life may not spring forth from their dark abode for many weeks but nevertheless they are quietly waiting for the right amount of moisture and radiant energy to manifest in all their glory. As in the barren spiritual landscape of our time, there are signs of new spiritual life arising - heralds of the return of the Green Man as the consort of the Divine Feminine into our world which so desperately needs them.

People hearing the Green Man's voice through conscious participation in the process of psychic photosynthesis are awakened to the radiant energy of the natural world and their souls begin to radiate the joyful richness and loving fullness of life. As more and more people hearken to his emerging presence, the Green Man will come out from behind the leaves and join with Sophia in the ecstatic dance of verdant life.

The Mystical Bypath

". . .by paths they have not known
I will guide them"

Isaiah 42:16

CHAPTER VIII: OPENING THE MYSTICAL BYPATH

"Our normal waking consciousness, rational
consciousness as we call it, is but one special type
of consciousness, whilst all about it, parted from it
by the filmiest of screens, there lie potential forms of
consciousness entirely different..."[1]

A simple walk through the woods can be a completely different experience for people according to their state of consciousness. One person, in the "normal" mode of consciousness, may be so distracted by thoughts and fantasies, discomfited by sensations of thirst or fatigue, or preoccupied with reaching the goal at the end, that she walks the entire trail without really perceiving anything beyond the general shapes of trees, underbrush, earth and rocks. Another person, with a more awakened consciousness, focuses on the surrounding sights, sounds and smells and becomes aware of the true life of the forest around her. She detects the small things which are passed by, unnoticed, by others – the tiny wildflowers among the ferns, the bird's nest hidden in the tree branches, the varied colors of the rocks in the stream. She looks beyond the obvious, noting the tracks and broken twigs which mark the presence of unseen animals; she sees beneath the surface appearances, recognizing the web of life which contains her as well as all the plants and animals of the forest. She may even become aware of the deeper Mystery which underlies all that she perceives; in the play of light and shadows, the rustling of the wind, the melody of the brook, and the song of the birds, she may glimpse the invisible Presence which is their source. In the same way, it is our consciousness that determines what our experience will be on the journey of life. We can live only on the surface, accepting material existence and rational thought as the sole "reality," or we can experience life in a deeper, more complex manner, perceiving the presence of God in all aspects of life. This is the basis of mystical consciousness.

Those who walk on the mystical bypath attain this heightened consciousness through the cultivation of the spiritual rather than the physical senses – the development of the "inner eye" and the "inner ear." In mystical consciousness the wisdom of the heart is emphasized more than logic and rational knowledge. The mystic shares the simple secret of Saint-Exupery's Little Prince: "It is only with the heart that one can see rightly."[2] The eros faculties of feeling and intuition enable one to look beneath the surface of life and perceive the underlying meaning of everyday experiences. This is the wisdom of the heart that Jesus imparted in his parables. His use of common experiences such as tending sheep, toiling in the fields, building a house, and ordinary objects such as a mustard seed, fig tree, and bread leaven pointed to the profound depth of meaning that can be found in daily life when one "sees with the heart."

Jesus Christ himself is the primary exemplar of mystical consciousness, whose claim to bring "abundant life" (John 10:10) refers to the spiritual riches that are available to the awakened soul. Following in the footsteps of their master, the apostles and saints of the early Christian Church also experienced the transformed consciousness of the mystic. Christian ritual and doctrine, which originally developed from the mystical experiences of these first Christians, became structured and formalized as the Church was institutionalized. Unfortunately, the numinous spiritual power at the core of Christian religion was lost to most travelers on the interstate highway of the Church as its mystical traditions were largely ignored. Indeed, mainstream churches today are more likely to emphasize social activities or humanitarian causes rather than direct spiritual experience. While these functions of the Church serve a very valid purpose, there is an even greater need to acknowledge the primary value of mystical consciousness in order to maintain a vital, living spirituality. Since the Christian Church has generally not fulfilled this need, it has been left to the pilgrim on the mystical bypath to seek the original spiritual **experience** rather than settling for the institutionalized dogma which was generated from someone else's experience of God. As the basis for personal spiritual experience, mystical consciousness is central to the journey on all of the bypaths which comprise the Path of ChristoSophia.

On the mystical bypath one encounters the essence which is the same underlying the outward forms of all the world's diverse religions. For it is the transformation of consciousness which lies at the heart of all true spiritualities. Thus one who travels the mystical bypath realizes the futility of arguing about the doctrines and practices of different religions, for the true purpose of them all is to point one toward the supreme goal of spiritual experience. As the great mystic Jacob Boehme instructs us,

> It is the greatest folly in Babel that the devil has made the world argue about religion so that they argue about self-made ideas, about the letter. The kingdom of God does not consist of any idea but of power and love…The letters all stand in one root, which is the Spirit of God, even as various flowers all stand and grow on the earth beside one another. None bites at the other because of colour, smell, and taste. They allow the earth and sun, the rain and wind and also heat and cold to do with them as they will. Each grows according to its own essence and characteristic.So it is also with the children of God. They have many gifts and much knowledge, but all of one Spirit.[3]

THE MEANING OF "MYSTICISM"

The term "mysticism" itself has been a subject for great argument through the centuries. It can mean so many different things to different people that the word itself may seem to lack any specific definition. It may be helpful in this regard to examine the origin of the word "mysticism." Its root is probably found in the Greek word "muein," meaning "to close the lips or eyes."[4] This reference suggests the nature of a secret, which is also found in the related word "mystery." In ancient Greece, the "mystery religions" were based on secret rites whose purpose was to bring about a transformation of consciousness in its initiates. Participants maintained a strict silence regarding cultic practices and teachings, thus preserving the mystery. Christianity itself actually began as a form of mystery religion, although it is apparent that through the centuries most of its adherents lost touch with the deeper mysteries of the faith. The Mediterranean and Near Eastern mystery cults in general were derived from even earlier forms of worship of the ancient Mother Goddess. Thus the source of the mysticism which was the essence of the mystery religions was the Divine Feminine. Because mysticism has always been linked to the feminine experience of eros, which by its very nature resists definition, it is no wonder that attempts to describe it have been enormously varied. For ultimately it is the **mystery** which is central to mysticism. Spiritual awakening involves the awareness of mystery and paradox as its fundamental experience; the essence of wisdom is accepting the mystery and living the paradox. As the psychologist Gerald May explains, "Mystery, regardless of its form, is a question… The more open the question is, and the deeper we can go into it without having to contrive an answer, the closer our awareness comes to the Original One."[5] For the traveler on the mystical bypath, searching for a precise answer to the meaning of mysticism is not as important as asking the questions and thereby opening oneself ever more deeply to the mystery. Then, instead of getting trapped in the debates regarding the definition of mysticism, we may truly listen to the mystics' descriptions of their own experiences which are as varied as the wildflowers which Boehme describes, but yet are rooted in the same essential Mystery. We then may follow the mystics on the bypath to our own personal encounter with Mystery, and thereby discover for ourselves the meaning of mysticism.

THE MYSTIC'S QUEST

The pilgrim on the mystical bypath will soon discover the central mystery of the unity of the One and the multiplicity of the manifestation. Learning how to live this paradox of unity and duality is essential to the mystic's quest. As Gerald May says,

> It is possible to conceptualize unity as being the fundamental reality that underlies, undergirds and becomes manifest, as duality... To be successful, any attempt to deal with the unity/duality dichotomy must preserve this paradox, for this is the only way in which realization of the existence of ultimate mystery can be protected... We must nurture a "both/ and" rather than an "either/or" attitude.[6]

For example, on the mystical bypath one may intuit the energy which is "behind" all created things, may in a sense "see" with the inner eye the vast web of energy which connects all things within the cosmos, but can also see with the physical eyes the forms and shapes that this energy takes in the earthly realm. We know that all that we see in the created world is not "ultimate reality" because our perceptions are based upon the structure of our sense organs and brain, yet at the same time it **is** real in the world of manifestation. In the same sense the unitive view, as the underlying essence of Reality, is true; and so is the dualistic view, which is the outward appearance of forms that this unity manifests in the physical world. The panentheistic view is also based upon this paradox for it recognizes the Divine as the transcendent One but also immanent within the multiplicity of creation.

The problem with our "normal" state of consciousness is that we perceive things only dualistically. Everything in the world exists by itself, separate from everything else, and often in opposition to others. This recognition of duality is the normal state as the human ego develops early in life, and the child gains a sense of ego-identity which separates him from the world around him and other people. Thomas Merton, a great mystic of our modern age, says, "It is a great mistake to confuse the **person** (the spiritual and hidden self, united with God) and the **ego**, the exterior, empirical self, the psychological individuality who forms a kind of mask for the inner and hidden self."[7] The development of the "I" breaks our original condition of unity; this may truly be seen as the root of "original sin" which results in humanity's expulsion from the Garden of Eden, the primordial paradise of wholeness. As long as we identify only with our ego, we cannot re-enter our original state of unity with God. One who lives solely in a "normal," dualistic state of consciousness is alienated from God and also from his own true Self.

Thus the basis for the mystic's quest is to regain the unitive experience of oneness with God. The psychologist William James, who made a ground-breaking study of individuals' religious experiences, describes his own experience of the mystical state in this way: "the keynote of it is invariably a reconciliation. It is as if the opposites of the world, whose contradictoriness and conflict make all our difficulties and troubles, were melted into unity."[8] When the discriminating, separating function of logos consciousness is suspended, the eros mode of consciousness can surface, bringing its perception of wholeness. It is this insight into unity which is the essence of the mystical state. Mystical consciousness, then, augments the ordinary state of dualistic consciousness, enabling the mystic to live the unity/duality paradox.

The transformation of consciousness which signifies the unitive state does not emphasize "the separate autonomy of the individual but a realization of one's essential rootedness in God and relatedness in creation. Its means are not willful mastery but willing surrender."[9] This is the issue which is fundamental to the spiritual path; in some traditions referred to as "ego-transcendence" but perhaps more clearly expressed in Western culture as "transformation of the ego," it entails bringing the ego into its proper relation with the Divine. The true essence of the spiritual life is to honestly say – and **mean** – "Not my will, but Thy will be done." This attitude reveals the transformation of the ordinary ego which desires "willful mastery" over other people and the natural world into the true Self whose "willing surrender" indicates its union with the Divine.

Although the destination of the mystical bypath is ultimately union with God, few are able to fully attain this goal in this lifetime. Therefore those who walk on the Path of ChristoSophia must guard against the belief that the mystical quest is only for a small group of people who have special spiritual gifts. For mysticism may also be described as "the immediate or direct **presence of God**."[10] Although many of the Christian mystics' descriptions of their raptures and ecstasies in the unitive state may seem impossible for our own mode of experience, these are not necessary to the mystical quest. The monastic way of life, which emphasized the silence and solitude that fostered such heights of mystical consciousness, is certainly antithetical to the environment of most modern people. However, for those on the mystical bypath it is possible to experience the presence of God in the New York subway as well as in the monastic retreat. In fact, it is exactly in those mundane activities of daily life – at work, as parents, with friends, while eating, drinking and lovemaking – that the mystical approach to life can be fully realized. For when we transcend our dualistic consciousness and perceive the sacred and the secular as one, then God is fully present. Evelyn Underhill describes the Christian mystic as "one for whom God and Christ are not merely objects of belief, but living facts experimentally known at first-hand; and mysticism for him becomes…a life based on this conscious communion with God."[11] Living in communion with God enables one to perceive the presence of the Divine in all things. The nature of the quest along the mystical bypath is this ever deepening awareness of God's continual presence, with occasional glimpses of mystical unity which offer spiritual nourishment along the way.

THE SUPPRESSION OF MYSTICISM IN WESTERN CULTURE

Christianity, which began as a mystery religion with baptism as its initiation rite, eventually became a religion for the masses when it was adopted as the official religion of the Roman Empire in the fourth century. As beliefs became institutionalized with the building of the interstate highway of the Church, Christians had to follow the authorized dogmas of Church authority rather than the messages from their own dreams, intuitions, and visions. Gnostic Christians, who cultivated the inner wisdom of their own spiritual experience, emphasized the mystical viewpoint in early Christianity. The primary goal of the gnostics, the transformation of consciousness which was shared with all the mystery religions, was displaced by Roman Christianity as it built its formal institutional structure of laws and doctrines. The suppression of gnostic Christianity in the fourth century was largely an attempt to barricade the mystical bypath of these seekers for inner wisdom. But in doing so, the Christian Church lost much of its power to effect spiritual transformation. Christianity came to emphasize the transcendent God, the search for the Divine outside ourselves, rather than the Divine within which the gnostics sought. However, mystical consciousness is an attribute of human beings which cannot be totally repressed, and pilgrims have sought the mystical bypath within Christian tradition throughout the Church's history. The Christian mystics – sometimes canonized as saints, sometimes denounced as heretics —revealed the ambiguity of the Church's response to the challenge that mysticism presented to the authority of the institution. For "the aspect of life rejected by the orthodox tradition 'goes underground' into the unconscious and reappears as mysticism, only to be rejected again by orthodoxy."[12] Yet it was also apparent that the mystics within Christian tradition were the ones who brought a renewal of spiritual vigor and vitality to the Church from their travels on the mystical bypath.

Another dominant factor in the suppression of mystical consciousness within Western culture stems from the advent of scientific materialism in the seventeenth century. The Age of Reason brought an emphasis on rational thought and control and a corresponding distrust of the irrational inner world. The development of science and a focus on the outer world replaced the medieval preoccupation with intuitive, imaginative thought and the spiritual world. When the universe came to be viewed as a machine, mystery was perceived as simply that which science had not yet explained. As the Christian Church in the West was influenced by the culture's prevailing materialist world view, it too began to emphasize worldly concerns – social action and ethical principles – more than spiritual experience. Even within the Roman Catholic Church, which had preserved its mystical heritage to a much greater degree than Protestant denominations, an erosion of belief in the spiritual mysteries took place. Much of the mystical teaching of the Church was denounced as simply "superstition." This rational, outer-directed world view also promoted the search for the "historical Jesus" which has prevailed in theology for the past two hundred years and the displacement of the "Cosmic Christ."[13] Scholars, armed with all the techniques of science, pursued a greater understanding of the man who inspired the development of Christianity, while leaders of the Church neglected the inner contact with the spiritual Christ who exists within the entire cosmos.

The paradigm shift that is occurring in Western culture today, however, has profound implications for the recovery of mystical consciousness. Foremost in our changing outlook is the recognition of the limitations of the mechanistic view of the universe. For just as contemporary science can aid the development of an ecological spirituality, it can also provide support for a mystical world view. The discovery of interconnectedness by quantum theorists and the holistic perception of complexity theory are consistent with the primacy of Unity in mystical consciousness. An understanding of the integration of mind and matter in the New Physics can provide the conceptual basis for a synthesis of mysticism with its focus on spirit and science with its study of nature.

This is especially important today because the lengthy suppression of mystical consciousness in Western culture has resulted in a condition of inner sterility for most people and spiritual stagnation within the Church. A great many people today are desperately yearning for spiritual **experience**. That essential nature of the human spirit which has been repressed for so long must periodically surface again, as it is doing in our time. This is the reason why the modern charismatic movements attract so many followers, for they provide an experience which is fueled by emotion and imagination. But many of these movements are regressive because eros is so dominant that rational, logical thought is dismissed. What we need today is an integration of the logos with the eros qualities; we need the scientific objectivity of the scholar combined with an openness to the reality of spiritual experience. We must not get trapped by the modern Western mind-set which accepts only rational thought and sense experience as "real," but we must also not yield to the temptations of pure fantasy and emotions untempered by reason. Because of the current condition of our culture, there are great possibilities for the seeker on the mystical bypath today to help bring about this much needed balance by integrating direct, personal spiritual experience with critical thinking and scientific understanding.

STAGES OF MYSTICAL EXPERIENCE

The mystical bypath is often referred to as the Threefold Path by Christian mystics. This schema, which was originally described by NeoPlatonist philosophers and later adopted by Christians, identifies the three stages of the mystical bypath as purgation, illumination, and union. Evelyn Underhill describes these stages this way:

> By "purgation" is usually meant the purification of character and detachment from earthly interests...
> By "illumination" is meant that peaceful certitude of God, and perception of the true values of existence in His light, which is the reward of the surrendered will...
> By "union" is meant that perfect and self-forgetting harmony of the regenerate will with God...Whereas in the earlier stages he saw and moved towards the life of the Spirit, now he finds himself to be immersed in it, inspired and dedicated in all his actions by the indwelling love of God.[14]

While this is a useful model for understanding mystical experience in the framework of Christian tradition, it is important that we not interpret the series of stages in a literal, concrete manner. This is always the danger inherent in logos conceptualizations of eros experience. For the spiritual life is an ongoing process rather than a final goal, and it cannot be delineated in finite, linear stages. The mystical bypath meanders here and there in a circuitous manner, spiraling in and out; it is not a straight track way to a final destination. It is best to think of the classical stages of mystical experience as "representative dimensions of spirituality" or "levels" that are not necessarily experienced in sequence.[15] From this perspective we can listen to the Christian mystics, those great souls who have traveled the pathways before us, and follow their guidance in our own exploration of these dimensions of spiritual experience.

Purgation

This aspect of spiritual experience is the one which is described first by Christian mystics because it denotes the necessity of preparation for the mystical journey. We make a grave mistake if we enter the mystical bypath expecting to find only bliss and light, for inevitably we will also encounter struggle and strife upon the way. In popular thought, mysticism is often viewed as an attempt to escape the hard facts of everyday existence by seeking solace in some "spaced-out" state of blissful peace. But actually nothing could be further from the truth. For when we embark upon the inner journey, we are bound to experience the darkness, the conflicts within ourselves, the "shadow" archetype of the Jungian psychologists and the "evil demons" of the mystics. As Morton Kelsey warns us, "In the spiritual world we can find not only greater beauty and creativity than in the physical one but also the reality of destructiveness and ugliness, of evil itself. One of the saddest misconceptions of the modern world is the notion that something that is spiritual must necessarily be good."[16] This is a problem that is readily apparent in the drug culture. Many people who are actually searching for spiritual experience today use drugs to induce "altered states of consciousness," and encounter the dark side of mystical awareness for which they are woefully unprepared. This is why it is necessary that we turn to the true mystics for guidance on how to prepare for the inner journey. Our best guide is Jesus Christ, who underwent the arduous preparation for his supremely spiritual life during the forty days he spent alone in the desert. During this time he practiced the disciplines of prayer and fasting, and confronted the temptations of the devil. We can see in the example of Jesus that inner preparation requires the dedication of time and solitude for spiritual practice. We can also understand the meaning of "purgation" as a preparatory step for mystical experience when we examine Christ's encounter with evil before he began his ministry. The trials that Jesus underwent in the wilderness marked his acknowledgement that his will belonged to God rather than his own ego. This journey out of egocentricity to a life centered on the Divine is the primary purpose of the purgative process. Along with Jacob Boehme we can pray for the goal of purgation: "conquer my 'I' in me."[17] In the wilderness Christ had to confront his own "shadow" or dark qualities when Satan tempted him to use his divine powers to produce material gain, perform supernatural actions, and achieve worldly conquest. These are all temptations which are familiar to those who possess spiritual power.

245

When Jesus says his final words to Satan: "Worship the Lord your God, and serve only him" (Matt. 4:10) the devil departs and angels appear to serve him. This indicates the completion of the process of ego transformation within Jesus; his refusal to succumb to his own ego desires, so cleverly presented by Satan, eventually leads to the overcoming of the darkness that is part of human nature. Now he is the Christ, the anointed one of God, whose ego is completely attuned to the Divine. In a similar way all who embark on the mystical bypath must confront the trials and temptations that occur when one first becomes aware of the primacy of the ego in ordinary consciousness. Evelyn Underhill describes how egocentricity is overcome in the process of purgation as "the disciplining and simplifying of the affections and will, the orientation of the heart."[18] Although few modern explorers of the mystical bypath will attempt to follow Christ's example of fasting for forty days in the wilderness, there are numerous possibilities in contemporary life for practicing the discipline and simplification that are necessary prerequisites to the transformation of the ego. Essentially the simplification of life requires the removal of the outer as well as the inner distractions of temporal life in order to make space for the Eternal to enter. Today we particularly have to deal with the outer impediments to spiritual life because Western culture is obsessed with distractions which feed the ego and starve the spirit. All of our technological advances such as phones, radios, television, cars and computers which are touted as making our lives "simpler" actually do just the opposite, taking more and more of our time and attention away from the inner life. A primary challenge for the person traveling on the mystical bypath today is to learn how to live in the world yet avoid the excessive and unnecessary distractions that are rampant in modern life. To do this requires the continual discipline of one's time and energy. It takes discipline to avoid such things as watching mindless television shows, succumbing to advertising appeals, spending endless hours playing computer games, engaging in addictive behaviors, and spending our lives in the pursuit of entertainment. Only when we have simplified our outer lives are we free to engage in the spiritual disciplines such as prayer, meditation, and contemplation which are timeless methods for eliminating the inner obstacles of ego desires and turning one's heart towards God.

One practice which can help in the process of simplifying our lives is to continually ask ourselves the question, "What is **essential**?" This is the basic question that life poses to us – the question of ultimate meaning and value – and our answer to this question can transform our consciousness. For the mystic, none of the outer things of life – whether wealth, status, home, job, even other people – are truly essential. Instead she would give the same answer as the mystical Little Prince: "What is essential is invisible to the eye."[19] When we orient our lives in the direction of this essential, invisible Spirit we can more easily let go of our concerns about worldly things. This is the practice of detachment, which is also crucial to the process of purgation. Evelyn Underhill defines detachment as "the refusal to anchor yourself to material things, to regard existence from the personal standpoint, or confuse custom with necessity."[20] All of these are ultimately means of detaching from the importance of one's ego. Attachment to material possessions, which is so strongly promoted in Western culture, keeps us firmly rooted in the ego as we spend our time and energy on getting more and more for ourselves and worrying about protecting what we already have. Jesus emphasizes the importance of non-attachment to worldly goods when he says, "Do not store up for yourselves treasures on earth, where moth and rust consume and where thieves break in and steal; but store up for yourselves treasures in heaven, where neither moth nor rust consumes and where thieves do not break in and steal. For where your treasure is, there your heart will be also." (Matt. 6:19-21) As Jesus points out in this verse, the key reason for detachment to earthly things is so that one's heart can be centered in God rather than the world. This is the reason that many Christian mystics have advocated a life of poverty – not because material goods are sinful, but because attachment to them hinders union with God. St. Francis is a prime example, for he dedicated himself to "Lady Poverty" so that all of his love would be directed towards the infinite God rather than the finite things of this world.

Detachment for the mystic also means that one must broaden one's view of life beyond the considerations of the ego. Instead of judging events as good or bad from the standpoint of how they affect me, we must seek the meaning in all manner of events by taking a deeper perspective, attempting to understand insofar as we are able how these events are consistent with the divine plan. We must view the problems and struggles of our own existence as opportunities to learn and grow in faith and wisdom, rather than yielding to fear, anger, or self-pity. Detachment from the personal vicissitudes of one's own life, which demonstrates ultimate surrender to God's will, is based on absolute trust that divine love and wisdom are at the heart of life. No matter how difficult our circumstances, we still believe with St. Paul that "all things work together for good for those who love God." (Romans 8:28)

Mystics have often attempted to use ascetic practices such as fasting, celibacy, poverty, and self-mortification to promote the process of purgation. Accounts of the austerities which early and medieval Christian mystics inflicted upon themselves often sound downright pathological to us today. While recognizing the necessity for discipline and simplification which are the basis for an ascetic lifestyle, it is also important to realize the subtle dangers which may arise in ascetic practices. Asceticism can be a stumbling block to true spirituality if it leads to a masochistic attitude towards the body and a negative view of the created world rather than joy and gratitude for all God's blessings. It is also possible for the pilgrim on the mystical bypath to become attached to spiritual practices and accomplishments. Then the ascetic lifestyle has exactly the opposite result of what was intended, inflating the ego with spiritual pride rather than diminishing the ego's importance. Mechtild of Magdeburg warns of these dangers when she says, "Those who would storm the heavenly heights by fierceness and ascetic practices deceive themselves badly. Such people carry grim hearts within themselves; they lack true humility which alone leads the soul to God."[21] The mystic must detach himself even from spiritual disciplines, viewing them not as ends in themselves but only as tools to help the ego surrender its will to God. As Thomas Merton says, "Ultimately the secret of all this is abandonment to the will of God in all things you cannot control, and perfect obedience to Him in everything that depends on your own volition, so that in all things, in your interior life and your outward works for God, you desire only one thing, which is the fulfillment of his will."[22]

Illumination

When walking in the woods early in the morning, occasionally one may see the Sun shining through the trees and illuminating hundreds of filaments of spider's web strung between the branches. The play of sunlight along the fibers appears like pulses of dancing energy. These strands of spider's web are always present but usually invisible; it is only at a particular moment, when the Sun shines on them and one's attention is completely focused upon them, that the magical dance becomes apparent to the eyes. In the same way, mystical illumination occurs when the invisible, spiritual world is made manifest to the human being whose attention is focused upon the Divine. Christ speaks of this process of illumination when he says, "Blessed are the pure in heart, for they will see God." (Matt. 5:8) Purgation can cleanse the "inner eye" and prepare the mystic to truly "see," but the actual experience of spiritual illumination is always a gift which is given by the grace of God. Only those who have purified their hearts of egocentricity are able to receive this "sudden gift of awareness, an awakening to the Real within all that is real; a vivid awareness of infinite Being at the roots of our own limited being."[23]

Just as one can see the light of the Sun either by looking at the shining spider's web or by gazing directly at the star in the sky, so the mystic can perceive the illuminating presence of the Divine within the natural world or as the transcendent Ground of Being. A panentheistic view of deity is central to the mystical bypath, for spiritual experiences of illumination reveal God as both immanent and transcendent. The mystical view is limited if it focuses only on nature, such as "pantheism" or "nature mysticism," but also if it accepts solely the spiritual world, ignoring or condemning the natural world. Julian of Norwich summarizes her mystical experience of the divine presence in this way: "He wants us to trust that he is constantly with us, and that in three ways. He is with us in heaven…drawing us up…and he is with us on earth, leading us…and he is with us in our soul, endlessly dwelling, ruling and guarding…"[24] Like Julian of

Norwich, the mystic can unite with the transcendent God in heaven, the God which penetrates nature on Earth, and the God which is immanent within the soul.

The Christian Church in general has emphasized only the first of these ways, directing the traveler on the interstate highway to look for God in heaven. However, as we have seen from our journeys on the nature bypath, the great Christian mystics such as Hildegard of Bingen and Francis of Assisi have also experienced the presence of the Divine within the natural world and loved God as He manifested through creation. The Eastern Orthodox saint of the fourth century, John Cassian, points out the importance of contemplating God in many ways:

> God is not only to be known in His blessed and
> incomprehensible being, for this is something which is
> reserved for his saints in the age to come. He is also to be
> known from the grandeur and beauty of His creatures…When
> we consider that he numbers the raindrops, the sand of the sea
> and the stars of heaven, we are amazed at the grandeur of His
> nature and His wisdom.[25]

This is a view which would be familiar to the Celtic Christians, who celebrated God's immanence in the world of nature. The Celtic Christian John Scotus Eriugena explicated this view in his concept of "theophany," that all creatures are a revelation of God who pours forth His divine essence through the manifest universe.[26] This is an example of the mystical view of cosmogenesis, which tends to understand creation as an emanation of the Godhead into the physical world rather than as a product which was created separate and apart from God. The word "emanate" derives from the Latin word "emanare," meaning "to flow"; the divine energies flow from the Source, creating and sustaining the world of nature. A cosmological view which perceives creation as the emanation of the Divine into the material realm supports the mystic's awareness of the divine presence within nature. This is the view expressed by the medieval German mystic Meister Eckhart : "the Father speaks the Son always, in unity, and pours out in him all created things."[27] Christ as the Word, the divine expression of God, flows forth into the world in the act of continual creation. Eckhart recognizes that the purpose of all things in the physical world is to communicate God's presence because they all contain the Word: "All created things are God's speech. The being of a stone speaks and manifests the same as does my mouth about God."[28] Eckhart tells us that those who listen with the "inner ear" can turn even to the stones which lie along the bypath for divine revelation.

This path to spiritual illumination, which leads us along "a way of seeing the world sacramentally,"[29] is referred to as the "Via Positiva" by Matthew Fox. On this path, mystical consciousness is marked by the awareness that God's Word and Wisdom – ChristoSophia – are inherent within every aspect of creation. This is the "original blessing" which the mystic experiences with joy and gratitude, giving thanks to God by practicing "the art of savoring" the delights of the created world.[30] One cannot be in a hurry when walking along this track of the mystical bypath, for one must take the time to closely observe, experience, and savor the beauty and pleasure of the natural world with which God blesses us. This experience of the Via Positiva was certainly the basis for Julian of Norwich's exclamation, "the fullness of joy is to contemplate God in everything."[31] Her awareness of God's presence in all things extends to even the natural processes of the human body, which were often so despised by Christian theologians. But instead she sees the blessing of God in all our physical functions: "He does not despise what he has made, nor does he disdain to serve us in the simplest natural functions of our body...For as the body is clad in cloth, and the flesh in the skin, and the bones in the flesh, and the heart in the trunk, so are we, soul and body, clad and enclosed in the goodness of God."[32]

Mystics often report their awareness of the divine presence within the created world as an experience of the feminine. As we have seen while traveling the feminine bypath, this is the Sophianic perception which unites the polarities of existence – nature and spirit, dark and light, temporal and eternal. This Sophianic perception, which is at the heart of mystical consciousness, is expressed by Jacob Boehme: "this visible world, with all its host and being, is nothing other than a counter-stroke of the spiritual world which is hidden in the material, elemental world just as the *tinctur* is in plants and animals."[33] The mystic lives the unity/duality paradox by perceiving the presence of the unchanging, eternal One within the changing forms of the multiplicity of created life. Philip St. Romain, a contemporary explorer of the mystical bypath, reports his transformed perception in this way:

> This "seeing-in-Christ" has brought a dramatic change in my
> experience of creation. No longer is there an unconscious
> sense of God's presence in creation; now it seems that
> creation itself is God-manifest. Trees are still trees, rivers are
> rivers, mountains are mountains. But they are also Christ.[34]

This is the radical shift in perception that is required in order to achieve the deep sense of relatedness to all creation. It is this Sophianic perception, the change in consciousness that is needed in order to avert the ecological disasters of our current age, that one may receive as the gift of illumination when one opens oneself to the mystery of the natural world.

This approach to spiritual illumination which recognizes the immanence of the Divine also emphasizes God's presence within the human soul. As Jungian psychologists in our modern age have so clearly demonstrated, the soul expresses itself through symbols and images. Therefore we may become aware of God's presence within the soul by paying attention to the symbols and images which spontaneously arise in dreams, visions, and forms of meditation which employ the visionary imagination. This track on the mystical bypath, which uses images as signposts to point the way to the Divine, is traditionally referred to as the "kathopathic" approach in spirituality. Although the way of imagery in mysticism has often been denounced, it is one of the paths in Christian tradition which may be especially valuable for people in our modern world. Carl Jung, a twentieth century pioneer in the study of symbolic imagery, has shown the immense value that symbols have for our psychological and spiritual condition. Symbols attempt to express that which is unknown. They arise from the unconscious and therefore help to bring greater wholeness to the psyche by providing a balance to the dominating rational consciousness. Symbols serve the process of inner transformation by helping us get in touch with the deeper, unrealized meanings and values in our lives.[35] In religious terminology, the unknowable Mystery which lies at the heart of life, penetrating our very souls, can be expressed only through the use of symbols. This is why Christ so often spoke in parables; through the use of symbols and imagery, he was attempting to communicate the truth of the divine Mystery in a language which could be understood by the soul. But Christ realized that the response for many who heard his parables was this: "seeing they do not perceive, and hearing they do not listen, nor do they understand." (Matt. 13:13) For symbolic imagery can only be understood through the eros functions of creative, intuitive insight. While many may hear the symbolic stories or see the images, only those who listen with the "inner eye" and hear with the "inner ear" of mystical consciousness will be able to interpret their deeper levels of meaning.

The use of images to stimulate mystical consciousness reached its height in the Eastern Orthodox practice of iconography. The purpose of the icon, a religious image which portrays Christ, the Virgin Mary, or the saints, is to help the believer get in touch with the Divine by looking through the image to the unknowable Mystery which it represents. As with all religious symbols, it is imperative for one to realize that the image is **not** the same thing as the Reality that it attempts to express. Failure to make this crucial distinction between the visible image and invisible deity results in idolatry.

Another problem which can arise with the use of religious imagery is that symbols lose their spiritual power to illuminate consciousness when they become literal and concrete. This has often been the case on the interstate highway of the Christian Church, where many symbols which point inward to the deep mysteries of the Christian faith have been reduced to mere outer signs which express only one accepted meaning. For example, the cross is a central symbol of the Divine in Christianity. The image of the cross can take many forms and have many different meanings, depending upon the consciousness of the one who gazes upon it. As a symbol, the Christian cross has tremendous power to help the believer contact the divine Mystery which it represents. However, when the cross is interpreted only literally as the physical cross of Calvary upon which Jesus died, it becomes a simple sign and loses the spiritual vitality of a true symbol. One of the tasks for the pilgrim on the mystical bypath is to help maintain the numinous power of living symbols in Christian tradition. Mystical illumination brings the gift of insight and imagination which can revitalize the ancient symbols and make them alive again in our modern world. The experience of illumination may also bring forth new symbols and imagery from the depths of the psyche which can recast the mysteries of the Christian faith in a manner that is appropriate for our current age.

In this way many of the great mystics have enriched the symbolic legacy of Christian tradition through the gifts of spiritual illumination that they were given in visionary experiences. For example, we have already shown how the cosmic images that Hildegard of Bingen received through her illumination by "the Living Light," as recorded in her book *Scivias* (*Know the Ways*), pointed to the mysteries of the cosmological tradition within Christianity. She also received revelations of the feminine dimension of God, especially in her visions of Sapientia (Wisdom), a beautiful woman who appeared to her in the form of a goddess. Julian of Norwich was another great visionary in the fourteenth century whose images have enriched Christian tradition. In one great episode of mystical illumination, which took place for a period of five hours on May 8, 1373, she beheld Christ's appearance in his Passion and received his revelations. Her meditations upon this mystical experience were set forth later in her book *Revelations* (or *Showings*.) As we have seen, Julian's visionary experiences brought an affirmation of God's love and the goodness of creation. She also directly encountered God as Mother; she stated, "God rejoices that he is our Father, and God rejoices that he is our Mother..."[36] Through these visions Julian infused Christianity with the Sophianic perception of the union of the masculine and feminine within the Divine. This is also shown in her description of the Trinity: "God almighty is our loving Father, and God all wisdom is our loving Mother, with the love and the goodness of the Holy Spirit, which is all one God, one Lord."[37] Her equation of the Second Person of the Trinity – Jesus – with "wisdom" and the feminine aspect of God indicates that Julian's mystical visions revealed to her the nature of ChristoSophia. Jacob Boehme, the German Protestant mystic of the early seventeenth century, also perceived the presence of the

Divine Feminine in his visionary trances. His first major experience of mystical illumination occurred in the simple activity of gazing at the reflection of the sunlight on a pewter dish; this episode initiated a series of visions, in which the divine Sophia served as the primary means of illumination for him. His book *The Way to Christ* records the dialogue between Sophia and the soul that took place during his mystical encounters with her. In it he provides instructions for the pilgrim on the mystical bypath who is seeking union with the Divine, whose appearance to Boehme was most intense in the image of the Virgin Sophia.

It is apparent from these few examples that the Divine Feminine has been able to reveal herself more fully to the mystics within Christianity than she could to the organized Church. Because it is the feminine dimension of the Divine which has been repressed in Christian tradition, this is the aspect which often breaks through into consciousness in the visionary images of mystical illumination. The symbols which arise from the depths of the mystic's unconscious point to the side of the deity which is virtually unknown to mainstream Christianity. In this way the illuminating visions of the mystic can serve all seekers on the Path of ChristoSophia by bringing greater wholeness to the Christian mythos.

Although Hildegard of Bingen, Julian of Norwich and Jacob Boehme are just a few representatives of the Christian visionary mystics, there are countless others whose inner voices and images have provided revelations that can guide the pilgrim on the mystical bypath to a greater understanding of the Christian mysteries. The value of these mystics' visionary experiences demonstrates the important role that symbolic imagery can play in mystical consciousness. However, there is another major pathway to mystical illumination. This one, which emphasizes the search for the unknown, transcendent God is traditionally referred to as the "apophatic approach" in mysticism. It recognizes that all images are inadequate to express the transcendent "otherness" of the "mysterium tremendum."[38] Pilgrims who tread this steep and strenuous path toward the Divine refer to God as the Abyss, the Ground, or even Nothingness. This is the path that leads into darkness because it is the ultimate acknowledgement of the divine Mystery. For "not-knowing is in fact the only truly proper attitude toward mystery."[39]

This approach originated with the NeoPlatonist philosophers of the third century, and was incorporated into Christian mysticism by Dionysius the Areopagite (also called Pseudo-Dionysius) in the sixth century. For Dionysius, the ascent of the soul to mystical illumination necessitates leaving behind reason and sensory perceptions in order to enter "the dark mystery of the divine."[40] In Dionysius is seen the dilemma of the mystic who attempts to describe his experience of the mystery of God which transcends all words and concepts. He uses the paradoxical language of negative rather than positive statements about God in order to point to the unknown and unlimited nature of the Divine.

The "negative" approach to mystical consciousness was embraced by the contemplative tradition within Christianity, which is the way of silence rather than imagery. Eastern Orthodox monks have maintained the practice of mystical contemplation for over a thousand years at their holy mountain of Mt. Athos in Greece. One of the Athonite monks refers to the writings of St. Gregory of Nyssa in this description of the mystical illumination that occurs on the apopathic way:

> Man sees at first the Light because he used to live in darkness...Yet, the more he approaches the Divine Essence the more he realizes the impossibility of beholding the divine nature and this is what the Fathers call 'radiant darkness'... this is the seeing that consists of not seeing, because that which is sought transcends all knowledge, being separated on all sides by incomprehensibility as by a kind of darkness.[41]

The true Light of God becomes a darkness for humans because they cannot fathom the divine Essence. The contemplative can only rest in the depths of this dark silence, letting go of all words and images which are wholly inadequate when one encounters the divine Mystery. The pilgrim on this path must finally resort to silence when attempting to communicate his mystical illumination, for all language falls far short of the experience of the transcendent God. As Meister Eckhart says,

> God is nameless, because no one can say anything or
> understand anything about him…If I say: "God is a being,"
> it is not true; he is a being transcending being and a
> transcending nothingness…So be silent about, and do not
> chatter about God; for when you do chatter about him, you
> are telling lies and sinning.[42]

The contemplative teaches us the importance of letting go of all our images of God, which are often simply projections of our ego and therefore block us from union with our eternal Ground. It is in this spirit that Eckhart says, "Therefore let us pray to God that we may be free of 'God.'"[43] It is only when we humbly acknowledge our total ignorance of God that we can, in the words of the modern contemplative Thomas Merton, "know **beyond** all knowing or 'unknowing.'"[44]

One of the best guides for pilgrims undertaking this arduous route along the mystical bypath can be found in a treatise written by an anonymous English mystic in the fourteenth century called *The Cloud of Unknowing*. It describes the contemplative mystical journey in this way:

> For when you first begin to undertake it, all you find is a
> darkness, a sort of cloud of unknowing; you cannot tell what
> it is, except that you experience in your will a simple reaching
> out to God…So set yourself to rest in this darkness as long
> as you can, always crying out after him whom you love. For
> if you are to experience him or see him at all, insofar as it
> is possible here, it must always be in this cloud and in this
> darkness.[45]

The author of this text stresses that it is only through love that one can reach out to God. He advises the seeker "to smite upon that thick cloud of unknowing with a sharp dart of longing love."[46] Because God is beyond all our mental concepts and sense perceptions, we must approach the Divine through love rather than the intellect. As the author states, "it is love alone which can reach God in this life, and not knowing."[47] It is eros – not logos – that is the means to mystical illumination in the dark cloud of unknowing.

St. John of the Cross, the well known Christian contemplative of the sixteenth century, extended the experience of divine darkness to refer to the point on the mystical journey that he called the "dark night of the soul."[48] The "dark night" aptly describes the suffering of the soul which experiences the absence of God. It is a common condition for those who have already traveled far upon the mystical journey and increasingly surrendered their will to God to be tormented by doubts about God's will or even his existence. However, this state of emptiness and desolation is only a stage on the spiritual journey that precedes the soul's ultimate union with the Divine; it is akin to the darkness before the dawn.[49] The purpose of this "dark night" is that it brings the process of purgation to its culmination, forcing the mystic to detach from even the spiritual pleasures which come from experiencing God's presence. St. John of the Cross's account can provide wise guidance for the pilgrim on the mystical bypath who experiences this condition. When one is immersed in the "dark night" experience, one must continue to trust in God even when bereft of all spiritual consolations. In the midst of loneliness and confusion, one must not succumb to despair, but instead must wait patiently for God with a loving heart. For when the work of the "dark night" is accomplished, the final attachments of the ego will be dissolved and the soul will be ready to receive the fullness of the Divine.

Matthew Fox refers to the way of darkness as the "Via Negativa," which "opens us to our divine depths."[50] As in the "dark night of the soul," pain and suffering can lead us to a deeper experience of the mystery of the Divine as well as our own souls. The "Via Negativa" is the path that Christ walked during his crucifixion; he experienced his own "dark night of the soul" when he cried out from the cross as darkness covered the land, "My God, my God, why have you forsaken me?" (Matt. 27: 46) It was shortly after this total emptying of himself that his soul left his body to reunite fully with God.

Many mystics have experienced Christ on the "Via Negativa" in the image of his wounded heart. In walking this path we must follow the lead of Christ and also allow our own hearts to be wounded so that we may deeply experience the suffering of earthly life – not only our own individual suffering, but also the suffering of humanity, the suffering of the creatures of Earth, and the suffering of Sophia as the Soul of the World. For it is only when one's heart is opened, through its wounding, that one can relate to the suffering of others.

The climax of mystical illumination occurs with the realization that the way of the light and the way of the dark are necessary complements to each other on the spiritual journey. Mechtild of Magdeburg describes this insight in her vision:

> Our Lord held two golden chalices in his hands that were both full of living wine. In the left was the red wine of suffering, and in his right hand the white wine of sublime consolation. Then our Lord spoke:...I give both out of divine love...noblest of all are those who drink both the white and the red.[51]

When we drink deeply of the red wine of sorrow as well as the white wine of joy we may share in the mystical illumination of the wholeness of life in both its light and dark aspects. Likewise we may recognize the unity of the Divine, who is revealed to us within the natural world and hidden from us within the deep Abyss. For it is only by going through the dark that we come to the light; it is only by going through Earth that we reach Heaven.

Mystical Union

This integration of the polarities of existence is the essence of mystical union. "In union, all is One, one is All, and this All/One is given completely in every timeless moment."[52] For the pilgrim on the mystical bypath, the supreme unitive state occurs when the soul and the Divine are joined as one. The great Christian mystics tell us that this union is always the result of God's grace. This blessed state of oneness with God can only be received as the gift that it is; there is nothing that we can do to bring it about except to willingly surrender to God's love. Teresa of Avila offers the following analogy: "the soul does nothing more in this union than does the wax when another impresses a seal on it. The wax doesn't impress the seal upon itself; it is only disposed – I mean by being soft."[53] At this stage of the mystical journey the soul must let go of all active striving and simply be receptive to the actions of the Divine upon it.

Thomas Merton describes the experience of mystical union in this way:

> The essence of the union is a pure and selfless love that
> empties the soul of all pride and annihilates it in the sight of
> God, so that nothing may be left of it but the pure capacity for
> Him...the only way to enter into that joy is to dwindle down
> to a vanishing point and become absorbed in God through the
> center of your own nothingness.[54]

After the final purgative experience of the "dark night," the soul is stripped of egocentric desires so that its emptiness may be filled purely with God. Just as the glory of the resurrection followed Christ's crucifixion, so the soul may experience the rebirth of mystical union after enduring the agonies of the "dark night" which bring death to the "I." Through the experience of "nothingness" the ego is dissolved so that the hidden Self, the ground of the soul, is revealed in its essential unity with the Divine Ground.

The primary model of mystical union is found in Jesus Christ, who proclaimed "The Father and I are one." (John 10:30) This statement reveals the mystery of the divine nature of Christ; for Jesus did not just intermittently experience union, but lived his life in a conscious state of oneness with God. The mystery of the Incarnation – in which the Divine became human – reveals the potential of all to share in Christ's unity with the Divine. As Irenaeus said in the second century, "God became a human being in order that human beings might become God."[55] This statement describes the Eastern Orthodox concept of theosis, or the deification of human beings. As Kallistos Ware explains:

> God's Incarnation opens the way to man's deification. To
> be deified is, more specifically, to be 'christified': the divine
> likeness that we are called to attain is the likeness of Christ.
> It is through Jesus the God-man that we men are 'ingodded,'
> 'divinized,' made 'sharers in the divine nature." (2 Pet. 1:4)[56]

Orthodox tradition distinguishes between the **essence** of the transcendent, hidden God and the **energies** of the manifest, immanent God. In mystical union the person unites with the divine energies but never the divine essence. In this way the mystic always remains a human being who experiences an "I-Thou" relationship with God rather than the dissolution of his identity within the Godhead.[57]

St. Paul recognized his own divinized state when he said, "it is no longer I who live, but it is Christ who lives in me."(Galatians 2:20) He still existed as the man Paul, but his "I" had been transformed into Christ-consciousness. All humans may share Paul's experience when the ego is displaced by the emergence of the hidden, true Self which is the image of the Divine or the "Cosmic Christ" within each of us.[58] Unity with God results from the awakening of Christ-consciousness, for this is the center of the soul where the Divine and human are one.

Deification occurs when one has experienced the "second birth" that Christ refers to in John 3:5: "no one can enter the kingdom of God without being born of water and Spirit." Through this baptism of the "living water," the true Self which is hidden in the depths of the soul is "born" into conscious awareness. The "second birth" results in a "new being" who realizes that his true identity is not the outer "I" but the deep Self which is also the inner Christ. One will still experience the trials and sufferings of earthly life, but now they will be perceived through this transformed consciousness. Deification is the proper state for all human beings since every soul is made in the image of the Divine; this is the "Good News" that Jesus Christ brought humanity through his Incarnation. However, it is a divine mystery which is still unrealized by most people. For although divinization is the birthright of all, it is also a gift which can only be received by those who have purified their hearts through the rigors of the spiritual journey.

Mystics have used a variety of images in their attempts to portray this ultimately indescribable unitive experience. Meister Eckhart followed an earlier mystical tradition in his graphic depiction of the deification process as the "birth of the Son in the soul":

> The Father gives birth to his Son in eternity, equal to himself.
> 'The Word was with God, and God was the Word.' (Jn 1:1); it

261

was the same in the same nature. Yet I say more: he has given
birth to him in my soul. Not only is the soul with him, and he
equal with it, but he is in it, and the Father gives his Son birth
in the soul in the same way he gives him birth in eternity…[59]

The Incarnation of Jesus Christ, which according to Christian
tradition occurred at one particular moment in history, is also
understood by the mystics to be an eternal process. Christ is
continually born within the human soul because the soul's ground is
one with the divine Ground. The mystical divinization of the human
being is complete when "he gives birth to me as himself and himself
as me and to me as his being and nature. In the innermost source…
there is one life and one being and one work."[60]

Eckhart's other major image for mystical union is the theme of
"breaking-through" to the Ground where the soul and the Divine are
one. In his description of the apophatic mystical way, he says that
the "spark in the soul…wants to go into the simple ground, into the
quiet desert, into which distinction never gazed, not the Father, nor
the Son, nor the Holy Spirit."[61] In this state of mystical union, the
soul breaks through all dualities to the One which lies even beyond
the Trinity. Transcending all the separations of ego-consciousness,
the mystic discovers "in this breaking-through…that God and I are
one."[62] This is the direct experiential awareness that the ground of
the soul is joined with the divine Ground.

Although the spiritual journey is commonly described as an
ascent up a ladder or a mountain, there are many images which
instead portray the unitive experience as a "sinking" or "flowing."
This emphasizes that the final stage of the mystical journey is not
achieved through assertive struggle, but instead depends upon
the passive process of "letting go." Meister Eckhart gives these
instructions to those who have reached this point in their spiritual
journey: "You ought to sink down out of all your your-ness, and
flow into his his-ness, and your 'yours' and his 'his' ought to become
one 'mine,' so completely that you with him perceive his uncreated
is-ness, and his nothingness, for which there is no name."[63]

All of these diverse images point to the truth that receptivity is
the key to mystical union. At this juncture on the mystical bypath
one can only cooperate with the process by opening one's heart

completely to the Divine and flowing with the actions of the Spirit within the soul. Nowhere is this receptive attitude better expressed than in the beautiful images which portray mystical union as the spiritual marriage of the soul with the Beloved. Erotic imagery is abundant in the mystical literature of all traditions, for it symbolizes in a powerful way the intimacy of the soul and God as experienced in the unitive state. As we have seen, the "hieros gamos" or sacred marriage is an archetypal theme; it appears in the union of the Goddess and the Green Man in pagan mythology and the union of Christ and Sophia in gnostic Christianity. The symbolism of the spiritual marriage found in the writings of medieval Christian mystics is reminiscent of the gnostic Christian ritual of the bridal chamber, in which the divine spark within the human soul reunites with its divine Ground, thus overcoming the illusion of separation.

Although the theme of the sacred marriage is found throughout Christian mystical literature, it reached its full development in the cultural milieu of the twelfth century. Mystics of this time, influenced by the language of love cultivated by troubadours, trouveres, and the Courts of Love, produced passionate poetic images of the love between God and human. Marriage, which represents the union of opposites, became a potent symbol which was used by the mystics to express the union of the feminine soul and the masculine Christ, the union of the human and the Divine.

Bernard of Clairvaux, a Cistercian monk of the twelfth century, was one of the major influences on this love mysticism in Christian tradition. He explored the theme of spiritual love primarily through his extensive sermons on *The Song of Songs*, the love poem of the Hebrew Bible which has furnished allegorical material for many mystics through the ages. Bernard interpreted the meaning of the "bride" in *The Song of Songs* as referring to both the Christian Church and the individual soul, but he emphasized the latter. This is why he exhorted his monks to prepare themselves inwardly as "brides" for the coming of Christ, the divine bridegroom. He explained the allegory in this way:

> The Bride...is the soul which thirsts for God...for no names
> can be found as sweet as those in which the Word and the
> soul exchange affections, as Bridegroom and Bride, for to

such everything is common, nothing is the property of one and not the other, nothing is held separately.[64]

Bernard used the symbol of marriage to denote the closeness of the soul and God in which there is no separation. Mystical union is symbolized by "the kiss of his mouth" (The Song of Songs 1:1) for "when we are joined with him in a holy kiss we are made one with him in spirit…"[65] This signifies the primacy of love in Bernard's mysticism, as the soul "pours herself out completely in love" in response to "the inexhaustible flow of love from his spring."[66] When the soul realizes the strength of God's love, it cannot help but love in return although human love can never approach the limitless depth of divine love. The soul then lyrically praises the joys of this mutual love which unites her with Christ:

> Happy is she to whom it is given to know the embrace of
> such tenderness! For it is nothing other than holy and chaste
> love, love sweet and tender, love as tranquil as it is true,
> mutual, close, deep love, which is not in one flesh, but which
> joins two in one spirit, making two no longer two but one
> (Mt. 19:5).[67]

But, just as human lovers must eventually part, so too does the Divine Lover take leave of the soul. However, God is never really absent even though the human being may not experience his presence. As Bernard explains, "let us understand that this is only how it feels to the soul; there is no movement of the Word. When the soul is aware of grace, she knows that the Word is with her. When she is not, she seeks him who is absent, and begs him to come to her…"[68] Bernard points out that mystical union is not a constant state while in this earthly realm; union with the Beloved alternates with periods of separation, when the soul aches in its yearning for God until the Lover returns.

Mechtild of Magdeburg in the thirteenth century repeated many of Bernard of Clairvaux's themes in passionate poetic images which express the mutual yearning between God and the soul. Mechtild was a member of the Beguine community, a group of women who pledged themselves to religious lives but were not members of an established religious order. This way of living, which combined worldly and spiritual life, laid the foundation for Mechtild's mystical experiences which joined sensual and spiritual imagery perhaps more than any other mystical writer. Her mystical treatise *The Flowing Light of the Godhead*, which records the visionary dialogue between God and her soul, marks a pinnacle of love mysticism within Christianity.

Mechtild's language, which is based in the tradition of Courtly Love, is an expression of pure eros for this is the only way that she can describe her ecstatic experiences of union with Love. The soul states her longing for God in this way:

> Lord, you are my lover,
> My desire,
> My flowing fount,
> My sun;
> And I am your reflection.[69]

God reciprocates this yearning as He "caresses the soul in six ways":

> You are my softest pillow,
> My most lovely bed,
> My most intimate repose,
> My deepest longing,
> My most sublime glory.
> You are an allurement to my Godhead,
> A thirst for my humanity,
> A stream for my burning.[70]

The soul who seeks union with the Beloved must travel the sevenfold path of love by passing beyond the temptations of the world and the desires of the ego. Then she puts on the three garments of the bride – humility, chastity, and her good name – and meets the Lord who leads her in a dance of praise so she can "leap with abandon...leap into love."[71] Finally the bride is prepared to join her Love in "the secret chamber of the invisible Godhead;"[72] here the bed has been prepared for her and she removes her clothing so that the soul will be naked before God. The moment of mystical union is thus described by Mechtild:

> Then a blessed stillness
> That both desire comes over them.
> He surrenders himself to her,
> And she surrenders herself to him…
> But this cannot last long.
> When two lovers meet secretly,
> They must often part from one another inseparably.[73]

Here Mechtild again echoes Bernard of Clairvaux's realization that experiences of union must be followed by separation in spiritual as well as human love. Mechtild experiences the "dark night" of doubt and loneliness after the ecstatic bliss of passionate love, but God consoles her by telling her where he will be in his absence:

> I am in myself in all places and in all things,
> As I always have been eternally,
> And I shall be waiting for you in the orchard of love
> And shall pluck for you the flowers of sweet union…[74]

Although the heights of the nuptial union cannot be sustained forever, the mystic realizes nevertheless that God, who is present in all things, is never truly absent. It is not the raptures of ecstatic union, but the faithful love of the soul for God – in both joy and sorrow – which is most important in the spiritual life.

Teresa of Avila, the Carmelite mystic of the sixteenth century, also had visionary experiences in which she received the blessing of spiritual marriage to Christ. Her text, *The Interior Castle*, is a systematic presentation of the stages on the spiritual journey which lead to this final unitive experience. Based on a vision of a crystal castle with seven dwelling places, she draws an analogy between it and the "interior castle" of the soul. One may enter the first three dwelling places through spiritual effort and the practice of virtues, but only God's grace can open the doors to the last four which reveal the essence of mystical experience. Entry into the fourth dwelling place marks the beginning of contemplative prayer and the fifth dwelling place brings the prayer of union. In the sixth dwelling place the soul meets with its Beloved and undergoes preparations for its betrothal which include visions and raptures as well as trials and affliction, including the woundings of love. It is in the seventh dwelling place, which exists in the center of the castle, that the consummation of the spiritual marriage takes place. Teresa explains that "this secret union takes place in the very interior center of the soul, which must be where God Himself is…"[75] She struggles to explain the indescribable mysteries of the spiritual marriage, making analogies with the union which takes place when rain falls into a river, a stream enters the sea, or two beams of light join upon entering a room. In all cases two seemingly independent entities merge completely so that there is no longer any separation between them. Even though trials and suffering still exist as long as one remains in the physical body, the soul which is spiritually wed to its Beloved remains at peace.

Jacob Boehme's treatise *The Way of Christ* also used his visionary experiences as the basis for a description of the stages of the mystical journey which culminates in the spiritual marriage. However, he differs from the preceding initiates of the bridal chamber by characterizing the Divine Lover as the Virgin Sophia. Boehme's statement that "Sophia has revealed Herself in the precious name JESUS as Christ"[76] expresses the same understanding of the Sophianic nature of Christ that was held by many in the earliest Christian communities. But it is in the form of the Divine Feminine that the Second Person of the Trinity presents herself to him:

> You will obtain the love of a kiss from the noble Sophia in the holy Name JESUS for She stands immediately before the soul's door and knocks and warns the sinner of (his) godless ways. If he desires Her love She is willing and kisses him with a beam of Her sweet love, by which the heart receives joy.[77]

Since this statement appears in the first treatise which focuses on "true repentance," it appears that Sophia woos the soul even on the first step of the spiritual journey. It is her love which leads him away from temptations and earthly attachments. The responsive soul will have her as a companion as he travels further upon the spiritual path which eventually leads to the consummation of the mystical marriage:

> Immediately the marriage with the Virgin Sophia begins
> when the two lovers receive each other in joy, and press into
> each other with completely inner desire, in the sweetest love
> of God. Then in a short time the marriage of the lamb is
> prepared when the Virgin Sophia (as the worthy humanity of
> Christ) is wedded with the soul.[78]

The love of Sophia – which is synonymous with love of Christ – is central to Boehme's mystical experience. He presents the divine Sophia, in images often reminiscent of those of the gnostic Christians, as the loving guide of the soul at the beginning of the spiritual journey as well as the treasure at its end.

Teresa of Avila summarizes the stages of mysticism by comparing the soul to a silkworm. Like the worm who spins its cocoon, we can build the dwelling place for Christ within the soul through our spiritual efforts in the first stages of the mystical journey. When we reach the point where we are blessed with the experience of union during prayer, our soul is transformed just like the silkworm that changes into a white butterfly. In the final stage of the mystical journey, when the soul is wed to Divine Love, its old ego-self dies and its nature is wholly transformed into the resurrected Christ. Teresa describes the final destination of the mystical bypath as "the place where the little butterfly…dies, and with the greatest joy because its life is now Christ. And that its life is Christ is understood better, with the passing of time, by the effects this life has."[79] Teresa points out that the interior life of prayer and the external life of action are two complementary aspects of the full mystical life. For the realization of mystical union brings greater responsibilities and more work in service to the Divine in all. Commitment to this work is based upon an emptying of the ego, thus deification allows the divine energies to flow without the obstructions that the ego usually raises. Jacob Boehme tells us that our "one single order" from God is to "give our wills to Him and allow His Spirit to work in us, playing and making what he wills. What he works and reveals in us we give to Him again as His fruits."[80] The true value of the mystical life is revealed in its "fruits" or effects in the outer world. The sweetest of these fruits are faith and love. For the pilgrim on the mystical bypath, faith is not adherence to some external system of belief, but instead consists of receptivity to the spiritual processes within the divine inner Self. Faith in the validity and value of these spiritual experiences opens one to the workings of God within the human soul. This is the true basis, then, of love. For one who has united with Christ, love is not based on duty to the external commandment "love one another," but is instead an authentic response of the heart which has experienced the unity of Self and Other. Thus the rhythm of the mystical life is union with the transcendent God alternating with service to the immanent God. The lives of all the saints exemplify this synthesis of interior mystical life and outward action which is grounded in love.

Meister Eckhart emphasizes the importance of the inner attitude with which one goes about his outer activities; the fruits of the mystical life grow from our **being** rather than our **doing**. For all actions are sacred when they arise from the divine Ground rather than the human ego. As Eckhart says, "It is not what we do that makes us holy, but we ought to make holy what we do."[81] Union with God brings an end to distinctions between the sacred and secular. Eating, sleeping, and mundane work all become holy activities when performed with the inner Beloved. As Thomas Merton says, "the saint preaches sermons by the way he walks and the way he stands and the way he sits down and the way he picks things up and holds them in his hand."[82] Deification results in the transformation of one's whole being whose effects are seen in every aspect of one's life. The divinized human being, through whose actions divine love flows into the world, no longer needs to seek an explanation for existence. He can simply **be** without asking "Why?" For as Meister Eckhart says, "he who lives in the goodness of his nature lives in God's love; and love has no why."[83] Life then becomes ultimately a celebration of the divine dance of life.

This is the dance which the gnostic Christians described in their hymn of Christ. The gnostic round dance symbolizes mystical consciousness, for the disciples who turn toward Christ in the center are actually turning toward the divine center within the Self. In mystical union one enters the center of the dance itself and becomes one with divine Love. Then there is no longer any separation between one's ego and divine Will. Through the process of deification one realizes one's position as both dancer and the center of the dance itself. This is truly the basis for spiritual transformation - as the dancer, one's will is aligned to the will of the Divine; in the center of the dance, one's will **is** the divine Will. Then there is no difference between work and play, sacred and secular, solitude and community, for all of one's life expresses the wholeness of the divine dance.

This description of an Orthodox monk of Mt. Athos illustrates the spiritual wholeness that is found at the end of the mystical journey:

> Living, therefore, in Christ he attains not only the unification
> of his whole inner world but also of the world around him.
> He overcomes all the divisions and he ascends to an even
> higher level than the one before the Fall; he becomes like the
> first Adam.[84]

The deified mystic attains the wholeness which allows him to return to the original state of paradisal unity, although now with the "higher level" of consciousness that he has obtained through the mystical journey. Primordial humanity, represented by Adam and Eve, existed in a state of unconscious union with God in the Garden of Eden. So it is in the beginning of life for all human beings, who have not yet developed a sense of ego separateness. The cause of the "Fall," Adam's disobedience to God, symbolizes the willfulness of the ego in every human being who experiences alienation from the divine Ground. The mystical journey leads to a transformation of the ego and ultimately to reunion with the Divine. So at the end of the mystical bypath is found the way to re-enter the garden of Paradise, but this time with the heightened consciousness of the mystic who is able to live the unity/duality paradox.

Jacob Boehme expresses the mystical insight that this return to the Garden reveals the presence of Sophia, for it is she who brings the perception of wholeness that is essential to mystical consciousness. He explains that Sophia's "pearl" was present in the beginning in Adam as the divine harmony, but the Fall from unity into fragmentation caused Adam to lose this precious pearl of wholeness. It is through the androgynous "new Adam" – the union of Christ and Sophia – that humanity will regain its original oneness with the Divine.[85] For Boehme, the mystical journey leads back to

Paradise where the soul who unites with ChristoSophia will receive the pearl of wisdom and wholeness.

MARKERS ON THE MYSTICAL BYPATH

In a culture such as ours' which relies on the powers of logos reasoning, people in general are spiritually illiterate and therefore unprepared for walking the mystical bypath. This is why it is necessary to look for the trail markers of those who have traveled the way before us, following the guidance of these Christian mystics as we explore the rough and sometimes dangerous trails of the mystical bypath. As we have seen, there are many different paths which one may take on the mystical journey, so the first task for the beginning pilgrim is to decide which track to set out on. It is important to keep in mind that the various approaches to mysticism are not exclusive; for example, St. Teresa of Avila used her visionary experience of the "interior castle" of the soul as a means for describing the contemplative journey into the "unknowingness" of God. People of differing temperaments will probably find different spiritual practices most useful. So the most important consideration in beginning the mystical journey is simply that: **begin!** Take the first steps on the mystical bypath from where one is and continue walking, always searching for the signposts which will lead one further along the way. After traveling a distance along this path, markers may appear which point to other trails that one might profitably explore. However, it is very important on the mystical journey not to cross from one trail to another without fully exploring the path that one has chosen. It is also important to realize that although there is no one "right path" on the mystical bypath, certainly some approaches are better than others. The spiritual explorer needs to beware of the dangers which may be found on the mystical bypath and assess the value of the path that she has chosen by the spiritual "fruits" which grow in her life; an increase in faith and love is the primary sign of the validity of any spiritual path.

Some of the most valuable signposts along the mystical bypath are those which guide us in the practice of prayer and meditation. These are the methods which have been used for centuries to develop

271

the spiritual faculties and transform consciousness. The basis for the meditative attitude that leads to mystical illumination is found in this verse in Psalms: "Be still and know that I am God." (Ps. 46:10) One must be still – cease the ordinary flow of physical and mental activity – in order to perceive the Reality which exists beneath the everyday reality of normal consciousness. Thomas Merton advises those who are embarking upon the spiritual journey to apply this attitude to every aspect of life:

> The best thing beginners in the spiritual life can do…is
> to acquire the agility and freedom of mind that will help
> them to find light and warmth and ideas and love for God
> everywhere they go and in all that they do. People who only
> know how to think about God during fixed periods of the day
> will never get very far in the spiritual life.[86]

While the goal of meditative practice is to develop this mystical consciousness which perceives the Divine in all of life, nevertheless periods of solitude are necessary in order to nurture this awareness. Those who have traveled far along the mystical bypath show us how important it is to set aside specific times for spiritual retreat from the world, on a daily basis as well as more intensive periods at longer intervals. This time for solitary prayer and meditation allows the roots of the soul to reach into the divine darkness and absorb the life-giving water and nutrients of the Spirit so that the flower of one's life and work can bloom when returning to the outer world.

Because of the suppression of the mystical bypath within Christianity, those who travel on the interstate highway of the Church seldom receive instruction in methods for prayer and meditation. Although this situation is changing somewhat today because of the work of visionary leaders within the Church who recognize the need that people have for deeper spiritual experience, it is still common for Christians to turn to Eastern religions or New Age practices to look for methods of meditation that they do not find within the Church. However, those who have explored the mystical bypath know that Christianity has a tradition of meditation practices which are as viable as those of Eastern religions with the additional value of being grounded in our own culture. Eastern Orthodoxy in particular is a repository of the Christian mystical tradition. Kyriacos Markides, a sociologist who went on his own pilgrimage to study the Orthodox monks who still perform their age-old spiritual practices on Mt. Athos, believes that this mystical tradition can play a central role in the revitalization of Christianity. The significance of the Mt. Athos monastery for contemporary Christians lies in its preservation of the experiential spiritual tradition of early Christianity which has been lost to most travelers on the interstate highway of the Church. Markides believes that the essential elements of this tradition, if adapted to our contemporary Western culture, can help Christians regain the vital, living spirituality that was characteristic of the early Christian community.[87]

One of the Orthodox pathways that can be especially beneficial for us to explore is the practice of "hesychia," the way of interior stillness and silence. The trail marker which points the pilgrim towards this inner stillness is the "Prayer of the Heart" or the "Jesus Prayer," which consists of repeating the phrase "Lord Jesus Christ, Son of God, have mercy on me a sinner." In Orthodoxy the "heart" symbolizes "the spiritual state of man's being, the human person as made in God's image – the deepest and truest self."[88] The purpose of the Jesus Prayer is to open one's heart – one's true Self – to the loving presence of God. The practice of this prayer consists of three levels, as described by Kallistos Ware:

> It starts as "prayer of the lips," oral prayer. Then it grows more inward, becoming "prayer of the intellect," mental prayer. Finally the intellect "descends" into the heart and is united with it, and so he prayer becomes "prayer of the heart"…At this level it becomes prayer of the whole person – no longer something that we think or say, but something that we are: for the ultimate purpose of the spiritual Way is not just a person who says prayers from time to time, but a person who is prayer all the time.[89]

This progression in the practice of prayer is illustrated in *The Way of a Pilgrim*, the story of an unknown nineteenth century peasant who faithfully persevered along this track of the mystical bypath by constantly reciting the Jesus Prayer as he literally walked across his native Russia. The narrative of his remarkable journey can serve as an inspiration for other pilgrims on the mystical quest, for he attained the final destination of the inner pilgrimage – a spiritual state in which the Jesus Prayer is repeated effortlessly and continuously within the heart even in the midst of all other activities.[90] In this transformed state of consciousness it is actually the inner Christ who is doing the praying. The Jesus Prayer has accomplished its purpose – "to unify the whole of man 'who has become fragmented' " – and bears its "wonderful fruit" of love, for "not only man himself is integrated, but (he) also feels the unity of mankind."[91]

The Prayer of the Heart is essentially an apophatic approach within Orthodox tradition, which ultimately seeks inner union with the Divine beyond any thoughts or images. Within Western Christianity, an attempt to renew the contemplative tradition is found in the practice of "centering prayer." Thomas Keating explains the essence of contemplative practice in this way:

> Contemplative prayer is a way of tuning in to a fuller level
> of reality that is always present and in which we are invited
> to participate. Some suitable discipline is required to reduce
> the obstacles to this expanded awareness. One way is to slow
> down the speed at which our ordinary thoughts come down
> the stream of consciousness. If this can be done, space begins
> to appear between the thoughts, enabling an awareness of the
> reality upon which they are resting.[92]

Centering prayer provides an entrance to the interior silence of contemplation. This method makes use of a sacred word – such as "God," "Jesus," "love," etc. – to help one practice detachment from thoughts and thus make this shift in consciousness. The sacred word is an "arrow" which points to God and expresses one's intention of opening to the Divine within.[93] Since the purpose of contemplative prayer is to rest in God, one should simply reach out towards God and place the sacred word gently into awareness when one is distracted from the inner silence by other thoughts. It does not need to be repeated continuously; it should be dispensed with when one is experiencing the presence of God in interior silence and returned to when thoughts inevitably come back. As Keating says, "the use of the sacred word is designed to foster the receptive attitude…it is simply an attitude of waiting for the Ultimate Mystery."[94] He stresses the importance of regular periods of prayer, suggesting two daily sessions of twenty to thirty minutes each. This is necessary in order to maintain a level of interior silence throughout the day so that the greatest benefits of contemplation can be realized in all aspects of one's life. For the pilgrim who perseveres on this path by regular and devoted practice of contemplative prayer, "The presence of God should become a kind of fourth dimension to all of life…The contemplative state is established when contemplative prayer moves from being an experience or series of experiences to an abiding state of consciousness."[95] Those who have taken the mystical journey of contemplative prayer to its furthest point report experiences very similar to the masters of the Jesus Prayer. One's prayer becomes increasingly the prayer of the Divine within, as contemplation becomes a continual state which unifies one's outer as well as inner life.

In addition to the trail markers which point the direction on the apophatic way, the spiritual seeker will also discover signposts on the kathopathic way of the mystical bypath. These markers have been made more visible in recent times due to the work of Jungian psychologists, who recognize the immense value of images as the language of the soul. Christians such as John Sanford and Morton Kelsey who have applied Carl Jung's concepts to the traditions of their faith have done a great deal to make the way of imagery on the mystical bypath more accessible. Morton Kelsey explains his reasons for exploring this path: "images open one not only to the depth of oneself, but also beyond to the world of the spiritual realities where one is able to come into contact even with the realm of the Divine."[96] Spiritual practices which open up this inner world of images are important means to experiencing God's presence within the soul.

The easiest way to begin to explore this inner world of symbolic imagery is by paying attention to one's dreams. That dreams serve as revelations of the Divine is a belief that is widely held among many different spiritual traditions. Many dreams are reported in the Bible, from Pharoah's dream which foretold seven years of famine, to Joseph's dream in which he was warned by an angel to take Mary and Jesus to Egypt to escape Herod's wrath. It is apparent from the records of numerous dreams that both the Jews and early Christians placed great significance upon the symbolic meaning of the dream. All of the major theologians of the early Church as well believed in the revelatory power of dreams.[97] The work of psychologists in our modern time can help us reconnect with the wisdom that earlier peoples found in their dreams. Carl Jung pointed out that dream symbols may arise from personal as well as archetypal elements within the psyche. Therefore, dream images can help us integrate parts of ourselves that may be blocking our psychological and spiritual growth; they also can reveal to us the universal world of the archetypes, which in spiritual terminology is known as the realm of the Divine. These archetypal dreams provide a means of access to divine revelation for us today in the same way that they have done for spiritual explorers throughout the centuries.

In addition to paying attention to the images which arise spontaneously in our dreams, we can also get in touch with inner images through various forms of meditation, for symbols produced in the dream and the imagination come from the same source. Although meditation with images has often been denigrated by Church authorities as well as some mystics who accepted only the apophatic approach, it nevertheless has been a well traveled way on the mystical bypath. Trail markers can be found in the tradition of "lectio divina," the reading of the Bible in medieval monasteries which produced responses in the imagination of the listener, and in the "Spiritual Exercises" of Ignatius Loyola which employ imaginative enactments of the life of Jesus. Contemporary psychological techniques such as "creative visualization" and "active imagination" are of great value in helping modern people get in touch again with the images of the inner world and using them for psychological and spiritual transformation. Morton Kelsey provides a very helpful guide to various types of imagery meditation based in Christian spirituality in his book *The Other Side of Silence*. He claims that "few things are much more important for the development of our spiritual life…than knowing the images that arise within us and meditating upon them."[98] There are several methods that he suggests to get in touch with these inner images. One is to focus on an outer stimulus such as a religious symbol, art work, or Bible passage, and allow it to unfold in the imagination. For example, one can step into a Biblical story in one's imagination, either as an observer of the events or even as one of the characters. This "re-living" of the story can lead to a much deeper understanding of the Scriptures and a closer relationship with the Divine. Through this method of visualization one can encounter once again the numinous power of the traditional images which have often become stale for us, and in this way help bring about the revitalization of Christian symbols which is so necessary today.

Another way of meditating with images is to begin within the imagination, practicing the quiet stillness of meditation until images begin to arise spontaneously. One then allows these images to unfold without trying to direct or control events. Following the meditation period, the symbolic meaning of the images may be explored in a similar manner to dream interpretation. Using this method of active imagination, one may engage in dialogue with figures who appear in the inner world and even receive guidance from them based on the wisdom that comes from the deep spiritual center of the psyche. In meditation the figure of Christ may appear and talk to us like He has with many mystics such as Mechtild of Magdeburg, or Sophia may converse with us as She did with Jacob Boehme.

Many mystics who have explored this meditative path have warned of the dangers that confront us in the imaginative realm, for here we also encounter the destructive forces of the psyche as well as the benevolent ones. When using images in meditation we must be especially careful to practice discernment and judge the insights we receive by their effects in our lives. We must be prepared to deal with the negative images which may arise because this is necessary to our spiritual growth. For as Kelsey says, "We can seldom seek the Holy unless we deal with the full depth of our souls."[99] Meditation with images provides another way to the inner transformation which leads to wholeness.

The images that arise spontaneously in meditation may also at times provide new symbols to represent the mysteries of the Christian faith for our time. This is because divine revelation is an ongoing process; the universal archetypes are expressed through symbols which reflect the person's individual psyche as well as culture and historical period. Thus, the symbols which arise from the spiritual depths of the seeker on the mystical bypath today may express the same truths of Christian tradition in different forms. As Matthew Fox tells us, "Every person needs to learn to trust his or her own images."[100] These images may possess immense value for the birth of the new mythos of our current age. Fox labels this way the "Via Creativa,"[101] and it celebrates art as meditation. Regardless of native talent, all persons are creative; the rendering of images which arise in meditation in an outward form such as painting, sculpting, poetry, or music can be a spiritual practice in itself. Art requires the full engagement of our eros faculties, and is therefore another approach to mystical consciousness.

Another marker on the mystical bypath which has become increasingly popular in recent years is the ancient symbol of the labyrinth, a unicursal path that leads in to a center and back out again. Lauren Artress, an Episcopal priest who has pioneered the restoration of this spiritual tool, claims that "the labyrinth is part of the rediscovery of the lost mystical tradition."[102] While the labyrinth has been an important symbol of transformation in many Earth-centered spiritual traditions – such as ancient Crete, Scandinavia and native America – it has also appeared widely in Christian tradition, often appearing on the walls or floors of medieval churches. The most notable example is Chartres Cathedral, where a classical labyrinth of eleven circuits is placed in the floor. In medieval times a pilgrimage through the labyrinth could serve as a substitute for those Christians who could not make the pilgrimage to Jerusalem.

Labyrinth at Chartres Cathedral 48 ft. in diameter

The labyrinth at Chartres, a cathedral dedicated to the Virgin Mary, points to ancient associations of the labyrinth with the Divine Feminine. The labyrinth is a form of the spiral, a pervasive symbol of the goddess in early cultures. In ancient Crete, the mysteries of the goddess were celebrated in the labyrinth, which was the place of rebirth.[103] The later Greek myth in which Ariadne provided the hero Theseus with the thread to lead him back out of the labyrinth also refers to the importance of the feminine in the symbolism of the labyrinth. Walking the labyrinth can be a very powerful method for helping us reconnect with this suppressed feminine dimension of the Divine. The simple process of quietly walking the path helps suspend our usual logos thinking and allows the eros intuitive function to arise. The practice of walking meditation can help integrate the body and soul, masculine and feminine consciousness, and the physical and spiritual worlds. The labyrinth is especially significant as a symbol on the Path of ChristoSophia because it links the ancient Earth mysteries with the Christian mystery. When one walks the labyrinth outdoors, as was done in its earliest forms, one gets in contact with the energies of the Earth and experiences the interconnectedness of all living things.

The labyrinth can also be walked as the Threefold Path of mystical Christianity. As Lauren Artress suggests, the path inward represents the process of purgation, as we quiet ourselves and release those things which block our communication with God; the center represents illumination, where we reach clarity; the path outwards represents union, in which we commune with the Divine and are empowered to return to service in the outer world. The labyrinth embraces both apophatic and kathopathic approaches to meditation; like the path inward and the path outward which converge at the center, these two mystical paths unite in the labyrinth. One may walk through the labyrinth using the "sacred word" to help reach the center point of interior silence, or healing and illuminating images may arise spontaneously as one walks. Regardless of the method used, the labyrinth demonstrates that the destination of the mystical journey is the same.[104]

The labyrinth may also represent the Path of ChristoSophia itself, which is not a linear path leading to an end point but instead spirals in and out in a circuitous manner. Walking the labyrinth thus becomes a metaphor for the mystical journey. One begins the path with intention and then simply keeps walking, putting one foot in front of the other without worrying about the outcome, in the sure knowledge that the destination will be reached. Walking the labyrinth can help us cultivate the receptivity that is an essential component of mystical consciousness. The spiritual seeker must walk the path with patience and perseverance, but trust that the Divine will lead one to the center.

The intertwining paths of the labyrinth symbolize the mystical life, where periods in the outer world alternate with periods of inner work. We do not completely recognize the connection between the paths while we are walking them, particularly on the outermost path where our attention is drawn outward beyond the labyrinth. It is in the center, the point of stillness where walking ceases, that one recognizes the pattern of interconnectedness. The center of the labyrinth corresponds to the Heart - the center of the true Self – of the mystic. As one enters the center of the labyrinth, one also enters the center of the divine dance. This is the center where the Divine Feminine is found at the source of life; where Sophia may be experienced as World Soul; where one meets the Beloved and encounters the Mystery. As one gazes upon the wholeness of the labyrinth from its center, one may experience the corresponding inner wholeness as perceived from the center of the soul. It is here that one may comprehend the message of the labyrinth for the spiritual life: "Return to the center, where all is connected."

THE OPENING OF THE MYSTICAL BYPATH

The mystical consciousness which in the past has been attained only by the few intrepid spiritual seekers is the harbinger of the divine union that is possible for all humanity. Because of the dire needs of our present time, we are witnessing an opening of the mystical bypath which has the potential to lead eventually to the transformation of human consciousness. Within Christian tradition this is seen as the possibility of divinization for all human beings, the birth of the "Cosmic Christ" within the soul which leads to identification with the divine Self rather than the human ego. Matthew Fox refers to this as the "Via Transformativa," the way which leads to a "new creation" not only within the individual soul but also within the world as a whole.[105] According to Evelyn Underhill, if all human beings were to undergo this journey into mystical consciousness, "the spiritual world would be actualised within the temporal world at last" which is "the true incarnation of the Divine Wisdom."[106] The process which began with Sophia's incarnation in Jesus Christ now continues within the human heart through the process of deification. The opening of the mystical bypath for all humanity may fulfill the prophecy that Sophia will arise within the heart of human beings and thus bring transformation to the world. This could truly be the form of the Second Coming – the second incarnation of Love and Wisdom – now within the transformed consciousness of humanity which reconciles the transcendent and immanent deity within the heart.

Sophia is the World Soul and the Soul of Humanity through whom all is connected. When she is realized, all people will live together in the fullness of peace and harmony; when the barriers of ego separateness are discarded, all will relate through their divine Self and only love will exist. This is the task of Sophia on Earth, and our task as her servants: to bring about the realization of our essential oneness with all of humanity and with all of nature, and thus to bring about the reign of Heaven on Earth. By traveling the mystical bypath, a spiritually evolved humanity may return to the paradisal Garden of wholeness and fulfill its divine purpose of reconciling the physical and spiritual worlds.

We can find great help for this task by following the signposts for the Kabbalah and the Holy Grail on the mystical bypath. These aspects of the hidden tradition are especially important today because they have provided guidance for many seekers of diverse backgrounds throughout history and thus transcend solely Christian spirituality. As such, the multifaceted spiritual dimensions of the Kabbalah and the Grail can be of immense value in our present world for opening the mystical bypath to all. It is these track ways on the Path of ChristoSophia that we will explore in the following chapters.

CHAPTER IX: THE MYSTICAL KABBALAH

Say to Wisdom, "You are my sister."
Join thought to divine wisdom, so she and he become one.[1]

One of the major signposts that the wayfarer should look for on the mystical bypath of the Path of ChristoSophia is the Jewish Kabbalah. At first this statement may seem paradoxical but the mystical essence of the Kabbalah speaks to the hearts of all true seekers whether they be Jew or Christian. The Kabbalah shows the way for modern pilgrims of any faith to actualize in their minds and hearts the reality of the interconnectedness of all things. The twentieth century Kabbalist scholar Gershom Scholem said: "In none of their systems did the Kabbalists fail to stress the interrelation of all worlds and levels of being. Everything is connected with everything else, and this interpenetration of all things is governed by exact though unfathomable laws. Nothing is without its infinite depths. . ."[2]

The mystic understands and embraces the seeming contradictions of the material world because she knows that underlying the dualism of all physical reality is the One, the Kabbalistic Ain-Sof. The Kabbalah is an invaluable aid to illuminating the mystical paradox of the transcendent and immanent God, unity and duality, the Unknowable God and knowable divine manifestation. Even though the origins of the Kabbalah are rooted in Jewish mysticism, our modern Western culture is in critical need of reestablishing contact with those origins because they provide a strong foundation for those seeking a deeper relatedness with all of creation. Knowledge of Kabbalistic concepts and practices enables the walker on the mystical bypath to quest more deeply into her surroundings. As Dion Fortune stated in *The Mystical Qabalah*, ". . .the Tree of Life is the best meditation-symbol we possess because it is the most comprehensive."[3]

It is important to remember that Christianity from its very beginning has been deeply embedded with Judaic thought and practice. Jesus was a practicing Jew and, according to an ancient esoteric tradition, after speaking with the elders in the Temple in Jerusalem at the age of twelve, he was sent by them to the Essene community where he remained until the beginning of his public ministry at age thirty.[4] At this community near the Dead Sea, Jesus supposedly studied the great mystical tradition of Judaism handed down orally from the time of Abraham. In the eyes of many believers, the mystical tradition that Jesus learned was the Kabbalah.

The term "Kabbalah" – alternately spelled Qabalah, Qabala, Cabala, Cabbala, Kabalah or Kabbala – means literally "tradition" or "that which has been received." Its very name, therefore, implies that the seeker must develop an attitude of openness and receptivity. For "this is what Kabbalah is and always has been, the way of opening, the way of becoming a receptacle for God, the way of being One with him."[5] The Kabbalah has provided a primary way of opening the mystical bypath within Judeo-Christian tradition and leading the seeker onward to union with the Divine.

HISTORICAL BACKGROUND

The origins of the Kabbalah are lost in the mists of the history of Judaism. Like all eros mystical terms, "Kabbalah" resists definition. Some people use the term as a synonym for Jewish mysticism in general while others say that the Kabbalah goes back to the Garden of Eden before the Fall when Adam and Eve received God's wisdom directly with pure and simple hearts. Others point to the Kabbalah as first being given to Abraham as part of his covenant with God. Still others refer to the Kabbalah as being the oral tradition given to Moses on Mt. Sinai at the same time that he received the written Law.

A number of scholars point out that the Kabbalah was derived from the mystical commentaries that were part of the Midrash (amplifications and interpretations of the Scriptures) that appeared in the first few centuries of the Common Era. Of particular interest were the midrashic commentaries of the Merkabah (Divine Chariot) mystics and the Bereshith (Creation) mystics who advocated the practice of meditation, visions, and ecstatic trance states to encounter the Divine. It is from the Bereshith tradition that the first Kabbalistic book appeared – the *Sefer Yetzirah* (*Book of Formation*). This short, enigmatic book is the source of one of the most central concepts of the Kabbalah – the thirty-two paths of Wisdom which consist of the twenty-two letters of the Hebrew alphabet plus the ten sefiroth, the divine emanations of God.

The writings of the Merkabah and Bereshith mystics spread to Italy and Germany and eventually France and Spain between the ninth and twelfth centuries. Around 1180 in France appeared the next important Kabbalistic text – the *Sefer ha-Bahir* (*Book of Brilliance*). The *Bahir* is the first Jewish mystical writing to use sexual symbolism to describe the Divine, a concept that is central in many latter Kabbalistic works. The *Bahir* also contains descriptions of the sefiroth as emanating from God in the form of a tree – the primary symbol of the later Kabbalah – the Tree of Life.

The man considered to be the first Kabbalist was the charismatic rabbi of Provence, Isaac the Blind (c.1165-c.1235). He systematized the ten sefiroth and originated the concept of God as *Ain-Sof* (Without End). The teachings of Isaac the Blind were transmitted by his disciples to circles of Jewish mystics in Catalonia which became the dominant center for Kabbalah until the Jewish Diaspora in 1492. One of the most renowned Spanish Kabbalists was Abraham Abulafia, the principal exponent of what came to be known as prophetic or ecstatic Kabbalah. He was the first Kabbalist to write specific manuals of meditation techniques. These techniques involved meditation on Sacred Names and the permutations of letters and numbers.

From Catalonia also appeared the most important text in the history of Kabbalah – the *Sefir ha-Zohar* (*Book of Splendor*). Most scholars believe that the *Zohar* was written by Moses de Leon between 1275 and 1290 although many Kabbalists prefer to think

285

of it as having originated in the second century. The *Zohar* is an immense collection of rabbinic tales, legends, parables, biblical and talmudic commentaries, and above all, mystic visions that are meant to inspire the faithful to journey up the Tree of Life through each of the sefiroth. The *Zohar* taught that every word of the Torah (the Five Books of Moses) had a secret divine meaning which it was the duty of the Kabbalist to uncover.

After the expulsion of the Jews from Spain in 1492, the Spanish Kabbalists scattered throughout Europe and the Near East. A major school of Kabbalah was established by émigrés at Safed in Galilee (in modern Israel). The principal Kabbalist at this school was Moses Cordovero (1522-1570), who taught an essentially panentheistic doctrine of the Ain-Sof and the ten sefiroth. Rabbi Isaac Luria traveled to Safed to study with Cordovero and with his visionary genius made the school the greatest center of Kabbalah in the sixteenth century. Luria developed the concepts of *tsimtsum* (the contraction of God), the "breaking of the Vessels," the Four Worlds, and *tikkun* (cosmic restoration and reintegration), all of which have been central to the modern practice and study of Kabbalah. Rabbi Luria's bold, mystical insights into the *Zohar* created a system of complex symbolism and terminology which has had a profound influence on Kabbalah to the present day.

Rabbi Luria's teachings became known to Kabbalists throughout Europe and the Holy Lands and especially in Eastern Europe and Russia. The charismatic peasant leader, Israel ben Eliezer, the Baal Shem Tov (Master of the Holy Name), instilled some of the basic concepts of the Kabbalah among the peasants of Eastern Europe in the eighteenth century. The Baal Shem Tov was the founder of modern Hasidism. Hasidic storytellers like Rabbi Nahman of Bratislov took the concepts of the Kabbalah and turned them into simple folk-tales that could be readily understood by even the most unlettered people. The Hasidic leaders became wonder-workers to the masses, who believed that they had magical powers. They helped end the people's suffering through dancing and singing and achieving the ecstasy of oneness with God.

Early Christian Kabbalists

Christian Kabbalism developed during the fifteenth century as the vigor of Florentine Renaissance thought swept away the stultified scholasticism of medieval Christian dogma. Under the inspiration of Marsilio Ficino, Florentine humanists began to search for "Truth" by rediscovering and reinterpreting the writings of ancient Greek, Roman, and Jewish thinkers. They were not trying to discredit Christian tradition but were seeking to strengthen the "Truth" of Christianity by showing how it encompassed Neoplatonic and gnostic teachings. In this endeavor, Renaissance humanists were drawn to many non-traditional sources such as the esoteric literature and secret teachings of Pythagoras, Hermes, Zoroaster, the "Chaldean Oracles" and, above all, the Kabbalah as ways to invigorate Christian tradition and practice. As Joseph Dan, the noted professor of Kabbalah at Hebrew University, stated: ". . .Christianity itself has to be revitalized by a renewed understanding of its ancient origins that has become possible by the revelation of new sources. These include, first and foremost, the Hermetic writings, and the Kabbalah is to be regarded as an integral part if not the oldest and most sacred – of these rediscovered pre-Christian sources of divine truth."[6]

Christian interest in the Kabbalah appears to have originated with Jews familiar with the Kabbalah who later converted to Christianity. As early as 1320, Abner of Burgos, a converted Jew, wrote about Christian doctrines that could be found in the Kabbalah.[7] Many other converts during the next century and a half were interested in finding Kabbalistic support for Christian doctrines. Pedro de la Caballeria, a Spanish Christian Kabbalist, published *Zelus Christi* in 1450 in which he referred to Christian elements in the *Zohar*.[8]

But the true Christian Kabbalah began with the Florentine humanist, Pico della Mirandella (1463-1494). In 1486 he published his *Nine-Hundred Conclusions* of which his "Cabalistic Conclusions" formed a significant part. Pico believed, as did the Jewish Kabbalists, that the Kabbalah contained the oral law given by God to Moses on Mt. Sinai. His understanding of Kabbalah was that ". . .the mysteries of the Law are concealed in the Divine Names and that one can unravel the mysteries through combinations of letters."[9] These "combinations of letters" were part of the traditional Kabbalistic methods of exegesis: *gematria* (numerology), *notarikon* (acrostics), and *themurah* (cryptography or permutation of letters) and Pico used them to prove that Christian doctrines predated Jewish ones. For example, by using *gematria* and *themurah,* Pico took the first word of the Torah in Hebrew, *Bereshith*, and uncovered the "hidden" meaning to be: "Son, Spirit, Father, their Trinity, complete oneness."[10] The same methods were used to explore the Kabbalistic teachings pertinent to the mysteries of the Incarnation, the Virgin Mother, Original Sin and the Holy Name of Jesus.

Pico sought to achieve a grand synthesis of Pythagorean, Kabbalistic, and Christian doctrines; in fact, he was essentially seeking a Renaissance "Grand Unified Theory" of all human knowledge. To do this, he immersed himself in the Kabbalistic system of correspondences, a holographic view in which an individual thing contains every thing. In the second proem to his *Heptaplus,* Pico states: "Whatever is in any of the worlds is at the same time contained in each, and there is no one of them in which is not to be found whatever is in each of the others."[11] Pico della Mirandola's trailblazing efforts in the Christian interpretation of Kabbalah had a profound influence on such sixteenth century thinkers as Johannes Reuchlin and Henry Cornelius Agrippa.

Johannes Reuchlin (1455-1522), a Swiss humanist and contemporary of Pico, began his study of the Kabbalah after Pico's "Conclusions" appeared. His first book on the Christian Kabbalah was *The Wonder Working Word* in 1494 and his magnum opus, *De arte cabalistica,* was published in 1517. In *De arte cabalistica,* Reuchlin developed a view of Christian Kabbalah far beyond what Pico expressed in the "Conclusions." While Reuchlin followed Pico's interest in the synthesis of Neoplatonic, Kabbalistic, and Christian doctrines, he created a new dimension for the Christian Kabbalah by blending it with astrology, magic, Hermeticism, and alchemy. He viewed the Kabbalah as a repository of ancient wisdom which, through a system of correspondences that included all knowledge, could serve as a guide to those seeking the Divine. As Joseph Dan states: "For him the Zohar, Gikatilla and Abulafia were as rational as Plato, Pythagoras and the Gospels. Esotericism, occultism and magic were not conceived, in his works and in the works of those who continued to develop the study of Christian Kabbalah, as inferior, superstitious doctrines, but as the keys to divine truth, inseparable from science and logic."[12]

The third great pioneering Christian Kabbalist was the German mystic and magician Henry Cornelius Agrippa (1487-1535). Agrippa became the most famous and influential of the early Christian Kabbalists because of his charismatic personality and the notoriety of his teachings. His most significant contributions to Christian Kabbalah were contained in *On Occult Philosophy* which was written in 1510 but not published until 1533 due in part to its controversial subject matter. In it, Agrippa showed the influence of Reuchlin's mystical view of the Kabbalah as a guide to universal truth, but went further than Reuchlin in his treatment of the esoteric, alchemical Kabbalah. Agrippa developed a Kabbalistic system of magical conjuration wherein the goal was to influence and even control natural forces. He took the tradition of *gematria, notarikon,* and *themurah* which he obtained from Reuchlin and applied it to everyday life. In his *On Occult Philosophy*, Agrippa states:

> There are, therefore, (in the Hebrew alphabet) one and twenty letters (*sic*) which are the foundations of the world, and of the creatures that are, and are named in it, and every saying and every creature are of them, and by their revolutions receive their name, being, and virtue. . .*hence voices and words have efficacy in magical works* (italics ours), because that in which Nature first exerciseth magical efficacy is the voice of God.[13]

It is important to keep in mind the difference between magic and mysticism when discussing the Kabbalah since the time of Agrippa. Magical conjuring such as that advocated by Agrippa is **not** part of the mystical bypath. The use of Kabbalah in the development of modern magical schools from those of Eliphas Levi in the nineteenth century to Alistair Crowley in the twentieth has created a modern misconception that all use of Kabbalah is for magical purposes. Magicians seek to control spiritual entities or forces, in contrast to those on the mystical bypath who seek the guidance and enlightenment of the spiritual realms to effect the Divine Will.

For those on the mystical bypath, the pioneering efforts of Pico, Reuchlin, and Agrippa have blazed a trail that can be of great benefit to all who seek wisdom and understanding. Their work has helped to open the mystical bypath by making the Kabbalistic doctrines and techniques, once known to only a small group of Jewish rabbis and mystics, accessible to all people in Western culture.

THE TREE OF LIFE

When we walk the mystical bypath, we are in a sense climbing the Tree of Life which is the predominate symbol of the Kabbalah. Dion Fortune explains the significance of the Tree of Life as follows:

> The curious symbol-system known to us as the Tree of Life
> is an attempt to reduce to diagrammatic form every force
> and factor in the manifest universe and the soul of man; to
> correlate them one to another and reveal them spread out as
> on a map so that the relative positions of each unit can be
> seen and the relations between them traced. In brief, the Tree
> of Life is a compendium of science, psychology, philosophy,
> and theology.[14]

In the Hebrew commentaries on the Garden of Eden, the Tree of Life has the significance of the "axis mundi," the cosmic or world tree, the source of all things. In the medieval Kabbalistic *Sefer ha-Bahir,* the Tree of Life is the All (*kol*), as is seen in the statement by God: "I am the one who planted this tree so that I and the whole world would delight in it. I established in it everything, and I called it All. . . I called [the tree] All for everything is dependent upon it and everything comes out from it, all need it, they gaze upon it and wait for it. From there the souls fly out. I was alone when I made it."[15] For the medieval Kabbalists, the Tree of Life was the central motif to the mystery of creation. As the concept of sefiroth evolved, the emanation of God through the ten sefiroth naturally became known as the Tree of Life. Avram Davis and Manuela Mascetti, in their book *Judaic Mysticism*, explain this concept for contemporary seekers: "The Tree of Life can be described in more modern terms as a holographic image, where each part of the image contains the whole. There exists a Tree of Life with ten sefirot everywhere, and it pulsates with God's golden light in everything."[16]

Ain-Sof and the Ten Sefiroth

"With Beginning, the unknown concealed one created the palace, a palace called God. The secret is: "With Beginning, _____ created God."[17]

The Tree of Life may only begin to be understood when put in relation to the Kabbalistic concepts of Ain-Sof (or "Ein-Sof") and the ten sefiroth. The term "Ain-Sof" means literally "without end." This is the ultimate divine One which Christian mystics such as Meister Eckhart attempted to describe as the Abyss, the Ground of Being, or Nothingness, and gnostics referred to as the "unknown God." We can only negatively try to define Ain-Sof because it is beyond all human comprehension: Ain-Sof is not Being or Non-Being and is not a part of human experience in any conceivable way; it has no human characteristics or qualities such as thought, reason, or imagination; its existence or non-existence cannot be debated; it cannot be discussed in terms of magnitude, essence, time, wisdom, goodness or any other human conception; it cannot be discussed even as spirit. As Charles Poncé states, "He can be neither understood by what He is not, nor by the idea of nothing. Neither approach works."[18]

The Tree of Life is a single, unified symbol representing the manifestation of the One God. Just as sunlight is pure white but when directed through a prism reveals the multitudinous colors of the rainbow, so the Tree of Life symbolizes the pure unity of Ain-Sof but when manifested through the ten sefiroth, the diversity of creation is shown. According to the *Zohar*:

He made ten lights spring forth from His midst, lights which shine with the form which they have borrowed from Him, and which shed everywhere the light of a brilliant day. The Ancient One, the most Hidden of the hidden, is a high beacon, and we know Him only by His lights, which illuminate our eyes so abundantly. His Holy Name is no other thing than these lights.[19]

The ten lights through which the Hidden One is made manifest are the sefiroth, which Caitlin Matthews describes as ". . .the ten essences or 'sapphires' of God's emanations. . .jewel-like light through which the different qualities of God's glory are manifest."[20] The sefiroth are analogous to the colors of the spectrum when sunlight shines through a prism. Their separate colors are invisible when looking at the pure light, but they can be said to be inherent in that light. The sefiroth are intimately connected with the emanation of the Ain-Sof – they continuously flow from the hidden, unmanifest source of light and are dependent on the source for their own refracted light. They all share equally in the pure divine light and only show a preponderance of the quality of their part of the spectrum. The sefiroth are as vessels that contain the light of Ain-Sof and at the same time they are made out of that light.

That there are ten sefiroth does not mean that there are ten parts or attributes of God, but that they are the effect of the divine emanation as humans can conceive of it. The ten sefiroth of the Tree of Life may also be considered as the fruits of the Tree. Each fruit contains the same essence and potential as all the other fruits but still has its distinct quality. Each fruit or sphere of the sefiroth on the Tree of Life represents a different aspect of Ain-Sof's emanation. This concept of the Tree of Life indicates that many early Kabbalists believed in the panentheistic nature of God as both transcendent (Ain-Sof) and immanent (sefiroth). Moses Cordovero was particularly concerned with the relation between Ain-Sof and the sefiroth as an expression of panentheism. ". . .(A)re they (sefiroth) God's substance or only *kalim* ("instruments" or "vessels")? Cordovero's answer to this question… the *Sefirot* are substance and *kalim* at the same time."[21] If Ain-Sof is transcendent and the sefiroth are immanent, a panentheistic view of God requires that the sefiroth must be consubstantial with Ain-Sof. Cordovero taught that God concealed Himself in the sefiroth when He emanated them in order that He be revealed – the sefiroth are Ain-Sof revealed. "The *Sefirot,* he argues, owe the source of their existence to *Ein-Sof*, but this existence is "hidden" in the same sense that the spark of fire is hidden in the rock until it is struck with metal."[22]

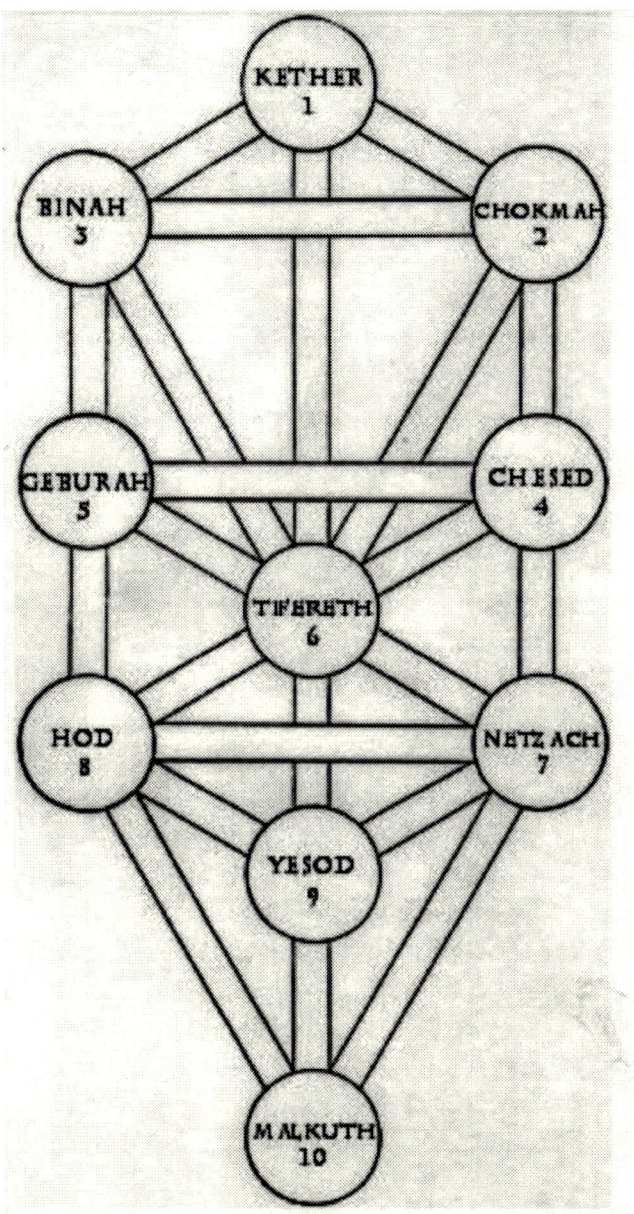

Diagram 1

wisdom is made here (handwritten in left margin)

The ten sefiroth are arranged in the glyph or symbol which is the Tree of Life, as shown in Diagram 1. The first point of the emanation of the Ain-Sof is *Kether* - Crown (#1) followed by *Chokmah* - Wisdom(#2) and *Binah* - Understanding (#3). These form the first triad or trinity called the Supernal Triad, the union of the Crown (Kether), the Father (Chokmah) and the Mother (Binah) from which all the other sefiroth are manifest. The next three sefiroth are *Chesed* – Mercy (#4), *Geburah* – Strength (#5), and *Tifereth* – Beauty (#6). They form the Moral Triad, the representation of the Ain-Sof's moral power. *Netzach* – Victory (#7), *Hod* – Splendor (#8) and *Yesod* – Foundation (#9) together are called the Creative Triad, the symbol of the Ain-Sof's reproductive power which creates the physical universe represented by the final sefiroth, *Malkuth* – Kingdom (#10).

The names of the sefiroth come from two verses in the Scriptures: "I have filled him with the spirit of God, with Wisdom, with Understanding, and with Knowledge" (Exodus 31:3). According to the *Sefer Yetzirah*, the spirit of God is Kether, and Wisdom and Understanding refer to Chokmah and Binah respectively. Knowledge is represented by what some Kabbalists call the "hidden Sefirah" – *Daath*, which is the result of the union of Wisdom and Understanding. Some versions of the Tree of Life show Daath between Binah and Chesed and always indicated by a dotted line. The remaining seven Sefiroth are named in the following verse from I Chronicles: "Yours O God are the Greatness (Chesed - Mercy [also called *Gedulah* – Greatness]), the Strength (Geburah), the Beauty (Tifereth), the Victory (Netzach), and the Splendor (Hod) for All (Yesod) in heaven and in earth; yours O God is the Kingdom (Malkuth). . ." (29:11).

The Supernal Triad points up towards its source in Ain-Sof since it is the effect of the Divine emanation as cause. This Primal Trinity is the source of all further manifestation and to some Kabbalists, both Jewish and Christian, this trinity is the God of the first chapter of Genesis. Some Christian Kabbalists look at this as the Trinity: Kether – Father, Chokmah – Son, and Binah – Holy Spirit. Since Binah is perceived by Kabbalists as the Supernal Mother, the feminine nature of the Holy Spirit is clearly revealed in this understanding of the Trinity. The other two triads point downward on the Tree of Life towards Malkuth because they channel the divine light or energy into the physical world. From the time of the early Kabbalists, Malkuth has been considered to be just as holy as Kether because Malkuth is the world in which the Divine is manifest. In fact, in the system of Four Worlds of Rabbi Luria, Malkuth in the higher world is Kether in the next lower world, so in a sense, Malkuth and Kether are one.

Some medieval rabbis condemned the early Kabbalists for destroying the unity of God by separating the Divine into ten qualities much in the same way that they condemned Christian theologians for the doctrine of the Trinity. Yet, to those on the mystical bypath, three-in-one or ten-in-one do not destroy the oneness of the Divine, but point to an ever richer and deeper way of spiritual union.

The Thirty Two Paths of Wisdom

The ten sefiroth can also be called the "Holy Names of Ain-Sof" because they are connected by the twenty-two letters of the Hebrew alphabet. The ten sefiroth themselves are said to represent the ten vowels of the Hebrew alphabet so the Tree of Life contains the entire Hebrew language as manifest by God. In the Kabbalah, the letters are as sacred as the sefiroth because God emanated all creation by them. As can be seen in Diagram 2, the ten sefiroth are connected by twenty-two paths each of which has a corresponding Hebrew letter. The sefiroth and the twenty-two connecting paths together form the Thirty-two Paths of Wisdom. We can consider each of the thirty-two paths to be interconnecting trails on the mystical bypath. On each trail, we encounter different scenery and topography but each trail is contained within the mystical bypath.

[handwritten marginal note, right side:] do letters have anound when God created?

[handwritten note at bottom:] what does the Hebrew language have to do with God? They got their alphabet from the Assyrians (Cedars of Lebanon)

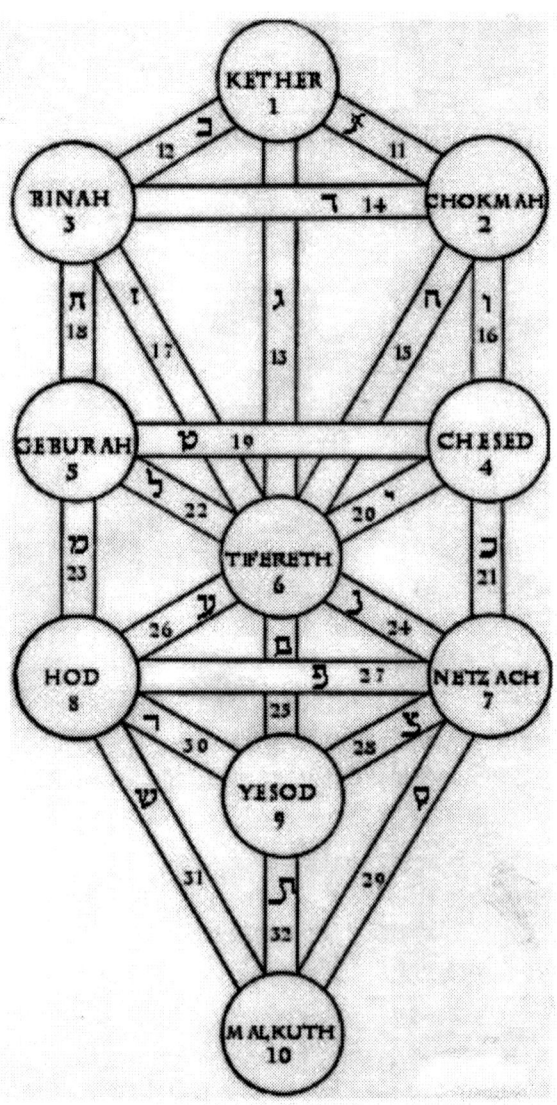

Diagram 2

Unlike our alphabet, the Hebrew letters each have a numerical and symbolic significance which permits a wealth of mystical insight and interpretation. Kabbalists to this day spend a great deal of time meditating on the letters of the Hebrew alphabet using the interpretative techniques of *gematria, notarikon,* and *themurah* to find the hidden meaning in the Scriptures. This is considered essential in order to help God with the redemption of the world.

According to mystical tradition, God has placed hidden levels of meaning in every word in the Scriptures which will be keys to enlightened humans in their acts of redemption with God. Each letter of the Hebrew alphabet has a numerical value so when letters form words, the words have a number derived from the combined value of the letters. Gematria is the method which relates different Hebrew words that have the same total number. For example, the Hebrew letters for the word Messiah are "MshICh": Mem = 40, Shin = 300, Yod = 10, and Cheth = 8 for a total of 358. The Serpent of Moses is "Nachash": Nun = 50, Cheth = 8, and Shin = 300 totaling 358. Therefore, the Messiah and the brazen serpent Moses lifted up in the wilderness have a close correspondence. Medieval Christian Kabbalists, using the method of gematria, taught that the figure of Christ on the cross was foreshadowed by the figure of the brazen serpent of Moses.[23]

Contemporary writers such as John Michell and Margaret Starbird have rediscovered the significance of the "numbers theology"[24] of gematria in the hidden tradition of Christian spirituality. Gematria was essential to the understanding of sacred texts by the early Christians until the practice was suppressed by the Church Fathers in their condemnation of Gnostic heresy.[25] Through her application of the ancient techniques of gematria, Margaret Starbird has uncovered a rich source of mystical insights that are especially illuminating for the seeker on the Path of ChristoSophia. For example, she refers to Christ's statement that "The Kingdom of God is like a grain of mustard seed." (Mark 4:30-31) Starbird points out that the gematria for "a grain of mustard seed" is 1746, which is the sum of 666, the male solar principle, and 1080, the feminine lunar principle. Thus, Jesus implied through gematria that the Kingdom of Heaven is the sacred union of masculine and feminine principles.[26] She also explains that the sum of the letters of "the Magdalene" is 153, the sacred number which links her to the Divine Feminine and the bride of Christ.[27] Through interpretations of the number symbolism of biblical verses such as these, Margaret Starbird reveals many of the hidden truths of the Gnostic Christians, such as the mystical role of Mary Magdalene and the significance of the sacred marriage.

↓ in what language

Another interpretative technique of Kabbalah that can be used to discover insights on the mystical bypath is notarikon, a system of acrostics of the Scriptural verse. For example, by taking the first letter of each word in a verse, the resulting word will have mystical significance. A famous example of notarikon used by Christians is the Greek phrase I*esous* Ch*ristos* Th*eou* U*ios* S*oter* (Jesus Christ, Son of God, Savior) which by acrostics becomes the word *ichthus* – the Greek word for fish. Thus, the fish became a primary symbol for early Greek-speaking Christians.

Themurah is also a system for seeking hidden meanings in biblical verses by using cryptographic methods. For example, the alphabet can be written in order on one line and then reversed on the next line (in English, a b c become z y x). This provides interesting insight into many Hebrew place names and proper names. An example can be found in Jeremiah 25:26 ". . .and the king of Sheshak shall drink after them." According to this formula, Sheshak (Shin, Shin, Kaph) becomes another name for Babel (Beth, Beth, Lamed). Thus, to the Kabbalist trained in themurah, there is a correspondence between Sheshek and Babel which must be investigated.[28] Since the Kabbalist can choose an infinite variety of permutations, the method of themurah can be used to prove just about any theological point.

[handwritten: So doesn't this pretty much discredit it?]

The Three Pillars

The ten sefiroth may also be arranged into three pillars. The Pillar of Mercy is light and on the right side of the Tree of Life as one looks at it and contains the three sefiroth Chokmah, Chesed, and Netzach. These three sefiroth are all considered masculine in nature based upon the top sefirah which is Chokmah. The Pillar of Judgment (Severity) is dark and on the left side and contains Binah, Geburah, and Hod which are considered feminine in nature. We see in these two pillars the Kabbalistic view that the totality of the Divine is composed equally of feminine and masculine elements. The Middle Pillar, called the Pillar of Equilibrium or Pillar of Mildness, consists of four sefiroth: Kether, Tifereth, Yesod, and Malkuth and is referred to as being androgynous.

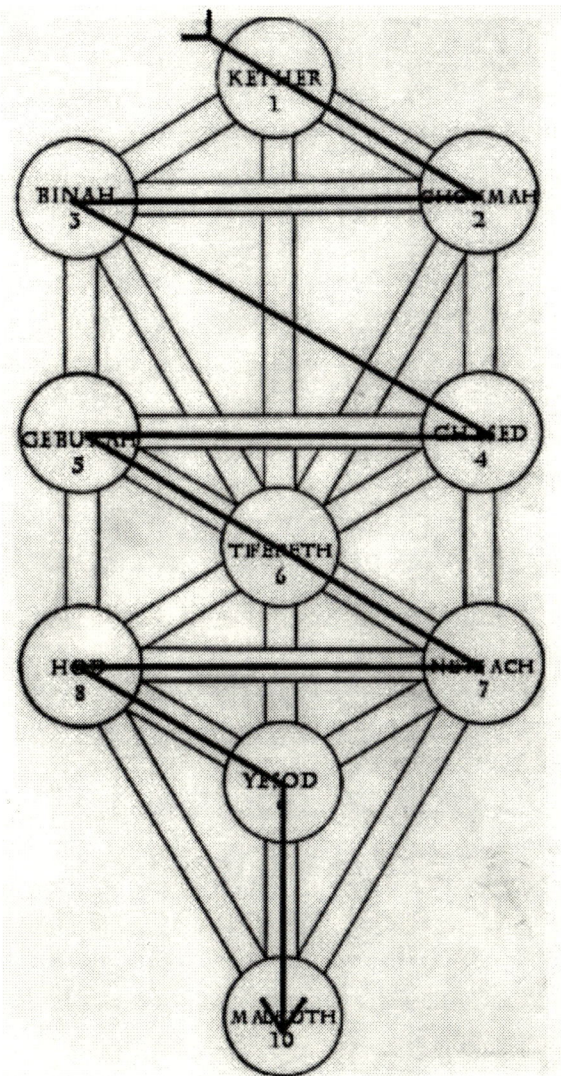

Diagram 3

In Diagram 3 a zigzag line connects the sefiroth. This is called the Lightning Flash which shows the order of emanation from Ain-Sof. It also illustrates how the Sefiroth alternate between the positive, negative, and equilibrated pillars. Dion Fortune states, "The two side Pillars, then, represent the positive and negative forces in Nature, the active and passive, the destructive and constructive, concreting form and free-moving force."[29]

The concept of the Three Pillars helps us to understand the nature of polarity, such opposites as feminine/masculine, eros/logos, dark/light, etc. While we might be tempted to call these opposites an example of duality, polarity is the more accurate term since the forces of the two outside pillars meet at the Middle Pillar and are balanced therein. The Chinese concepts of Yin and Yang relate very well to the Three Pillars; Yin, the dark, feminine quality is symbolized by the Pillar of Judgment while Yang, the light, masculine quality is symbolized by the Pillar of Mercy. The Pillar of Equilibrium represents the Chinese concept of the Tao, the Way, the principle of balance or equilibrium. The Tao can be said to coalesce through the central sefirah of the Pillar of Equilibrium, Tifereth, the divine essence of harmony, beauty, and balance.

Tifereth As the Cosmic Christ

Tifereth is the central sefirah of the Tree of Life. Paths to all the other sefiroth lead to and from Tifereth. The significance of this is explained in the following passage from the *Sefer Yetzirah*: "The Sixth Path (Tifereth) is called the Mediating Intelligence, because in it are multiplied the influxes of the Emanations; for it causes that influence to flow into all the reservoirs of the blessings with which they themselves are united."[30] Tifereth is located in the center of the Middle Pillar of Equilibrium, and therefore harmonizes the potencies of the Right and Left Pillars. Tifereth serves as the Great Mediator, transmuting all the inflowing potencies into pure harmony and balance which stabilizes the other sefiroth. From all this, one begins to realize the mystical insight that Tifereth cannot be thought of as a single sefirah, but rather only in its links with the other sefiroth. Its function is to transmute and transform, similar to the purpose that the human heart serves in the body.

It is through Tifereth that Ain-Sof manifests to humanity, therefore this central sefirah is the "Christ-centre"[31] of the Tree of Life. Pilgrims on the Path of ChristoSophia are especially drawn to the sefirah Tifereth because it is here that we contact the Cosmic Christ, the eternal "I – am" within us all. Tifereth is called Shemesh, the Sphere of the Sun, by some Kabbalists. This indicates that Tifereth is the life-force behind all physical creation. Just as the very cells of our bodies or those of all life-forms are dependent on the physical sun, the very existence of the material universe is dependent on the life-force of Tifereth, the Sun behind all suns. The Path of ChristoSophia leads to the sefirah Tifereth as the realm of the Cosmic Christ, the divine Son whose power animates and sustains the physical world.

Tifereth is also the center of the six sefiroth below the Supernal Triad of Kether, Chokmah, and Binah. These six sefiroth are the archetypal worlds that directly influence Malkuth, the material world of our existence. One could say that these archetypal realms are the Kingdom of Tifereth since one of the common images associated with Tifereth is the King. This is the Kingdom of Heaven that Jesus refers to so often in his parables, and where, as the Cosmic Christ, he reigns as Lord and King. These six central sefiroth are also referred to by some Kabbalists as the Archetypal Man, Adam Kadmon. Christ as the "Son of Man" is the divine image of humanity as a synthesis of these six potencies.

Tifereth is the sefirah of Incarnation – the manifestation of Ain-Sof to creation. The mystery of the Incarnation is symbolized by the image of a child, also ascribed to Tifereth. All of the sacrificed gods of antiquity such as Osiris, Dionysus, and Mithras are also attributed to Tifereth. To those on the mystical bypath, Tifereth expresses the essence of the Crucifixion and the Resurrection. Thus Tifereth contains the image of the life pattern of Christ – from the incarnation of the Divine within the human Jesus of Nazareth, to the sacrifice and rebirth of Christ as the archetypal Green Man.

Tifereth means "Beauty" but there is another Hebrew name for this sefirah which perhaps describes its qualities even better: *Rachmim,* "Compassion." Compassion is the union of strength with love. It is certainly possible to "love too much" in the sense of smothering another person with affection and attention. And too much strength or power can easily become cruelty. But compassion can know no excess. Compassion is helping others from a position of strength, not by sympathizing with them. Compassion expresses balance and harmony; thus, Tifereth harmonizes Chesed (Mercy, Love) with Geburah (Strength, Power). Looking at the Gospel accounts of the life of Christ, it can be seen that he was always expressing compassion to those he touched. In fact, the life of the historical Jesus embodied the way humanity can express the qualities of Tifereth.

The *Zohar* helps us to understand how Tifereth is the Kabbalistic equivalent of the Cosmic Christ. Two mythical descriptions within it describe the Cosmic Christ:

> The Blessed Holy One has one son who shines from
> one end of the world to the other. He is a great and
> mighty tree, whose head reaches towards heaven and
> whose roots are rooted in the holy ground.
> (*Zohar* 2:105a)[32]

The Blessed Holy One in this sense is Ain-Sof whose "one son" is Tifereth, the Cosmic Christ, who manifests the Ain-Sof in all creation. Tifereth can also be seen to be a "great and mighty tree" – the Tree of Life from Kether (heaven) to Malkuth (holy ground) – since Tifereth connects with all the other sefiroth.

> The mystery of the word is written concerning the mystery
> on high: "What is His name? What is the name of His son,
> if you know?" (Proverbs 30:4) That name is known: *YHVH
> Zeva'ot* is His name. The name of His son? Israel is his name,
> as it is written: My first-born son, Israel." All the keys of
> faith hang from Israel. He praises himself, saying: "*YHVH*
> has said to me: 'You are My son'" (Psalms 2:7). Indeed it is
> so, for Father and Mother have crowned him and blessed him
> with countless crowns; they have commanded everyone:
> "Kiss the son!' (Psalms 2:12). Kiss the hand of this son!" As
> if it were possible, He has given him power over all, for all
> will worship him. "Lest he turn angry" (Ibid.). For he has
> been crowned with judgment and compassion. Judgment
> for one who deserves judgment; compassion for one who
> deserves compassion. All the blessings of above and below
> belong to this son. (*Zohar* 3:191b)[33]

Daniel Matt comments on the above passage: "The son is not earthly Israel but its divine archetype, the central sefirah called Beauty of Israel. . .The author of the Zohar is translating Christological formulations into the language of kabbalistic myth."[34] The "divine archetype" is the Cosmic Christ. *YHVH* or the Tetragrammaton is the sacred name of the deity that is associated with Tifereth; it refers to the manifest Ain-Sof and the Cosmic Christ which transcends the historical Jesus. We call the Cosmic Christ "ChristoSophia," to better indicate the androgynous nature of the Divine. To the Kabbalists, this androgynous deity was the union of Tifereth with Malkuth or Shekhinah on the Middle Path. A great deal of Kabbalistic literature discusses the nature of this union dating all the way back to the *Bahir* in the twelfth century. In order to understand the androgynous deity, it is first necessary to discuss the Shekhinah, the Divine Feminine in the Kabbalah.

The Divine Feminine in the Kabbalah

A tradition which recognizes and honors the Divine Feminine has probably always existed within the outwardly patriarchal, monotheistic structure of Judaism, as documented by Raphael Patai in his book *The Hebrew Goddess*. As we have already seen in the Christian religion, the presence of the Divine Feminine emerges on the mystical bypath where the heart of the seeker is more open to her revelation. In Judaism, with its emphasis on the logos qualities of the Law, it is primarily the Kabbalah which provides access to the eros characteristics of the feminine. Understanding the significance of the feminine dimension of deity that one encounters on the mystical path of the Kabbalah can greatly enrich our insights regarding the role of the Divine Feminine within the Christian mystical tradition.

The primary reference to the feminine aspect of God in mystical Judaism is the "Shekhinah." This term is not found in the Bible, but appears in the Talmud in approximately the first century B.C.E. where it refers to God's "indwelling" or "presence" in the world.[35] This concept of the Shekhinah derives from the passage in Exodus 40:38 which refers to the "glory" of God as the cloud which hovered over the Tabernacle. In the earliest writings, the Shekhinah is simply the physical manifestation of God and the feminine gender of the noun has no significance. The concept of the Shekhinah appears to have originated in an attempt to reconcile the paradox of divine transcendence and immanence; the Jewish rabbis perceived a need to distinguish between God who cannot be known by the perception of the senses and his physical manifestation, the Shekhinah.[36] The statement "There is no place that is empty of the Shekhinah, not even the thornbush," proclaims the belief that God, who is transcendent, is also present in all aspects – even the lowliest – of the physical world.[37]

The further development of the concept of the Shekhinah into a representation of the Divine Feminine first appears in the mystical Kabbalah. As Gershom Scholem says, "The presentation of the Shekhinah as female element - simultaneously mother, bride, and daughter – within the structure of the Godhead constitutes a very meaningful step..."[38] The culmination of feminine imagery for the Shekhinah occurs in Kabbalistic writings of the Middle Ages, corresponding to the emergence of the feminine in Western Christendom as seen in the visionary experiences of medieval mystics who traveled the bypaths as well as the rise of the Cult of the Virgin within the Church itself. It appears that both Christians and Jews were responding at this time to a need to bring greater wholeness to an exclusively masculine God-image. As the *Zohar* states:

> "Male and female He created them."
> From here we learn:
> Any image that does not embrace male and female
> Is not a high and true image.[39]

Here the statement in Genesis forms the basis for an androgynous concept of deity that is central to the *Zohar*, in which the Shekhinah portrays the feminine side of God.

The characteristics of the Kabbalistic Shekhinah resemble those of Sophia in many ways. The Shekhinah is the name of the tenth and final sefirah, Malkuth. This is the manifestation of Ain-Sof, the transcendent and unknowable Divine, in the physical world. Gershom Scholem says, "The final Sefirah descends to the earthly realm in the guise of the Shekhinah mentioned in the Talmud and the 'Wisdom' of the Bible. She is no longer merely God's presence, but is now a specific factor in his self-manifestation."[40] The immanent deity – whether referred to as the Shekhinah or Sophia – is perceived by both Jewish and Christian mystics as feminine in nature.

The creative power of the Divine Feminine, to which the Hebrew Bible alludes in its description of Sophia as first creation and co-creator with God, is greatly expanded in the Kabbalistic portrayal of the Shekhinah. Here the feminine sefirah Binah, also referred to as the "upper Shekhinah," is the primal maternal Womb which is the source of creation. Binah originates "the process of emanation whereby the inner world of the Godhead is brought forth and expressed as an active force."[41] This force eventually manifests through the sefirah Malkut, the "lower Shekhinah," where it "permeates and vivifies all of the worlds that are outside of the Godhead."[42] Thus the Shekhinah contains within herself the forms of every created thing and is the source of the continually renewing energies which maintain all of creation.[43] The insight that all things are already contained and prefigured in the Shekhinah is expressed in references to Her as the "Orchard of Holy Apple Trees," in which "the apple trees are the sefirot from Chesed to Yesod, which fill Her"[44] and as the "Rainbow," for "she displays the colors of the sefirot."[45] These names for the Shekhinah are also images frequently associated with Sophia which symbolize the manifestation of the Divine in creation.   *"Jesus Christ the Apple Tree"*

The dual nature of the Divine Feminine shown in Kabbalistic references to the "upper Shekhinah" of the sefirah Binah and the "lower Shekhinah" of the sefirah Malkuth is reminiscent of gnostic images of the "upper Sophia" who resides in the Pleroma and the "lower Sophia" who has fallen into the world. A central theme of both of these mythologisms is the "exile" of the Divine Feminine, which has many levels of symbolic meaning. From a historical perspective, the Jews believed that the Divine as the Shekhinah always accompanied the people of Israel and thus shared in their exile. From an archetypal perspective, the "exile of the Shekhinah" has profound cosmic significance as a symbol of the separation of the created world from its divine source. Baring and Cashford explain the meaning of the Shekhinah's exile in this way:

> The image of exile…is not only associated with her failure to return to the Holy Land, but with her exile from the godhead,

> as if her being immanent in creation had cut her off from her 'other half," her transcendent source and spouse…As long as her exile lasts, creation is cut off from the transcendent deity.[46]

Kabbalistic tradition teaches that this condition is due to "Adam's fall," which was caused by his exclusive worship of the Shekhinah and failure to recognize the unity of the sefiroth.[47] Thus Adam's sin, interpreted by Kabbalists as the sin of separation, is the archetypal condition of the human soul which experiences separation from divine Unity. The Shekhinah, as the manifestation of God in creation, is also the divine ground of the human soul. Her "exile" from the godhead is the fate of all human souls. The experiences of exile that the people of Israel have suffered throughout history are symbolic of the universal condition of "exile" which the Shekhinah shares with all of humanity.

The Divine Androgyne

The exile of the Shekhinah also refers to the separation which exists within the archetypal Divine; the androgynous deity imaged by the Kabbalists is broken apart and the feminine half of God suffers in a state of exile. A condition of cosmic wholeness and harmony can be restored only by the reuniting of the Shekhinah with her divine masculine counterpart. The "sacred marriage" archetype is central to Kabbalistic symbolism in its representation of the union of the Shekhinah and Tifereth as the feminine and masculine aspects of God. The joining of Tifereth and the Shekhinah unites Heaven and Earth, the sun and moon, spirit and nature.

The union of Tifereth and Shekhinah is a major theme in Kabbalah, especially in the *Zohar.* In the commentary "Abram, the Soul-Breath" (*Zohar Hadash* 22c-d, 23a), Tifereth is referred to as "the mirror that shines." In his notes to this passage, Daniel Matt states "This image. . .designates *Tif'eret,* the Blessed Holy One, the central *sefirah* and divine mate of *Shekhinah.* The soul-breath is born from the union of *Tif'eret,* her father, and *Shekhinah,* her mother."[48] The soul-breath (note it is feminine) is our "vitality," the inner essence of our being. Tifereth, the mirror that shines, radiates the divine essence to Shekhinah who is called "a mirror in which all colors appear. This is the mirror that does not shine."[49] It is the union of the polarity between Tifereth and Shekhinah that allows us to access the Divine. It is through Shekhinah that the pilgrim starts the ascent of the Tree of Life. She provides the vision for the prophets by filtering the light of the sefiroth above her so that mortals may perceive it. Hence, she does not shine herself but transmutes the divine essence so we are not blinded by it. The shining light of Tifereth would blind us so we need the union of Shekhinah and Tifereth in order to perceive the Divine.

Another example of the divine androgyne is found in "The Secret of the Sabbath" (*Zohar* 2:135a-b):

> The Secret of Sabbath:
> She is Sabbath!
> United in the secret of One
> to draw down upon Her the secret of One.[50]

"She is Sabbath" refers to Shekhinah as the Queen entering the palace at the beginning of the Sabbath celebration. She is coming to unite with the King, Tifereth, through the devotions of the faithful. As Daniel Matt states in his commentary to this verse: "This secret of One is *Tif'eret*, the Holy King, joined together with the *sefirot* surrounding Him. *Shekhinah* and *Tif'eret* must each be whole before their union: 'The Blessed Holy One [*Tif'eret*], One up above, does not sit on His Throne of Glory [*Shekhinah*] until She becomes like Him through the secret of the One: One in One'. . . .' *YHVH* is One and His Name is One' (Zechariah 14:9)"[51]

The Kabbalistic concept of the union of Tifereth and Shekhinah closely parallels gnostic myths of the sacred union of Sophia and Christ and mystical visions of the marriage of the feminine soul and Christ. When Tifereth is interpreted as a symbol of the Cosmic Christ, the sacred marriage of Tifereth and the Shekhinah in the Kabbalah resonates with the union of Christ and Sophia on the Path of ChristoSophia.

The Kabbalistic view also reclaims the holiness of the body and sexuality. For human sexuality mirrors the divine order, and marriage between man and woman symbolizes the "sacred marriage" between the masculine and feminine aspects of God. In Kabbalism, lovemaking between husband and wife is viewed as a primary spiritual practice; when approached with right intention, the sexual act can facilitate the divine union which restores harmony to the cosmos. For this reason married couples are expected to engage in sexual intercourse on the eve of the Sabbath as a means of actualizing and celebrating the divine marriage.[52] However, sexual behavior is just one way that human beings can influence the cosmic order. Any savoring of physical pleasures and the blessing of life are expressions of thanksgiving for the divine gifts in life – the "Via Positiva" of the medieval mystics. The Baal Shem Tov in particular emphasized the corresponding Kabbalistic viewpoint, for he taught that "a key means to transcend our daily cares is to wholeheartedly savor our physical pleasures. He insisted that our sensual needs must not be denigrated, but prized and hallowed."[53]

The Kabbalah's image of the Divine Feminine can help illumine the way for the pilgrim on the mystical bypath. The role of the Shekhinah in the Kabbalists' cosmological view supports the mystical perception of the divine presence in every aspect of creation and the interconnectedness of life. For "through the radiant light of the Shekhinah everything is linked to everything else, as if connected through a luminous skein of being…What is called nature is therefore the epiphany of the Divine."[54] For Kabbalists, every human action has profound effects in the divine realm; every righteous action promotes the union of the Shekhinah and Tiferet, and every sinful action disrupts their union.[55] Thus the Kabbalah stresses that the supreme purpose of traveling on the mystical bypath is to work as "co-creators" with the Divine in the task of reuniting Heaven and Earth.

The Doctrine of *Tikkun*

The task of reuniting Heaven and Earth is called *tikkun* by Kabbalists. *Tikkun* means cosmic reunification or restoration and is a term first used by Isaac Luria in the sixteenth century. *Tikkun* involves the "raising of the holy sparks," which became lost at the "breaking of the vessels" of the sephiroth during creation. The need for *tikkun*, according to Rabbi Luria, originated in this breaking

[handwritten margin note: this really sounds like gnosticism]

308

of the vessels as the primordial light poured forth from Ain-Sof. The emanating sefiroth could not contain this light and, while the Supernal Triad was undamaged, the six central sefiroth from Chesed through Yesod shattered. The early Lurianic Kabbalist Israel Sarug beautifully summarizes the mystery of the breaking of the vessels:

> Traces of the light adhered to the shards of the shattered
> Vessels. This may be compared to a vessel full of oil.
> If it breaks and the oil spills out, a bit of the liquid adheres
> to the shards in the form of drops. Likewise in our case,
> a few sparks of light adhered. When the shards descended
> to the bottom of the world of actualization, they were
> transformed into the four elements – fire, air, water, and earth –
> from which evolved the stages of mineral, vegetable, animal,
> and human. When these materialized, some of the sparks
> remained hidden within the varieties of existence. You should
> aim to raise those sparks hidden throughout the world,
> elevating them to holiness by the power of your soul.[56]

The final sentence of Rabbi Sarug's analogy illustrates the cosmic purpose of *tikkun*. Here is where the creation of humankind has its purpose: to repair the break in the divine unity by "raising the sparks." This is done by acts of virtue and by living in harmony with the natural world, using the gifts of the kingdoms appropriately, thereby releasing the sparks to return to the divine unity.

Therefore, the entire universe, including all animate and inanimate things, contains these "holy sparks" which consist of the primordial light from Ain-Sof. These sparks are contained in "shells" or "husks" in the physical universe and must be liberated. As so aptly put by Rabbi David Cooper in his inspiring book, *God is a Verb,*

> Our task, according to Luria, is to release each spark from
> the shell and raise it up, ultimately to return it to its original
> state. The way these sparks are raised is through acts of
> lovingkindness, of being in harmony with the universe, and
> through higher awareness. The ramifications of this teaching
> are enormous. In each moment of existence we have the
> potential to raise holy sparks. If we are unaware of this

ability and are spiritually asleep, then we do not accomplish much, for the medium through which sparks are raised is consciousness itself. . .everything in daily life presents sparks locked in husks awaiting release.[57]

In a sense, we may say that the most basic purpose of human existence is to participate in *tikkun*. We have an opportunity to work to restore the divine unity by the way we live our lives. According to Kabbalah, by consciously seeking to release sparks, we not only aid others and the world at large, we mend our own souls. We **must** transform our consciousness, because in so doing, we are releasing sparks and bringing about healing to all of creation.

There is a beautiful Sukkoth practice which illustrates how *tikkun* is expressed by ritual as a central responsibility of Jewish people – and, by extension, all pilgrims on the mystical bypath:

> During the holy days of Sukkot, one of the primary rituals
> is to hold an unopened palm branch, a citron, and myrtle
> and willow branches, and shake them in the six directions.
> This is viewed by Kabbalists as a way to bring a *tikkun*, a
> mending, to the separation caused by the physical universe.
> The palm branch represents a *vav*, the number six, and the
> citron (a lemonlike fruit) represents the Tree of Knowledge
> in its most "beautiful" state of unity and undifferentiation –
> when it is united with the Tree of Life. During the ritual
> shaking, the six directions are mystically drawn into the
> citron, representing the person's heart. The intention of the
> ritual is to break through the illusion of separation and to
> return to the unity of the symbolic garden.[58]

Whether by rituals such as this, or by our prayers and meditations, or by daily acts of kindness, we can and must express *tikkun*. The pilgrim on the mystical bypath, by the very act of walking on the path, is participating in the divine activity of *tikkun*.

MEDITATION ON THE TREE OF LIFE

For the pilgrim on the mystical bypath, the Tree of Life is unequalled as a rich source of concepts and images for meditation.

We can describe the act of meditation as a technique to bring about a state of altered consciousness. Rabbi David Cooper states:

> Higher and lower realms of consciousness are not separated by space; rather, they are dimensions that represent a proximity of relationship to ultimate truth. The higher the consciousness, the less there is an illusion of separateness. Earth represents a level of consciousness. Everything on this level has its likeness in higher consciousness. There is no object, however small, that does not have its counterpart in other realms. So when the thing below bestirs itself, the result is a simultaneous stimulation of its likeness above. The two realms form one interconnected whole.[59]

[handwritten margin note: this is like Greek philosophy]

So when we meditate using the Kabbalah, we are embarking on an activity to connect that which is below with that which is above. This is like the meditative practices of the ancient Hebrew prophets – they raised their consciousness until they could impinge upon the divine consciousness, thus bringing the higher consciousness "down to earth." After the Age of the Prophets, which ended in the fifth century BCE, it was the concern of Kabbalists ("those who receive") to continue receiving divine enlightenment through rigorous methods of meditation. Many Kabbalists believe that Rabbi Shimon bar Yochai in the second century of the Common Era wrote or compiled the *Zohar* from the direct inspiration of the prophet Elijah while deeply meditating for thirteen years in a cave.[60]

[handwritten margin note: right, people believe whatever they want to]

Kabbalists use many methods of meditation, both apophatic and kathopathic. Apophatic meditation employs the sacred letters, words, and Divine Names as springboards into the upper regions of the Spirit. Many of the apophatic methods require years of intense study, mastery of Hebrew, and single-minded dedication in order to achieve even a modicum of enlightenment. These methods involve the tools of *gematria, notarikon,* and/or *themurah*, memorization of long passages of Divine Names in Hebrew, and close supervision by a trained Kabbalist. Obviously, the vast majority of pilgrims on the mystical bypath are not able to commit themselves to this protracted study, and will find the Kabbalistic kathopathic meditational techniques most useful. This form of meditation is based upon "the kabbalistic principle that our imaginations are connected with higher realities."[61]

Kathopathic meditation uses mental images built up within the imagination or taken from one's own dreams, or images that may be selected from external sources such as sacred signs and symbols. If the image is from an external source, it must resonate in some way with the personal psyche since it will be used as a vehicle to enter into the realm of the Spirit. If there is no internal resonance, the symbol or image will be like a car low on fuel; it won't go very far! Thus, when we use external images or symbols, we must make them a part of our psyche by contemplating them with focused attention. It is very similar to the concept of active imagination that is a central technique used in dream analysis by the Analytical Psychology school of C. G. Jung.

Jewish Kabbalistic Meditation

Jewish Kabbalists developed many forms of meditation which became the basis for the Western Mystery Tradition, the term most frequently used to describe the nineteenth and twentieth century amalgam of Christian Kabbalah, Hermeticism, Rosicrucianism, etc. Because the Western Mystery Tradition provides the seeker with most helpful signposts on the mystical bypath today, it is important to understand their primary origin in the meditational practices of the medieval Jewish Kabbalists.

Abraham Abulafia in the thirteenth century was the first Kabbalist to write down many of the meditation practices of the earlier Merkabah and Bereshith mystics. He also created many new techniques which exerted great influence for many centuries. Many of these techniques may have been inspired by the practices of Christian mystics as he had meetings with many of them to discuss their insights and methods. In his treatise *Key of Wisdoms*, Abulafia states:

> There is no question that there are individuals among the Christians who know this mystery. They discussed the mysteries with me and revealed that this is unquestionably

their opinion, whereupon I judged them to be among the
most pious of the gentiles.[62]

We know that Abulafia had many contacts with Christians
during his career and that there must have been a certain cross-
fertilization of ideas about meditation practices, even though there
was no agreement about basic theology. Abulafia was writing during
the great medieval flowering of mysticism in Christianity and Islam
as well as Judaism and was familiar with many diverse practices.
He taught the "Method of Sefirot" (kathopathic) as separate from
the "Method of Letters" (apophatic). He wrote about ascending
the "ladder of the Sefirot" but warned people not to think of the
Sefiroth as separate entities which he felt was the principal danger of
visualizing sefirothic images.[63] Abulafia has very specific warnings to
those who seek to travel the mystical bypath. He discouraged people
younger than middle age from attempting Kabbalistic meditation
because they were too tied to the body. In the *Book of Blendings* ,
Abulafia made the very modern observation about the psychological
dangers of spiritual dilettantism:

> Your mind will be confused, your thoughts confounded,
> and you will not find any way to escape the reveries of your
> mind. The power of your imagination will overwhelm you,
> making you imagine many utterly useless fantasies. Your
> imaginative faculty will grow stronger, weakening your
> intellect, until your reveries cast you into a great sea. You
> will not have the wisdom ever to escape from it, and will
> therefore drown.[64]

Abulafia gives very specific instructions on how to meditate
which are pertinent for any type of meditation:

> Make yourself right. Meditate in a special place, where
> your voice cannot be heard by others. Cleanse your heart
> and soul of all other thoughts in the world. Imagine at this
> time, your soul is separating from your body, and that you
> are leaving the physical world behind, so that you enter the
> Future World, which is the source of all life distributed to
> the living. [The Future World] is the intellect, which is the

313

source of all Wisdom, Understanding and Knowledge,
emanating from the King of Kings, the Blessed Holy One.[65]

His reference, "The Future World," is to Kether, the Crown
and first sefirah of the Tree of Life. Wisdom, Understanding, and
Knowledge refer to Chokmah, Binah, and Daath respectively.
Thus we see the sefiroth as they may be used in a more apophatic
meditation.

Along with many of his contemporaries, Abulafia was distrustful
of the power of the imagination and hence advocated more apophatic
methods using the Divine Names and the inherent power of the
Hebrew letters. And yet, in the following passage from his *Life of the
Future World*, he tells his students to imagine God and His angels as
if they were human beings sitting or standing in the presence of the
meditator and communicating directly with him:

> Then take in your hand a tablet and some ink. These
> will serve as your witnesses that you are coming to
> serve God with joy and good heart. Then begin to
> permute a number of letters. You may use only a few,
> or you may use many. Transpose and permute them quickly,
> until your heart is warmed as a result of these permutations. . .
> From these permutations, you will gain new knowledge that
> you never learned from human traditions nor derived from
> intellectual analysis. . .Then prepare your inner thoughts to
> depict God and His highest angels. Depict them in your heart
> as if they were human beings, sitting or standing around you.
> You are in their midst, like a messenger whom the King and
> his servants wish to send on a mission. You are ready
> to hear the words of the message. . .from His mouth. . .[66]

As can be seen, Abulafia viewed the Hebrew alphabet as a path
to the Divine by suspending the rational associations of words made
up of the letters. By spontaneously creating new combinations
of letters, the voice of divine inspiration could penetrate directly
into the soul of the mystic and thus what begins as an apophatic
meditation becomes an ecstatic kathopathic vision of the Divine.

Also in the thirteenth century, there appeared a small text called
The Gate of Kavanah. In this book, *Kavanah* is a form of meditation

requiring the concentrated visualization of the sefiroth and different types of light. Basically, this is a combination of apophatic and kathopathic forms of meditation since the individual visualizes herself ascending various levels of light to finally arrive at the *Ain Sof Aur* (Infinite Light):

> When a person sets his mind on something, its essence
> returns to him.
> Therefore, if you wish to pray, or if you wish to grasp the
> true nature of an idea, do the following:
> Imagine that you yourself are light, and that all of your
> Surroundings, on every side, are also light.
> In the middle of this light is a Throne of light.
> Above this Throne is a light called *Nogah* (Glow).
> Facing this is [another] Throne. Above [the second Throne]
> Is a light called *Tov* (Good).
> You are standing between the two. . .
> Now turn yourself to the right of it, and there you will find
> [another] light. This is a light that is called *Bahir* (Brilliant).
> To its left you will [also] find a light. This is a light called
> *Zohar* (Radiant).
> Above these two, directly between them, is a light called
> *Kavod* (Glory).
> Around it is a light called *Chaim* (Life).
> Above it is the Crown.
> This is the light that crowns the desires of the mind and
> illuminates the paths of the imagination, enhancing the
> radiance (*zohar*) of the vision. . .
> It is hidden from those who stray from the path of this light. . .
> The true path is straight, depending on the concentration
> (*kavanah*) of the individual. . .
> He can then probe very deeply, and break away from the
> crooked path. Through the power of his meditation, the
> individual can then blaze a new path.[67]

This long passage gives an indication of how the visualization of the lights of the sefiroth was done by the early Kabbalists. The six lights mentioned in the passage correspond to the six sefiroth from Chesed to Yesod. It is interesting to note that two of the lights in the above meditation are the names of two of the most important meditational Kabbalistic texts: *Bahir* (Brilliant) and *Zohar* (Radiant).

It wasn't until the next generation that the first true meditation book on the ascent of the Tree of Life appeared. It was *Gates of Light* by Joseph Gikatelia (1248-1323). In it, Gikatelia combines the ten sefiroth with the ten Divine Names. One ascends the Tree of Life from Malkuth to Kether by meditating upon and communing with the Divine Name for each sefirah. The *Gates of Light* became a basic primer for meditating on the Tree of Life for many centuries. A famous prayer by the great sixteenth century Kabbalist Rabbi Joseph Tzayach (1505-1573) reflects the *Gates of Light*:

> *Ehyeh Asher Ehyeh,* Crown me (*Kether*).
> *Yah,* grant me Wisdom (*Chokmah*).
> *Elohim Chaim,* grant me Understanding (*Binah*).
> *El,* with the right hand of His Love, make me great (*Chesed*).
> *Elohim,* from the Terror of His Judgment, protect me (*Geburah*).
> *YHVH,* with His mercy, grant me Beauty (*Tifereth*).
> *Adonoy Tzevaot,* watch me Forever (*Netzach*).
> *Elohim Tzevaot,* grant me beatitude from His Splendor (*Hod*),
> *El Chai,* make his covenant my Foundation (*Yesod*).
> *Adonoy,* open my lips and my mouth will speak of Your praise (*Malkuth*).[68]

This beautiful and succinct prayer is an excellent way for the pilgrim on the mystical bypath to begin any meditation – it focuses the attention on the sefiroth and, more importantly, connects one with the divine power found in each of the Holy Names of God.

Rabbi Moshe Cordovero, leader of the Kabbalistic school at Safed in the sixteenth century, associated specific colors to each sefirah in addition to the Divine Names. He warned, however, that one should not think of the sefiroth as separate from Ain-Sof. In his *Garden of Pomegranates*, he states:

> In many places in Kabbalistic texts and the Zohar, we
> find that various colors parallel the Sefirot. One must
> be very careful and not imagine that this is to be taken
> literally. Color is something physical, used to describe
> the physical world, and [the Sefirot], which are spiritual

should not be described with physical properties. . .these colors allude to the results that are transmitted from the highest Roots. . .There is no question that the colors can thus serve as a door to the dynamics of the Sefirot. . . colors can serve as a channel for the forces that are transmitted from on high.[69]

The *Gates of Light* also had a very profound influence upon the sixteenth century Christian Kabbalists like Johannes Reuchlin and Henry Cornelius Agrippa. It became the basis for many texts of the practical Kabbalah and eventually the books of the Western Mystery Tradition which are almost entirely devoted to the kathopathic uses of the Tree of Life.

Meditation in the Western Mystery Tradition

The basic kathopathic method of meditation on the Tree of Life is called "pathworking," or "ascending the Tree" – terms that came into use in the seventeenth century in the various schools of the Western Mystery Tradition that arose from the Kabbalistic teachings of Christian Knorr von Rosenroth, Robert Fludd, and Thomas Vaughan. At the same time, there was great interest by many practitioners in the symbolism of the tarot deck of cards which had become "rediscovered" in much the same way that the Kabbalah had been by Pico and Reuchlin. It did not take the practical Kabbalists of the Western Mystery Tradition long to combine the tarot cards with the Tree of Life. Since the tarot deck has twenty-two "court" cards (known as the major arcana), it became obvious that these cards could correspond to the twenty-two letters of the Hebrew alphabet and thereby "fit" onto the twenty-two paths that connect the ten sefiroth on the Tree of Life. Once this association was made, a wealth of archetypal imagery was available for pathworking meditation. See Diagram 4 for a synthesis of many of the most common images.

Diagram #4

The following correspondences, images, names, and symbols have come down to the present through the Western Mystery Tradition in the late 19th and early 20th centuries. The color of each sephirah is based upon the "Queen" scale of the World of Briah.

<u>Kether</u> – The Crown #1 (Pure white brilliance)
Archangel: Metatron

An ancient bearded king in profile	The primum mobile
Ancient of Days	The first swirlings
Ptah	The Point of Living Light
Zeus	The Central Point
Wotan	The Smooth Point
The crown	The Primordial Point
The swastika	The White Hand
God	The Vast Countenance
Macroprosopos	The Point within the Circle

<u>Chokmah</u> – Wisdom #2 (Gray)
Archangel: Ratziel

A bearded male figure	The phallus
Father	The Inner Robe of Glory
Man	The Great Sea
Thoth	The zodiac
Neptune	The standing stone
Odin	The tower
Athena	The Uplifted Rod of Power
Lingam	The straight line
Logos	

Binah – Understanding #3 (Black)
Archangel: Tzaphkiel

The Outer Robe of Concealment	Woman
Nephthys	The Great Mother
Cybele	A mature woman
Demeter	A matron
Frigga	The throne
Saturn	Vesica Piscis
Juno	The chalice
Yoni	The cup

Daath – Knowledge (hidden) (Silvery gray)
Archangels of the Four Directions

Uranus	The condemned cell
Asteroids	The empty room
Janus	The second mountain
The Abyss	A grain of corn
The solar disk with wings	The caduceus
The upper room	The prism
Sirius, the Dog Star	The Gateway to Nirvana

Chesed – Mercy #4 (Blue)
Archangel: Tzadkiel

A mighty crowned and enthroned king	The solid figure
Isis	The tetrahedron
Poseidon	The pyramid
Wotan	The equal-armed cross
Jupiter	The orb
The shepherd's crook	The scepter
The unicorn	The wand

Geburah – Strength #5 (Scarlet red)
Archangel: Khamael

A mighty warrior in his chariot	The five-petaled Tudor rose
Horus	The pentagon
Ares	The sword
Hades	The spear
Thor	The scourge
Mars	The chain
Basilisk	The dragon

Tiphereth – Beauty #6 (Golden yellow)
Archangel: Raphael

A majestic king	The lamen	The phoenix
A sacrificed god	The Rosy Cross	The King
Ra	The Calvary Cross	The truncated pyramid
Apollo	The child	The cube
Adonis	The lion	

Netzach – Victory #7 (Emerald green)
Archangel: Hanael

A beautiful naked woman	The lamp
Hathor	The girdle
Aphrodite	The lynx
Freya	The rose
Venus	

Hod – Splendor #8 (Orange)
Archangel: Michael

A hermaphrodite	The apron
Anubis	The jackal
Hermes	The names and words of power
Mercury	The versicles
Loki	

Yesod – Foundation # 9 (Violet)
Archangel: Gabriel

A beautiful naked man, very strong	The sandals of ceremony
Shu	The elephant
Diana	The moon
Perfumes	Sandals

Malkuth – Kingdom #10 (Citrine, olive, russet, and brown)
Archangel: Sandalphon

A young woman, crowned and enthroned	The sphinx
Seb	The altar of the double cube
Persephone	The equal-armed cross of the Ceres
The four elements	The magic circle
The triangle of evocation	

There have been many books written in the past hundred years about the connection between the Tree of Life and the tarot. Two books that have not been surpassed for their clarity and wealth of archetypal images are Dion Fortune's *The Mystical Qabalah* and Gareth Knight's *Practical Guide to Qabalistic Symbolism*. The most appropriate tarot decks for meditating with the Kabbalah are the

Paul Foster Case deck and the Rider-Waite deck although there are many others that can be useful too.

The twenty two paths that connect the sefiroth can also be said to represent states of consciousness in contrast to the ten sefiroth which represent the natural forces of creation. Thus we meditate on the Tree of Life by raising our consciousness as we ascend the Tree on each path. Keep in mind that "Kabbalah" means "to receive," so when one begins a meditation on the Tree of Life, one must be receptive. One uses the signposts on the paths on the Tree of Life which are the archetypal images used by countless people before us, both Jewish and Christian Kabbalists as well as seekers of the Western Mystery Tradition. Each personal meditation on a path adds to the spiritual essence to be found on that path by other pilgrims.

Pathworking

To begin meditation for pathworking, one should always begin with a centering prayer or ritual for protection and inspiration. Pathworking may begin at any point on the Tree of Life although one should begin with the sefirah that is at the base of the path that one intends to travel. For the purpose of pathworking, sefiroth are considered paths in themselves so one might wish to journey in the path of the sefirah itself. However, ascending the Tree usually indicates the intention of traveling from one sefirah to the next higher one. For example, if the meditator seeks to travel the twenty-fifth path that connects Yesod with Tiphereth, she would begin in the sefirah Yesod. One common way of meditating on a sefirah is to create a mental image of a temple that contains the attributes of that sefirah. For instance, a temple for Yesod would include lunar symbols, violet light, the archangel Gabriel, etc. This can be as simple or as detailed as the power of one's imagination wishes to make it. However, the purpose of creating these images is not the images in themselves but for the connection they make between one's psyche and the spiritual energy represented by the sefirah. An experienced pathworker can connect with the energy of a sefirah very rapidly and then embark on the exploration of the selected path. To do this, one may envision a literal path leading from the temple in the direction of the next sefirah. On the other hand, one can visualize

321

the tarot card as a gateway onto the path. This is where active imagination can be very valuable. By looking at the card, one can make it come alive just as if the tarot image were a photograph. One can put oneself into the picture, so to speak, and imagine walking and conversing with the figure depicted on the card. The tarot card associated with the twenty-fifth path connecting Yesod to Tifereth is named "Temperance." In the Case and Rider-Waite decks, the figure is that of Michael, the archangel of the Sun and the Christian saint who dispels the chthonic darkness of outworn forms. Conversing with such a powerful archetype might appear to be daunting but St. Michael is in everyone's psyche and he is an infallible guide. The main purpose of active imagination is to allow an inner dialogue to occur in which often valuable insight may be obtained. One should remember to thank the inner figure before continuing on the path.

At first, it may seem strange to think of carrying on a conversation with a "separate" entity within one's psyche. Of course, the inner figure is just that, part of one's own being. Even though the figure may have first appeared on a tarot card, once it has been internalized, it serves as part of one's inner world. The thirty-two paths and all their complex imagery are found within each person's psyche so there are an astronomical number of possible inner figures and images one may contact.

At this point in the pathworking, the meditator may wish to return rather than continuing on to the end. This is fine, since it is the process of walking the path that is important, not reaching the "end" of the path. If one decides to continue to the end of the path at the next sefirah, one can envision that as another temple, a castle, a garden, a pool, a glowing sphere of color, or a specific image associated with that sefirah. The sefirah at the end of the twenty-fifth path is Tifereth, the Bridegroom of Shekhinah. In building the image of a temple for Tifereth, its attributes would include solar symbols, golden yellow light, a majestic king, a child, etc. One may create many detailed images for this sefirah, too, keeping in mind that detailed images are not the central purpose of pathworking. In any event, one should not discontinue the meditation until one has contacted the energy at the sefirah at the end of the path, or returned to and reconnected with the energy of the initial sefirah. At the end of the pathworking, one can envision oneself walking away from the inner temple or place and returning to the temporal world. A final prayer of thanksgiving should close the meditation followed by time to write down the experience in one's meditation journal. This last is very important since it provides a place to return to contemplate the wider picture from many meditations.

Ascending the Tree of Life

The pilgrim on the mystical bypath will find a well marked map pointing the way on the "ascent of the Tree." The journey begins at Malkuth which is also the Shekinah, the Gateway to the Divine. She leads the way through Yesod to Tifereth, her Bridegroom, who is the Cosmic Christ. Since our physical bodies exist in Malkuth, that is the sefirah in which we must begin our ascent. Malkuth represents the physical world and all the natural forces of which it is made. The nature bypath of the Path of ChristoSophia exists in Malkuth. The Celtic saints, as they trod the nature bypath and contemplated the divine within nature, were experiencing Malkuth. The first step on the ascent, then, is the recognition of the presence of God in the natural world. On the Tree of Life, we take this step on the path from Malkuth to Yesod, which is called the thirty-second path. To this path is attributed the last letter of the Hebrew alphabet, *tav*, which means mark or cross. In the Scriptures, Jesus says that the last shall be first, so our first step on the path is the last letter. Jesus also tells us to take up our cross and follow Him; it is appropriate that we begin our journey by taking our cross with us, our limitations so to speak, as we aspire to enter the upper worlds. The cross of Jesus has been associated with a tree since the apostolic times. Christians of the first two centuries often referred to the cross of the crucifixion of Jesus as a tree. For example, *The Gospel of Truth* states, "He was nailed to a tree (and) he became a fruit of the knowledge of the Father."[70] Christ becomes the fruit of the tree by which act he overcomes the onus of the fruit of the Tree of Knowledge eaten by Adam and Eve. Those who eat of Christ's fruit from the tree of the cross will gain the new knowledge and gladness of heart. Thus, the pilgrim taking up his cross (*tav*) as he begins his ascent is nourished by the fruit of Christ from the cross.

PATHWORKING FROM MALKUTH TO TIFERETH

The following is an example of a pathworking from Malkuth to Tifereth via the thirty-second path through Yesod and the twenty-fifth path to Tifereth. This is sometimes referred to as the "Path of the Arrow" because it goes straight up the Middle Pillar of the Tree of Life. It is a fundamental way on the Path of ChristoSophia because it is here that the Divine Feminine as the Shekhinah unites with the Cosmic Christ.

You may use the imagery of this meditation to help you become familiar with the method of pathworking, or you may use it as a model for developing your own images based upon the symbolic associations with the sefiroth and the paths that you are working with. Find a quiet, peaceful place where you will be undisturbed for at least an hour and still your mind in whatever way works best for you. Don't neglect to use a centering prayer for protection and inspiration on your inner journey.

Envision yourself in a natural environment. It may be any place where Nature predominates. Imagine yourself as a Celtic saint on the nature bypath, leaning against the trunk of an ancient oak tree which shelters your primitive beehive hut. Your temple is the clearing in which you sit: the tall trees are the vaulting, their trunks the supporting columns. The sunlight filtering through the leaves is the stained-glass windows and the birdsong, the humming of the insects, and the babbling of a small brook are the chanting of the choir. The smells of the rich earth, the fragrant air, dew-laden wildflowers are the incense. You sit receptively, soaking in all the myriad impressions of Sophia/Shekhinah, because this is her world of enchantment. (We are part of this world every day but we live in it with blinders on, seeing it as "through a glass darkly" because we rarely open ourselves to receive her gifts.) Reflect on her beauty, feel the profound depth of her presence, the interconnectedness of all creation from the most distant galaxy to the tiniest gnat buzzing around your head. Reflect – feel – be at peace – in harmony with all creation.

From this state of peaceful harmony, you feel a quiet, yet insistent, yearning to find that which is hidden behind the natural world. You

324

arise and see a path that you've never noticed before leading from your clearing into an unknown part of the woods. You pick up your stout oak walking staff and begin leisurely walking along the path which has been hitherto hidden. Your sense of yearning deepens and you slightly quicken your pace as you see a small clearing ahead. In the center of the clearing is a naked androgynous figure who is dancing in a labyrinth with a graceful, yet energetic, complex pattern of steps. When the figure reaches the center, while still dancing, she calls to you to come to her in the center by following the path of the labyrinth. You hesitate, not knowing how to do such a complicated dance, but she encourages you and you begin to enter. As you progress around the labyrinth, you become more assured with the dance steps and by the time you arrive in the center, you feel confident. You join her in the dance and as you grasp her hands, you suddenly find yourself aware of the "energy of life" which continually creates the physical world. You also become aware that this energy connects you with all creation.

At this point, you may ask her whatever questions that you feel are pertinent. Her answers you will bring back with you to reflect upon at a later time. You ask to be shown the way to the Temple of the Moon. She indicates that when you retrace your steps to the beginning of the labyrinth, you will come out in the temple of Yesod, the Moon. You thank her for her insights and assistance and begin going back out of the labyrinth. As you do so, you realize that it is night time and a full moon is lighting up the labyrinth. As you gaze at the moon, you become aware of the ebb and flow of the energy of life. There is a time for growth and a time for decay. As you leave the labyrinth, you find yourself in a structure that appears to be made of some kind of violet magnetic energy beams. You can see objects but you can also see right through them. The roof of the temple is a large dome with a circular opening (oculus) to the sky. The light of the full moon shines through the oculus onto a round altar on which stands a chalice. You go over to the altar and look into the chalice. You see sacred primary water which reflects the light of the full moon. As you look at the reflection, you become aware that the light you see in the chalice is a reflection of the moonlight which is reflected sunlight. You ponder the meaning of this and resolve to reflect upon it when you return. As you turn away from the altar, you are startled to realize that you are not alone. A dark-robed figure has been standing behind you while you gazed in the chalice. He tells you to pick it up and drink the primary water. You do so and you feel the magnetic-like energy flowing through every cell of your body. You realize that you are resonating with the energy of the moon. You feel the flux and reflux of life and become conscious of the polarity of "As above, so below." You also realize the need to reflect more deeply on this when you return.

You now may ask the robed figure whatever questions you feel are pertinent with the understanding that you will ponder the answers at a later time. You ask where the gateway to the twenty-fifth path is and the figure points to the oculus of the dome. As you look up, you see that there is brilliant sunlight pouring through the oculus and that a great white-robed angel is hovering in the sky, beckoning for you to rise up to him. You thank your robed temple guide and feel yourself ascending on a shaft of pure brilliance. As you rise up you see a vista of indescribable beauty. Every thing that you direct your gaze at has an aura of rainbow light emanating from it: trees, plants, rocks, streams, insects, birds, animals, and human beings – all are radiant in the brilliant prismatic hues of the rainbow. You find yourself standing on a mountain peak next to Michael. He tells you that he is the guide for all those who are seeking spiritual insight. You realize that he is the higher octave of the androgynous dancer you met in the labyrinth and that he, too, is androgynous. It is through the archangel Michael that the divine light of the Cosmic Christ is transmuted into physical existence. He reminds you that your physical eyes only perceive light, not the objects-in-themselves. If that is true on the physical plane with physical light, how does one see the divine light? He tells you to reflect on the deep significance of this from a spiritual perspective when you return.

As you have with the other figures on your journey, you may now ask Michael questions that are pertinent to your life. As you gaze at the archangel, you see above him a rainbow coruscating with rapidly vibrating waves of brilliant color, so bright, that you must turn your eyes away. Michael tells you that the end of the path to Tifereth lies beyond the rainbow in the Heavenly City. It will be necessary for you to flow over the rainbow bridge on the ray of color that you most resonate with. You thank Michael for his guidance and inspiration and begin to flow on your color ray. You arrive in the Heavenly City through the gate of your color and are welcomed by the gatekeeper. He informs you that you must state your purpose for seeking entrance to the city. You realize that this is very significant because, you infer, that you will be allowed to see only that which you are ready to see based upon your stated purpose and spiritual development. You reflect deeply on what you have experienced thus far on your journey and realize why you seek entrance to the realm of Tifereth. You state this to the gatekeeper who smiles and tells you how to gain entrance to that place in the Heavenly City. You are led to it by two golden yellow-robed guides who walk on either side of you. They are very compassionate and understanding and welcome you as a citizen. They are thankful that you have brought the wisdom of Sophia/Shekhinah with you to be united with the love of the Cosmic Christ. You are to witness the uniting of Tifereth with Malkuth which will manifest the loving-wisdom of ChristoSophia into all of creation. This union is an indescribable mystery which happens beyond all comprehension so you will not be consciously aware of it but you will have the loving-wisdom of ChristoSophia placed in your heart to bring back to those on the physical plane you come into contact with.

After attending the mystery of the Divine hieros-gamos, you are led back to the gate and given the necessary sustenance to safely see your return via the paths on which you traveled. As you return, you briefly share with the figure from each path what you experienced on the path above. When you return to your temple of Nature in Malkuth, you sit quietly, leaning against the trunk of oak tree, and slowly, peacefully return to your temporal place and time.

Offer a closing prayer of thanksgiving and then restore the energy of your body with bread and wine mixed with warm water. Write down all that you recall of your journey in your meditation journal. Don't worry about the details – focus on the general themes. In ensuing meditations, you may return to this meditation and re-enter any path and seek clarification or further insight from the figures you encountered. The most important step is to keep up the pathworking on the Tree of Life. It will provide you with inexhaustible insight and inspiration which you can then share with others along the mystical bypath.

CHAPTER X: THE HOLY GRAIL

There the great mystery is written
Which is called the Grail.[1]

It is the Grail which has been the most powerful symbol on the mystical bypath for nearly a thousand years. Because of its eros qualities, the Grail cannot be controlled by any organizational structure or confined to any philosophical system. Therefore it has never been accepted as an official signpost for those traveling on the interstate highway of Christianity. Instead, the quest for the Grail has always taken place on the bypaths where the individual pilgrim accepts challenges and hardships in his search for an inner experience of the Divine, as opposed to collective belief in the dogmas of the institutional Church.

The numinous symbol of the Grail, which lures the seeker on the mystical bypath forward in his quest, is so uniquely powerful because it fuses together many of the elements of Christian tradition which are hidden on the bypaths: Gnosticism, Celtic Christianity, the Kabbalah, and especially the Divine Feminine. Yet the significance of the Grail goes even more deeply than this, for it is also a symbol which integrates the ancient wisdom of the pagans with the "new revelation" of Christ. As Emma Jung points out, the symbol of the Grail is the manifestation of an underlying archetype which appears in the mythologies of most cultures: the "miraculous vessel" which may provide a renewal of life, youth, healing, strength, wisdom, or transformation.[2] This universal symbol of eros thus seems to be extremely important in the psyche of human beings. For the Grail quest symbolizes the yearning of humanity: the yearning to return to Paradise before the Fall, the yearning for inner wholeness, the yearning for union with God. It is this universal yearning of humanity for "something more" to complete our broken fragmented selves, when not consciously understood, that leads us on the illusory quests for power, fame, wealth, sex, and all the variations of addictive behaviors. It is only when this yearning is understood for what it truly is - the soul's response to the Divine which seeks it - that the true quest can begin. Thus the Grail becomes the goal of the mystic's quest.

SOURCES OF THE GRAIL MYTH

The term "Grail" itself is ambiguous and its etymological origin is unclear. Some possible derivations for the word include the Latin "gradale" or "gradalis," meaning a deep plate or dish; the Old French "greal" or "grasal," meaning a vessel or cup; and the French "grassale," meaning a basin.[3] Similarly, the form that the Grail takes varies from one story to another: it may appear as a stone, cauldron, dish, platter, cornucopia, vessel, cup or chalice. The meaning of the Grail changes just as its form changes. Thus the modern day Grail seeker, like the Grail knight of the past, first encounters the dark forest of confusion where shapes shift and multiple pathways appear. For the many legends of the Grail comprise a vast network of paths seeming to lead in different directions, which however intersect at the center: the central theme of the mystery of the Grail.

The Grail stories which we are most familiar with today were written over approximately fifty years during the late twelfth and early thirteenth centuries. However, these works were based on much earlier oral versions of the myth which comprise the "Matter of Britain," as the legends and folklore surrounding King Arthur are known.[4] Pre-Christian sources which are of particular importance for understanding the symbolism of the Grail are the early Celtic myths which come to us from Ireland, Wales, Cornwall and Brittany.

A primary image of the Grail in Celtic mythology is the magical cauldron. For example, the Irish Dagda's cauldron provided

330

limitless food, the Welsh Bran's cauldron brought the dead back to life, and Ceridwen's cauldron contained the drink of inspiration.[5] The cauldron is a deeply feminine image because all that it provides - nourishment, rebirth, intuition and wisdom - are functions of the feminine. The guardians of the Grail in its form of cauldon or cup are also feminine in Celtic mythology, representing the Goddess of the Land who is called Sovereignty. She is often depicted in her role as the Black Goddess, and the quest of the Celtic hero results in marriage to her. This represents the Sacred Marriage, the union of the King and the Land as Sovereignty, and the integration of the masculine and the feminine which results in the fruitfulness of body and soul.[6]

The tragedy which results from the disruption of this sacred union is recounted in *The Elucidation*, a very moving tale which has particular significance for our modern day. The Realm of Logres (Britain) is depicted originally as a paradise in which the inner and outer worlds are in harmony. Sacred wells and springs in the land are attended by maidens who offer a golden cup to all travelers that provides whatever food and drink is desired. The golden cup is a form of the Grail as a limitless source of sustenance, which parallels the plenitude of nature to be found in this paradisal world. This condition of blessed abundance is disrupted, however, when the evil King Amangons rapes one of the well maidens and steals her golden cup. His men follow his example and the maidens of the wells, guardians of the Grail, go into hiding and are seen no more. The loss of the "voices of the wells" causes the Realm of Logres to become a barren wasteland where the waters dry up and all growth withers. No longer can be found the Court of the Rich Fisherman, "he that once made the land bright with his treasures."[7] The quest of the Grail hero is to seek this Court of Joy, the Earthly Paradise, so that the waters will flow freely and the Earth will be green again. It appears that this can only be accomplished by re-establishing the union between the King and the Goddess of the Land.

We find ourselves today in the land which has lost the maidens of the wells. When the golden cup of the Grail was stolen, the experience of wholeness - the interconnectedness of humans and the natural world - was lost. The rape of the well maidens caused a disruption of the harmony between the masculine and feminine, and consequently between the outer and the inner worlds. This theme parallels the "rape of nature" which has been a dominant characteristic of Western culture, for the story also symbolizes the dominance of patriarchal consciousness with its emphasis on aggressive power which is a major cause of our current "wasteland."

During the Middle Ages there was a brief reappearance of the feminine as the "voices of the wells" were heard in the love songs of the troubadours and trouvères and in the Grail tales of the poets. Because of the predominance of the Christian Church in society at this time, many of the legends of the Grail which were written in the late twelfth and early thirteenth centuries were strongly influenced by Christianity. However, much of this influence actually came from the hidden tradition of the bypaths: Celtic Christianity through which percolated the earlier pagan Celtic images of the Grail, and gnostic Christianity with its feminine representations of the Divine. As Emma Jung suggests, the rapid development of the Grail mythology during the Middle Ages and its immense popularity was due to the psychological need "to complete the Christ-image by the addition of features which had not been taken sufficiently into account by ecclesiastical tradition."[8] Thus the symbol of the Grail as it reappeared to the Christian populace of the West in the Middle Ages was an attempt by the psyche to integrate the polarities of good and evil, masculine and feminine, spirit and nature which had been split apart in institutional Christianity. Under the influence of Christianity the Grail as Celtic cauldron was transformed into the cup which was used by Christ at the Last Supper and subsequently the chalice of the Eucharist. This new image of the Grail as a relic of Christ's blood appeared for the first time in the story *Joseph of Arimathea* which was part of the *Roman de L'Estoire dou Graal* trilogy attributed to the Burgundian poet Robert de Boron.[9] This tale begins with the story told in the apocryphal Gospel of Nicodemus. After the crucifixion, Joseph of Arimathea goes to Pontius Pilate and obtains Christ's body and the cup which he had used during the Last Supper. While preparing Christ's body for burial in his own tomb, Joseph catches the blood which flows from the wounds into the cup and takes it to his home. When the Jewish authorities discover that

Christ's body has disappeared, they throw Joseph into prison. In de Boron's version, Christ appears to him while he is imprisoned and brings him the cup, informing him that he is to be its guardian and instructing him in the symbolism of the mass. Joseph remains there for forty-two years, during which time he is sustained physically and spiritually by the Grail. After his release Joseph goes into exile with a small company of Christians. After a number of years they experience famine and the Holy Spirit tells Joseph that this is due to the sinful lust of some members of his community. He is instructed to set up a table replicating the table of Christ's Last Supper, where an empty place called the "siege perilleux (dangerous seat)" is to be kept as a representation of the seat that Judas left when he betrayed Christ. Joseph's brother-in-law Brons is instructed to catch a fish to place on the table beside the cup, and because of this Brons becomes known as the Rich Fisher. Only the worthy are able to sit at the table and have their desires satisfied, while those full of lust are turned away. Here the Grail is shown to have the power of discrimination. Joseph is later divinely commanded to give the Grail to Brons, who will be the first of the three Grail guardians of his lineage. It is Brons who is instructed to take the Grail to Britain.[10] Thus, in this first Christian rendition of the Grail myth, de Boron presents the claim that the holy relic which contains Christ's blood found its resting place in Britain.

In other legends it is Joseph of Arimathea himself who brings the relics of Christ to the Isle of Avalon (Britain) in the form of two cruets containing the blood and sweat of Christ, which he had caught during the crucifixion. He is also reputed to be the founder of the first Christian church in Britain, established at Glastonbury, which was dedicated by Christ himself to his mother Mary. From these stories derived the claim that the Celtic Christian Church, since it traced its authority to Joseph of Arimathea, was independent of the Church of Rome, which it in fact preceded.[11]

It is also apparent that much of the magical, fantastic quality of the Grail stories is a reflection of the Celtic spirit. The transformation of the Celtic Grail legends into their Christian versions was achieved largely because of the basic differences between Celtic and Roman Christianity. Pagan elements of the Grail myth could be more readily incorporated by Celtic Christianity which had integrated the earlier nature religion into its rituals and symbolism. The Celtic concept of the Otherworld which overlays our everyday physical world infused the Christian Grail stories with an aura of the magic of the supernatural. Many of the spiritual adventures of the knights take place in the wild places of nature, where they encounter many marvels, strange creatures, and mysterious visions. This is characteristic of the nature mysticism of Celtic Christianity, which did not separate the spiritual and the natural worlds as did the Roman Church. The forest hermit who gives aid to the knight, a very common character in the Grail stories, appears to be none other than the old Celtic Christian holy man. The hermit's solitary spiritual quest mirrors that of the knight's solitary quest for the Grail. Both reflect the Celtic Christian emphasis on the individual rather than the institutional Church.[12]

Themes of Celtic mythology are particularly recognizable in the medieval versions of the Grail story which feature Perceval as the Grail hero. The French poet Chretien de Troyes, who wrote *Le Conte del Graal* in approximately 1180, casts Perceval in the mold of the Celtic hero whose quest leads him into the Otherworld where he witnesses many wondrous phenomena and encounters strange and supernatural events.[13] Yet the pagan Celtic elements in this story mix with Christian allegory, for Perceval is also cast as a savior figure whose role parallels that of Christ.[14] This fusion of pagan and Christian symbolism is reminiscent of their synthesis in Celtic Christianity.

Perceval is portrayed by Chretien as a fool, a simpleton, a "country bumpkin." He is reared solely by his mother who hopes to protect him from his father's fate of death in battle by keeping him ignorant of the ways of the world. However, one day the naive youth meets five knights in the forest who he assumes must be angels because of their wondrous splendor. Needless to say, he follows them to King Arthur's court, thoughtlessly leaving his mother behind to die of grief. Thus Perceval starts out on his quest as the archetypal fool, a role which carries deep spiritual significance. Often in mystical symbolism the seeker is the "fool," which conveys the paradoxical truth that wisdom is attained only by the one who appears foolish to the world, who follows his own narrow path rather than the broad

road of convention, who maintains a free mind that is open to all possibilities. It is this very "foolishness" which is seen in Christ's death on the cross, and the underlying wisdom which is ultimately revealed in the resurrection. Here again, Perceval's role as the fool is symbolic of Christ.

It is Perceval, the naive fool, who responds to the challenge of the Red Knight rather than the King or his experienced knights. That this task falls to the newcomer Perceval is an indication that the court of King Arthur is suffering a physical and spiritual malaise, which appears to be due to the King's lack of union with the Queen. The role of Guinevere as Sovereignty, the Goddess of the Land, and the theft of her golden cup by the Red Knight hearken back to earlier Celtic themes in the Grail myth. However, it is not King Arthur but Perceval, untrained as he is in the arts of warfare, who performs the heroic act of defeating the Red Knight and returning the golden cup to the Queen. Perceval then leaves King Arthur's court to pursue many other adventures. He meets the seasoned knight Gornemant who instructs him in the conventional skills of knighthood and chivalry. One of his admonitions to the naive youth is to refrain from being too talkative, a piece of seemingly wise advice which will have major repercussions on Perceval's future destiny. After awhile Perceval leaves Gornemant to belatedly seek his mother, but instead he finds the beautiful Blancheflor, who he marries after defeating her enemies. Eventually Perceval leaves again to look for his mother, and this time comes upon the Grail Castle, which is invisible to all except those who are worthy. At this point Perceval has clearly entered the Celtic Otherworld which is invisible except to those who are "foolish" enough to perceive what most humans do not see. Here he meets the Fisher King who has a wound in his thighs that will not heal. This is symbolic of a wound in the sexual organs, indicating that the King is impotent. During the delightful evening in the castle, Perceval witnesses the procession of the Grail hallows: a knight carrying a sword, a squire bearing a white lance that drips blood, a damsel carrying a golden grail, and another damsel carrying a silver carving dish. Despite his great curiosity about the wonders that he is witnessing, Perceval heeds the advice of his mentor Gornemant and keeps his silence. He does not ask his burning questions about the meaning of the procession or who the Grail serves. When he awakens in the morning he finds that he is alone in an empty castle. Returning to the forest, he meets a maiden who provides him with the dark wisdom that comes from looking deeply at one's faults and failures. She berates him for not asking the question of who the Grail serves, for the wounded King would be healed if only this question were asked. She further informs him that all of this misery is caused by his thoughtlessness toward his mother, who had died of grief because of him.

The deeply sorrowful Perceval returns to King Arthur's court after many further adventures, where the Loathly Hag appears and also publicly condemns him for failing to take action when he had the opportunity to ask about the Grail. She reiterates that the King's wound will not heal and the land will lie in waste because of Perceval's silence. Perceval then vows to quest until he finds an answer to the question of the Grail, and he does so for five years. During this time he completely forgets about God, until finally on Good Friday he meets a holy hermit in a chapel in the forest and confesses his sins. He learns that the hermit is his mother's brother, his uncle, and he stays with him to receive communion on Easter. This is the last action of Perceval in Chretien's tale, which was left unfinished. A number of continuators attempted to complete his narrative, but we will now turn to the story of Perceval (or Parzival) which was written around 1210 by the Bavarian knight Wolfram von Eschenbach.

Wolfram's *Parzival*, although based on the work of Chretien, differs significantly from it in several major respects. This is the Grail myth which speaks most clearly to modern people because of its psychological and philosophical complexity. Wolfram combines traditional Celtic elements of Grail mythology with Eastern ideas which pervaded Europe during the Crusades. Gnostic, Kabbalistic and alchemical symbolism are all featured within Wolfram's fascinating narrative.[15]

A major difference in Wolfram's version is the nature of the Grail itself. He describes the Grail as the "lapis exilis," the small or paltry stone, which had been brought to Earth by the angels who remained neutral during the war between God and Satan. The Grail is renewed every Good Friday by a white mass wafer which is brought by a dove from heaven to the stone. From this the Grail obtains its power to provide abundance. Wolfram emphasizes the functions of the Grail in preserving youth and providing whatever food or drink is desired. Here again we see associations of the Grail with pagan fountains of youth and cauldrons of plenty. In this version the Grail is clearly connected to the Earthly Paradise. For "the Gral was the very fruit of bliss, a cornucopia of the sweets of this world and such that it scarcely fell short of what they tell us of the Heavenly Kingdom."[16] It resides in Munsalvaesche (the Grail Castle) under the guardianship of the Templars. Those who are destined to be servants of the Grail, both men and women who come from many countries, are revealed by an inscription which appears on the stone and then disappears once it has been read.

Parzival's refusal to ask the question about the Grail is due not to ignorance but to a lack of compassion in Wolfram's story, for Cundrie in the role of Black Goddess accuses him of being indifferent to the wounded King Anfortas's suffering which his question would have eased.[17] Thus the blame for his sin of omission seems to fall even more heavily upon Parzival in this version. Furthermore, he does finally rectify his error. He must first fight his final battle, which happens to be with his pagan, piebald brother Fierefiz. When Parzival's sword breaks, Fierefiz throws his own away and then they realize that they are indeed brothers. After their reconciliation they return to the court of King Arthur, where Cundrie reappears and gives Parzival the happy news: "The Inscription has been read: you are to be Lord of the Gral!"[18] She takes him and his chosen companion Fierefiz to the Grail Castle to heal the King and restore the land. Parzival finally asks the question, "Dear Uncle, what ails you?"[19] Through this act King Anfortas is made well again. Since no answer is actually given in the narrative, it is apparent that it is the compassionate act of asking the question which is most important for the restoration of wholeness to the King and the land.

The figure of Perceval (Parzival) as the Grail hero is supplanted by the purely Christian knight Galahad in *The Queste del Saint Graal*. This narrative, which contains many of the elements of the Grail myth which are best known today, was written about 1200 as one of the five stories of the Vulgate Cycle. Although the authorship of *The Queste* is attributed to the English cleric Walter Map, many scholars have pointed out that the emphatically Christian world view presented in this version is probably due to the influence of Cistercian monks.[20] For this is a version of the Grail myth in which the earlier Celtic elements have been largely suppressed, although they can still be detected by the discerning eye, and the ideals of ascetic medieval Christianity have been consciously emphasized. Because of this a new Grail hero, the "Perfect Knight" of Christianity, has to take over the dominant role from Perceval who exhibits too many pagan features in his character.

Galahad is clearly presented in *The Queste* as a parallel to Christ. His very name originates from the Biblical "Gilead," which is a mystical reference to Christ. As a perfectly virtuous, pure man, he has achieved the condition previously attained only by Christ. He fulfills the Messianic prophecy as the long awaited redeemer of the Kingdom of Logres.[21] In Galahad's first appearance at King Arthur's court at Camelot he is introduced as "The Desired Knight...through whom the enchantments lying on this land and other lands are to be loosed."[22] The pronouncement of his lineage from the House of David and Joseph of Arimathea also clearly links him to Christ. Galahad's uniqueness is further shown in his ability to sit in the great Seat of Danger, for no man since the time of Christ has been able to master this seat until his coming.

The appearance of the Grail at Camelot significantly occurs on Pentecost, the anniversary of the date when the Holy Spirit descended upon Jesus's disciples with the sound of rushing wind and brightly burning tongues of fire. (Acts 2:1-4) In this recreation of the Pentecostal drama, a booming clap of thunder and radiant sunbeam fills the hall of Camelot and the knights are illumined by the grace of the Holy Spirit. The Holy Grail then appears, covered with a white cloth, and glides through the air, providing each knight with whatever food he desires. Then the holy vessel vanishes just as mysteriously as it had appeared.

**Stained glass window of the Holy Grail in
St. John's Chapel, Tréhorenteuc, Brittany, France**

In this scene the Holy Grail is clearly connected with the Holy Spirit, and symbolizes Divine Love as the grace which is freely given just as the desired food is provided abundantly by the vessel. The knights respond to this numinous experience of God's love by pledging themselves to the quest for the Holy Grail. The initial divine vision, which came unexpected and unsought, was the impetus for the conscious decision to seek again this mystical vision. But the knights must pursue this quest alone, for they are truly undertaking the solitary journey of the mystic. The tests and trials and temptations which they must undergo symbolize the challenges of the dedicated spiritual life which purify and strengthen the soul. As the narrative recounts the adventures of Galahad, Perceval, Bors, Gawain, Hector, and Lancelot, we see different forms of the mystical journey and varying degrees of fulfillment of its goal.

Finally it is only three of the original knights - Galahad, Perceval, and Bors - who prove themselves worthy to achieve the quest. They arrive at the Castle of the Maimed King at Corbenic, and he welcomes Galahad as the knight he has been waiting for to relieve his suffering. Then a man appears from Heaven, borne on a throne by angels, and is identified as Josephus, the first Christian bishop who had been consecrated by Christ himself in the holy city of Sarras. His throne is placed by a table upon which sits the Holy Grail, and the angels carry into the room candles, a red cloth, and a bleeding lance which they place beside the Grail. Josephus officiates at the Grail Mass, and as he raises the host from the holy vessel, the knights perceive the mystical vision of Christ in the form of a child entering the bread. When the bread is placed again in the vessel, an image of the crucified Christ arises from the Grail and he addresses the knights, telling them that their spiritual attainments have earned them the right to perceive in part the mystery of the Grail. He says, "the knights of this castle and many more beside have been filled with the grace of the Holy Vessel, but never face to face as you are now."[23] Christ himself feeds them with the holy food, and then reveals to them the innermost secret of the Grail: "it is the platter in which Jesus Christ partook of the paschal lamb with His disciples."[24] As he ate with his original disciples at the table of the Last Supper, now he has eaten with the knights, who are his new apostles, at the table of the Holy Grail. Christ tells them that one day they will see the Grail even more plainly in the holy city of Sarras, and instructs them to go there with the Grail because Logres is no longer worthy of it. Galahad heals the Maimed King with blood from the dripping lance, and then the three blessed knights board the Ship of Solomon where they again find the table with the Grail. They sail to Sarras where they escort the Grail to the spiritual palace. One day, after many other adventures, the three knights again see Josephus by the holy vessel. He is reciting the mass of the Mother of God, and beckons Galahad to look into the Grail to see what his soul has so fervently desired. As the true and perfect knight contemplates the great mystery of the Grail he exclaims, "Now I see revealed what tongue could not relate nor heart conceive...I see the wonder that passes every other!"[25] Galahad has fulfilled the ultimate goal of his quest, has experienced the bliss of mystical union with the Divine, and so his wish for death is granted. His soul is carried by joyous angels to Heaven, where a hand appears and takes away the Grail and the lance. Since that time they have been seen no more in this earthly realm.

The Queste translates the Grail myth into a medieval Christian allegory which provides a model for the mystical bypath. Galahad is the supreme example of the soul who has undergone the rigors of the solitary quest and attained ultimate union with God. His ecstatic vision of pure bliss cannot be told because it is the deep mystery of the Grail which is beyond all words, concepts, and rational thought. In this profound Christian version of the myth, the Grail mystery pertains to the mystery of the Eucharist, the mystery of the divine presence within the bread and wine of ordinary life. As in the celebration of the Eucharist itself, the perception of the Grail mystery - whether it is the partial illumination of the Grail knights or the ultimate mystical union of Galahad - must be an experience of eros. Galahad is the exemplar and the inspiration to those who dedicate themselves to the quest for the Grail on the mystical bypath.

These summaries of just a few of the many Grail stories reveal the diversity as well as the intriguing commonalities which confront us as we seek to penetrate the secrets of the Grail. Since these are among the Grail myths which are particularly relevant to us today, they will be used as the basis for our further examination of the meaning that the symbolism of the Grail and the hero's quest has for the seeker on the Path of ChristoSophia.

THE GRAIL SYMBOL

The Grail is the cauldron of healing and rebirth, the cup of inspiration and wisdom, the cornucopia which provides a never-ending supply of food, the chalice which contains the blood and water of transformation. The Grail is the fullness of creation, the great round of the cosmos, the container of the essence of life. Ultimately, the Grail is the great Mystery. As such, we will never be able to fully grasp its meaning while in this earthly realm. Yet the ongoing quest for the Grail today involves exploring its many layers of symbolic meaning in our attempt to discover the ever deeper levels of the mystery of the Grail. These are the mysteries of eros, the archetypal energies of the feminine. All of the forms that the Grail takes are deeply feminine images. On the bypaths where the quest for the Grail takes place, the feminine has had the opportunity to break through in the mystical symbolism of the Grail in a manner which was not possible on the interstate highway of the institutional Church.

The Grail as Life's Abundance

As Emma Jung says, "the woundrous vessel" is "the primal image of the mother."[26] At the most basic level the mother provides physical sustenance for her children, whether she be human or goddess. This aspect of the Grail can be seen in the Celtic image of the cauldron of the Mother Goddess with its never-ending supply of food and drink, as well as in the golden cup of the well maiden which miraculously provides whatever nourishment is desired. This same motif appears in *Parzival*, where it is the Grail as stone which physically sustains the Grail guardians at Munsalvaesche. The theme of maternal giving which is represented in these Grail images parallels the abundance of the natural world which is celebrated in the Hebrew scriptures. The Grail in this aspect is the source of the "Original Blessing," as life's goodness is called in creation-centered spirituality.

342

The Grail as Womb and Tomb

The Mother Goddess also is the source of both the womb and the tomb, for it is she who initiates the cycles of life, death and rebirth. The life and death-giving aspects of the Grail are seen in the Celtic goddess Ceridwen, "whose womb became a tomb for Gwion and a womb for Taliesin,"[27] whose cauldron could provide both death and rebirth. The Grail is Mother Earth, in whose soil new life grows from the seeds of death and decay. The Grail is the "world egg" as depicted in Hildegard of Bingen's vision of the origin of the cosmos, and it is the womb of the Virgin which gave birth to the Divine in human form. The Grail is the human womb, the state of being which precedes earthly life; it is also the cosmic womb, the state of being prior to the creation of the universe. The Grail is the uroboric state of being which gives rise to continuous becoming. It is the container for the cosmic dance, the divine energies which pour forth in the creation of the universe and withdraw in its dissolution. The Grail symbolizes the potential for life in its image as egg and womb, but also the potential for rebirth from death, for the renewal of life, which is found in its image as tomb.

The Grail as the Chalice of Christ

The representation of the Grail as simultaneously the womb and tomb of the Mother Goddess is transformed on the mystical Path of ChristoSophia into the primary Christian image of the Grail as the vessel containing the redemptive blood of Christ. The same symbolism is seen in Robert de Boron's *Joseph of Arimathea* as in the Celtic stories of life and rebirth from the Grail of the Goddess. The blood which Joseph collected from the wounds of Christ represent his death on the cross, as did the tomb which Joseph buried him in. But the chalice which contains the sacrificial blood of Christ becomes the womb which gives new life to the faithful during the ritual of the Eucharist. Likewise, Joseph's tomb in which Jesus was buried becomes the Holy Sepulchre, the womb for the resurrection of Christ. Thus there is a strong connection between the burial tomb of Christ and the cup which contains his blood. The Eucharist, as the central sacrament of Christianity, is based on this mystery of the Grail. From ancient times, blood as the principle of life has been thought to possess magical qualities. It has often been identified with the soul, the essence of life. Thus the Eucharistic chalice which contains the blood of Christ has such numinous power because it in effect holds within it the "soul-substance" of Christ, the essence through which he mystically continues to live.[28] When we drink from the chalice, we take within us this essence of Christ and therefore are also able to participate in the resurrected life.

The promise of resurrection which the chalice of Christ offers us is, on one hand, similar to the immortality procured through immersion in the cauldron or drinking from the cup of the Goddess. In both cases the Great Mother gives her gift of eternal life through the "living water" that she offers. Christ's gift of immortality also appears to be bestowed by water as well as by his blood. When he meets the Samaritan woman at the well, which is another image of the Grail, he offers her the "gift of God" which is the "living water." (John 4:10) This is the water which never ceases to quench one's thirst; it provides for abundant and eternal life. In this scene there is a resonance between Christ and the maiden of the well who offered her Grail filled with abundance to all who asked. A representation of the Grail of living water may also be seen in the baptismal font; followers of Christ who immerse in its waters are initiated into eternal life in a manner similar to those selected by the Mother Goddess who submerge in the cauldron of immortality. The importance of both blood and water in the Grail mysteries of Christian tradition may be the basis for the legendary story that Joseph of Arimathea brought two cruets, containing the blood and water of Christ, to Glastonbury.

The Grail as Transformation

The meaning of the Grail of Christ as a vessel for salvation, however, lies much deeper than simply physical immortality. For ultimately the Grail is a "vessel of spiritual transformation."[29] Drinking from the chalice of Christ's blood in the Eucharistic ritual brings about a spiritual renewal that has its analogue in the knights who succeed in their quest for the Grail. As Emma Jung has suggested, the meaning of the Grail as a symbol of transformation can be better understood through its connection with alchemical symbolism. The medieval study of alchemy developed at approximately the same time as the Grail stories were written and also attempted to further develop the image of Christ, so it is no wonder that the symbolism of the Grail myths closely corresponds to that of medieval alchemy.[30] The Grail story which most clearly reveals its alchemical connections in its rich and complex symbolism is Wolfram's *Parzival*. Many scholars have identified the Grail in its form as the "lapis exilis," or poor stone, with the alchemical Philosopher's Stone. Although on the surface the alchemists' goal was to turn base metal into gold, their underlying intent was to bring about a transformation of the psyche. In the Alchemical Great Work, "the baser elements of humanity are transformed into spiritual gold."[31]

Emma Jung's discussion of the symbolic meaning of Wolfram's "lapis exilis," which is based on her husband Carl Jung's study of the psychological symbolism of alchemy, emphasizes its potential for spiritual transformation. The alchemical stone represents "the inner spiritual man,"[32] the spark of the Divine which is found within each human being. It symbolizes the descent of God into human form in the person of Jesus Christ. But the term "lapis exilis" refers to the insignificance of the stone and therefore suggests that the divine is present in **all** human beings, not just Christ. "The Lapis may therefore be understood as a symbol of the inner Christ, of God in man. Looked at from this point of view, the stone represents a further development of the Christ symbol, reaching downwards into matter."[33] A similar idea is expressed in the Gnostic Gospel of Thomas, when Jesus says, "Lift up the stone and you will find me there."[34] The Grail as stone conveys the truth that the spiritual is hidden within the most material of objects in the physical world.

The Grail is thus a form of the "hidden treasure" motif which is so common in fairy tales and myths. In its image as the "lapis exilis," the treasure which is hidden symbolizes something of great value which is concealed within matter. In terms of the human soul, this hidden treasure is the inner divine nature which has the potential to transform one's whole being; it represents the mystical process of deification which is possible for all human beings. The difficulty of discovering this transformative power within the soul is shown in the stories of the Grail quest where the holy object appears only at certain times and can be found only by the Grail hero who submits to the challenges and hardships of the quest.[35]

This hidden treasure within the human soul which is represented by the Grail is called the "Self" by Jungian psychologists. The "Self" is an archetype which denotes "the psychic totality of the human being."[36] We usually identify with just our ego consciousness, our sense of individual identity, but the Self represents much more than just the ego. It is the sum total of **all** the aspects of the psyche, including both the conscious and the unconscious. Dreams, fantasies and specific psychological techniques can help us become aware of these aspects of the psyche other than the ego.

Jung also points out that the figure of Christ is a significant, although problematical, symbol of the Self in Western culture.[37] The Grail seeker today must include Christian tradition in his quest because it has provided the Western psyche with its major symbol of the Self for almost two millenia. However, the image of Christ which is projected on the interstate highway of Christianity - the male Son of God who brings light to the world in a manner similar to the ancient "Sun Gods" - is an incomplete symbol of the Self. An image of Christ which includes the feminine and the darkness, which are essential to the totality, remains to be found on the mystical bypath.

It is the Self which underlies the process of individuation, the journey towards wholeness in which all aspects of the psyche are developed and integrated. This process involves a reconciliation of the opposites within the psyche: good and evil, masculine and feminine, thinking and feeling. This is a journey which is never completed however, for individuation is an ongoing **process** rather than a final goal which can ever be achieved. The Self as the archetype of wholeness is, therefore, "present in us as a potentiality."[38] In this sense it is symbolized by the Grail, that hidden treasure within the psyche which appears only when we commit ourselves to the process of individuation. This is the journey of the soul that the seeker embarks on in the Grail quest.

The quest for individuation is a modern psychological concept which parallels the mystic's ancient quest for illumination and union with God. In both cases the seeker's journey leads to a transformation of consciousness - the mystical transformation of the ego or the psychological integration of the ego and the Self. Thus the Grail is also a vessel which symbolically contains the waters of illumined consciousness. Many forms of the Grail, from the Celtic cauldron which dispensed wisdom and inspiration, to the gnostic krater which contained gnosis or the knowledge of God, to the Christian chalice which provided spiritual enlightenment, primarily perform this function of transforming human consciousness. The pilgrim on the mystical bypath who drinks from this Grail of wisdom will attain enlightenment as the realization of the inner Christ, which results in the mystical experience of union with the Divine.

The Grail as Sophia

The Chalice of Christ which contains the wisdom of illumined consciousness is also the Cup of Sophia. Within her is found the mystery of eros: the paradoxical wisdom which transcends our rational thinking. For, as Caitlin Matthews says, "The Grail is a prime symbol of Sophia."[39] It is this Grail of Wisdom which can bestow healing and wholeness to our world today.

As a symbol of Sophia, the Grail continues its traditional representation of the feminine side of God. The Grail has always been associated with the feminine, as we have seen in the ancient Celtic images of the Goddess with her cauldron and the maidens of the wells. Both the vessel, as the chalice of the Last Supper, and the stone, as the "lapis exilis," are derived from primary symbols for the Great Goddess.[40] The theme of feminine authority over the Grail is further developed in the medieval stories in which it is woman who serves as the bearer of the Grail. In this role the Grail-bearer who tends the sacred relic is similar to the ancient female priestess of the goddess rather than the male priest who administers the sacrament in the institutional Church. Feminine imagery is also seen in the frequent associations of the dove and the Grail. For example, in *Parzival* the white dove is the source for the renewal of the Grail. The dove, sacred to the ancient Goddess, became a symbol of the Holy Spirit in Christian iconography and thus is one of the hidden images of Sophia in Christian tradition. The appearance of the dove

347

with the Grail clearly shows the connection between these two symbols of the Divine Feminine.

The chalice of Christ's blood which symbolizes the presence of God in the physical world also points us to the Divine Feminine which penetrates all of creation. Thus the Grail represents the spiritual essence of life which infuses nature. This is Sophia in her aspect as World- Soul, "she through whom everything in the outer world has qualities of interiority."[41] In gnostic mythology Sophia divided herself into the Heavenly Sophia and the Sophia who remained in exile in the material world. This is Sophia as "the soul of the world," perhaps best symbolized in the Grail image of the "lapis exilis," the stone which appears worthless but contains the secret of the divine presence within matter. In the gnostic myth, Sophia created the four elements of air, earth, fire and water. Thus the elements are the body of Sophia in her terrestrial form, and are her creative powers in the physical world. The Grail is the Cup of the World, the divine container of the elements which gives form to the natural world. It bestows the gift, like Sophia herself, of renewal and regeneration of the world.[42] A major theme of the Grail stories is the loss of this Grail, the loss of the Soul of the World, and the devastation of the land which ensues. Caitlin Matthews points out this connection in *The Elucidation*, where the maidens of the wells are the "voices of Sophia in her aspect of World-Soul."[43] Their retreat from the outer world and withdrawal of the nourishing golden cup is symptomatic of our lack of recognition of the Soul of the World. When we are once again able to hear Sophia's message through the voices of the well maidens, the Grail will be restored and the world will be renewed. The Court of Joy will be found and paradise will reign on Earth. This connection of the Grail with the "Earthly Paradise" has been a traditional feature within the Grail legends.[44] This paradisal realm on Earth, the dream which humanity has longed for through the ages, is to be achieved by Sophia's creative work within the material world when we recognize her presence within it.

The paradoxical nature of Sophia's Cup is that while it provides limitless nourishment, it is at the same time an **empty** vessel. For the Grail is the receptive feminine ground from which all nature arises. The mystery of the Grail is that it contains **all things** and yet it contains **no-thing.** It contains everything within it, for we project our own psyches into the Grail and can thus obtain whatever we desire. But if we gaze long enough into the Grail, following the meditative practice of the mystic, we may see the essential Emptiness - the Void which lies before creation and beyond mortality. And when the Void becomes the vessel of our experience in the earthly realm, we experience both the joy and the pain of life. These polarities of existence are expressed in all of the images of the Grail: the cauldron of the Goddess which gives both life and death; the World-Soul which experiences both Wasteland and the Court of Joy; and the chalice of Christ's blood which represents the suffering of Good Friday and the ecstasy of Easter.

The Grail contains both the light and the dark aspects of existence which arise from the emptiness of the Void, thus symbolizing the wholeness of the Great Goddess. The two sides of existence are a major theme in Wolfram's *Parzival*, which begins with a reference to the "black" and the "white," the "motley...magpie"which combines these two colors in its plumage, and "Heaven" and "Hell" which can be found equally in man.[45] Images which unite the light and the dark abound in the story, including the white and the black army that Parzival's father fights and Parzival's own brother Feirefiz who is both white and black. In this story the Grail as "lapis" was brought to Earth by the neutral angels, those who sided with neither God nor Satan during the great War in Heaven. Thus they symbolize the middle way, the path between the polarities of good and evil. And the alchemical Philosopher's Stone which has been associated with the Grail as "lapis" also "represents a light-dark unity of the divine opposites."[46] It is very important for the Grail hero to recognize the dark side of the Grail, because, like all seekers on the mystical bypath, he can encounter grave dangers in the realm of the sacred if he has not undertaken the necessary preparation.

The dark side of the Grail which corresponds to the fear and pain of mortal life refers to the realm of the Black Goddess. Recognizing Sophia in her role as dark goddess helps us to accept the draught from the dark side of the Cup of Life, realizing the ultimate unity of the light and the dark in the Grail. This is the revelation that the mystic experiences when the "dark night of the soul" is joined with the light of illumined consciousness. As John Matthews says, "At the nexus point, in the heart of the Grail, is a point of harmony, of resolution, of polarity, which is brought about through the interaction of the darkness and light which surrounds the Grail."[47] The dark side of the Grail is not evil when it is acknowledged and understood. It can become dangerous and evil when it is not accepted, when it is split apart from its unity with the light, and especially when it is projected externally into the world. The necessity of accepting the dark side of the Goddess, and thus the darkness of life, is shown in the many Grail stories which require the Grail hero to kiss or marry the ugly crone or "loathly lady." Sophia aids this process of spiritual enlightenment, as "Wisdom sends forth her call to the knights, who become her lovers. Disguised as a hideous hag, she guides them to embrace their own darkness and transform it through love."[48] For this is the wisdom of the Grail: to be able to hold both the dark and the light, without being torn by destructive conflict. This can be our experience when we drink from both the dark and the light sides of the Grail, and feel a sense of unity with the Soul of the World in her suffering as well as her joy. We can drink deeply from both sides of the Cup of Life, experiencing fully the happiness and the sorrow in our own life, and feeling our connection to all other souls in their pain as well as their joy. This is ultimately the experience of compassion.

The Grail as ChristoSophia

The Christian Grail as a feminine symbol of the chalice of Christ's blood also represents the union of the masculine and feminine divine images of Christ and Sophia. Recognizing the Grail as a symbol of ChristoSophia satisfies the need to further develop the Christ symbol by incorporating the material world and the dark side of the Divine. This is the task which has been so emphasized by Emma Jung in her psychoanalytic study of the Grail.[49] The union of Sophia with Christ in Grail symbolism integrates the feminine face of God with the masculine, thereby including nature and the dark side of existence in our image of deity.

The Sophianic nature of Christ is one of the great hidden secrets of the Grail which can be discovered by the seeker who travels on the bypaths. The deeper meanings of the Grail reveal this central key to its secret. The mystical meaning of blood is that it carries the life-essence or spirit of the individual. So the Grail as a container for Christ's blood carries the spirit of Christ, which in this case is the Holy Spirit.[50] The Holy Spirit is also a representation of Sophia, so the blood of Jesus which is infused with the Holy Spirit can be seen as symbolic of the unity of ChristoSophia. This is the deeper meaning behind the understanding that Christ's blood in the chalice represents the presence of God in the world. Thus the Grail has kept the secret known to many early Christians, that Jesus Christ was the incarnation of Sophia. As the chalice of Christ's blood contains the essence of Christ which is still alive in our world, it conveys the early Christians' understanding of the resurrected Christ's presence in the world as Sophia-Spirit.

Another image of ChristoSophia contained within Grail symbolism can be derived from this statement by Emma Jung: "The Grail really forms a quaternity in which the blood contained within it signifies the Three Persons of one Godhead, and the vessel can be compared to the Mother of God."[51] The Mother of God, while usually designating Mary in Christian terminology, can also be seen as Sophia in her role of archetypal Mother Goddess. In this sense the vessel representing the Divine Feminine is the container for the Trinity. The Grail itself can be compared to Sophia as the **ousia**, or divine substance, of the Russian Sophiologists. It is **in** Sophia, as the vessel of the Grail, that the Father, Son, and Holy Spirit have their Being. The differentiated wholeness of ChristoSophia is clearly seen in the image of the vessel and its contents, which are interdependent yet at the same time are distinct from each other.

The secret of ChristoSophia is also revealed in the importance of both water and blood in the Grail mysteries of Christian tradition. Sophia provides the living water of Wisdom and Christ provides the sacrificial blood of Love; when combined within the chalice, the water and blood signify the mystical union of Christ and Sophia within the Grail of the world - the Loving Wisdom of ChristoSophia.

This is the great mystery of the Grail: that the blood of Christ is Sophia's essence of life. The chalice of ChristoSophia is the mystical container for the divine elixir of life. This is the mystery which lies at the heart of Christian tradition: the wine-blood which is received in the Eucharist is Sophia's gift of life - the immortal life of the Spirit which is already present in the material world. The wine/blood which fills the chalice is the kingdom of the Holy Spirit, the kingdom of wholeness, the kingdom of ChristoSophia. This is the meaning of Christ's statement in the Gospel of Thomas, "The kingdom of the father is spread out upon the earth, and men do not see it."[52] When we drink from the Grail of ChristoSophia our eyes are opened and we perceive the mystery; then we realize that we already live in this kingdom for we discover that it exists within us and in all of creation.

THE QUEST FOR THE GRAIL

The central myth of Western culture since the Middle Ages is the quest for the Grail. The basic motif from medieval to modern Grail stories is that something of priceless value has been lost and can be recovered only by a hero who must undergo many dangerous trials. This theme flourishes today in books and films as much as it did in the poems and songs of troubadours of the Middle Ages. The prevalence of the Grail theme today indicates that this symbol still speaks deeply to the psyche of the modern human being. The psychological and spiritual issues which gave rise to the Grail symbolism of the Middle Ages have not yet been resolved in Western culture. A primary image of this unsolved problem is the Wasteland.

The Wasteland

A major theme in most Grail stories, from *The Elucidation* to *Parzival*, is that the loss of the Grail results in a wasting of the land. This theme is particularly relevant today; one of the great poems of the twentieth century, *The Wasteland* by T. S. Eliot, shows the connection between our modern condition and the condition symbolically portrayed in the medieval Grail stories. For our world today does seem in many ways to be a wasteland: the spiritual aridity of modern life is paralleled by the environmental devastation that is rapidly disrupting the cycles of life on our planet.

The land that the Grail hero travels through is symbolic of the soul. Thus the presence of the Wasteland indicates a barrenness in the soul, a condition which is especially common today. For the great suffering in the soul of modern humans is the pervasive sense of loss of any meaning and purpose to life. While science and technology have often seemed to be our modern day Grail, providing abundantly for our physical needs, we have also found the dark side to this Grail. One of its dark aspects is the loss of the cosmological view of past ages which perceived God as present within the created world and human beings as participants with the Divine in living on this Earth. For when the divine presence is no longer recognized in the world and human life ceases to have any spiritual purpose, the soul and the world both become a wasteland.

The Grail legends of medieval Christianity arose in response to the suppression of eros, which was necessary in order to construct the interstate highway of Christianity. As the Christian Church formalized its doctrines and established a priestly hierarchy, the logos signposts directing the collective toward law and authority were erected on the highway of the interstate Church. The eros markers which pointed toward the individual's mystical, intuitive experience of the Divine within were forcibly removed so that they often could be found only on the spiritual bypaths. The Grail imagery which flourished during the Middle Ages was an attempt to compensate for the one-sided logos development of the Christian Church by symbolically revealing the eros qualities of Christian tradition which had been suppressed for so long.

The loss of the feminine in Western culture is the major problem which is the cause of the Wasteland. The rise of patriarchy and the suppression of women in the history of the West is mirrored in the story describing the rape of the well maidens and the subsequent loss of the golden cup. This situation is again depicted in the historical development of Christianity, when women's leadership roles were suppressed and the "feminine voice" was lost to the Church just as the "voices of the wells" were lost to the Western world. When the voices of women were no longer heard, the Divine Feminine also went into hiding, and the Grail disappeared with her. Western culture suffered the tragic loss of the experience of wholeness and the vision of connectedness which is the essence of feminist spirituality.

The fragmentation of the world and of the soul which ensued is seen in the separation of spirit and matter, God and nature, within the theology of the interstate Church. The perception of the physical world as "lower" than the spiritual world, and in some cases even "evil," was further augmented by the view of mechanistic science that the cosmos was an inanimate, clocklike machine. When the Divine Feminine and her Grail disappeared from the consciousness of the Western world, a view of the cosmos developed that lacked any divine presence or purpose. This is the mindset that we have inherited today, and it is the source for our current destruction of the living Earth and her creatures. For we no longer recognize the soul inherent in the natural world. Sophia in her aspect of World-Soul has hidden, like the maidens of the wells, in response to the injuries suffered from the dominance of masculine consciousness, the rational, analytical thought of Western science and technology. Nor do we any longer admit to consciousness our natural intuitive, mystical response to sacred places on the Earth. Because of this our souls live in a wasteland which is bereft of magic, wonder, and enchantment, and we perpetrate the wasting of the land of our planet Earth because we do not recognize the presence of the Divine within her.

The Wasteland is the culmination of humanity's loss of Paradise. In Judeo-Christian tradition, Paradise as the Garden of Eden symbolizes the original state of wholeness and undifferentiated consciousness. When humanity, represented by Adam and Eve, ate the apple which gave them "knowledge of good and evil," they "fell" from the Paridisal consciousness of unity to the condition of ego-consciousness in which they experienced themselves as separate from each other, from the rest of creation, and from God. This recognition of duality which results from eating the apple is analogous to the withdrawal of the Grail of wholeness, since humanity's innate connection with the natural world is severed. This is the duality which, according to Matthew Fox, is truly the "original sin."[53] For it is the sin of separateness, seeing everyone and everything as objects outside of ourselves, that is the root cause of our violence toward others and destruction of the world. The perception of duality between self and other leads to a sense of alienation, and the lack of compassion which results from this alienation produces the Wasteland in our souls and on the Earth.

The Garden of Eden myth expresses the human condition of alienation which occurs with the development of ego consciousness. The Christian story of the incarnation of the Divine in the human form of Jesus of Nazareth brought the "good news" which could overcome this sense of separation. However, as the medieval Grail stories attest, the experience of wholeness and unity has not yet been achieved by humanity. The condition of alienation is even much more dramatically present in our current world, where most modern people do not have an authentic mythos to live by. The Wasteland of our current age also results from the lack of this guiding story to give a sense of purpose and meaning to our lives. Without a myth to connect us with the Divine and the world around us, the soul of the modern human is a stunted and shriveled version of the vibrant, fertile one that it could be.

The Wasteland of the human soul and the planet Earth is reflected in the image of the Wounded King. A central motif in the stories of the Grail is a King who has a wound that will not heal. The wound is usually in the "thigh" or the genitals, indicating that it is a sexual wound and the King is impotent. The wounding of the King is the cause of the barrenness of the land. This theme recalls the ancient Celtic belief that the King had to be united to the Goddess of the Land, as Sovereignty, to insure health and prosperity for all of his kingdom. The withdrawal of the Grail, the retreat of the Divine Feminine, causes a rupture between the King and Sovereignty which is symbolized by his wound. Western culture which is dominated by masculine consciousness suffers a wound which it cannot heal by itself, and nature becomes a wasteland. Joseph Campbell refers to the meaning of the Grail King's wound when he says, "The Christian separation of matter and spirit, of the dynamism of life and the realm of the spirit, of natural grace and supernatural grace, has really castrated nature..."[54]

The Wounded King symbolizes every human being who is "wounded" by being "cut off" from the original state of wholeness.

All of us, as we grow from infancy and develop our egos, are wounded in this sense. But the souls of modern human beings suffer much greater wounding from the suppression of the eros qualities of instinct and intuition. In this way we become infertile, like the Wounded King, and experience the soul as a wasteland which lacks inspiration, vitality and creativity. In this state we also experience a sense of impotence to solve the ecological and spiritual crises which confront us. The common plaint of modern humans is, "But what can I do?" In our wounded state we do not perceive the presence of the Grail and therefore cannot avail ourselves of its healing properties.

The dualistic split which has occurred in Christianity is also seen in the association of the suffering Grail King with the figure of Christ. The Grail King represents the image of Christ which is dominant in the collective consciousness, the image of the Savior King which has been presented on the interstate highway of the Christian Church. The "wounding" of this Christ image is caused by the Church's "cutting off" all physical, instinctual, and sexual attributes from its portrayal of Christ. The repression of the feminine has rendered Christ incomplete and lacking the wholeness of the archetypal divinity. Here the meaning of the King's sickness is that the image of Christ has consequently lost much of its numinous power to attract and transform the soul of the believer.[55] The medieval Grail legends imply that the image of Christ portrayed on the interstate highway of the Church was even then outworn and in need of renewal. This is even more the case today, when many people are finding that traveling on the interstate highway of Christianity does not satisfy their needs for an authentic spirituality. The "wounding" of the Christ image remains an unresolved problem in Christianity. Because the Grail King "cannot himself solve the problem within the structure of the outlook he personifies," he must "await a successor who shall free him."[56] Likewise the Christian Church will not be able to heal the Wounded King and restore fertility to the Wasteland with the dualistic viewpoint which is still dominant today. Instead, the "successor" to the Christ image, which will restore the archetype of wholeness, may be found by the seeker who quests for the Grail on the Path of ChristoSophia.

The Hero's Quest

Christ is the archetypal Grail hero whose role as the Savior requires him to go through the necessary suffering in order to complete his quest which involves the restoration of the lost Paradise to humanity. This task is mirrored in the quests of the Grail knights to find the Grail which will heal the Wounded King and restore fertility to the Wasteland. In a deeper sense their quest involves the restoration of Sovereignty, as Goddess of the Land, to her rightful place and union with the King. Thus the Grail quest is ultimately a search for the feminine as Divine Queen and World-Soul. She is represented by all the female figures that the Grail knight meets on his journey - the lovely maidens in distress, the fairies from the Otherworld, the old crone "wise women." All of these feminine figures represent aspects of the Divine Feminine and the Grail knight must receive the help of these women, beautiful and terrible alike, if he is to be successful in his quest. He must drink from the cup of living water offered by the Grail maidens, which provides access to the inner world; he must listen to the "voices of the wells" in the form of dreams, visions, feelings and intuition; he must accept the dark side of the feminine by kissing the ugly old hag. Finally, if the hero proves worthy of these tasks, he will meet the Queen who gives him the Grail, the sacred symbol of the Divine Feminine which can restore the wholeness of Paradise to the land.

As Caitlin Matthews says, "We trivialize the Grail quest if we think of it only in terms of spiritual attainment. It is nothing other than Sophia's sign of wholeness, where duality is restored to unity, where the fragmentations of the Fall are mended."[57] For the loss of Paradise symbolized in the Garden of Eden myth refers to the expulsion from paradisal wholeness to a state of duality. It is the sense of connection, of union, of oneness that we lose as we develop ego consciousness. The paradox of life is that as we grow in consciousness we can embark on the quest to rediscover our connection with this lost Paradise. This is the meaning of the Grail quest: the quest for wholeness within the self and mystical union with the Divine and with the world.

This is the quest which is initiated by the question, "Who am I?" For regardless of whether the knight appears to be questing for fame, fortune, a woman, or a sacred relic, at a deeper level the Grail quest is a journey to discover one's true self. This is the quest we all undertake when we begin to question our own meaning and purpose in life. The Grail knight must travel deeply into the forest all by himself, on uncharted paths, to pursue this quest; likewise the seeker must delve deeply into the psyche, entering the unknown, to discover who he truly is. And as the Grail knight discovers untold marvels on his quest, so the seeker discovers the awesome wonders of the soul. The Grail knight finds out that there is much more territory to explore beyond the Wasteland, and the seeker realizes that his being consists of much more than just the ego of everyday consciousness. In psychoanalytic terms this is the quest for the Self, the search for one's true individuality and wholeness. The Grail hero undergoes the transformative quest of individuation, in which the ego unites with the Self. The consciousness of duality is transformed into the unitive consciousness of the mystic. The higher and lower selves are integrated, and the seeker who attains the Grail recognizes the presence of the Divine within. Wolfram's Parzival best exemplifies this struggle toward wholeness, whose source is the Grail. After his final battle he unites with his black and white brother Feirefiz, indicating a reconciliation of the light and dark aspects of existence whose images have recurred throughout the pages of the story. His quest which leads him to the Grail as "lapis exilis" ultimately results in his realization of the inner Grail, the alchemical stone of the Self through which he experiences the union of opposites within and without. The fulfillment of Parzival's quest mirrors the mystic's vision which perceives the bright luminosity of the Grail present in all persons and all things, united with the dark "cloud of unknowing" which precedes and permeates it. Thus the illumined soul of the mystic comprehends the paradox of the Grail mystery by recognizing its presence in all.

The fulfillment of the Grail quest brings the attainment of the second Paradise, symbolized by the apple orchard which in ancient times was sacred to the Goddess. The apples of healing and wisdom were found in such sacred places as Avalon (the Island of Apples), the Isles of the Blest, and the Celtic "Land of the Living."[58] In the second Paradise to which the Divine Feminine has returned, the apple of Sophia which provides the wisdom of wholeness will replace the apple of Eve which brings sin as the consciousness of duality. This is the same Sophianic wisdom which is obtained from the living water of the Grail, the wisdom which reconciles the opposites. In the second Paradise of the restored Wasteland, nourished by the water of Sophia's Grail, the dualities of earthly existence will once again be united: masculine and feminine, light and dark, human and divine, spirit and nature. This paradise is not the same as the original Garden of Eden, however, which consisted of a wholeness prior to ego development. That is the paradisal condition of the infant in the womb. In the transformed paradise, wholeness is an achievement of the differentiated consciousness of a highly developed ego. The transformation of consciousness which is needed to restore the paradisal unity of Sophia is that of the mystic's transcendence of ego or the individuated person's uniting of the ego with the Self.

The Grail Question

As shown in many of the Grail stories, a central feature of the quest for transformation involves the art of asking questions. Here again we see the significance of Sophia to the quest, for the Grail knight must acquire wisdom in order to know when and what to ask. The nature of the question is of extreme importance, for it determines the form and focus of the quest and delineates the path that one will take. The initiating question "Who am I?" is related to the further all important questions of the quest: "Who does the Grail serve?" and "Dear uncle, what ails you?"

The central issue in Perceval's quest is that he fails to ask the healing question, "Who does the Grail serve?" This major question which must still be asked today regards the purpose of the Grail. Perceval failed to ask the essential question which would have healed both the King and the land because he adhered to the admonition of his tutor that he refrain from asking questions. Although this appears to be a commendable act of deference to authority, it was not the appropriate action for this situation. Perceval's failure lay in his blind obedience to the social rules of conduct, rather than following the deeper instinctive wisdom of his own eros nature. The major task of the Grail hero is to achieve a higher level of consciousness than the conventional man; he must go beyond his cultural conditioning to discern the true nature of any situation and have the courage to ask the needed questions. This is the task which Perceval failed and which ultimately falls to the modern pilgrim on the mystical bypath who searches for the meaning of the Grail. Some possible answers to Perceval's unasked question is that the Grail serves the individual questor who follows the path of the heart; it gives its Loving Wisdom to those solitary seekers of the Divine Feminine, not to collective organizations which are still based on a patriarchal model of authority. The Grail of ChristoSophia transcends the conventional Eucharistic cup which is limited by sectarian divisions for it serves all of creation as the divine source of unity and wholeness. Today's Grail guardians, who have achieved consciousness of this unity, are served by the Grail and at the same time act in its service. They form the evolutionary edge of humanity's ascent to consciousness, as referred to by Teilhard de Chardin, which recognizes the unity of all creation through divine love. Thus the Grail of ChristoSophia serves the entire world, the Earth and all her creatures, through the loving hearts of those Grail guardians who have recognized its divine presence within themselves.

The servants of the Grail are those who have also thoughtfully asked the question that perplexes Parzival: "Dear uncle, what ails you?" For this is the question that we really ask of ourselves: what ails our own soul, our culture, our Earth? Caring enough about the suffering within the world and our own selves to ask this question marks the beginning of spiritual transformation. For Parzival's initial failure to ask this question was a sign of his callousness toward suffering, and his subsequent asking of the question signaled "the act of compassion that comes instinctively out of an individual who lives his or her own authentic life."[59] It is this act which proceeds from the heart which initiates the healing process within the world and within the soul. For it is love which leads to the transcendence of ego and the ultimate experience of union. Parzival's Grail question denotes the turning away from selfishness to service which is based on the recognition that the Grail quest is not for oneself alone but for the world - all other people, creatures and beings, and the World-Soul herself.

THE RETRIEVAL OF THE GRAIL

Another essential Grail question which we must have the courage and compassion to ask and act upon today is: "How do we return the Grail to the world?" For in most of the Grail stories the sacred relic is withdrawn from Earth or is concealed so that it can no longer be seen by mortals. This symbolizes its movement into the inner world; thus the quest for the Grail today must take place on the mystical bypath which leads into these inner realms. The task for the modern Grail hero who travels on the Path of ChristoSophia is to restore the Grail to a world which is in such dire need of it.

The Age of the Holy Spirit

The withdrawal of the Grail from the earthly realm also signifies the repression of eros which has occurred after each brief blossoming of the feminine in past ages. The Grail will be recovered when the time is ripe for a full flowering of Sophia's Tree of Life, and it appears that this is beginning to happen in our current age. As Emma Jung points out, the three successive Grail guardians in de Boron's story, Brons and his son and grandson, correspond to the three historical ages of Father, Son, and Holy Spirit in Joachim of Floris' mystical view. The Age of the Father refers to the original state of undifferentiated consciousness, the Age of the Son brings the conflict which comes with increased consciousness, and the Age of the Holy Spirit leads to the recovery of the first stage of inner wholeness. However, this third age is not a regression to the original unitive consciousness of the first phase, but instead involves a conscious submission of the ego to the Spirit and a faith based on personal experience rather than authority or collective systems of belief.[60] Whereas Adam's sin was to eat of the fruit of the Tree of Knowledge, Perceval's sin lay in **not** asking the question which would have imparted the sacred wisdom. Thus, in the Age of the Holy Spirit, the retrieval of the Grail requires the seeker to accomplish the supreme task of transformed consciousness based on an individual relationship with God.[61] Perceval's quest for the Grail is also a quest for the wisdom to be attained through an inner experience of the Divine, for the Grail acts as a mediator whereby the individual can hear the voice of God **personally** and **directly**.[62] The Grail is the inner wisdom or "gnosis," and the retrieval of the Grail today requires retracing the ancient steps of the gnostics in opening the soul to divine wisdom. Thus the Age of the Holy Spirit is also the Age of Sophia and the Age of the Grail.

The Receptive Attitude

The personal, inner experience of the Divine which is the hallmark of Sophia's wisdom is beautifully expressed in Galahad's culminating numinous vision as he gazes into the depths of the Grail. This is the supreme mystical experience which blesses the seeker who recovers the Grail. The attainment of the goal of the Grail quest, however, is achieved through the paradox of action and receptivity, which in traditional Christian terminology is known as "works" and "grace." The Grail stories colorfully recount all the actions that the knights must undertake on the quest, all the trials they confront and tasks they must achieve. But ultimately the vision of the Grail is bestowed as a gift, requiring a receptive attitude rather than striving. The Cistercian allegory *The Queste* makes clear that Galahad's beatific vision is given to him by the grace of God. The Grail which symbolizes divine grace is freely offered to all people, but its attainment depends upon the soul's capacity to receive it. Only three knights are spiritually capable of achieving the quest for the Grail, and only Galahad is pure enough to actually experience the Grail's ultimate mystery.[63] The tests and temptations of the questing knights serve the purpose of purifying and preparing their souls to receive the supreme gift of God's grace.

The knight's heroic adventures, based on the focused striving of masculine consciousness, serve to develop a strong and competent ego to deal with the challenges of the quest. But eventually the knight must let go of his hard won ego and experience the flow of feminine consciousness in order to receive the gift of the Grail. For after all of the knight's struggles and battles, the revelation of the Grail comes unexpectedly and miraculously. Because striving and receptivity are both necessary to attain the Grail, discerning the appropriateness for action or non-action is a major lesson to be learned on the quest, as shown in the question test of Parzival. The development of humility and compassion is so important for the Grail knight because these are qualities of the soul which are integral to the feminine mode of consciousness.

Like the knights of the medieval Grail stories, today we must also develop a dynamic balance between assertive striving and receptive flowing in order to retrieve the Grail. We must carefully prepare ourselves for the spiritual quest, courageously embark on the first solitary steps into the unknown, and competently meet the challenges which confront us along the way. But we must also maintain a receptive attitude, as emphasized by the mystics such as Meister Eckhart, which allows us to empty the ego so that we can follow the inner promptings of the Divine which guide us on the quest and perceive the Grail when it is given to us. The retrieval of the Grail today especially depends upon cultivating this attitude of receptivity because this is the mode of consciousness which has been suppressed for so long with Western culture's denial of the feminine.

The receptive nature of the soul can be likened to that of the flower whose seed germinates in the darkness of the earth while its blossoms unfold to the sun. We need to acknowledge and honor the processes going on unconsciously in the depths of the psyche and aid them through conscious attention to the dream images, intuitions and synchronicities which arise, bringing forth into the world the hidden treasures of the soul. The Grail quest is the quest of daily life which, when rooted in this process, achieves the goal in the manner of the unfolding of the flower blossoms - simply responsive to the light of the Sun rather than willful striving, like the soul's centering and flowing in the Spirit. Both aspects of growth, the germination of the seed and flowering of the bud, are nonegoistic; they represent the processes of individuation or enlightenment through which the Grail is attained.

The Grail Vision

The mystery of the Grail, which is open to all but revealed only to those who are capable of perceiving it, is "the secret essence of the soul of the world."[64] This is the cosmic dance which arises from the emptiness of the Grail and fills it with the entirety of creation. It is the vision of Divine Love and Wisdom at the center of the cosmos, a vision so wondrous to mortal eyes that "tongue could not relate nor heart conceive."[65] The seeker attains the Grail through experiencing this unitive vision, which leads to the "new perception" of Sophia: seeing the soul in the material world, seeing beyond appearances to their secret essence, and ultimately recognizing Sophia in all things. It is through this truly significant change in perception that the Grail will be restored to the world. Then we will realize that contemplating the soul of the world is more important than changing it, celebrating the Earth is more important than controlling it, and being is as important as doing.

The wisdom of Sophia, the wisdom which comes from the feminine attitude of receptivity, is necessary in order to perceive the vision of the Grail. For just as the Wounded King did not perceive the Grail and therefore his land lay in waste, so most people today are not aware of the Grail which could bring wholeness to their souls and thus heal the Earth. We also need the wisdom of Sophia to deal with the dark side of the Grail constructively. For the Grail has the power of discriminating judgment, as shown in the members of Joseph of Arimathea's company who were turned away from the Table of the Grail because of their sinful lust. The Grail can be dangerous for those who attempt to aggressively seize it for their own selfish purposes of power or control. Many knights who are spiritually unworthy in this manner meet with injury or even death in the Grail stories. In our modern world we are especially confronted with the dark side of the Grail because science and technology have allowed us to harness the powers of creation for our own egoistic uses. We attempt to control the processes of life through genetic engineering and the primal energy of the cosmos through nuclear physics. It is imperative that we acquire the wisdom of Sophia in order to deal with the dark powers that our hubris has unleashed.

The Grail of Sophia brings the vision of wholeness which reconciles the light and the dark. This Grail is "an image of the unity of creation - the reality of which compassion is in humanity the prime expression."[66] This is the compassion which integrates the light and dark aspects of the Grail by encompassing the depths of grief and heights of joy. It is the compassion which comes from the recognition that there is ultimately no separation between self and other; it is this compassion based on the vision of connectedness which lies at the heart of feminist spirituality. This is the Grail vision which is needed to propel us beyond our egoistic strivings for power and control to embrace our role as co-creators with the Divine in the restoration of our current Wasteland.

The key to the retrieval of the Grail is to recognize that it is **already** in the world; we simply have to perceive its presence. The mystical vision of the Grail reveals to us Sophia as the divine presence which is within all persons and every created thing. The gift of the Grail is the experience of union with the Divine Sophia as one becomes conscious of the divinity within oneself. The Grail will be returned to the world through experiencing its healing and transforming power, and through realizing one's unity with the Grail of all creation. Once we do this we will perceive the Grail which is ever-present and thereby restore it to the realm of human consciousness.

The Empowerment of the Grail

The wholeness and unity which are experienced in the Grail vision leads to the empowerment of the Grail in our lives. The retrieval of the Grail involves enabling these empowering energies of the Grail to emerge into the world and thus transform it. As David Spangler says, "Transformation comes from...an energy that derives from the unity of all things...This is an energy of pure being...The energy truly opens up our identities and our realities to new possibilities... It is a spirit of playfulness, a spirit of delight and wonderment, a spirit of discovery, exploration, and unconditional power. It is not striving to be any particular thing, for it is all things. This makes it the essence of abundance."[67] This is the empowering energy of the Grail, the energy of divine love and wisdom. When this energy is activated within our souls, we experience its manifestation in the outer world as the abundance of life. The greatest gift of the Grail is spiritual abundance, the wealth of the soul that Jesus spoke of when he said, "I came that they may have life, and have it abundantly." (John 10:10) Jesus as the archetypal Grail hero brings the chalice of living water to Earth and offers us the spiritual abundance of life.

When we attain the Grail vision of the cosmic dance of creation, we are empowered to become partners in this dance. It is through the creative powers of the inner Grail of our own souls that we can become co-creators with the Divine in bringing transformation to the world. For when we discover the Grail within ourselves we become open to all the potentials it contains - all the possibilities that can arise from its emptiness. Likewise we realize all the potentials within ourselves and in the world. With this heightened awareness we are able to actualize more of these possibilities in our lives and in the world. But the ultimate empowering gift of the Grail is the recognition of pure Being - beyond all desires of the ego - and the ability to act from this state of Being. In this state we gain the power to serve as channels for the divine energies of the Grail to pour into the world. This is the state of mystical union to which the apostle Paul refers when he says, "it is no longer I who live, but it is Christ who lives in me." (Galatians 2:20) Paul is no longer existing in his ego but in the divine center of Being within his soul. In this state the soul then becomes the receptive vessel, the Grail, which is filled with the divine Spirit and gives it to the world. It is in this way that we truly receive the abundance of the Grail, for it is in experiencing the Grail within - experiencing union with the Divine - that all of our needs are fulfilled. This was the mystical experience of Galahad and the reason that he prayed for death, because after his vision of the Grail he had no other earthly desires. His ascension to Heaven symbolizes his spiritual wholeness which is the ultimate empowerment of the Grail.

THE GRAIL: SOPHIA'S RE-EMERGENCE IN THE NEW MYTHOS

The theme of the empowering Grail which was so popular in medieval myth reveals the possibilities for transformation which were present in the culture of the Middle Ages. However, the brief flowering of the feminine at that time was repressed and the Grail was again lost to the Earth, which became increasingly more of a Wasteland with each passing century. Emma Jung says, "The Grail has the characteristic of those hidden treasures of which it is said that from time to time they 'blossom,' and that when they do the moment has then arrived when they can be brought to the surface. Should this fail to occur they will disappear again."[68] The extremely one-sided development of masculine consciousness, which led to the horrors of the twentieth century, is now causing the "hidden treasure" to "blossom" again to compensate for the dreadful lack of eros in Western culture. So we find ourselves today at a similar turning point as in the Middle Ages, when the Divine Feminine is making her return and bringing the Grail again to human consciousness. The critical questions which face the Grail seeker today are: Will the Grail quest be completed in our era? Will the Grail finally be restored to the earthly realm? Or will the forces of repression win again? For if we again fail to return the Grail to Earth, we can be assured that it will once more disappear, with even more disastrous results for our planet and all of life.

However, there is great hope in the potential for retrieving the Grail in our time for a number of reasons, of which a major one is the cultural paradigm shift that is now occurring. We are living through a time of major transformation in beliefs, attitudes, and values which provides an opening for the Grail to return as well as a desperate need for its empowerment to face the challenges of our modern culture. Joachim's Age of the Holy Spirit, the Age of Sophia, the Age of the Grail, appears to be the cultural phase that we are now entering, characterized by the individual seeker on a spiritual journey. The quest for the Grail is an expression of this age, for it takes place on the spiritual bypaths rather than the interstate highway of the Church. The secularization of our present age may also be a surprisingly positive feature for the retrieval of the Grail. For although the loss of spiritual meaning seems to be the root cause of the wasteland of modern life, this very condition of secularization may be necessary in order for Joachim's visionary Age of the Holy Spirit to be fully realized. It is only because the authoritarian Church has lost the monolithic power that it wielded in the Middle Ages that today's Grail seekers can recover the hidden treasures on the spiritual bypaths without being condemned to burn at the stake for heresy. Secularization has produced a fragmentation of society and a freedom of thought which will make it much more difficult to repress the spiritual energies which are emerging today than it was in the Middle Ages.

Perceval's quest for the Grail, which is a quest for Sophia's wholeness, symbolizes the condition of the seeker in the Age of the Holy Spirit. Perceval is destined to play the role of the third Grail guardian, the one who achieves the heightened consciousness that transcends conflicts to a recognition of inner wholeness. However his failure to accomplish this task signifies that the transition to the Age of the Holy Spirit remained unfulfilled in the Middle Ages. Perceval renounced the world and failed to return the Grail to the Round Table, and thus the Spirit was separated from the natural world.[69] This symbolizes the cause of the ills which beset our Western world. This interpretation of Perceval's quest is especially clear in the version of Chretien de Troyes which remained unfinished, perhaps indicating the unresolved nature of the problem. Whether because of the patriarchal values and attitudes of the Middle Ages or because of the dominance of the authoritarian Church, the masculine hero could not achieve the synthesis required to return the Grail to the world.

The unfinished nature of the quest in the medieval Grail stories indicates that the quest continues in our time. The quest for wholeness is always a **process** rather than a final point of completion. The quest to bring wholeness to the Christ symbol by including the elements of darkness and the feminine has been left woefully incomplete since the Middle Ages. Likewise, the quest for Sophia is unfinished, for she remains a hidden presence within Christian tradition. Both of these quests, which are really mirror images of the **one** quest of the Grail stories, have been left for our modern age to complete. The quest of Western culture today is for a revitalized mythos containing the new symbols of wholeness which will satisfy the psychological needs and spiritual yearnings of modern humanity.

The Grail myth can lay the foundation for this new mythos because the Grail is **the** symbol for our time. Since the Grail symbol connects the ancient wisdom of the pagan past and the mysteries of Christianity, it is a key to the emerging mythos which will synthesize the significant spiritual truths of Western culture without regard to the divisions of doctrine or sect. In addition, the Grail represents a and can be easily adapted into Christian ritual by seeing the communion cup as the Grail

synthesis of the bypaths of Christian tradition - the nature, feminine, and mystical bypaths - and therefore is the spiritual symbol which lies at the heart of the Path of ChristoSophia. The seeker on the Path of ChristoSophia who retrieves the hidden treasure of Christian tradition, the Grail, brings the new mythos its central symbol of wholeness which includes nature, the feminine, and mystical consciousness.

Because the Grail is a symbol of the Divine Feminine, the completion of the Grail quest in our present age entails the re-emergence of Sophia in the new mythos. Caitlin Matthews points out that "The Grail's withdrawal is like Sophia's retirement to her place of waiting."[70] Therefore the retrieval of the Grail corresponds with the return of Sophia as the Divine Feminine to her central position within the mythic consciousness. The masculine image of God which has dominated Western culture for the past two millennia is no longer viable in our modern world or in the psyche of modern humans. The new form for the God-image must include the feminine if the wasteland of modern life and spirituality is to be renewed. But since the major theme of the Grail myth is the reuniting of the Goddess and the King, the new myth must be based upon a true synthesis of the masculine and the feminine. The age-old union of the King and the Queen, the Hero and the Goddess, can be translated into Christian tradition in the form of ChristoSophia. The heroic knight who possesses the Grail symbolizes the Christ in his union with Sophia. As we have seen, the Grail itself is a symbol of ChristoSophia. The quest for this Grail must take place on the spiritual bypaths, for it will not be found on the interstate highway of Christianity.

It is the Grail as the symbol of ChristoSophia which will bring healing to the Wounded King by providing the feminine complement that he so desperately needs. This is the Grail which can "complete the Christ-image"[71] by uniting the world of the feminine, nature, and darkness with the world of the masculine, spirit, and light. It is the Grail which symbolizes the Jungian Self, the archetype of wholeness, by uniting the opposites within the Western psyche's image of the Divine. The Grail of ChristoSophia will bring greening to the barren Wasteland through its eros qualities of imagination and feeling. This is the "viriditas" or "greening power" that Hildegard of Bingen associates with the Divine. The living waters of the Grail can restore the green growth to the land which has been decimated by the logos emphasis on control and power, as well as the fertile green vitality to the soul which has become parched and impotent in our secular, technological world. It is in this respect that the relationship of Christ as the Green Man with Sophia is central to the emerging mythos. When the Divine Feminine re-emerges in human history, the Green Man as the sacrificed and reborn God will also reappear as part of the same archetypal complex.[72] Within Christian tradition this means that Sophia's re-emergence in the new mythos will entail a corresponding emergence of Christ as Green Man into consciousness. He is the Green Man in whom Sophia's secret of creation, the life-essence, the soul of the world, lies hidden. Christ as the Green Man has kept the mystery of the Grail. In the new myth the Grail hero will serve as the prototype of Christ as the Green Man; the time has come for him to "free the waters" by returning the Grail of Sophia, which he has kept hidden for so long, to the world so that it can now "green" the Earth. This role is foreshadowed in Parzival, who symbolizes Christ, for he "is called the Green One, who restores the waters of life to the earth."[73] In his role as Green Man, Christ can transmit the wisdom of Sophia to us. This is similar to the early Christian view that Christ, as the incarnation of Sophia, conveyed her wisdom to the world. However in the new myth, the wisdom that Christ as Green Man will bring is the Sophianic perception of wholeness.

The new mythos will emerge through the process of "psychic photosynthesis,"[74] the "greening" of the psyche, the Sophianic process at work within the soul, which is ultimately the Grail quest. The new mythic symbols will arise through this photosynthetic process as the water of wisdom - Sophia - combines with the light of love - Christ - to bring forth the greenery of life to our world again. The union of Christ and Sophia will create the new myth, now living, growing and fertile, which will emerge from the dark soil of the unconscious. Thus the Grail which was removed into Heaven in the medieval myth will be retrieved from the Earth herself as the new myth arises from the depths. The task of the seeker on the mystical bypath today is to aid in the process of birthing this new myth through prayer, meditation, and ritual. For the Grail is truly **within** us; we only need to enter into the Grail Castle of our own soul to discover it and bring it back to the outer world with us. The Grail will manifest again on Earth when enough people have undertaken this quest for the Grail within their souls and brought the inner Grail to consciousness. Then the world will finally heed the message of Sophia:

> The search for the Grail begins in the ordinary world, in your everyday life. But remember that the ordinary world is not 'ordinary' if you have eyes to truly perceive it, and everyday life is not 'everyday' if you have the heart of wisdom. The path of the Grail leads you to see the 'ordinary' world as Sophia's dance of rainbow colors, and recognize 'everyday' life as your part of the dance.

CHAPTER XI: THE PATH OF CHRISTOSOPHIA

Keep on walking on this road, where you can become
more human and more divine.[1]

Just as a national transportation system requires both the
interstate highway and the byroads, so a vital Christianity needs the
institutional Church and the bypaths which comprise the Path of
ChristoSophia. Since many of these bypaths have been little used
and are overgrown, those who explore them today must in effect be
trailblazers. They must work to clear the bypaths so that they may
be more readily traveled by others. For it is particularly in times of
transformation such as our current cultural crisis that the wisdom
which can be found on the Path of ChristoSophia is most needed.

DANGERS OF THE BYPATHS

Those who begin walking on the Path of ChristoSophia must
take the risk of following an unknown path into unfamiliar territory.
There are very real dangers inherent in walking the spiritual bypaths
just like there are in hiking wilderness trails. The spiritual seeker
who sets forth on the bypath without preparation faces much greater
dangers without the structure of the Church to mitigate them, just as
a walk in the woods without compass or knowledge of wilderness
survival is much more dangerous than a journey along a well-traveled
road. However, it is important to not be overcome by fear. As fear of

the unknown, especially that which is "wild," limits our experience of the Earth and our instinctual selves, shutting us off from many experiences of beauty and wonder, so fear of walking the bypaths can limit our spiritual experience and prevent the realization of our complete selves. In order to walk the Path of ChristoSophia we must be aware of the potential dangers and prepare for them, and then have the courage to explore the less traveled trail.

The dangers that one faces on the spiritual bypaths are graphically illustrated by the trials of the knights who set forth on the Grail quest. Deep in the forest they must battle dangerous animals and monsters, encounter enchantments and bewitchings, and undergo severe tests and temptations. All of these struggles symbolize the arduous journey into the inner world which one takes on the spiritual bypath, where one encounters the destructive forces of the psyche as well as the benevolent ones. As the Grail knights had to fight the dangers of the wild forest, the accounts of Christian mystics describe in detail their ubiquitous battles with the demons. The rituals of the Church help to control these powerful forces, which in their full intensity can be shattering to the psyche. Experiences of the numinous – whether light or dark - can completely overcome the ego; the "death" of many of the Grail questors is mirrored in the stories from numerous spiritual traditions of those who "died" after encountering the Divine.

Just as the Grail heroes often became "enchanted" or "bewitched" and lost their way on the quest, so a common problem for the traveler on the spiritual bypath is to lose touch with "reality." The enticement of the inner world can be so alluring that one may find it difficult to function in the mundane world. Like the Celtic hero who succumbs to the enchantment of the fairies and unknowingly spends years delighting in the pleasures of the Otherworld, only to find when he returns to earthly reality that his quest has been interrupted, so the authentic quest on the Path of ChristoSophia may be deterred by an unbalanced flight into the inner world and a lack of grounding in the outer world.

The severe tests of fortitude and grave moral temptations that the Grail heroes faced during their quest symbolize the necessity of overcoming the dangers of egotism which are commonly

374

experienced by those who have already traveled some way on the bypaths. Many who have acquired a degree of spiritual power and enlightenment through their inner quests succumb to the feeling of being "special" and more "spiritually evolved" than others. One who has experienced the numinous power of the Divine may develop a dangerous inflation of the ego in which he believes that he is **the** spokesperson for God – and may even act as though he **is** God. The Church, through its organizational structure of checks and balances, is often able to suppress the disruptions of individual egotism; the individual who walks on the spiritual bypath lacks these institutional controls. Because of this, one of the greatest dangers that the spiritual seeker must avoid is the charismatic leader who wields authoritarian power over others. Cults which have ended in death for their members, such as Jonestown and Heaven's Gate, are just a few of many examples throughout history which demonstrate the profound danger in handing over one's autonomy and freedom of choice to an authoritarian leader of a spiritual group.

All of these dangers on the spiritual bypaths, like the perils which beset the questing Grail knights, can obstruct one's journey on the Path of ChristoSophia. We must not yield to the glamours of enchantment in the inner world because the task for one who walks on the Path of ChristoSophia is to live both a spiritual and a fully embodied life in this world. Likewise, we must not succumb to the temptation of egotism because the spiritual journey necessitates a never-ending process of ego transformation in which the divine light is seen ever more clearly within all people. Finally, we must not surrender the responsibility for our own inner quest to an outside authority, because it is only through the individual journey that deification can be realized and the Cosmic Christ born within the soul.

Recognizing these risks that are inherent in the spiritual quest makes us realize the importance of preparing to cope with these dangers. One of the surest ways of promoting our safety when walking on the Path of ChristoSophia is to follow those guides who have gone before us. Christian mystics throughout the ages have given us maps of the territory through which the bypaths lead, and we can continue to invoke their aid in our own journeys. The Kabbalists in particular have provided us with a very comprehensive map of the Path of ChristoSophia in the symbolic Tree of Life. In fact, the Kabbalah is immensely valuable for the spiritual seeker because the "pathways" of the Kabbalistic Tree have been so well traveled.

Our most important guides, as well as companions, on the Path are Christ and Sophia themselves. Andrew Harvey's visionary statement, "I am the journey and the traveler,"[2] indicates that Christ is both the path itself and the guide, the one who has traveled the way before us. Harvey points out that Jesus does not ask us to believe in him as a "savior" but as "path-blazer" – "one who has opened a path for others to follow."[3] Jesus himself traveled the spiritual bypaths rather than the interstate highway of Judaism which carried the mass populace of Jews in his time. Today Jesus is the primary trailblazer on the bypaths: he shows us the way on the feminine bypath as ChristoSophia in his union with the Divine Feminine; he shows us the way on the nature bypath as the Cosmic Christ which is the divine presence within all of nature; he shows us the way on the mystical bypath as the prime exemplar of mystical consciousness for he lived in the Heart of the Divine. On the Path of ChristoSophia we follow Jesus as our guide through his life and teachings rather than the dogmas or rules of the Church. We attempt to follow the way he shows us of love and compassion, courage and self-sacrifice, eros and wisdom. The historical Jesus, whose task it was "to birth the eternal Christ,"[4] is our guide to follow on the Path of ChristoSophia in displaying those actions which spring from an inner experience of Christ-consciousness.

As we prepare to begin our inner quest on the Path of ChristoSophia, it is imperative that we invoke divine protection from the threats that endanger us along the way. Consciously aligning oneself with the divine Center of love and wisdom is important before commencing any inner work. Meditation sessions can begin with a centering in the Kabbalistic Tifereth, the sefirah of the Cosmic Christ. As we focus on the golden light of Tifereth surrounding us, we can ask for protection and blessing during our meditation by using the Kabbalistic "Cross of Light."

The Cross of Light

Imagine yourself standing peacefully in a tranquil setting. Breathe deeply and slowly and still your thoughts as you say the following. Envision the light of Tifereth flowing out in the directions as you say them.

> *Let there be Peace, Love, Harmony, Joy, and Wisdom*
> *Among all Creatures, Beings, and Humankind*
> *Before me, behind me,*
> *To the right of me, to the left of me,*
> *Above me, within me, beneath me, and all about me,*
> *Peace - - Peace - - Peace.*

Then say the Lord's Prayer. The following version reflects the union of the masculine and feminine aspects of deity which are found on the Path of ChristoSophia:

> *Our Mother – Father, Who art in Heaven and all Creation,*
> *Hallowed be Thy Name. Thy Kingdom come, Thy Will be done,*
> *on Earth, as it is in Heaven. Give us this day our daily bread,*
> *and forgive us our trespasses, as we forgive those who trespass*
> *against us. Lead us lest we fall into temptation, and deliver us*
> *from evil.*

At this point, take the right hand, with the thumb and first two fingers held together and the ring and little fingers pressed against the palm, and raise it to a point three or four inches over your head. Envision a bright pool of the light of Tifereth over your head and dip your thumb and two fingers into it, drawing the light down to your forehead as you say the word *Ateh*. Continue the movement of your right hand downwards and touch your abdomen as you say the word *Malkuth*, visualizing the light of Tifereth following the movement of your hand and descending right through your genitals into the earth between your feet. Without stopping the movement of your hand, raise it to your right shoulder and say the words *Vi Geburah* and then cross to your left shoulder saying the words *Vi Gedulah* still visualizing the light of Tifereth following the motion of your hand.

377

Then immediately place your hands with palms together in front of your heart, visualizing the light as a brilliant miniature sun between them as you say *Le Olam*. You may then repeat the Cross of Light in English if you wish, saying "For Thine is" in place of *Ateh*, "the Kingdom" in place of *Malkuth*, "the Power" for *Vi Geburah* and "the Glory" for *Vi Gedulah*, and Amen for *Le Olam*. At this point you may offer any prayer for protection, guidance, and inspiration. After your prayer, repeat the opening verse *"Let there be Peace, Love, Harmony, Joy, and Wisdom"* etc., visualizing the light of Tifereth as before. At this point, you are ready to begin your meditation and can assume the position that you find most conducive for that purpose.

We can also use the prayers of Christian mystics who have traveled the way before us as models when confronting the trials and temptations of the quest. For example, the mystic Jacob Boehme, who knew well the dangers which beset the "thorny way" of the spiritual bypath, invoked Christ's aid as his guide in this prayer:

> O Lord Jesus Christ, I fly to You under Your cross.
> Oh dear Emmanuel, take me, and lead me to You
> through your own pilgrim's path that You traveled
> in this world...[5]

Celtic Christians also were very aware of the perils that lie in the spiritual as well as the physical world. Their response to these threats was to continually appeal through prayer and ritual to the Trinity, the Virgin Mary, and the blessed saints for protection from the dangers of the inner and the outer world. For example, the famous *lorica* ("breastplate") of St. Patrick, which symbolizes the shield of protective armor, invokes the protection of the company of Heaven against inner as well as outer enemies. The *lorica* can serve as a model for developing our own prayers for protection, such as the following stanza:

> I bind unto myself today
> The strong name of the Trinity
> By invocation of the same
> The Three in One and One in Three.[6]

We can also adapt the practice of the Celtic Christian "encircling prayer" in which one uses the index finger of the right hand to draw a circle of spiritual fire around oneself and the immediate environment and prays for protection:

> The Sacred Three
> My fortress be
> Encircling me
> Come and be round
> My hearth and my home.[7]

Rituals such as these help us to be aware of the constant presence of the Divine within and around us and the power which is always available to aid us as we confront the dangers of the spiritual quest.

Prayers for guidance as well as protection are necessary preparations for the pilgrim who walks on the Path of ChristoSophia. Receptivity to divine guidance entails surrender to the divine will, which is the primary means to avoid the perils of egotism that so often befall the explorer of spiritual realms. On the Path of ChristoSophia the emphasis must always be on spiritual service rather than spiritual power. Here again we turn to Christ as our guide through his response to the depths of his despair in the Garden of Gethsemane – "**Thy** will be done." As we follow Christ, our journey on the spiritual bypath will often be into the darkness of "not-knowing" that he experienced during the Crucifixion. We will often have to travel far beyond our rational beliefs to a faith based on radical trust in the Divine. It is this ultimate trust, even amid our deepest doubts and fears, which surrenders the ego so that the true Self can emerge to serve as a channel for the Divine to act within the world. When this occurs, synchronicities commonly appear and events unfold far beyond what we can even imagine.

The radical trust of the pilgrim on the Path of ChristoSophia is based on the promise that "all things work together for good for those who love God." (Romans 8:28) It is this ego-transforming trust that gives us the courage to travel upon the unknown bypath without the signs of the highway to clearly guide the way. On the bypath it is easy to seemingly lose the direction and end up in a place that we hadn't planned. But if we continually pray for guidance and are open and receptive to the workings of the Divine, in retrospect the synchronistic nature of these "false turns" is apparent. For we find that we ended up not where we planned – yet exactly where we needed to be!

WALKING THE PATH OF CHRISTOSOPHIA

Packing the Backpack

As the hiker of the wilderness trail packs a backpack with the necessities for survival, so must we carry a backpack containing the essential items which are needed for our spiritual journey. In preparing to walk on the Path of ChristoSophia we pack our backpack with only those things which are essential to Christian tradition, leaving behind the patriarchal containers within which its Mysteries have been encased. In a similar way Jesus attempted to reform the religion of his time by keeping that which was essential to Jewish tradition and discarding the accretions which falsified its true spirit. Our task today is to sort through the doctrines, symbols and practices of Christianity and retain the essential elements of Christian tradition as we search for their deeper meanings which have remained hidden on the bypaths. This is a task which must be undertaken with humility for it requires wisdom and discernment. But it is a task which is vitally necessary if the great cultural split between the spiritual and the physical, the masculine and the feminine, is to be healed. For many of the accretions of Christianity which have accumulated through the past two thousand years are a hindrance or even harmful in our current world, such as views of "original sin" that denigrate the feminine and the natural world.

The essential core of Christianity, around which the early Christian community coalesced, is the central Mystery of Christ's Passion, the crucifixion and the resurrection. This is the essence of Christian tradition which must accompany the pilgrim on the bypaths, where a different meaning may be discovered than on the highway of the Church. For on the Path of ChristoSophia the Mystery of the Christian Passion refers to the crucifixion and resurrection of **both** Christ and Sophia; here one meets the crucified and risen Lord as ChristoSophia.

Sophia is present with Christ in the crucifixion and continues to share in his suffering. Sophia as the Soul of the World suffers today in the exploitation of the Earth and her creatures, and she shares in the suffering of all those who have been oppressed by patriarchal power. Sophia, as the divine spark which is hidden within the material world, suffers with all of humanity as it yearns to reunite with its divine source.

Sophia also shares in the resurrection with Christ. As Jann Aldredge-Clanton says:

> From the beginning the theology of the Christian movement identifies the resurrected One not only with the Spirit of God but also with the Sophia of God...The specific physical form of the historical Jesus, including gender and race, was not part of the essence of the resurrected Christ-Sophia. More important than the physical reality was the spiritual reality of the risen One...Resurrection thus results in a new creation, unlimited by time, culture, race, and gender.[8]

It was the disciples' encounter with the resurrected ChristoSophia which converted this small group of fearful, confused followers of Jesus into a joyful, confident community committed to spreading the "Good News" of Christ's resurrection throughout the world. For it was not the historical person Jesus of Nazareth that the disciples met on the road to Emmaus or in the upper room in Jerusalem, but instead they apprehended the divine glory of the One in the risen ChristoSophia.

The "Good News" of the resurrection is also seen on the Path of ChristoSophia as a joyous proclamation of the "original blessing"[9] of God. Jesus did not die for our sins because it was preordained that a sacrifice was needed to atone for "original sin"; rather, he died because the darkness of human ignorance and selfishness – the mark of the ego when it is separated from the Divine – prevailed and did not understand his message of love. This then is the "original sin" – the "shadow" which is found in all human beings that turns destructive when we do not live out of our divine wholeness. The essential meaning of Christ's crucifixion is that he died for us out of boundless divine love – not as a sacrifice for our sins to propitiate God the Judge, but as a result of human sin which now, as then, separates us from the divine center of Love and Wisdom. The crucifixion of Jesus reveals that the Divine fully shares in the suffering of the earthly realm; ChristoSophia continues to suffer today with all of creation when sin sets human beings apart from the Divine. The resurrection of ChristoSophia reveals the illusion of our ordinary sense of "reality" that separates us from other creatures and the cosmos. This is the central illumination that we gain when we walk on the Path of ChristoSophia – the realization of divine Love at the center of the universe and our own beings. The actualization of this love within our hearts is the process that we undertake when we follow Jesus as our guide on the Path. This is the transformative process that underlies deification; the "Good News" of the resurrection is precisely this revelation that all human beings have the potential to follow Jesus in becoming a "Christ."

Whereas the interstate highway of the Church emphasizes that **belief** in Christ's crucifixion and resurrection is essential, the bypaths lead to **participation** in the Passion of ChristoSophia. When we consciously open ourselves to the suffering of the world and undergo the transformation of the ego into the divine Self, we directly experience the power of the crucifixion and resurrection on the Path of ChristoSophia. This was the primary experience of the original disciples that initiated the early Christian community. Thus, "living" the Passion of ChristoSophia within one's own being is the core experience in Christian tradition that has the power to transform the human being and thus heal the world. This deeper meaning of the Passion is the essential revelation of Christianity; it is the culmination of the "alternative wisdom" of Jesus as described by Marcus Borg: "The alternative wisdom of Jesus sees the religious life as a deepening relationship with the Spirit of God, not as a life of requirements and reward."[10] Jesus proclaimed an "alternative wisdom" that emphasized love and compassion rather than the "conventional wisdom" of his culture that stressed rules and regulations.[11] It is these eros qualities which are central to the message of Jesus – the wisdom and love of ChristoSophia that he manifested on Earth – that are essential to carry in our backpack as we walk with him as our guide on the Path.

Blazing the Trails

Since the bypaths of Christianity have been blocked and even destroyed through the process of building the interstate highway of the Church, those who walk on the Path of ChristoSophia must blaze the trails in order to make the bypaths more accessible to spiritual seekers today. Trailblazers on the Path of ChristoSophia can reopen the barricaded bypaths by recovering aspects of the hidden tradition of Christianity within Sophiology, Gnosticism, Celtic Christianity, Kabbalism, and Grail mysticism. However, the journey on the Path of ChristoSophia is not a return to the past; we must travel forward, **through** Christianity, taking with us the essential elements of Christian tradition as we create new blazes on the Path. In this way we can rebuild those bypaths which have been destroyed through the centuries, and mark the trails with fresh blazes in the form of new modes of worship and ritual which honor the feminine, celebrate the natural world, and develop mystical consciousness.

Blazing the trails on the Path of ChristoSophia is of utmost importance because through this process we will discover and reveal the new mythos which Christianity requires if it is going to be a vital tradition in the future. As Carl Jung has emphasized, the basic myth of a culture must be renewed in each age if it is going to continue to bring healing and meaning to people's lives. In times of transformation a "new assimilation of the traditional myth"[12] is required which builds upon the historical foundations of the culture as it adapts to current conditions. The renewal of the Christian myth which our culture so desperately needs today will be found more easily on the Path of ChristoSophia where revelation is an evolving process, rather than on the interstate highway of the Church where the myth has become rigidified in dogmatic beliefs and practices.

A major function of the renewed Christian mythos must be to heal the split between religion and science which has steadily widened since the Age of Reason in the seventeenth century. Since today science provides the primary way of knowing about our world, a religious viewpoint that conflicts with scientific discoveries is no longer viable for our modern culture. Instead, the new mythos must acknowledge both science and religion as two different, but complementary, ways of perceiving reality. Trailblazers such as

Teilhard de Chardin and Thomas Berry have led the way in showing us how to revision the Christian myth so that Christianity and modern science can mutually enrich each other. The tools of contemporary science – empirical observation and analytical reason – can combine with the ancient spiritual practice of visionary imagination to blaze the Path of ChristoSophia in our current age.

The new mythos, which is gestating even now, will be born as we share our discoveries on the Path of ChristoSophia. This myth, which will arise from our collective experiences on the feminine, nature, and mystical bypaths, will function like a new graft onto the tree of Christianity. Its roots are the same – reaching deep into the ground of Christian tradition – yet it will form a new tree; the new mythos will grow as the Tree of Wisdom, the revelation of the divine Sophia who has been hidden within Christian spirituality. For the bypaths will lead us to Sophia if we return to a true understanding of mythology, as advocated by Carl Jung – a living, vital mythology which engages our whole being, our heart and soul, and not just our mind.

Once we meet Sophia on the Path we must aid the ongoing process of her revelation within the world. Because Sophia is an "unfinished presence in the New Testament,"[13] blazing the trail means that we must open the way for Sophia to fully reveal herself and transform the world. In the new mythos Sophia must emerge in the full power of the Divine Feminine, which has been repressed through countless centuries of patriarchal power. Susanne Schaup refers to the necessity of this empowerment of Sophia:

> If she is to become an active force again, a redemptress
> in this time of history, she will have to regain the "Isis power"
> of the Goddess of Heaven, the sovereign eroticism of Astarte,
> the maternal anger of Demeter…She desires to be reborn as
> a new collective symbol of the Feminine Divine.[14]

As long as the Christian Church remains bound to the patriarchal paradigm, Sophia cannot take her position as equal feminine counterpart to the masculine deity. Today it is still only on the spiritual bypath that she can be seen with the full power and glory of the ancient goddess.

As Sophia reveals herself on the bypaths in the totality of the archetypal Feminine, the new mythos will provide an image of the *hieros gamos* or sacred marriage to symbolize deity. An image of the union of Divine Feminine and Divine Masculine – foreseen in Hildegard's vision of the embrace of Wisdom and Father God, the gnostics' myth of the marriage of Sophia and Christ, and the Kabbalists' concept of the union of Shekhinah and Tifereth– will emerge as a central symbol to represent the integration of masculine and feminine polarities within the godhead. The exclusively masculine Christian Trinity must also be revisioned to reflect this union. One possible form that the Trinity may take in the new mythos is a reconceptualization of the first person as Mother-Father God, the second person as ChristoSophia, and the third person as both masculine and feminine Holy Spirit.

The union represented by ChristoSophia will also serve the important function in the new mythos of completing the Christ-image which has remained incomplete until our present day. Carl Jung has emphasized the importance of bringing wholeness to the image of Christ because it is the prime symbol of the Self in Western culture. The archetype of the Self is symbolized by the "marriage quaternio,"[15] the union of the masculine and the feminine, and the light and the dark. ChristoSophia fulfills the symbol for the Self archetype which has been evolving in Western culture, for ChristoSophia integrates the polarities of the feminine and the darkness which have been excluded in the traditional Christian image of Christ. The emergence of ChristoSophia in the new mythos as a symbol which unites the opposites will aid human beings today in the process of individuation. ChristoSophia can lead us to greater wholeness by helping us to integrate the "shadow" within instead of projecting it onto others or the Devil, and by helping us to develop our feminine nature and thus actualize the eros function in our lives.

The renewal of the Christian myth must also restore this necessary eros dimension to Christianity. As Susanne Schaup says, "The time has come for an all-embracing erotic vision of life in the sign of Sophia."[16] The dangerous excess of the logos function in our culture can be balanced by an infusion of eros through a symbolic image of deity which unites the feminine with the masculine. A mythology which celebrates the eros function of the instincts will help us regain a reverence for sexuality and the human body; a mythology which embraces the eros qualities of feeling and intuition will help us recover a sense of connectedness with Mother Earth and all her creatures. In this way the new mythos will bring healing to our fragmented, alienated world by emphasizing the relatedness of eros.

Trailblazers on the Path of ChristoSophia who discover these elements of the new mythos on their spiritual journeys must mark the trail with the fresh blazes of symbols and rituals that will guide others to this living mythos. While we can rediscover some of the trail markers that were hidden on the bypaths through historical and archaeological research today, there is much of early Christian teaching and practice that we do not have available. Therefore we must search directly on the inner path, using the visionary imagination to gain access to the archetypal world, and in this way recover the symbolism which has been lost. Blazing the trail on the Path of ChristoSophia involves giving form to the symbols of wholeness which the new mythos yields, such as images of the Divine Feminine and the sacred marriage. As we have seen, the primary symbol of the renewed myth is the empowering Grail, which is returning in many forms today through the collective psyche to heal our current Wasteland. Representations of these symbolic images through poetry, painting, music, dance, sculpture, woodworking, and other arts and crafts serve as markers on the trail so that others may also discover the new mythos. Art serves a spiritual purpose for the seeker on the Path of ChristoSophia, just as it did for the Celtic Christians. Their exquisitely sculptured high crosses and illuminated manuscripts expressed the spiritual images of their time; in the same way, artwork today can reveal the sacred symbols that are emerging into consciousness. However, we must guard against the common tendency to avoid this task because we believe we do not possess artistic talent. In earlier societies, such as the Celts and the Native Americans, art was a natural expression of spirituality. People simply rendered the sacred images in a concrete form as they arose, regardless of artistic ability or training. A return to this personal enactment of the archetypal symbols which emerge in dream or meditation can help us truly "live" the new mythos as we aid its birth in our culture.

Another major task for trailblazers on the Path of ChristoSophia is to embody the emerging mythic images in new modes of worship which honor the feminine, nature, and mystical consciousness. This work is also a form of art, for it requires the use of eros creativity. Trailblazers such as Miriam Therese Winter, Aurora Terrenus, Susan Cole, and Jann Aldredge-Clanton are pointing the way to Sophia's rebirth in the new mythos through their creation of prayers, rituals and liturgies that honor the Divine Feminine. Their ideas are excellent resources for us to use as guiding markers on the Path of ChristoSophia, but may be even more invaluable as models for inspiring us to open to our own creative depths and allow Sophia to emerge in whatever form she desires within us. Then we can continue the work of these trailblazers in creating worship settings and structures which include both the feminine and masculine dimensions of deity.

Changes in worship must also occur in order to reflect the primacy of eros in the new mythos. In traditional church services the congregation is usually passive and nonparticipatory, and worship involves primarily the logos activities of reading the Bible, reciting prayers, and listening to sermons. On the Path of ChristoSophia, new forms of worship are evolving which engage the eros qualities of playfulness, spontaneity, and creativity. As the new mythos is a harbinger of wholeness, so worship is emerging on the Path of ChristoSophia which involves the whole person – mind, body, and soul. Most important is everyone's participation as an equal part of an interconnected whole. Matthew Fox, as one who has blazed the trail to guide us in new ways of worship, says:

> We need to worship in circles again, preferably on the soil of
> Mother Earth whenever possible. Circles invite all creatures
> to be part of the grateful event and they allow the humans
> present to look each other in the eye while rounding and
> connecting themselves in step with the universe.[17]

Because the circle and the Earth are primary symbols of the Divine Feminine, worship which takes place outdoors in a circle is an especially meaningful way to honor Sophia. This setting also encourages us to use our physical bodies and our instincts to connect with the Divine, which are necessary elements if we are to include eros in our worship.

Performing music, singing and dancing are all expressions of eros which are very important to a fully embodied worship experience. Ancient peoples used to emulate the cosmic dance in their ceremonial dances, and in this way helped to keep the Earth energies in harmony. Because this important ritual is seldom done anymore, the trailblazer on the Path of ChristoSophia must recreate the music and dance that reflects and energizes the cosmic patterns. We can refer to the gnostic round dance as an example of a ritual which expresses the image of wholeness in motion. By once again performing these sacred dances we can become partners with ChristoSophia in the dance of life and co-creators on Earth of the divine patterns of the cosmos.

Walking the labyrinth is another ancient practice which is reappearing as a very powerful ritual today. The labyrinth, which had its source in pagan societies where it was associated with the goddess, was later appropriated by the Christian Church where it appeared in splendor on the floors of the great medieval cathedrals such as Chartres and Amiens in France. The current re-emergence of the labyrinth as a tool for worship reflects the renewal of the Christian mythos, for the circular journey through the spirals of the labyrinth helps us connect at a deep level with Sophia and our eros nature. This process of "walking meditation" is similar to the sacred dance in that the physical body is the means to achieve union with the Divine. In fact, these practices were often combined in the past as people danced their way through the labyrinth. These ancient uses of the labyrinth for dance, procession, and ritual can be adapted by those who are creating new forms of worship on the Path of ChristoSophia. One such trailblazer is Lauren Artress, who has dedicated herself to the recovery of this hidden Christian tradition. The labyrinth, which symbolized the actual practice of Christian pilgrimage in the Middle Ages, also provides us today with a concrete way of enacting the symbolic journey of the soul.

Prayer and ritual which celebrate the sacredness of everyday life, the home, and the family – all in the domain of the feminine – are also vital aspects of worship on the Path of ChristoSophia. The purpose of the renewed Christian mythos is to achieve wholeness – the wholeness of humans and the natural world, and the wholeness of spirituality and everyday life – by lifting the world of nature and mundane life into the realm of the sacred. Our best guides to follow for attaining this holistic perception are the Celtic Christians, who acknowledged God's presence in every place and in all activities. We can emulate their performance of rituals and prayers throughout the day in which they invoked divine blessing on all of their everyday activities such as working, eating, sleeping, and traveling. We can also practice this daily devotion of the Celtic Christians by conducting simple rituals such as lighting a candle, repeating a Bible verse, or saying a prayer as we engage in our everyday activities. Creating these moments of "sacred time" throughout the day helps us remember that **every** moment is sacred. Likewise, we can follow the example of the Celtic Christians in honoring the home – the foundation of daily life – as sacred. No matter how humble their dwelling, the early Celts recognized it as the abode of unseen spirits which Christians later perceived as the company of Heaven who also dwelt with them on Earth. For the Celts the hearth was an especially sacred place, and many prayers still exist for kindling and smooring (banking) the fire. A modern fireplace can serve a similar function in creating a sacred center within the home. Even without a fireplace, "sacred space" can be created any place within the home. A small shelf which holds a candle and meaningful spiritual artifacts can serve as an altar in any room and become a center for prayer, meditation, and ritual within the home. Such areas of "sacred space" within the home can serve to constantly remind us of the sacredness of **every** place.

Worship of the Divine in the places of daily life also extends to the natural world around us. In addition to the intimate spirituality which the Celtic Christians practiced in the home, they also often worshipped out of doors rather than in a church building. Rituals at outdoor shrines, devotions at the high crosses which marked the landscape, and pilgrimages to sacred natural places such as wells, streams, and mountains, were all adaptations of the spiritual practices of their pagan ancestors. The Celtic Christians retained the spirit of the pagan Celts who perceived the Divine in all things; therefore, it was natural for them to worship the immanent God in nature. Thomas Moore refers to paganism as "the soul's natural religion"[18] and states that "the problem with churches and temples as the only places of religion is that they tend to be merely spiritual, and they don't speak directly to the soul."[19] Christianity has in general emphasized the realm of the spirit by revering only the transcendent God, and this attitude is reflected in the church building that takes us away from the outer world in order to worship. On the Path of ChristoSophia worship instead celebrates the immanent as well as the transcendent deity, and so reconciles Christian tradition with elements of pagan religion that satisfy the soul. For help in this task we can look to those Christians in such places as Iona and Ballintubber Abbey who are blazing the trails today by preserving and revivifying the worship practices of their Celtic heritage.

It is essential to restore the Earth wisdom of pagan cultures through meaningful rituals in order to develop a truly ecological spirituality. One of the ways that we can do this is to return to the celebration of the seasonal festivals which mark the turning points of the year. The ancient Celts marked the cycle of the year with eight sacred celebrations. The solar festivals of the solstices and equinoxes held great symbolic importance as the light of the Sun alternately diminished and increased throughout the year. Some of the remnants of these pagan symbolic associations can be seen in the date of Christmas which is close to the Winter Solstice, marking the birth of the Sun in the darkest time of the year, and the date of Easter which is close to the Vernal Equinox, marking the beginning of the Sun's ascendancy over the darkness. The Celtic lunar festivals were held at the midpoint between the equinox and solstice: Samhain on November 1; Imbolc on February 1; Beltane on May 1; Lugnasadh on August 1. Several Christian festivals have also derived from them, such as All Saints' Day on November 1 and Candlemas on February 1. Retrieving the earlier pagan associations of these "holy days" can deepen their meaning for us, and celebrating the ancient solar and lunar festivals can bring about a creative blending of Christian and pagan traditions. For example, Samhain marks the Celtic Feast of the Dead when the gates are open to the Otherworld; in a Christian context, All Saints' Day provides an opportunity to celebrate spiritual intimacy with the company of Heaven in the manner of the Celtic Christians. The Celtic festival of Imbolc which marks the first return of the light and honors the Goddess Brighid was later transposed into the Christian Candlemas which honors the Divine Feminine as St. Bridget. Beltane is the ancient festival of Spring which celebrates the archetypal union of the Goddess and the Green Man that insures the fertility of the land. In Celtic lands the union of feminine and masculine was represented in many forms such as Maid Marian and Robin Hood, and today can be seen as the union of Sophia and Christ. Lughnasadh celebrates the bringing in of the harvest at the summer's end, and in our modern world provides a special occasion to give thanks for the blessings of one's life. Blazing the trail on the Path of ChristoSophia includes creating prayers and rituals which reinterpret the ancient solar and lunar festivals through the new mythic image of ChristoSophia as the symbol for the sacredness of the natural world. When we restore the ritual significance of these festivals in our contemporary world, we will once again connect at a visceral level with the world of nature through our observation of the seasonal cycle.

On the Path of ChristoSophia we must also restore the practices of earlier peoples that venerated the Earth as a living being by honoring the spirits of nature and sacred places on the land. Nigel Pennick describes this traditional view:

> The landscape is filled with places where spirit is present. Every time we experience it, this presence encourages us to make an imaginative act that personifies the place to us. Then we perceive its qualities as a personality. This is the *anima loci*, the place-soul. When this is acknowledged and honored, ensouled sacred places come into being. Our actions enshrine the *anima loci*, bringing the unseen into physical presence.[20]

Pagan Celts perceived the soul of the place as gods and goddesses, which Celtic Christians translated into saints and demons. Regardless, the essence of the place remained the same despite different spiritual interpretations.[21] Today we may view the "anima loci" as local manifestations of Sophia as World-Soul, the spirit of the Divine which dwells in every thing in nature. Just as the Celtic Christians followed their pagan predecessors in honoring these spirits at natural sacred places such as springs, trees, rivers, and mountains, so should we learn to recognize and honor the spirits which inhabit our natural surroundings. Discovering the sacred places in our own environment requires a spiritual sensitivity that we have to relearn as modern human beings; it requires the Sophianic perception which sees the Divine in all of nature. As we develop this openness and receptivity to the spirits of nature, we begin to get a special "feeling" from certain places or may even have spiritual experiences at them. We can then commune with the spirit of the place and pay attention to images which arise through the visionary imagination. We can relate further to the "anima loci" by creating a shrine that personifies its essence. This may take any number of forms, such as a pile of special stones at the base of a tree, a statue or sacred artifact in a garden, a candle and flowers by a spring. The purpose of such nature shrines is to manifest the inner archetypal energies in the outer world. Prayers and rituals which are conducted at these shrines serve to further enhance the "anima loci," which is a form of "spiritual gardening."[22] This is an important way that we can work as co-creators with Sophia to restore *viriditas* to our world, "greening" both the human soul and the World Soul. As in all gardening, "spiritual gardening" involves a reciprocal process between human beings and the land. Earlier peoples knew how important it was for human beings and the spirits of nature to cooperate for the benefit of both. Our imaginative acts and conscious actions help to ensoul the land, bringing harmony and thus healing to the Earth. In turn, our planting and nurturing of the spiritual seed within the land brings forth the fruit of heightened consciousness, inspiration, and wholeness. Through this process of ensouling the land, we aid Sophia in her return to conscious awareness and we in turn become one with nature.

Another important aspect of this process is to restore the Celtic Christian practice of pilgrimage to sacred places, which remains a living tradition in some areas to this day. Making the "rounds" to holy places such as stone crosses, rock cairns, standing stones, springs and wells, and performing ritual observances at each "station" is still practiced in many parts of Ireland. This is another very valuable form of embodied prayer which we can model by making the "rounds" in the sacred landscape of our own surroundings. We can make a ritual circuit around nature shrines that we have created in our own yards. We can also make a journey around the sacred places that we recognize in our immediate environment such as an old tree, a rock formation, a stream, or hill. In addition, we might emulate the Celtic Christian pilgrimage to the summit of a holy mountain. Climbing any mountain with a reverent attitude is another form of walking meditation which opens us to an experience of the sacred.

Pilgrimage to holy sites in foreign lands, a supremely important spiritual practice for earlier Christians, can be reinstated today as a further means of honoring Sophia as World-Soul. Reframing our travels as pilgrimages rather than as vacation tours opens us to the spiritual illuminations and experiences that are part of the sacred journey. For example, when we make a pilgrimage to the Celtic Christian holy places of Ireland, Cornwall, Wales, and Brittany, we are imbued with the sacred energy of the place that has been ensouled through the spiritual devotions of generations of worshippers. Likewise, we can help to re-energize these sacred sites through our own prayers and rituals. Earlier peoples would bring an offering such as flowers or stones to honor the spirit guardian of a sacred place, and tie a rag or ribbon to a tree which overhangs a holy well as they made their prayers. These practices, which have never entirely died out in Celtic lands, are being restored today and are immensely valuable in resacralizing the land. Spiritual acts such as these which deepen our relationship with the "anima loci" of the sacred site are especially important at those ancient holy places on the land where the spirits are no longer recognized by most people.

This is a critical task especially for those of us who live on the North American continent, since most of the sacred areas of our own land are no longer honored. While pilgrimage to another country can be very beneficial, our primary responsibility is to help once again ensoul our native land. Native Americans, like the Celtic peoples, have always honored the land as sacred. We can gain many valuable insights regarding the sacred places and the spiritual beings of this land from our aboriginal ancestors who once inhabited the places where we now live. By integrating the Earth wisdom of our Native American forebears with the new Christian mythos we follow the example of the Celtic Christians who synthesized the wisdom of their pagan past with the new revelation of Christ.

A land such as ours which is no longer recognized as sacred is the Wasteland of the Grail myths. By restoring the ancient practices of building nature shrines and making pilgrimages which renew the sacred places of the land, we can help to return the Grail to Earth. For ultimately the energy of the Grail is the energy of the Earth; it is the energy of Life, which is the same in the supernal and the earthly realms. Trailblazers on the Path of ChristoSophia must lead the way to recognize this energy in Heaven and on Earth and to "live" this light so that Heaven and Earth meet within.

Joining Other Pilgrims on the Bypaths

Although the quest on the Path of ChristoSophia is by necessity often solitary, we can find aid in our journey by joining others on the bypaths and forming a spiritual community. Walking with other pilgrims is of great help in coping with the dangers of the bypaths. Relationships can help keep us grounded in the outer world as we pursue the inner quest, and working with others is a primary way to overcome egocentricity. Several dedicated seekers who walk on the Path together can aid the emergence of ChristoSophia to a far greater extent than their few numbers would indicate. For Christ promised, "Where two or three are gathered in my name, I am there among them." (Matthew 18:20) Even a small group of people who gather in the name of ChristoSophia can help the Divine Masculine and Feminine to manifest.

Pilgrims on the Path of ChristoSophia form small, decentralized groups which are organized around spiritual practice, unlike the mass travelers on the interstate highway of Christianity who form groups that are organized around the institution of the Church. Because the personal spiritual journey is emphasized on the bypaths, the purpose of the spiritual community is for seekers to share their discoveries, learn from other members of the group, and support each others' individual quests. The community has to remain small in order to provide an atmosphere of intimacy so that these purposes can be fulfilled. This is in stark contrast to the organized Church which has the primary purpose of maintaining the institution; therefore, attracting increasingly greater numbers of people and bringing in more money are major goals. The epitome of this approach to Christianity is found in the huge "mega-churches" today, where ever- increasing expansion is a major function just like the continual widening of lanes on the interstate highways.

The spiritual community on the Path of ChristoSophia also differs from the traditional Church in that power is shared equally among all members. Decisions are reached through cooperation and consensus rather than by authorities in the Church hierarchy. In the spiritual community there is no distinction between leaders and followers; there are no priests or clergy, and no laypeople. Nor are there distinctions based upon gender; equal participation by men and women reflects the egalitarian union of the masculine and feminine which is emphasized in the new mythos. This approach overturns the hierarchical, patriarchal structure of the Church which was based on the model of Roman society, and allows the feminine values of sharing and cooperation to flourish.

In the spiritual community on the Path of ChristoSophia, everyone participates according to his or her own unique gifts and abilities. This form of organization empowers people to develop their own spirituality and helps avoid the ego problems which often arise among religious authority figures. The structure of the spiritual community is best represented by the circle, an ancient symbol of the feminine, rather than the masculine pyramid of the institutional Church. As we have seen, the circle is also an ideal form in which to celebrate worship on the Path of ChristoSophia, for it encourages creative participation by all members and heightens the synergistic effects of the group energy.

This type of spiritual community is not simply a "New Age" idea, but is actually the oldest form of Christianity. The Jesus movement, which was the earliest Christian community, consisted of small, informal groups of disciples who met in homes. Women often played leadership roles within these early "house churches." Even after the interstate highway of Christianity was built, small spiritual communities continued to coexist which have been the primary guardians of Christianity's hidden tradition. For example, gnostic Christian groups emphasized the individual seeker's quest for gnosis through inner experience rather than the spiritual authority of a religious hierarchy. Celtic Christians also formed small communities which emphasized individual autonomy rather than a centralized, bureaucratic Church. Women generally had more opportunity for diverse roles, especially positions of authority, within these spiritual communities than they did in the institutional Church. Our task on the Path of ChristoSophia today is to complete the work that these earlier Christian groups began by developing an authentic spiritual community composed of true individuals.

Honoring the unique spiritual quest of each individual seeker means that the spiritual community on the Path of ChristoSophia remains free of established doctrines and dogma. Prescribed systems of belief limit inner experience and thus deter the personal spiritual journey. Seekers on the Path of ChristoSophia respect each others' insights and experiences, knowing that revelation is a continuing process. However, this does not mean that every spiritual discovery is believed to be equally valid. Since one of the benefits of the spiritual community is to help its members remain grounded while engaged in inner work, each individual's spiritual experience must also be considered in the light of common sense and reason. Open-mindedness must be combined with critical thinking to assess the value of individual revelation.

The nondogmatic character of the spiritual community also does not imply a "smorgasbord" approach to spirituality in which we simply take those things that we like from a variety of religious beliefs and practices. The problem with this syncretistic approach is that it usually leaves the seeker with only a shallow and superficial experience of religious traditions that are immensely rich and deep. Once we have made a commitment to a spiritual path, it is important to follow that tradition as far as we can in order to experience its profound spiritual depths. The old tradition may be revisioned in new ways as times change and human consciousness evolves; nevertheless, the essential aspects of the tradition provide the foundation for the spiritual journey. The spiritual community on the Path of ChristoSophia recognizes the wisdom that Christianity shares with all authentic religions, and can draw inspiration from other sources such as Eastern and Native American spiritualities. Seekers on the Path of ChristoSophia do not see Christian religion as exclusive; rather, they have committed themselves to exploring Christian tradition as the framework for expressing this eternal and universal spiritual wisdom.

Sophia leads the spiritual community on the Path by transcending the limitations of dogma, for Sophia as Wisdom herself cannot be confined to any religious tradition or form. Unfortunately, there are some who argue today about whether Sophia is to be found in Christ or in the Virgin Mary, whether she is an emanation of God or a Goddess in her own right. But as the feminine face of the godhead, Sophia cannot be limited by logos conceptualization or classification. She has the important function of showing the connections and realizing the whole – transcending all dualities, dichotomies, and fragmented thinking. The spiritual community on the Path of ChristoSophia recognizes that Sophia expresses the universal archetype of the Great Goddess in a manner consistent with, but not limited to, Christian tradition.

Sophia brings the vision of the Grail which is the truth that each authentic religion attempts to express; it is the perennial wisdom, the essence of all true religions. But each religious tradition is an incomplete embodiment of the Grail, for the Grail is too vast to be encapsulated by any form of doctrine or symbol. Those who have experienced the Grail within know that this is true and therefore can honor different manifestations of the Grail Truth as it appears in various religions. This is not a syncretistic approach to religion, but a recognition that all the world's authentic religions reveal different facets of the one Grail. This recognition is the basis for the spiritual community on the Path of ChristoSophia which supports each person's search for the wisdom of the Grail, with the understanding that the search is never over and wisdom is never complete.

This is the reason that we must join other pilgrims and share the stories of our own personal journeys on the Path of ChristoSophia. As we weave together all of our spiritual experiences, insights, and images, like individual threads, we are creating the tapestry through which the new mythos will be revealed. As the Christian mythos originally developed within the small groups of early Christians who joined together to share their faith in the first centuries after Christ's death and resurrection, so the renewal of the Christian mythos in our modern era will take place within the spiritual community on the Path of ChristoSophia. It is here that Sophia will return in her full power and join with Christ in the sacred wedding that reunites the feminine and the masculine.

The ultimate task of the spiritual community is to aid the birth of ChristoSophia within the human heart and the realization of the heavenly kingdom on Earth. Although this seems to be a completely daunting task, it does not need to be accomplished by human beings alone. The earthly community receives help in this task from the beings of the spiritual realm that Christians have often referred to as the "company of Heaven" or the "communion of saints." Like the Celtic Christians, we too can be aware of the unseen spirits that surround us and invoke their aid in the enormous task that lies before us. In this way the spiritual community on Earth can consciously work with the community of Heaven to create the transformation that our culture so desperately needs.

This transformation must begin within the spiritual community itself. This means that seekers on the Path of ChristoSophia must attempt to realize the ideal of a spiritual community on Earth that mirrors the community of Heaven. This is a true "community of spirit" in which all live together with Christ and Sophia in the fullness of love and harmony. In this image of the community of Heaven we find the model for the true spiritual community and the ideal of a spiritually evolved humanity. This condition can only be realized when each individual's quest leads to a recognition of the deep Self that is rooted in the Divine and shared by all human beings. With this awareness comes the loosening of the ego barriers that separate us from each other, so that a loving community of authentic individuals can develop. This insight also brings the realization that while we are embodied in the earthly realm, our deep Selves are also living in the heavenly realm. Those in the spiritual community who gain this understanding then realize their oneness with the community of Heaven and comprehend the true significance of their task as co-workers with the "company of Heaven."

These insights are much further developed in the remarkable spiritual visions of Daniel Andreev, the 20th century Russian Christian mystic whose description of the multiple planes of existence is recorded in his book *The Rose of the World*. For Andreev, each plane is a material world that differs according to its dimensions and time streams.[23] His complex, mystical cosmology goes far beyond the simple, traditional view of Heaven and Hell, and is consistent with the contemporary view in theoretical physics that hypothesizes the existence of "parallel universes." Andreev's vision of the coming birth of the Divine Feminine provides a possible model for the new myth that is needed to renew Christian spirituality in our time. He states:

> A mysterious event is taking place in the metahistory
> of contemporary times: new divine-creative energy is
> emanating...Zventa-Sventana we call Her, She Who is the
> Brightest and All-Good, the expression of the Feminine
> Hypostasis of the Trinity...Her birth will be mirrored in our
> history as...the founding of the Rose of the World.[24]

This foretelling of the appearance of Zventa-Sventana echoes the prophecy that the Second Coming will in fact take the form of a Divine Woman – Sophia in our terminology. Her advent will bring forth the blossoming of the "Rose of the World," the future pan-religion that treasures the truth of each authentic religion as "a precious jewel belonging to all humanity."[25] In Andreev's beautiful vision, all the religions of Light will form the petals of the flower that is known as the Rose of the World. Instead of viewing religious differences as the source for judgment and hatred, we will instead honor the various truths to be found in the diversity of humanity's religions, and unite as we follow our own individual religious paths in seeking the higher spiritual Truth to which each authentic religion can lead us. Andreev describes the Rose of the World as the "amalgamation of all religions of Light in order to focus their combined energies on fostering humanity's spiritual growth and on spiritualizing nature.

Co-belief with all peoples in their highest ideals – that is what its wisdom will teach."[26] As the Rose of the World blossoms, humanity will fulfill its evolutionary purpose of transformation into a state of peace, love, and harmony. This is how the Second Coming of Christ appears in the new mythos: as ChristoSophia – Divine Love and Divine Wisdom – arises within the human heart, the Rose blossoms in the heart of humanity.

Completing the Journey

Those seekers who walk on the bypaths can aid the realization of this new mythos, for the Path of ChristoSophia is the path with a heart; it is on this path that we may discover the eros treasures of Christianity's hidden tradition. Jesus himself used the image of the heart to refer to "an internal transformation brought about by a deep centering in God."[27] The journey on the Path of ChristoSophia leads to this "internal transformation" which is the true essence of Christianity. The path with a heart does not follow the linear course of masculine consciousness, but instead it circles through the labyrinthine spiral of the feminine. Like the labyrinth, the Path of ChristoSophia leads inward to the center of the soul as well as outward to the world of all creation. At the center of this labyrinthine path, where the central Mystery is found, is the Loving Wisdom of ChristoSophia. This is the mystery of the inner transformation that lies at the center of the path and in the heart of the seeker. It is through this center that we may re-enter the garden of Paradise, and recover the pearl of wholeness in the heart that has been transformed by the journey.

Like the intertwining patterns of Celtic knotwork, the Path of ChristoSophia weaves together the feminine, nature, and mystical bypaths; it unites the Earth wisdom of our ancestors with Christian tradition. And like the continuous coils of the Celtic knot, there is no fixed end point to the spiraling journey. For on the Path of ChristoSophia, the path and the goal are the same. When one completes the journey to the still point at the center, then one may find this wisdom of Sophia:

One searches on the bypaths
 for what is already found;

The quest lies in uncovering
 that which has always been there;

And in asking the question
 which has already been answered;

When one truly understands this,
 then one has found Wisdom.

ENDNOTES

NOTES FOR PREFACE

1. Carlos Castaneda, *The Teachings of Don Juan: A Yaqui Way of Knowledge* (New York: Pocket Books, 1974), p. 11.

NOTES FOR CHAPTER ONE

1. Carl Jung, *Modern Man in Search of a Soul* (New York: Harcourt Brace Jovanovich, 1933), p. 218.
2. Riane Eisler, *The Chalice and the Blade* (San Francisco: Harper San Francisco, 1987), p. xvii.
3. Denise L. Carmody and John T. Carmody, *Mysticism* (New York: Oxford University Press, 1996), p. 10.
4. Carl Jung, *The Secret of the Golden Flower: Commentary* (New York: Harcourt Brace Jovanovich, 1962), p. 118.
5. *"Millennium: An Ecology of the Mind"* PBS Video, Biniman Productions Limited, 1992.
6. Carl Jung, *Man and His Symbols* (New York: Dell Publishing Company, 1968), pp. 59; 87.
7. Elaine Pagels, *Adam, Eve and the Serpent* (New York: Vintage Books, 1989), p. 152.
8. Isabel Florence Hapgood, *Service Book of the Holy Orthodox-Catholic Apostolic Church* (New York: Syrian Antiochian Orthodox Archdiocese, 1965), p. 100.

9. Willis Barnstone, *The Other Bible* (San Francisco: Harper & Row, 1984), p. xix.

10. Margaret Starbird, *The Woman With the Alabaster Jar* (Santa Fe: Bear & Company, 1993), p. 66.

11. Martin Palmer, *Living Christianity* (Rockport, Massachusetts: Element Books, 1993), p. 10.

12. Gregory Bateson, *Mind and Nature: A Necessary Unity* (New York: E. P. Dutton, 1979), p. 17.

13. Arthur Versluis, *TheoSophia* (Hudson, New York: Lindisfarne Press, 1994), p. 11.

14. Jean Houston, *Godseed: The Journey of Christ* (Wheaton, Illinois: Quest Books, 1992), p. 126.

15. Houston, p. 164.

16. Carl Jung, *Aion: Researches into the Phenomenology of the Self* (New York: Pantheon Books, 1959), pp. 37; 39.

17. Emma Jung and Marie-Louise von Franz, *The Grail Legend* (Boston: Sigo Press, 1980), p. 156.

18. Carl Jung, *The Secret of the Golden Flower: Commentary*, p. 83.

19. Thomas Moore, *Care of the Soul* (New York: HarperCollins, 1992), p. 212.

20. Moore, p. 212.

21. Starbird, p. 73.

22. Jean Houston, *A Mythic Life* (New York: HarperCollins, 1996), p. 101.

23. Thomas Berry, *The Dream of the Earth* (San Francisco: Sierra Club Books, 1990), pp. 116-117.

24. Carl Jung, *Modern Man in Search of a Soul*, p. 204.

25. Carl Jung, *The Undiscovered Self* (New York: Mentor Books, 1957), p. 123.

26. Elaine Pagels, *Adam, Eve and the Serpent,* p. 64.

27. Joseph Campbell, *Myths to Live By* (New York: Bantam Books, 1972), pp. 261-2.

28. Matthew Fox, *The Coming of the Cosmic Christ* (San Francisco: Harper San Francisco, 1988), pp. 7-8.

29. Fox, p. 92.

30. Fritjof Capra and David Steindl-Rast, *Belonging to the Universe* (San Francisco: Harper San Francisco, 1991), pp. xi-xv.

NOTES FOR CHAPTER TWO

1. Susan Cole, Marian Ronan and Hal Taussig, *Wisdom's Feast: Sophia in Study and Celebration* (Kansas City: Sheed & Ward, 1996), p. 6.
2. Ann Belford Ulanov, *The Feminine in Jungian Psychology and in Christian Theology* (Evanston: Northwestern University Press, 1971), p. 304.
3. Riane Eisler, *The Chalice and the Blade* (New York: Harper Collins Publishers, 1988), p. 120.
4. Susan Haskins, *Mary Magdalen: Myth and Metaphor* (New York: Harcourt Brace and Company, 1993), p. 30.
5. Karen Jo Torjesen, *When Women Were Priests* (San Francisco: HarperSanFrancisco, 1993), p. 5.
6. Colleen Murphy, "Women and the Bible," *The Atlantic Monthly* (Aug. 1993): pp. 45; 60.
7. Margaret Starbird, *The Woman With the Alabaster Jar: Mary Magdalene and the Holy Grail* (Santa Fe: Bear & Co. Publishing, 1993), p. xix.
8. Torjesen, p. 114.
9. Torjesen, p. 38.
10. Torjesen, pp. 156-7.
11. Elaine Pagels, *Adam, Eve, and the Serpent* (New York: Vintage Books, 1989), pp. 99, 143.
12. Pagels, p. 125.
13. Mary Condren, *The Serpent and the Goddess: Women, Religion, and Power in Celtic Ireland* (New York: HarperCollins Publishers, 1989), p. 17.
14. Condren, p. 97.
15. Condren, p. 165-177.
16. Torjeson, p. 234.
17. Condren, p. 180.
18. Condren, p. x.
19. Erich Neumann, *The Great Mother* (Princeton: Princeton University Press, 1963), p.3.

20. Joan Engelsman, *The Feminine Dimension of the Divine* (Philadelphia: The Westminster Press, 1979), pp. 154-156.
21. Torjesen, p. 211.
22. Mary Daly, *Beyond God the Father* (Boston: Beacon Press, 1973), p. 19.
23. Engelsman, p. 156.
24. James M. Robinson, "Very Goddess and Very Man: Jesus' Better Self," *Images of the Feminine in Gnosticism*, ed. Karen L. King (Philadelphia: Fortress Press, 1988), p. 123.
25. Murphy, p. 41.
26. Elisabeth Schussler Fiorenza, *In Memory of Her* (New York: Crossroad, 1992), p. 12-13.
27. Fiorenza, p. 55.
28. Fiorenza, p. 56.
29. Fiorenza, p. 41.
30. Fiorenza, p. 53.
31. Fiorenza, p. 52.
32. Fiorenza, p. 56.
33. Ann Belford Ulanov, *The Female Ancestors of Christ* (Boston: Shambhala, 1993), p. 90.
34. Ulanov, p. 29.
35. Ulanov, p. 43.
36. Ulanov, p. 52.
37. Ulanov, p. 69.
38. Ulanov, p. 91.
39. Miriam Therese Winter, *WomanWord* (New York: Crossroad, 1992), p. xiii.
40. Winter, p. 163.
41. Winter, p. 187.
42. Winter, p. 224.
43. Winter, p. 28.
44. Winter, p. 29.
45. Elisabeth Schussler Fiorenza, "In Search of Women's Heritage," *Weaving the Visions: New Patterns in Feminist Spirituality*, ed. Judith Plaskow and Carol P. Christ (San Francisco: Harper & Row, 1989), p. 35.
46. Torjesen, p. 33.

47. Haskins, p. 10-11.
48. Fiorenza, "In Search of Women's Heritage,", p. 35.
49. Fiorenza, *In Memory of Her*, p. 54-55.
50. Torjesen, p. 5-6.
51. Torjesen, p. 33.
52. Fiorenza, *In Memory of Her,* p. 169-170.
53. Torjesen, p. 2.
54. Miriam Therese Winter, *WomanPrayer WomanSong* (New York: Crossroad, 1993), p. 7.
55. Winter, *Woman Prayer WomanSong*, p. 7.
56. Cole et. al., p. 9.
57. Phyllis Trible, *God and the Rhetoric of Sexuality* (Philadelphia: Fortress Press, 1978), p. 22.
58. Fiorenza, *In Memory of Her*, p. 44.
59. Barbara G. Walker, *The Woman's Encyclopedia of Myths and Secrets* (San Francisco: Harper & Row, 1983), p. 279.
60. Miriam Therese Winter, *WomanWisdom* (New York: Crossroad, 1993), p. xiii.
61. Winter, *WomanWisdom*, p. xiii.
62. Starbird, p. 154.
63. Julian of Norwich, *Showings*, trans. Edmund Colledge and James Walsh (New York: Paulist Press, 1978), p. 296.
64. Arthur Versluis, *TheoSophia* (Hudson, New York: Lindisfarne Press, 1994), p. 146.
65. Cole, et. al., p. 6.

NOTES FOR CHAPTER THREE

1. Erich Neumann, *The Great Mother* (Princeton: Princeton University Press, 1963), p. 331.
2. Susan Cole, Marian Ronan and Hal Taussig, *Wisdom's Feast: Sophia in Study and Celebration* (Kansas City: Sheed & Ward, 1996), p. 9.
3. Sergei Bulkagov, *Sophia: The Wisdom of God* (New York: Lindisfarne Press, 1993), p. 21.
4. Raphael Patai, *The Hebrew Goddess* (Detroit: Wayne State University Press,1967), p. 26.

5. Asphodel P. Long, *In a Chariot Drawn by Lions: The Search for the Female in Deity* (Freedom, CA: The Crossing Press, 1993), p. 137.

6. Elisabeth Schussler Fiorenza, *In Memory of Her* (New York: Crossroad, 1992), p. 133.

7. James L. Crenshaw, *The Oxford Companion to the Bible*, ed. Bruce M. Metzger and Michael D. Coogan (New York: Oxford University Press, 1993), p. 802.

8. Joan Engelsman, *The Feminine Nature of the Divine* (Philadelphia: The Westminster Press, 1979), pp. 74, 81, 83.

9. Fiorenza, p. 133.

10. Engelsman, p. 95.

11. Fiorenza, p. 190.

12. Engelsman, pp. 111-119.

13. Engelsman, pp. 107-109.

14. Elaine Pagels, *The Gnostic Gospels* (New York: Vintage Books, 1981), p. 62.

15. Samuel D. Cioran, *Vladimir Soloviev and the Knighthood of the Divine Sophia* (Ontario: Wilfrid Laurier University Press, 1979), p. 21.

16. Bulgakov, p. 35.

17. Bulgakov, p. 66.

18. Bulgakov, pp. 34, 37.

19. Long, p. 172.

20. Ean Begg, *The Cult of the Black Virgin* (New York: Penguin Books, 1985), p. 130.

21. Michael Grosso, *Visions of Mary and Psychic Evolution,* Gnosis No. 13, Fall 1989, p. 50.

22. Cole, Ronan and Taussig, p. 44.

23. Cole, Ronan and Taussig, p. 46.

24. Fiorenza, p. 133.

25. Matthew Fox, *Original Blessing* (Santa Fe: Bear & Company, 1983), p. 44.

26. Thomas Moore, *Care of the Soul* (New York: HarperCollins, 1992), p. 141.

27. J. E. Cirlot, *A Dictionary of Symbols* (London: Routledge & Kegan Paul Ltd., 1962), pp. 35-36.

28. Christopher Bamford in Bulkagov, p. xvii.
29. Cioran, p. 259.
30. Bulkagov, p. 71.
31. Carl Jung, *Two Essays on Analytical Psychology* (New York: Pantheon Books, 1953), p. 195.
32. Riane Eisler, *The Chalice and the Blade* (New York: HarperCollins, 1988), p. xvii.
33. Arthur Versluis, *TheoSophia* (New York: Lindisfarne Press, 1994), p. 61.
34. Versluis, p. 151.
35. Jean Houston, *Life Force* (Wheaton, Illinois: Quest Books, 1993), p. 38.
36. Cioran, p. 26.
37. Versluis, p. 23.
38. Cioran, p. 51.
39. Bulgakov, p. 17.
40. Fiona MacLeod, *Iona* (Edinburgh: Floris Books, 1982), p. 20.
41. Caitlin Matthews, *Sophia* (London: Mandala, 1991), p. 320.
42. Cole, Ronan and Taussig, p. 59.
43. Aurora Terrenus, *Sophia of the Bible* (Santa Cruz, CA: Celestial Communications, 1988), p. 79.
44. Cole, Ronan and Taussig, p. 96.
45. Cole, Ronan and Taussig, pp. 116-122.
46. Jann Aldredge-Clanton, *In Search of Christ-Sophia: An Inclusive Christology for Liberating Christians* (Mystic, CT: Twenty-Third Publications, 1995), p. 114.
47. Jann Aldredge-Clanton, *Praying with Christ-Sophia: Services for Healing and Renewal* (Mystic, CT: Twenty-Third Publications, 1996), p. 134.

NOTES FOR CHAPTER FOUR

1. James M. Robinson, Ed., *The Nag Hammadi Library* (San Francisco: Harper San Francisco, 1988), "The Gospel of Thomas," trans. Thomas D. Lambdin, p. 129.
2. June Singer, *The Gnostic Book of Hours: Keys to Inner Wisdom* (Harper San Francisco, 1992), p. xix.

3. Elaine Pagels, *The Gnostic Gospels* (New York: Vintage Books, 1981), p. xix.
4. Pagels, p. 155.
5. Kurt Rudolph, *Gnosis: The Nature and History of Gnosticism* (San Francisco: Harper & Row, 1987), p. 276.
6. Rudolph, p. 300.
7. Rudolph, pp. 302; 305.
8. Pagels, p. 142.
9. Hans Jonas, *The Gnostic Religion* (Boston: Beacon Press, 1963), p. 179.
10. Anne Baring and Jules Cashford, *The Myth of the Goddess: Evolution of an Image* (New York: Arkana, 1991), pp. 634; 636.
11. James M. Robinson, Ed. *The Nag Hammadi Library* (HarperSanFrancisco, 1988).
12. Singer, p. xxi.
13. Singer, p. xx.
14. Pagels, p. xx.
15. David Fideler, *Jesus Christ, Sun of God: Ancient Cosmology and Early Christian Symbolism* (Wheaton, Illinois: Quest Books, 1993), p. 131.
16. James M. Robinson, Ed., *The Nag Hammadi Library,* "The Gospel of Philip," trans. Wesley W. Isenberg, p. 150.
17. Stephan A. Hoeller, *Jung and the Lost Gospels* (Wheaton, Illinois: Quest Books, 1989), p. 87.
18. Gilles Quispel, "Gnosis and Psychology," in *The Rediscovery of Gnosticism, Vol. I*, Ed. Bentley Layton (The Netherlands: E. J. Brill, 1980), p. 22.
19. Giovanni Filoramo, *A History of Gnosticism* (Cambridge: Mass.: Basil Blackwell, 1990), trans. Anthony Alcock, p. 143.
20. Pagels, p. 38.
21. Pagels, p. 37.
22. Robinson, "The Gospel of Philip," p. 142.
23. Robinson, "The Gospel of Thomas," p. 126.
24. Pagels, p. 61.
25. Pagels, p. 59.
26. Pagels, pp. 59; 68.

27. Pagels, p. 59.
28. Jonas, pp. 180-181.
29. Baring & Cashford, p. 621.
30. Carl Jung, *Psychology and Religion: West and East* , 2cd Ed. (Princeton: Princeton University Press, 1969), p. 190.
31. Robinson, "The Apocryphon of John," p. 105.
32. Robinson, "The Gospel of the Egyptians," p. 209.
33. Robinson, "The Gospel of Philip," p. 143.
34. Robinson, "The Thunder: Perfect Mind," p. 297.
35. Robinson, "The Thunder: Perfect Mind," p. 297.
36. Robinson, "The Thunder: Perfect Mind," pp. 297-299.
37. Robinson, "The Apocryphon of John," p. 107.
38. Robinson, "The Apocryphon of John," p. 108.
39. Robinson, "The Apocryphon of John," p. 108.
40. Robinson, "Trimorphic Protennoia," p. 513.
41. Robinson, "Trimorphic Protennoia," p. 513.
42. Robinson, "Trimorphic Protennoia," p. 513.
43. Rudolph, p. 83.
44. Hoeller, p. 106.
45. Robinson, "The Exegesis on the Soul," p. 192.
46. G.R.S. Mead, *Pistis Sophia* (New York: The Theosophical Publishing Society, 1896), p. 139.
47. Rudolph, p. 154.
48. Jung, p. 29.
49. Jonas, p. 196.
50. Robinson, "The Sophia of Jesus Christ," p. 231.
51. Robinson, "The Sophia of Jesus Christ," p. 231.
52. Jonas, p. 196.
53. Jean Houston, *Godseed: The Journey of Christ* (Wheaton, Illinois: Quest Books, 1992), p. 66.
54. Robinson, "The Gospel of Philip," p. 150.
55. Robinson, "The Apocryphon of John," pp. 116-117.
56. Robinson, "The Hypostasis of the Archons," p. 164.
57. Robinson, "The Hypostasis of the Archons," p. 164.
58. Robinson, "The Hypostasis of the Archons," p. 165.
59. Robinson, "The Hypostasis of the Archons," p. 165.
60. Robinson, "The Testimony of Truth," p. 455.

61. Mary Condren, *The Serpent and the Goddess: Women, Religion, and Power in Celtic Ireland* (San Francisco: HarperCollins, 1989), p. 8.

62. Robinson, "The Gospel of Philip," p. 151.

63. Robinson, "The Gospel of Philip," p. 145.

64. Susan Haskins, *Mary Magdalen: Myth and Metaphor* (New York: Harcourt Brace & Co., 1993), p. 40.

65. Robinson, "The Gospel of Philip," p. 148.

66. Robinson, "The Dialogue of the Savior," p. 252.

67. Robinson, "The Gospel of Mary," p. 525.

68. Robinson, "The Gospel of Mary," p. 525.

69. Robinson, "The Gospel of Mary," p. 526.

70. Karen L. King, "Introduction to the Gospel of Mary," *Nag Hammadi Library,* p. 524.

71. Robinson, "The Gospel of Mary," p. 526.

72. Robinson, "The Gospel of Mary," p. 527.

73. Ean Begg, *The Cult of the Black Virgin* (London: Penguin Books, 1985), p. 129.

74. Baring & Cashford, p. 597.

75. Pagels, p. 16.

76. Baring & Cashford, p. 633.

77. Baring & Cashford, p. 632.

78. Robinson, "The Thought of Norea," p. 446.

79. Singer, p. 97.

80. Haskins, p. 34.

81. Pagels, p. 72.

82. Rudolph, p. 211.

83. Tertullian, *De praescriptione* 41. 2-6, cited in Filoramo, p. 173.

84. Haskins, pp. 392-393.

85. Pagels, p. 72.

86. Rudolph, p. 271.

87. Robinson, "The Gospel of Philip," p. 151.

88. Robinson, "The Gospel of Philip," p. 151.

89. Jung, p. 397.

90. Robinson, "The Gospel of Philip," p. 152.

91. Hoeller, p. 207.

92. Rudolph, p. 245.

93. Robinson, "The Gospel of Philip," p. 160.

94. Robinson, "The Gospel of Philip," p. 154.

95. Rudolph, p. 230.

96. Rudolph, p. 241.

97. Robinson, "The Gospel of Philip," p. 144.

98. Cited in Rudolph, p. 242.

99. Rudolph, p. 242.

100. Jung, p. 276.

101. Edgar Hennecke, *New Testament Apocrypha, Vol. Two* (Philadelphia: The Westminster Press, 1964), "Acts of John," p. 230.

102. Jung, p. 276.

103. Hennecke, "Acts of John," pp. 228-229.

104. Jung, p. 280.

105. Hennecke, "Acts of John," p. 230.

106. Rudolph, p. 251.

107. Elaine Pagels, *Adam, Eve and the Serpent* (New York: Vintage Books, 1989), p. 59.

108. Hoeller, p. 233.

109. Pagels, *The Gnostic Gospels*, p. 168.

NOTES FOR CHAPTER FIVE

1. Thomas Berry, *The Dream of the Earth* (San Francisco: Sierra Club Books, 1990), p. 81.

2. Rosemary Radford Ruether, *Gaia & God: An Ecofeminist Theology of Earth Healing* (San Francisco: HarperSanFrancisco, 1992), p. 205.

3. Ruether, p. 3.

4. Ruether, p. 207.

5. Bruce M. Metzger and Roland E. Murphy, ed., *The New Oxford Annotated Bible* (New York: Oxford University Press, 1991), p. 3.

6. Denis Edwards, *Jesus the Wisdom of God: An Ecological Theology* (Maryknoll, New York: Orbis Books, 1995), p. 69.

7. Edwards, p. 78.

8. Edwards, p. 82.

9. Edwards, pp. 75-76.
10. Ruether, p. 229.
11. Edwards, p. 137.
12. Ruether, p. 127.
13. Ruether, pp. 128-132.
14. Elaine Pagels, *Adam, Eve and the Serpent* (New York: Vintage Books, 1988), pp. 130-133.
15. Ruether, p. 137.
16. Matthew Fox, *The Coming of the Cosmic Christ* (San Francisco: HarperSan Francisco, 1988), p. 109.
17. Barbara Newman, *Sister of Wisdom: St. Hildegard's Theology of the Feminine* (Berkeley & Los Angeles: University of California Press, 1987), p. 42.
18. Fritjof Capra, *The Turning Point: Science, Society, and the Rising Culture* (New York: Bantam Books, 1982), p. 53.
19. Ruether, p. 237.
20. Barbara Newman, "Introduction," *Hildegard of Bingen Scivias,* trans. Mother Columba Hart and Jane Bishop (Mahwah, NJ: Paulist Press, 1990), p.10.
21. Newman, "Introduction," p.11.
22. Newman, *Sister of Wisdom,* p. 21.
23. Newman, "Introduction," p. 14.
24. Newman, "Introduction," p. 14.
25. Newman, *Sister of Wisdom,* p. xvii-xviii.
26. Newman, *Sister of Wisdom,* p. 69-70.
27. Newman, *Sister of Wisdom,* p. 65.
28. Newman, "Introduction," p. 16.
29. Hildegard of Bingen, *Scivias,* trans. Mother Columba Hart and Jane Bishop (Mahwah, NJ: Paulist Press, 1990), p. 36.
30. Erich Neumann, *The Great Mother* (Princeton: Princeton University Press, 1972), p. 328.
31. Matthew Fox, *Illuminations of Hildegard of Bingen* (Santa Fe: Bear & Co., 1985), p. 36.
32. Fox, p. 36.
33. Hildegard of Bingen, p. 94.
34. Hildegard of Bingen, p. 93.
35. Hildegard of Bingen, pp. 94; 96.

36. Fox, p. 30.
37. Fox, p. 32.
38. Lauren Artress, *Walking A Sacred Path: Rediscovering the Labyrinth as a Sacred Tool* (New York: Riverhead Books, 1995), p. 15.
39. Hildegard of Bingen, pp. 465-466.
40. Hildegard of Bingen, p. 465.
41. Newman, *Sister of Wisdom*, p. 49.
42. Thomas of Celano, *St. Francis of Assisi,* trans. Placid Hermann (Chicago, Illinois: Franciscan Herald Press, 1988), p. 72.
43. Thomas of Celano, pp. 69; 72; 270.
44. Thomas of Celano, pp. 55-56; 71-72; 270.
45. Thomas of Celano, pp. 54; 72.
46. Thomas of Celano, p. 73.
47. Thomas of Celano, pp. 55-56; 274; 321.
48. Francis of Assisi, *Francis and Clare: The Complete Works*, trans. Regis J. Armstrong and Ignatius C. Brady (New York: Paulist Press, 1982), p. 38-39.
49. Matthew Fox, *The Coming of the Cosmic Christ* (San Francisco: HarperSanFrancisco, 1988), p. 113.
50. Thomas of Celano, p. 270.
51. Regis J. Arnstrong and Ignatius C. Brady, "Introduction," *Francis and Clare: The Complete Works* (New York: Paulist Press, 1982), p. 16.
52. Ruether, p. 192.
53. Nigel Pennick, *Celtic Sacred Landscape* (New York: Thames & Hudson, 1996), p. 177.
54. Capra, p. 54.
55. Mathews, Nieves H. De Madariaga, *Francis Bacon, Slave-Driver or Servant of Nature?,* 22 Dec. 2004 <http://www.sirbacon.org/mathewsessay.htm>
56. Rene Descartes, *Discourse on Method and Meditations*, trans. L. J. Lafleur (New York: The Bobbs-Merrill Company, 1060), p. 24.
57. Capra, p. 60.
58. Capra, pp. 61-62.
59. Capra, p. 66.

60. Thomas Berry, *The Dream of the Earth* (San Francisco, California: Sierra Club Books, 1988), p. 16.
61. Capra, p. 15.
62. Capra, p. 47.
63. George S. Viereck, "What Life Means to Einstein," *Saturday Evening Post* (26 Oct. 1929): p. 117.
64. Ruether, p. 249.
65. Capra, p. 47.
66. Fritjof Capra, *The Tao of Physics: An Exploration of the Parallels Between Modern Physics and Eastern Mysticism* (Berkeley: Shambhala, 1975), p. 18.
67. Freeman Dyson, *Disturbing the Universe* (New York: Harper & Row, 1979), p. 252.
68. Capra, *The Turning Point*, p. 265.
69. James Gleick, *Chaos: Making a New Science* (New York: Viking, 1987), p. 114.
70. J. E. Lovelock, *Gaia: A New Look at Life on Earth* (Oxford: Oxford University Press, 1987), pp. 11-12.
71. Capra, *The Turning Point*, p. 304.
72. Pierre Teilhard de Chardin, *The Phenomenon of Man* (New York: Harper & Row, 1959), p. 258.
73. Teilhard de Chardin, p. 151.
74. Teilhard de Chardin, p. 181.
75. Teilhard de Chardin, p. 259.
76. Teilhard de Chardin, pp. 293-294.
77. Teilhard de Chardin, pp. 264-265.
78. Teilhard de Chardin, p. 297.
79. Brian Swimme and Thomas Berry, *The Universe Story* (New York: HarperCollins, 1992), p. 2.
80. Swimme and Berry, p. 5.
81. Thomas Berry, *The Dream of the Earth,* p. 81.
82. Berry, p. 81.
83. Swimme and Berry, pp. 15; 245.
84. Berry, p. 21.
85. Swimme and Berry, p. 220.
86. Matthew Fox, *Original Blessing* (Santa Fe, N.M.: Bear & Co., 1983), p. 11.

87. Fox, p. 12.
88. Fox, pp. 37-49.
89. Fox, p. 90.
90. Matthew Fox, *The Coming of the Cosmic Christ* (San Francisco: Harper, 1988), p. 8.
91. Fox, *The Coming of the Cosmic Christ*, p. 7.
92. Fox, *Original Blessing*, p. 18.
93. Fox, *The Coming of the Cosmic Christ*, p. 145.
94. Anthony Duncan, *The Lord of the Dance* (Toddington, Glos.: Helios Books, 1972), p. 9.

NOTES FOR CHAPTER SIX

1. Quoted in Christopher Bamford and Wm. Parker Marsh, *Celtic Christianity: Ecology and Holiness* (Hudson, NY: Lindisfarne Press, 1982), p. 70.
2. Bamford and Marsh, p. 2.
3. Bamford and Marsh, p. 6.
4. John T. MacNeill, *The Celtic Churches: A.D. 200 to 1200* (Chicago: University of Chicago Press, 1974), p. 10.
5. MacNeill, p. 17.
6. MacNeill, p. 16.
7. MacNeill, p. 18.
8. James F. Kenney, *The Sources for the Early History of Ireland: Ecclesiastical* (York: Octogon Books, 1966), p. 171.
9. Bamford and Marsh, p. 17.
10. Caitlin Matthews, *The Celtic Tradition* (Longmead: Element Books Ltd., 1989), p. 35.
11. Shirley Toulsen, *The Celtic Alternative: A Reminder of the Christianity We Lost* (London: Rider Books, 1987), p. 2.
12. Bamford and Marsh, p. 11.
13. Edward C. Sellner, *Wisdom of the Celtic Saints* (Notre Dame, Indiana: Ave Maria Press, 1993), p. 22.
14. Quoted in Iain MacDonald, ed. *Saint Patrick* (Edinburgh: Floris Books, 1992), p. 58.
15. Robin Flower, *The Irish Tradition* (Oxford: Clarendon Press, 1947), p. 42.
16. Flower, p. 54.

17. Flower, p. 61.
18. Flower, p. 61
19. Flower, p.63.
20. Flower, p. 63
21. Alexander Carmichael, *Carmina Gadelica*, (Hudson, NY: Lindisfarne Press, 1992), p. 105.
22. Quoted in Bamford & Marsh, p. 19.
23. Quoted in Oliver Davies and Fiona Bowie, eds. *Celtic Christian Spirituality* (New York: Continuum Publishing Co., 1995), p. 43.
24. John Scotus Eriugena, *The Voice of the Eagle*, trans. Christopher Bamford (Hudson, NY: Lindisfarne Press, 1990), p. 37.
25. Eriugena, p. 82.
26. Eriugena, p. 83.
27. Flower, p.42
28. Iain MacDonald, ed. *Saint Brendan* (Edinburgh: Floris Books, 1992), p. 47.
29. Iain MacDonald, ed. *Saint Columba* (Edinburgh: Floris Books, 1992), p. 37
30. Kenneth Hurlstone Jackson, *A Celtic Miscellany* (London: Penguin Books, 1971), p. 279.
31. Miranda Green, *Celtic Goddesses* (New York: George Braziller, 1996), pp.199-200.
32. Iain MacDonald, ed. *Saint Bride* (Edinburgh: Floris Books, 1992), p. 33.
33. Iain MacDonald, ed. *Saint Bride* (Edinburgh: Floris Books, 1992), p. 10.
34. Toulsen, p. 124.
35. Toulson, p. 126.
36. Alexander Carmichael, *Celtic Invocations: Selections from Volume I of Carmina Gadelica* (Noroton, Conn.: Vineyard Books, 1972), p. 577.
37. Carmichael, p. 194.
38. Toulsen, p. 132.
39. Toulsen, p. 126.
40. Toulsen, p. 126.

41. James M. Robinson, gen.ed. *The Nag Hammadi Library in English,* rev. ed., (San Francisco: HarperSanFrancisco, 1988), p. 135.

42. Michael Herity, *Gleanncholmcille* (Dublin: Elo Press Ltd., 1933), p. 17.

43. Herity, p. 17.

44. Michael Dames, *Mythic Ireland* (London: Thames & Hudson, 1992), p. 167.

45. Harry Hughes, *Croagh Patrick* (Westport: Harry Hughes, 1991), p. 8.

NOTES FOR CHAPTER SEVEN

1. Quoted in Carl Jung, *Mysterium Coniunctionis* (Princeton, N.J.: Princeton University Press, 1974), p. 113.

2. William Anderson, *Green Man: The Archetype of Our Oneness With the Earth* (San Francisco: HarperSanFrancisco, 1990), p. 33.

3. Caitlin & John Matthews, *The Western Way,* v. 1 (London: Arkana , 1985), p. 36.

4. Ronald Hutton, *The Pagan Religions of the Ancient British Isles* (Oxford: Basil Blackwell, Ltd., 1991), p. 166.

5. Anderson, p. 50.

6. Lewis Spence, *The History and Origins of Druidism* (London: Aquarian Press, 1971), p. 76.

7. Sir James Frazer, *The Golden Bough*, (New York: Macmillan & Co., 1963), p. 392.

8. Frazer, p. 439.

9. Frazer, pp. 449-450.

10. Anne Baring and Jules Cashford, *The Myth of the Goddess* (London: Arkana, 1993), p. 411.

11. Baring & Cashford, p. 147.

12. Frazer, pp. 349-350.

13. Baring & Cashford, p. 211.

14. Caitlin Matthews, *Arthur and the Sovereignty of Britain* (London: Arkana, 1989), pp. 17, 20, 36.

15. C. Matthews, p. 299.

16. Baring & Cashford, p. 148.

17. Edwin O. James, *Origins of Sacrifice* (London: Kennikat Press, 1971), p. 53.
18. James, p. 63.
19. James, p. 66.
20. James, p.72.
21. Kathleen Basford, *The Green Man* (Ipswich: D. S. Brewer, 1978), plate 2a.
22. Basford, plate 2b.
23. John Matthews, *Gawain: Knight of the Goddess* (Wellingborough: Aquarian Press, 1990), p. 20.
24. John Matthews, *Robin Hood* (Glastonbury: Gothic Image Publications, 1993), p. 65.
25. John Matthews, *Robin Hood*, p. 3.
26. John Matthews, *Robin Hood*, p. 117.
27. Edwin O. James, *Seasonal Feasts & Festivals* (London: Thames & Hudson, 1961), p. 289.
28. Anderson, p. 46.
29. Basford, plates 6-10.
30. Stuart Piggott, *The Druids* (New York, Thames & Hudson, 1975), p. 79.
31. Anderson, p. 40, fig. 26.
32. Anderson, p. 41, figs. 27, 28.
33. Anderson, p.54.
34. Anne Ross, *Pagan Celtic Britain* (New York, Columbia University Press, 1967), p. 67.
35. Anderson, p. 56.
36. John Matthews, *Robin Hood*, p. 3.
37. Basford, p. 12, plate 14.
38. Basford, p. 12.
39. Anderson, p. 96.
40. Anderson, p. 95.
41. Anderson, p. 80.
42. Anderson, p. 81.
43. Anderson, p. 86.
44. Anderson, p. 85.
45. Robin Flower, *The Irish Tradition* (Oxford, Clarendon Press, 1947), p. 20.

46. Baring & Cashford, p. 597.
47. Baring & Cashford, p. 584.
48. Baring & Cashford, p. 592.
49. Baring & Cashford, p. 664.
50. Anderson, pp. 163-164.
51. ____ *Celebration: Christmas Fanfares & Carols* (New York: Nimbus Records, 1991), liner notes.
52. Anderson, p. 163.
53. Anderson, p. 163.

NOTES FOR CHAPTER EIGHT

1. William James, *The Varieties of Religious Experience* (New York: Simon & Schuster, 1997), p. 305.
2. Antoine de Saint-Exupery, *The Little Prince* (New York: Harcourt Brace Jovanovich, 1971), p. 70.
3. Jacob Boehme, *The Way to Christ* (New York: Paulist Press, 1978), p. 165.
4. Dan Cohn-Sherbok and Lavinia Cohn-Sherbok, *Jewish and Christian Mysticism: An Introduction* (New York: Continuum, 1994), p. 2.
5. Gerald G. May, *Will and Spirit: A Contemplative Psychology* (San Francisco: Harper & Row, 1982), p. 312.
6. Ibid., p. 262.
7. Thomas Merton, *New Seeds of Contemplation* (New York: New Directions, 1972), p. 280.
8. James, p. 306.
9. May, p. 27.
10. Bernard McGinn, *The Foundations of Mysticism* (New York: Crossroad, 1992), p. xvii.
11. Evelyn Underhill, *The Mystics of the Church* (New York: Schocken Books, 1964), p. 10.
12. Anne Baring and Jules Cashford, *The Myth of the Goddess* (New York: Penguin Books, 1993), p. 479.
13. Matthew Fox, *The Coming of the Cosmic Christ* (San Francisco: HarperSanFrancisco, 1988), p. 78.
14. Underhill, pp. 26-27.
15. May, p. 169.

16. Morton Kelsey, *The Other Side of Silence: Meditation for the Twenty-First Century* (New York: Paulist Press, 1997), p. 53.

17. Boehme, p. 36.

18. Evelyn Underhill, *Practical Mysticism* (Columbus, Ohio: Ariel Press, 1914), p. 65.

19. Saint-Exupery, p. 70.

20. Evelyn Underhill, *Practical Mysticism*, p. 91.

21. Quoted in Matthew Fox, *Original Blessing* (Santa Fe, New Mexico: Bear & Co., 1983), p. 201.

22. Merton, pp. 192-193.

23. Merton, p. 3.

24. Julian of Norwich, *Showings*, trans. Edmund Colledge and James Walsh (New York: Paulist Press, 1978), p. 280.

25. Saint John Cassian, "On the Holy Fathers of Sketis and on Discrimination," *Prayer of the Heart: Writings from the Philokalia*, ed. G. E. H. Palmer, Philip Sherrard, and Kallistos Ware (Boston: Shambhala, 1993), p. 12.

26. John Scotus Eriugena, *The Voice of the Eagle*, trans.Christopher Bamford (Hudson, NY: Lindisfarne Press, 1990), p. 82.

27. Meister Eckhart, *The Essential Sermons, Commentaries, Treatises, and Defense*, trans. Edmund Colledge and Bernard McGinn (New York: Paulist Press, 1981), p. 205.

28. Eckhart, p. 205.

29. Matthew Fox, *Original Blessing*, p. 90.

30. Fox, p. 52.

31. Julian of Norwich, p. 237.

32. Julian of Norwich, p. 186.

33. Boehme, p. 221.

34. Philip St. Romain, *Kundalini Energy and Christian Spirituality* (New York: Crossroad, 1995), p. 107.

35. Carl Jung, *Two Essays on Analytical Psychology* (Princeton: Princeton University Press, 1966), p. 291.

36. Julian of Norwich, p. 279.

37. Julian of Norwich, p. 293.

38. Kallistos Ware, *The Orthodox Way* (Crestwood, NY: St. Vladimir's Seminary Press, 1998), p. 14.

39. May, p. 240.

40. Cohn-Sherbok & Cohn-Sherbok, p. 101.
41. Archimandrite Hierotheos Vlachos, *A Night in the Desert of the Holy Mountain*, trans. Effie Mavromichali (Levadia: Birth of Theotokos Monastery, 1991), pp. 116-117.
42. Eckhart, pp. 206-207.
43. Eckhart, p. 200.
44. Merton, p. 2.
45. *The Cloud of Unknowing*, Ed. James Walsh (Ramsey, NJ: Paulist Press, 1981), p. 121.
46. *The Cloud of Unknowing*, p. 131.
47. *The Cloud of Unknowing*, p. 139.
48. St. John of the Cross, *Dark Night of the Soul*, trans. E. Allison Peers (New York: Image Books, 1990), p. 33.
49. Cohn-Sherbok & Cohn-Sherbok, p. 128.
50. Fox, *Original Blessing*, p. 130.
51. Mechtild of Magdeburg, *The Flowing Light of the Godhead* (New York: Paulist Press, 1998), p. 77.
52. May, p. 249.
53. Teresa of Avila, *The Interior Castle* (Mahwah, New Jersey: Paulist Press, 1979), p. 96.
54. Merton, p. 182.
55. Quoted in Fox, *The Coming of the Cosmic Christ,* p. 109.
56. Ware, p. 74.
57. Ware, p. 23.
58. Fox, *The Coming of the Cosmic Christ*, p. 65.
59. Eckhart, p. 187.
60. Eckhart, p. 188.
61. Eckhart, p. 198.
62. Eckhart, p. 203.
63. Eckhart, p. 207.
64. Bernard of Clairvaux, *Selected Works* (Mahwah, New Jersey: Paulist Press, 1987), p. 231.
65. Bernard of Clairvaux, p. 223.
66. Bernard of Clairvaux, p. 273.
67. Bernard of Clairvaux, p. 274.
68. Bernard of Clairvaux, p. 253.
69. Mechtild of Magdeburg, p. 44.

70. Mechtild of Magdeburg, p. 48.

71. Mechtild of Magdeburg, p. 59.

72. Mechtild of Magdeburg, p. 62.

73. Mechtild of Magdeburg, p. 62.

74. Mechtild of Magdeburg, p. 95.

75. Teresa of Avila, p. 178.

76. Boehme, p. 45.

77. Boehme, pp. 43-44.

78. Boehme, p. 70.

79. Teresa of Avila, pp. 92-93; 179.

80. Boehme, p. 165.

81. Eckhart, p. 250.

82. Merton, p. 193.

83. Eckhart, p. 59.

84. Vlachos, p. 22.

85. Boehme, p. 154.

86. Merton, p. 216.

87. Kyriacos Markides, *Riding With the Lion: In Search of Mystical Christianity* (New York: Viking, 1994), p. 353.

88. Ware, p. 115.

89. Ware, p. 123.

90. *The Way of A Pilgrim and A Pilgrim Continues His Way*, trans. Helen Bacovcin (New York: Image Books Doubleday, 1992), p. 41.

91. Vlachos, pp. 47; 107.

92. Thomas Keating, *Open Mind, Open Heart: The Contemplative Dimension of the Gospel* (New York: Continuum, 1997), p. 37.

93. Keating, p. 50.

94. Keating, p. 50; 72.

95. Keating, p. 75.

96. Kelsey, p. 176.

97. Kelsey, p. 211.

98. Kelsey p. 161.

99. Kelsey, p. 274.

100. Fox, *Original Blessing*, p. 203.

101. Fox, *Original Blessing,*, p. 175.

102. Lauren Artress, *Walking A Sacred Path: Rediscovering the Labyrinth as a Spiritual Tool* (New York: Riverhead Books, 1995), p. 136.

103. Baring and Cashford, pp. 135-137.

104. Artress, pp. 26-30.

105. Fox, *Original Blessing*, p. 247.

106. Underhill, *Practical Mysticism*, p. 187.

NOTES FOR CHAPTER NINE

1. Daniel C. Matt, *The Essential Kabbalah* (San Francisco: HarperSanFrancisco, 1996), p. 112.

2. Gershom Scholem, *On the Kabbalah and Its Symbolism* (New York: Schocken Books, 1965), p. 122.

3. Dion Fortune, *The Mystical Qabalah* (London: Ernest Benn, Ltd, 1935), p. 2.

4. Fortune, p. 4.

5. Herbert Weiner, *9 ½ Mystics: The Kabbala Today* (New York: Collier Books, 1969), p. 6.

6. Joseph Dan, "The Kabbalah of Johannes Reuchlin & Its Historical Significance" in *The Christian Kabbalah*, ed. by Joseph Dan (Cambridge, Mass.: Harvard University Library, 1997), p. 56.

7. Gershom Scholem, "The Beginnings of the Christian Kabbalah" in *The Christian Kabbalah*, ed. by Joseph Dan (Cambridge, Mass.: Harvard University Library, 1997), pp. 26-28.

8. Philip Beitchman, *Alchemy of the Word: Cabala of the Renaissance* (Albany: State University of New York Press, 1998), p. 102.

9. Chaim Wirszubski, *Pico della Mirandola's Encounter with Jewish Mysticism* (Cambridge, Mass.: Harvard University Press, 1989), p. 129.

10. Klaus Reichert, "Christian Kabbalah in the Seventeenth Century" in *The Christian Kabbalah*, ed. by Joseph Dan (Cambridge, Mass.: Harvard University Library, 1998), p. 131.

11. Quoted in Reichert, p. 133.

12. Dan, p. 81

13. Quoted in Bietchman, p. 81.

14. Fortune, p. 13.
15. Quoted in Elliot R. Wolfson, *Along the Path* (Albany: State University of New York Press, 1995), p. 71.
16. Davis & Mascetti, p. 183.
17. Matt, *The Essential Kabbalah*, p. 53.
18. Charles Poncé, *Kabbalah* (San Francisco: Straight Arrow Books, 1973), p. 96.
19. Poncé, p. 101.
20. Caitlin and John Matthews, *The Western Way, Vol. 2: The Hermetic Tradition* (London: Arkana Books, 1986), p. 91.
21. J. Ben-Schlomo, "Moses Cordovero" in *Kabbalah* by Gershom Scholem (New York: Meridian Books, 1978), p. 401.
22. Gershom Scholem, *Kabbalah* (New York: Meridian Books, 1978), p. 149.
23. Poncé, pp. 170-171.
24. Margaret Starbird, *Magdalene's Lost Legacy: Symbolic Numbers and the Sacred Union* (Rochester, Vermont: Bear & Co., 2003), p. 3.
25. Starbird, p. 3.
26. Starbird, p. 58.
27. Starbird, pp. 139; 141.
28. Poncé, p. 172.
29. Fortune, p. 58.
30. Fortune, p. 188.
31. Fortune, p. 191.
32. Daniel Matt, trans., *Zohar: The Book of Enlightenment* (New York: Paulist Press, 1983), p. 19.
33. Matt, *Zohar*, p. 19.
34. Matt, *Zohar*, p. 20.
35. Gershom Scholem, *On the Mystical Shape of the Godhead* (New York: Schocken Books, 1991), p. 141.
36. Raphael Patai, *The Hebrew Goddess* 3rd enl. ed. (Detroit: Wayne State University Press, 1990), pp. 99-100.
37. Scholem, *On the Mystical Shape of the Godhead*, p. 149.
38. Scholem, *On the Mystical Shape of the Godhead*, p. 160.
39. Matt, *Zohar*, p. 55.
40. Scholem, *On the Mystical Shape of the Godhead*, p. 164.

41. Scholem, *On the Mystical Shape of the Godhead*, p. 181.
42. Scholem, *On the Mystical Shape of the Godhead*, p. 181.
43. Scholem, *On the Mystical Shape of the Godhead*, pp. 178-180.
44. Matt, *Zohar*, p. 245.
45. Matt, *Zohar*, p. 251.
46. Anne Baring and Jules Cashford, *The Myth of the Goddess* (London: Arkana/Penguin, 1993), p. 641.
47. Gershom Scholem, *Major Trends in Jewish Mysticism* (New York: Schocken Books, 1974), p. 232.
48. Matt, *Zohar*, p. 219.
49. Matt, *Zohar*, p. 80.
50. Matt, *Zohar*, p. 132.
51. Matt, *Zohar*, p. 257.
52. Edward Hoffman, *The Way of Splendor* (Boulder, Colo.: Shambhala, 1981), pp. 83-85.
53. Hoffman, pp. 77-78.
54. Baring and Cashford, p. 640.
55. Matt, *Zohar*, p. 219.
56. Quoted in Matt, *Essential Kabbalah*, p. 97.
57. David A. Cooper, *God is a Verb* (New York: Riverhead Books, 1997), p. 29.
58. Cooper, p. 306.
59. Cooper, p. 36.
60. Aryeh Kaplan, *Meditation and Kabbalah* (York Beach, Maine: Samuel Weiser, Inc., 1985), p. 28.
61. Cooper, p. 269.
62. Kaplan, p. 64.
63. Kaplan, p. 78.
64. Kaplan, p. 80.
65. Kaplan, pp. 88-89.
66. Kaplan, p. 96
67. Kaplan, pp. 119-120.
68. Kaplan, pp. 165-166.
69. Kaplan, pp. 179-180.
70. James M. Robinson, ed. *The Nag Hammadi Library in English*, rev. ed. (San Francisco: HarperSanFrancisco, 1988), p.41.

NOTES FOR CHAPTER TEN

1. Quoted in Emma Jung and Marie-Louise Von Franz, *The Grail Legend* (Boston: Sigo Press, 1986), p. 147.
2. Jung and Von Franz, pp. 113-114.
3. Jung and Von Franz, p. 116.
4. Caitlin Matthews, *Arthur and the Sovereignty of Britain* (London: Arkana, 1989), p. 6.
5. Jung and Von Franz, p. 114.
6. Caitlin Matthews, *Sophia: Goddess of Wisdom* (London: Mandala, 1991), pp. 208-211.
7. Quoted in Caitlin Matthews, *Arthur and the Sovereignty of Britain* (London: Arkana, 1989), p. 251.
8. Jung and Von Franz, p. 104.
9. Jung and Von Franz, p. 315.
10. Jung and Von Franz, pp. 302-316.
11. Roger Sherman Loomis, *The Grail: From Celtic Myth to Christian Symbol* (Princeton: Princeton University Press, 1991), pp. 261-264.
12. Gareth Knight, *The Secret Tradition in Arthurian Legend* (Wellingborough, Great Britain: The Aquarian Press, 1983), p. 247.
13. Loomis, p. 47.
14. Jung and Von Franz, p. 77.
15. Anne Baring and Jules Cashford, *The Myth of the Goddess: Evolution of an Image* (London: Arkana, 1993), p. 653.
16. Wolfram von Eschenbach, *Parzival*, trans. A. T. Hatto (New York: Penguin Books, 1980), p. 127.
17. Loomis, p. 207.
18. Von Eschenbach, p. 387.
19. Von Eschenbach, p. 395.
20. Jung and Von Franz, p. 32.
21. P. M. Matarasso, trans. *The Quest of the Holy Grail* (New York: Penguin Books, 1969), p. 17.
22. Matarasso, p. 37.
23. Matarasso, p. 276.
24. Matarasso, p. 276.
25. Matarasso, p. 283.

26. Jung and Von Franz, p. 113.
27. C. Matthews, *Sophia: Goddess of Wisdom*, p. 213.
28. Jung and Von Franz, p. 156.
29. Erich Neumann, *The Great Mother* (Princeton: Princeton University Press, 1963), p. 326.
30. Jung and Von Franz, p. 101.
31. John Matthews, *The Elements of the Grail Tradition* (Dorset, Great Britain: Element Books, 1990), p. 54.
32. Jung and Von Franz, p. 157.
33. Jung and Von Franz, pp. 157-158.
34. James M. Robinson, ed., "The Gospel of Thomas," *The Nag Hammadi Library* (San Francisco: HarperSanFrancisco, 1988), p. 135.
35. Jung and Von Franz, pp. 130-132.
36. Jung and Von Franz, p. 98.
37. Jung and Von Franz, p. 99.
38. Jung and Von Franz, p. 133.
39. C. Matthews, *Sophia: Goddess of Wisdom*, p. 220.
40. Baring and Cashford, p. 653.
41. Robert Sardello, *Facing the World with Soul* (New York: HarperPerennial, 1994), p. 16.
42. Sardello, p. 16.
43. C. Matthews, *Sophia: Goddess of Wisdom*, p. 216.
44. Loomis, p. 211.
45. Von Eschenbach, p. 15.
46. Jung and Von Franz, p. 151.
47. J. Matthews, p. 91.
48. Baring and Cashford, p. 654.
49. Jung and Von Franz, p. 19.
50. Knight, p. 246.
51. Jung and Von Franz, p. 339.
52. Robinson, p. 138.
53. Matthew Fox, *Original Blessing* (Santa Fe, N.M.: Bear & Co., 1983), p. 49.
54. Joseph Campbell, *The Power of Myth* (New York: Doubleday, 1988), p. 197.
55. Jung and Von Franz, pp. 195-196.

56. Jung and Von Franz, p. 212.

57. C. Matthews, *Sophia: The Goddess of Wisdom*, p. 217.

58. Jung and Von Franz, pp. 343-344.

59. Baring and Cashford, p. 654.

60. Jung and Von Franz, pp. 317-322.

61. Jung and Von Franz, p. 335.

62. Jung and Von Franz, p. 324.

63. Matarasso, pp. 15-16.

64. Sardello, p. 19.

65. Matarasso, p. 283.

66. Jules Cashford, "Joseph Campbell and the Grail Myth," John Matthews, ed. *The Household of the Grail* (London: The Aquarian Press, 1990), p. 211.

67. David Spangler, *Everyday Miracles: The Inner Art of Manifestation* (New York: Bantam Books, 1996), p. 81.

68. Jung and Von Franz, p. 195.

69. Jung and Von Franz, pp. 322; 389.

70. C. Matthews, *Sophia: Goddess of Wisdom*, p. 219.

71. Jung and Von Franz, p. 104.

72. William Anderson, *The Green Man: The Archetype of Our Oneness With the Earth* (London: HarperCollins, 1990), p. 21.

73. Baring and Cashford, p. 653.

74. Anderson, p. 163.

NOTES FOR CHAPTER ELEVEN

1. Jean-Yves Leloup, *The Gospel of Mary Magdalene* (Rochester, Vermont: Inner Traditions, 2002), p. 80.

2. Andrew Harvey, *Son of Man: The Mystical Path to Christ* (New York: Jeremy P. Tarcher, 1998), p. 95.

3. Harvey, p. 60.

4. Harvey, p. 85.

5. Jacob Boehme, *The Way to Christ* (New York: Paulist Press, 1978), trans. Peter Erb, p. 53.

6. Ian Bradley, *The Celtic Way* (London: Darton, Longman and Todd Ltd, 1993), p. 45.

7. Bradley, p. 47.

8. Jann Aldredge-Clanton, *In Search of Christ-Sophia: An Inclusive Christology for Liberating Christians* (Mystic, CT: Twenty - Third Publications, 1995), pp. 56-57.

9. Matthew Fox, *Original Blessing* (Santa Fe, New Mexico: Bear & Company, 1983), p. 46.

10. Marcus J. Borg, *Meeting Jesus Again for the First Time* (New York: HarperCollins, 1995), p. 86.

11. Borg, pp. 69-70.

12. Jung, p. 181.

13. Susan Cole, Marian Ronan and Hal Taussig, *Wisdom's Feast: Sophia in Study and Celebration* (Kansas City: Sheed & Ward, 1996), p. 46.

14. Susanna Shaup, *Sophia: Aspects of the Divine Feminine* (York Beach, ME: Nicolas-Hays, Inc. 1997), p. 136.

15. Jung, p. 64.

16. Schaup, p. 212.

17. Matthew Fox, *The Coming of the Cosmic Christ* (San Francisco: HarperSanFrancisco, 1988), p. 217.

18. Thomas Moore, *The Reenchantment of Everyday Life* (New York: HarperPerennial, 1997), p. 277.

19. Moore, p. 277.

20. Nigel Pennick, *Celtic Sacred Landscapes* (New York: Thames & Hudson, 1996), p. 13.

21. Pennick, p. 9.

22. Pennick, p. 14.

23. Daniel Andreev, *The Rose of the World* (Hudson, New York: Lindisfarne Books, 1997), p. 114.

24. Andreev, p. 357.

25. Andreev, p. 53.

26. Andreev, p. 67.

27. Borg, p. 86.

SELECTED BIBLIOGRAPHY

Aldredge-Clanton, Jann. *In Search of Christ-Sophia: An Inclusive Christology for Liberating Christians*. Mystic, CT: Twenty-Third Publications, 1995.

Aldredge-Clanton, Jann. *Praying with Christ-Sophia: Services for Healing and Renewal*. Mystic, CT: Twenty-Third Publications, 1996.

Anderson, William. *Green Man: The Archetype of Our Oneness With the Earth*. San Francisco: HarperSanFrancisco, 1990.

Anonymous. *Meditations on the Tarot: A Journey Into Christian Hermeticism*. Trans. Robert Powell. New York: Jeremy P. Tarcher, 2002.

Artress, Lauren. *Walking A Sacred Path: Rediscovering the Labyrinth as a Sacred Tool*. New York: Riverhead Books, 1995.

Bamford, Christopher. *An Endless Trace: The Passionate Pursuit of Wisdom in the West*. New Platz, NY: Codhill Press, 2003.

Bamford, Christopher and Wm. Parker Marsh. *Celtic Christianity: Ecology and Holiness*. Hudson, NY: Lindisfarne Press, 1982.

433

Baring, Anne and Jules Cashford. *The Myth of the Goddess.* London: Arkana, 1993.

Basford, Kathleen. *The Green Man.* Woodbridge, Suffolk, UK: D. S. Brewer, 1996.

Begg, Ean. *The Cult of the Black Virgin.* New York: Penguin Books, 1985.

Berry, Thomas. *The Dream of the Earth.* San Francisco: Sierra Club Books, 1990.

Borg, Marcus J. *Meeting Jesus Again for the First Time.* New York: HarperCollins, 1995.

Carmichael, Edward C. *Carmina Gadelica,* Hudson, NY: Lindisfarne Press, 1992.

Cole, Susan, Marian Ronan and Hal Taussig, *Wisdom's Feast: Sophia in Study and Celebration.* Kansas City: Sheed & Ward, 1996.

Cooper, David A. *God is a Verb.* New York: Riverhead Books, 1997.

Douglas-Klotz, Neil. *The Hidden Gospel: Decoding the Spiritual Message of the Aramaic Jesus.* Wheaton, IL: Quest Books, 1999.

Eckhart, Meister. *Wandering Joy: Meister Eckhart's Mystical Philosophy.* Trans. Reiner Schürmann. Great Barrington, MA: Lindesfarne Books, 2001.

Edwards, Denis. *Jesus the Wisdom of God: An Ecological Theology.* Maryknoll, New York: Orbis Books, 1995.

Fideler, David. *Jesus Christ, Sun of God: Ancient Cosmology and Early Christian Symbolism.* Wheaton, IL: Quest Books, 1993.

Flinders, Carol Lee. *Enduring Grace: Living Portraits of Seven Women Mystics.* New York: HarperCollins, 1993.

Fortune, Dion. *The Mystical Qabalah.* London: Ernest Benn, Ltd, 1935.

Fox, Matthew. *The Coming of the Cosmic Christ.* San Francisco: HarperSanFrancisco, 1988.

Fox, Matthew. *Illuminations of Hildegard of Bingen.* Santa Fe: Bear & Co., 1985.

Fox, Matthew. *Original Blessing.* Santa Fe: Bear & Co., 1983.

Freke, Timothy and Peter Gandy. *The Jesus Mysteries.* New York: Three Rivers Press, 1999.

Freke, Timothy and Peter Gandy. *Jesus and the Lost Goddess.* New York: Three Rivers Press, 2001.

Griffiths, Bede. *Return to the Center.* Springfield, IL: Templegate, 1976.

Harvey, Andrew. *Son of Man: The Mystical Path to Christ.* New York: Jeremy P. Tarcher, 1998.

Haskins, Susan. *Mary Magdalen: Myth and Metaphor.* New York: Harcourt Brace, 1993.

Hoeller, Stephan A. *Jung and the Lost Gospels.* Wheaton, IL: Quest Books, 1989.

Houston, Jean. *Godseed: The Journey of Christ.* Wheaton, IL: Quest Books, 1992.

Jung, Carl. *Man and His Symbols.* New York: Dell Publishing Co., 1968.

Jung, Carl. *Psychology and Religion: West and East,* 2nd Ed. Princeton: Princeton University Press, 1969.

Jung, Emma and Marie-Louise Von Franz. *The Grail Legend.* Boston: Sigo Press, 1986.

Kaplan, Aryeh. *Meditation and Kabbalah.* York Beach, ME: Samuel Weiser, Inc., 1985.

Keating, Thomas. *Open Mind, Open Heart: The Contemplative Dimension of the Gospel.* New York: Continuum, 1997.

Kelsey, Thomas. *The Other Side of Silence: Meditation for the Twenty-First Century.* New York: Paulist Press, 1997.

Knight, Gareth. *A Practical Guide to Qabalistic Symbolism.* Boston: Red Wheel/Weiser, 2001.

Leloup, Jean-Yves. *The Gospel of Mary Magdalene.* Rochester, VT: Inner Traditions, 2002.

Leloup, Jean-Yves. *The Gospel of Philip: Jesus, Mary Magdelene, and the Gnosis of Sacred Union.* Rochester, VT: Inner Traditions, 2003.

Mack, Burton L. *The Lost Gospel: The Book of Q & Christian Origins.* New York, HarperCollins, 1993.

Markides, Kyriacos. *Riding With the Lion: In Search of Mystical Christianity.* New York: Viking, 1994.

Matthews, Caitlin. *Sophia.* London: Mandala, 1991.

Matthews, Caitlin and John Matthews. *Walkers Between the Worlds: The Western Tradition from Shaman to Magus.* Rochester, VT: Inner Traditions, 2004. (Revised edition of *The Western Way*)

Merton, Thomas. *New Seeds of Contemplation.* New York: New Directions, 1972.

Moore, Thomas. *Care of the Soul.* New York: HarperCollins, 1992.

Newman, Barbara. *Sister of Wisdom: St. Hildegard's Theology of the Feminine.* Berkeley & Los Angeles: University of California Press, 1987.

Pagels, Elaine. *Adam, Eve and the Serpent.* New York: Vintage Books, 1989.

Pagels, Elaine, *Beyond Belief: The Secret Gospel of Thomas.* New York: Random House, 2003.

Pagels, Elaine. *The Gnostic Gospels.* New York: Vintage Books, 1981.

Robinson, James M., Ed. *The Nag Hammadi Library.* San Francisco: HarperSanFrancisco, 1988.

Scholem, Gershom. *On the Mystical Shape of the Godhead.* New York: Schocken Books, 1991.

Schussler Fiorenza, Elisabeth. *In Memory of Her.* New York: Crossroad, 1992.

Sellner, Edward C. *Wisdom of the Celtic Saints.* Notre Dame, IN: Ave Maria Press, 1993.

Singer, June. *The Gnostic Book of Hours: Keys to Inner Wisdom.* San Francisco: HarperSanFrancisco, 1992.

Smoley, Richard. *Inner Christianity: A Guide to the Esoteric Condition.* Boston: Shambhala, 2002.

St. John of the Cross. *Dark Night of the Soul.* Trans. Mirabai Starr. New York: Riverhead Books, 2002.

Starbird, Margaret. *Magdalene's Lost Legacy: Symbolic Numbers and the Sacred Union.* Rochester, VT: Bear & Co., 2003.

Starbird, Margaret. *The Woman With the Alabaster Jar.* Santa Fe: Bear & Company, 1993.

Steiner, Rudolf. *How to Know Higher Worlds.* Great Barrington, MA: Anthroposophic Press, 1994.

Swedenborg, Emanuel. *Heaven & Hell.* New York: Swedenborg Foundation, 1984.

Swimme, Brian and Thomas Berry. *The Universe Story.* New York: HarperCollins, 1992.

Teilhard de Chardin, Pierre. *The Phenomenon of Man.* New York: Harper & Row, 1959.

Terrenus, Aurora. *Sophia of the Bible.* Santa Cruz, CA: Celestial Communications, 1988.

Torjesen, Karen Jo. *When Women Were Priests.* San Francisco: HarperSanFrancisco, 1993.

The Way of A Pilgrim and A Pilgrim Continues His Way. Trans. Helen Bacovcin. New York: Image Books Doubleday, 1992.

Ulanov, Ann Belford. *The Feminine in Jungian Psychology and in Christian Theology.* Evanston, IL: Northwestern University Press, 1971.

Underhill, Evelyn. *Practical Mysticism.* Columbus, OH: Ariel Press, 1914.

Versluis, Arthur. *TheoSophia.* Hudson, NY: Lindisfarne Press, 1994.

Ware, Kallistos. *The Orthodox Way.* Crestwood, NY: St. Vladimir's Seminary Press, 1998.

Winter, Miriam Therese. *WomanPrayer WomanSong.* New York: Crossroad, 1993.

Winter, Miriam Therese. *WomanWisdom.* New York: Crossroad, 1993.

Winter, Miriam Therese. *WomanWord.* New York: Crossroad, 1992.

THE CHRISTOSOPHIA COMMUNITY

If you are interested in learning more about the ChristoSophia Community, you may write to the authors at:

> P. O. Box 611
> Morganton, Georgia 30560
> U. S. A.

Visit our Website at ChristoSophia.org

Printed in the United States
80482LV00004B/49-54

9 781420 834925